Seshat History of Moralizing Religion, Vol. 1: Historical and Comparative Perspectives

Edited by Jennifer Larson, Jenny Reddish, and Peter Turchin

Seshat Histories II

Beresta Books

Seshat: Global History Databank

Beresta Books
Published by BERESTA BOOKS LLC
Chaplin, Connecticut, U.S.A.

THE SESHAT HISTORY OF MORALIZING RELIGION, VOL. 1: HISTORICAL AND COMPARATIVE PERSPECTIVES / Edited by Jennifer Larson, Jenny Reddish, and Peter Turchin

Cover design by Marta Dec
Layout and typesetting by Grzegorz Laszczyk
Indexing by Chandan Singh
Cover illustration by Kinsey Hotchkiss

Copyright © 2025 Beresta Books
All rights reserved. This book may not be reproduced in whole or in part without permission from the publisher.

Financial assistance for the research and writing of this book was provided by grants from the John Templeton Foundation, the Austrian Research Promotion Agency (FFG), the Tricoastal Foundation, the Economic and Social Research Council, and the European Union Horizon 2020 Programme for Research and Innovation. The editors were supported in their work by the Evolution Institute, the University of Oxford, Kent State University, and the Complexity Science Hub, Vienna.

Cover illustration: adapted from the "weighing of the heart" scene in the Papyrus of Hunefer, c. 1300 BCE, © Kinsey Hotchkiss.

ISBN:
Paperback   978-1-967343-00-3
Ebook   978-1-967343-01-0
This book is part of a set, ISBN 978-1-967343-04-1

Library of Congress Cataloging-in-Publication Data
The Seshat History of Moralizing Religion, Vol. 1: Historical and Comparative Perspectives / Edited by Jennifer Larson, Jenny Reddish, and Peter Turchin
p. cm.
Includes bibliographical references and index
1. World history. 2. History, ancient. 3. Religion and politics. 4. Kings and rulers – religious aspects. 5. Social evolution. I. Title.

Contents

Figures ... v
Tables ... vi
Notes on Contributors ... vii
Editors' Preface
    Jennifer Larson, Jenny Reddish, and Peter Turchin ... xi

Part I.
Understanding Moralizing Supernatural Punishment and Reward ... 1

Introduction — *Harvey Whitehouse* ... 3
Historical Questions — *Jennifer Larson* ... 25

Part II:
Moralizing Religions and Moralizing Supernatural Punishment and Reward ... 45

Hinduism — *Arunjana Das* ... 47
Rabbinical Judaism — *Tamás Biró* ... 69
Christianity — *István Czachesz* ... 91
Buddhism — *Mark Stanford* ... 105
Manichaeism — *Paul C. Dilley* ... 123
Islam — *Aria Nakissa* ... 133

Part III:
Comparative and Analytical Perspectives ... 153

Evolutionary Approaches to Moralizing Supernatural Punishment and Reward Beliefs in the Americas — *R. Alan Covey* ... 155
Great and Little Traditions — *Mark Stanford* ... 177
Hebrew Bible Traditions — *Jutta Jokiranta* ... 191
"We Don't Want to Hear Any More About Jesus": Christian Expansion and Immanentist Indifference — *Jenny Reddish* ... 207
The Evolution of Moralizing Supernatural Punishment: Empirical Patterns — *Peter Turchin* ... 227

Index ... 253

Figures

Part III.
    Chapter 5, Figure 1. Proportion of Seshat polities for which
        MSP data are coded as "unknown," as a function
        of the sophistication of information systems (Info)   246
    Chapter 5, Figure 2. Statistical association between MSP and Info   246
    Chapter 5, Figure 3. Correlation matrix between MSP
        and other variables reflecting various aspects
        of the sociocultural evolution of polities   247
    Chapter 5, Figure 4. Statistical association between MSP
        and sociopolitical complexity (SPC1)   247
    Chapter 5, Figure 5. Logistic regression models showing
        the probability of moralizing supernatural punishment
        as a function of social complexity   248
    Chapter 5, Figure 6. Mapping the evolution of MSP in space and time   249

Tables

Part I.
    Chapter 2, Table 1. Levels of MSP in immanentist religions in the 33 regions of our World Sample   29

Part III.
    Chapter 1, Table 1. Some reconstructed dates for North American societies   158
    Chapter 1, Table 2. External influences on moralizing beliefs in the Americas   160
    Chapter 1, Table 3. Temporal dimensions of religious beliefs in the EA [Ethnographic Atlas]   162
    Chapter 5, Table 1. Summary of the supernatural moral punishment/reward variables used in constructing the measures of MSP used in the analysis   231
    Chapter 5, Table 2. Four causal scenarios that can give rise to pairwise correlations   236
    Chapter 5, Table 3. Regression results with MSP_{t+1} as the response variable   239

Notes on Contributors

Tamás Biró is an Assistant Professor at ELTE Eötvös Loránd University, Budapest, and Associate Professor at OR-ZSE Jewish Theological Seminary – University of Jewish Studies, Hungary. A linguist and Hebrew studies scholar, he defended his PhD in Computational Linguistics in Groningen in 2006. His fields of interest include formal models of optimality theory, cognitive approaches to Jewish rituals, Hebrew and Semitic linguistics, and the history of the Neolog Jewish movement in Hungary. The author acknowledges the support of the Hungarian National Research, Development and Innovation Fund (NKFIH) under the National Research Excellence Programme's Advanced grant no. 150128.

R. Alan Covey is Professor of Anthropology at the University of Texas–Austin and a Research Associate in the Division of Anthropology at the American Museum of Natural History. Covey's archaeological and ethnohistoric research explores the dynamics of ancient and early modern empires, focusing on the Inca Empire and early colonial Peru. His current book project examines the interplay of state and local economics across the Andes during the period of Inca rule.

István Czachesz is a Professor at the Department of Archaeology, History, Religious Studies, and Theology at UiT The Arctic University of Norway. His research interests include Christian origins, the cognitive science of religion, and cultural evolution. He recently authored *Cognitive Science and the New Testament: A New Approach to Early Christian Research* (Oxford, 2017) and edited *Network Science in Biblical Studies*, a special journal issue of *ASE* (2022).

Arunjana Das is a PhD candidate in the Department of Theology and Religious Studies in Georgetown University, Washington, DC. Her research interests include Vaiṣṇava studies, Hindu–Christian comparative theology, and religious approaches to war, peace, and nonviolence.

Paul Dilley is the Erling B. "Jack": Holtsmark Associate Professor in the Classics and the DEO (chair) of the Department of Religious Studies at the University of Iowa. His research focus is the religions of late antiquity, particularly early Christianity and Manichaeism, with an approach that combines philology, both analog and digital, with cultural history, including cognitive studies.

Jutta Jokiranta is Professor of Hebrew Bible/Old Testament and Cognate Studies at the University of Helsinki, Faculty of Theology (2018–) and Vice Dean for Research. She has expertise in Qumran (Dead Sea Scrolls) studies and Early Judaism. Her research interests include social changes within late Second Temple Judaism, ritual studies, social identity construction in ancient religious movements, ethnicity, archaeology of Hellenistic and Roman Palestine, cognitive science of religion, conceptualization of divinity, and transmission of traditions. She is the author of *Social Identity and Sectarianism in the Qumran Movement* (Brill, 2013) and coeditor of the Brill series Studies on the Texts of the Desert of Judah (STDJ, 2022).

Jennifer Larson is Professor of Classics at Kent State University. Her research interests include ancient Greek mythology and religion, the cognitive science of religion, and early modern book history.

Aria Nakissa is a lecturer in the Faculty of Islamic Studies and Faculty of Social Sciences, Indonesian International Islamic University. His research focuses on religion and law in Muslim societies, using approaches from history, anthropology, and cognitive science.

Jenny Reddish is Lead Editor for Seshat: Global History Databank. She has worked for Seshat since 2016, contributing to projects on the Axial Age, sociopolitical crises through history, and the long-term dynamics of social complexity. She is the coeditor with Dan Hoyer of the *Seshat History of the Axial Age* (2019). Her background is in archaeology and anthropology, and she is particularly interested in comparative approaches to religion and ritual.

Mark Stanford is an Associate of the Asia Research Institute, National University of Singapore and a Research Affiliate at the Centre for the Study of Social Cohesion, University of Oxford. His research focuses on the role of moral psychology in the cultural evolution of cooperation.

Peter Turchin is Project Leader at the Complexity Science Hub, Vienna, a Research Associate at University of Oxford, and Emeritus Professor at the University of Connecticut. He is a founding director of the Seshat: Global History Databank. Currently, he is investigating a set of broad and interrelated questions. How do human societies evolve? In particular, what processes explain the evolution of ultrasociality – our capacity to cooperate in huge anonymous societies of millions? What processes are responsible for the resilience of complex societies to external and internal shocks? What causes political communities to cohere, and what causes them to fall apart?

His books include *End Times* (2023), *Ultrasociety* (2015), *Ages of Discord* (2016), and *The Great Holocene Transformation* (forthcoming).

Harvey Whitehouse is Professor of Social Anthropology at the University of Oxford, Director of the Centre for the Study of Social Cohesion, and a founding director of Seshat: Global History Databank. His research focuses on the role of ritual, religiosity, and social cohesion in the evolution of sociopolitical complexity. His books include *Inside the Cult* (Oxford University Press [OUP], 1995), *Arguments and Icons* (OUP, 2000), *Modes of Religiosity* (AltaMira, 2004), *The Ritual Animal* (OUP, 2021), and *Inheritance: The Evolutionary Origins of the Modern World* (Penguin Random House and Harvard University Press, 2024).

Editors' Preface

Jennifer Larson, Jenny Reddish, and Peter Turchin

This project came about as a companion to the quantitative studies of moralizing supernatural punishment and reward (MSP) conducted by Seshat: Global History Databank, an international collaboration of researchers interested in "big data" approaches to difficult historical problems. Seshat asks questions such as these:

What factors drove the rise of complex societies?
What kinds of crises destroy societies and under what circumstances?
What is the relationship between ritual behavior and group cohesion?
How do environment, climate, and culture interact over time?

The Seshat studies tied to the two volumes of *The Seshat History of Moralizing Religion* asked, "Did the presence of MSP drive the rise of complex societies in world history?" – and we concluded that it did not.

In order to begin to answer such questions, it is necessary to represent cultural information in units appropriate for quantitative analysis, but quantitative data must be complemented by more nuanced and detailed accounts. Ideally, these analytical narratives justify the coding decisions for the quantitative studies, while standing on their own as contributions to world history. The cultures included in Volume Two reflect a carefully selected sample chosen for diversity, both geographically and with respect to social complexity (see Turchin et al. 2018[1]), for the purposes of quantitative study. Unavoidably, the length of the analytical narratives and their "thickness of description" vary according to how extensively the cultures in question have been documented. In order to complement the world sample of analytical narratives at the heart of the project, we commissioned three introductory essays dealing with the goals and methods of Seshat: Global History Databank (Whitehouse, Volume One, Part I, Chapter 1; Larson, Volume One, Part I, Chapter 2; François, Volume Two); six essays exploring MSP in the major moralizing religions of the world (Volume One, Part II, Chapters 1-6); and four essays offering comparative, analytical, and methodological perspectives on the presence and/or absence of MSP in world traditions (Volume One, Part III, Chapters 2-6).

---

1 Turchin, Peter, Thomas E. Currie, Harvey Whitehouse, Pieter Francois, Kevin Feeney, Daniel Mullins, Daniel Hoyer, et al. 2018. "Quantitative Historical Analysis Uncovers a Single Dimension of Complexity That Structures Global Variation in Human Social Organization." *Proceedings of the National Academy of Sciences of the United States of America* 115 (2): e144-e151. doi: 10.1073/pnas.1708800115.

We are aware of no other effort to describe MSP at the level of detail attempted here. Inevitably, as a first attempt, our work has certain limitations, and in the interest of transparency, we feel that it is important to acknowledge them.[2] The most important limitation concerns our use of "legacy" ethnographic literature in descriptions of certain Indigenous peoples in our sample. In the case of Chuuk, for example, we were advised to leave out the material rather than risk printing an account that draws on biased colonialist sources, fails to capture all the nuances of Chuukese culture during the time period in question, and does not directly involve members of the descendant Chuukese community in its creation. Similar criticisms can be made of several accounts of Indigenous cultures included in Volume Two. Leaving them out of this global analysis, however, would be equally problematic in terms of inclusiveness and representation within our sample. Furthermore, it is a fundamental principle of Seshat to avoid applying the code "unknown" when at least some relevant evidence is available, even if that information is partial or biased in ways that require careful interpretation. Rather than eliminate all sources of information that do not rise to the highest standards, we have preferred to take legacy ethnography into account while including necessary caveats about its use.

We aspire to enlist more members of descendant communities in the data review activities leading to descriptions of their cultures. We acknowledge that only a few such collaborations have occurred in the making of the present volume; yet our database is constantly evolving, and recruitment of new experts is a permanent goal. It is important also to recognize that significant differences, difficult to reconcile, may arise between our conceptual framework, which assumes the possibility of etic, comparative approaches grounded in the scientific method, and the ways in which various Indigenous peoples perceive and categorize themselves. As Seshat grows and expands its community of contributors and experts, we will continue our efforts to build and analyze the global record in ways that are representative, respectful, and ethical.

This book has been many years in the making, and many people have generously contributed their time and expertise to it. As well as our authors and Seshat research assistants, we would like to thank the researchers who gave feedback on various chapters: Peter Bol, Axel Kristinsson, Árni Daníel Júlíusson, Peter Peregrine, Kevin White, Kristen Syme, Clark Barrett, Santiago Giraldo and Kyle Clark. Thanks are also due to Shamila Swamy (our copy-editor), Grzegorz Laszczyk (typesetter), Marta Dec (cover designer), Chandan Singh (indexer), and to Kinsey Hotchkiss, who created the illustration on the cover. We are especially grateful to Alan Strathern for peer-reviewing both volumes.

---

2   We thank Alan Covey for his insights on the matters addressed in this preface.

Part I.
Understanding Moralizing Supernatural Punishment and Reward

These chapters contextualize the project within the broader aims of the Seshat: Global History Databank and identify key methodological and historical questions.

Chapter 1

Introduction

Harvey Whitehouse

Moralizing religions postulate supernatural agents or forces that systematically reward virtuous behavior and punish transgressions across a broad range of human affairs, from sexual conduct to repayment of debts and from expressions of respect to acts of charity. Although the world religions of today are all "moralizing" in this sense, such religions are relatively rare both in the ethnographic record of the world's surviving Indigenous cultures and in the history of religions over the millennia. The latter religions are at best only tangentially concerned with how humans act toward each other. They are far more preoccupied with how humans behave toward their gods, spirits, and ancestors and how to manage the supernatural forces responsible for desired outcomes in domains such as health, prosperity, and fertility. Failure to behave in the right way toward the powers that be, rather than toward other human beings, is generally the main concern of traditional religions. Over the ages, much human effort has been invested in pleasing and placating capricious deities and ancestors, whose appetites for sacrificial offerings and other acts of devotion require continual vigilance and labor to assuage. Thus, the dominant theme in the religions of human societies cross-culturally and over the ages is the idea that supernatural agents and forces should be dutifully and respectfully managed, often under the guidance of expert cosmologists and visionaries, in order to prevent or ameliorate misfortune and to ensure that the world around us continues to operate in a manner conducive to human survival and flourishing.

However, many of the religious practices adopted to please and placate the gods have also contributed to the human capacity to cooperate, including the promulgation of rituals that bind groups together, inspiring acts of loyalty and self-sacrifice that might otherwise be impossible. Indeed, this capacity of religion to generate strong prosocial commitment has been regarded by some social theorists as the most salient feature of belief in the supernatural – even to the extent that religion may be seen as a way of conceptualizing through sacred symbolism the priority of the social order as a transcendent source of regulation and stability (Durkheim 1912; Haidt and Graham 2009). However, it is important not to confuse the prosocial effects of religious beliefs, norms, and practices that act as identity markers and devices for cohesion in groups (Whitehouse 2021b) with beliefs in supernatural agents or forces who punish transgressors and reward the virtuous (Norenzayan et al. 2016). In the present volume, we reserve the term *moralizing religion* for the latter and not the former.

Moralizing religions commonly postulate "high gods" (Watts et al. 2015) or "big gods" (Norenzayan 2013), who are believed to take a keen interest in the morality of human affairs and to exercise power to penalize the wicked and confer blessings on the righteous (see also Turchin, this volume, Part III, Chapter 5). Numerous efforts have been made to establish the emergence and distribution of such god concepts using a variety of methods. For example, some researchers have sought to analyze the distribution of beliefs in moralizing gods cross-culturally using ethnographic data (Johnson 2016; Norenzayan 2013; Swanson 1960), while others have tried to establish how and when such beliefs emerged using historical and archaeological data on particular regions and phases of history, such as Scandinavia during the Viking periods (Raffield et al. 2019) or the rise of Eurasian empires (Baumard et al. 2015). Still others have sought to infer the emergence of beliefs in moralizing gods from language phylogenies (Watts et al. 2015). Despite the diversity of approaches, researchers tend to agree that moralizing religions are associated with large-scale, complex societies rather than small-scale, traditional ones:

> Whereas there is little dispute that foraging societies possess beliefs in supernatural agents, these spirits and deities are quite different from those of world religions, with only limited powers and circumscribed concerns about human morality. It appears that interrelated religious elements that sustain faith in Big Gods have spread globally along with the expansion of complex, large-scale human societies. This has occurred despite their rarity in small-scale societies or during most of our species' evolutionary history. (Norenzayan et al. 2016: 3)

A key question then becomes how and why such a peculiar form of belief came to dominate the religious landscape in today's world.

Addressing the puzzle of moralizing religions

According to the big gods theory, moralizing religions – in which deities take an active interest in how people behave with one another and punish wrongdoing – helped to drive the evolution of sociopolitical complexity in world history. The earliest version of this theory proposed that big gods contributed to the initial rise of social complexity with the advent of farming during the Neolithic transition: "Big Gods were one critical causal factor that contributed to the rise of large groups unleashed by agriculture" (Norenzayan 2013: 120–1). A subsequent version of the theory, however, proposed that big gods emerged and spread much later – in larger-scale complex societies – as part of a package of features that coevolved together to support cooperation among relative strangers (Norenzayan et al. 2016). The rationale behind both variants of the big gods theory is that moralizing religions increase the levels of prosocial commitment necessary to limit the harmful effects of cheating, defection, and freeriding in interactions where the reputational costs of selfishness are low because the parties to transactions are relatively anonymous and secular sanctions difficult to impose. However, the theoretical basis for this rationale remains controversial (Schloss and Murray 2011) and the evidential basis inconclusive (McKay and Whitehouse 2015). A major alternative hypothesis is that moralizing religions first appeared much later than exponents of the Big Gods Hypothesis supposed, alongside the rise of transcendentalist teachings (Strathern 2019), in turn arguably part of a package of features associated with the so-called Axial Age (Bellah 2011; Jaspers 1948). Believed by some to be a turning point in world history associated with the flowering of new, universalistic ethical philosophies and religions, the Axial Age spawned a host of novel beliefs in moralizing supernatural agents and forces, perhaps prompted by increasing levels of affluence (Baumard et al. 2015). Another theory, however, is that moralizing religions allowed multiethnic empires to achieve unity around shared norms and thus outcompete more brittle social formations relying on top-down oppression by powerful elites (Whitehouse et al. 2019).

To help shed light on these debates, Volume One of *The Seshat History of Moralizing Religion* attempts to explore the evidence from world history using a qualitative approach. The rich and detailed data set brought together in this volume allows us to investigate the above assumptions empirically. One reason why this is necessary is that many of the arguments summarized above have been based on rough proxies for the presence of moralizing religions, extracted from data sets that were never designed for that purpose. In Part I of this volume, we introduce a variety of theories intended to explain the rise of moralizing religions, and describe the development of new methods to test those theories based on the quantification of patterns in the data on world history. In Part II, we focus on the handful of moralizing religions that arose and spread in the Middle East and Asia: Hinduism, Zoroastrianism, Judaism after 70 CE, Christianity, Buddhism, Manichaeism, and Islam. Our aim is to try to trace out the pathways that led to the extraordinarily wide distribution of followings of these major religions and how these patterns of spread helped to promulgate beliefs in moralizing supernatural punishment and reward. Part III is a collection of essays offering comparative perspectives on the evolution of moralizing religions. In Volume Two, we detail the appearance of moralizing religions in a stratified sample of world regions, associated with the 10 world regions covered by the Seshat: Global History Databank. As Pieter François's introduction to Volume Two explains, our approach was designed to maximize diversity in the sample, allowing the Seshat team to quantify the relationships between changes in moralizing religion and the rise of sociopolitical complexity in world history using sophisticated statistical methods. The Seshat method of analyzing world history is not an alternative to rigorous qualitative historiography and archaeology. On the contrary, the former relies on, and is derived from, the latter. *The Seshat History of Moralizing*

Religion constitutes an effort to assemble in one place much of the qualitative evidence on which the data coding used for statistical analyses of the role of religion in the evolution of sociopolitical complexity relies (Turchin et al. 2022, 2023a, 2023b; Whitehouse et al. 2023).

The universal foundations of wild religion

A wide corpus of research in the cognitive science of religion suggests that certain features of religious thinking and behavior emerged naturally as a consequence of our evolved psychology (e.g., Boyer 1994; McCauley 2011; White 2021). For example, the idea that higher-level cognitive functions (beliefs, desires, memories) persist after the physical body expires seem to occur in all the known cultures of the world, past and present, expressed in beliefs in life after death, spirit possession, and other forms of mind–body dualism. One possible explanation for the universality of afterlife constructs is provided by the simulation constraint hypothesis (Bering 2006), which proposes that while we can simulate the absence of lower-level perceptual functions, such as sight and hearing (e.g., by covering our eyes and ears), we cannot expunge from our minds the things we know or want or remember. So we are content to accept that the body and its perceptual functions can come to an end but are far less able to entertain the cessation of all mental processes, preferring to imagine them persisting in a bodiless form. Other cognitive predispositions and susceptibilities have been proposed to explain the universality of a variety of other recurrent features of religion, such as creation myths (Kelemen 2004), overdetection of agency in natural phenomena (Barrett 2004; Guthrie 1995), the need to repeat particular rituals and imbue others with high levels of sensory pageantry (McCauley and Lawson 2002), and the tendency to remember and pass on ideas about minimally counterintuitive agents and processes, such as invisible spirits, flying witches, and weeping statues (Boyer 2001). All such constructs are associated with "wild religion" – the kinds of religious beliefs and practices that emerge and spread naturally in human populations in the absence of explicit teaching or institutional supports (Boyer 2019).

One rather obvious feature of wild religion is that it is deployed as a way of managing problems that purely instrumental theories and methods do not satisfactorily resolve. Most forms of misfortune fall into this category. For example, when people fall ill or their crops fail, the immediate causes may be perfectly transparent – they came into contact with another sick person, or a drought caused the crops to wither and die. But people also intuitively seek explanations for more opaque and distal elements in the causal chain – for example, why they happened to encounter the sick person instead of being somewhere else or what prevented the rain from falling for such an extended period. This is illustrated by the anthropologically famous example from the Azande people of South Sudan, who explained the tragic deaths of people sitting in the shade of a granary as witchcraft. The Azande were fully aware that the supports of the structure had been weakened by termite infestation and this certainly caused the collapse, but they argued that the reason it gave way at the precise moment when particular people were sitting beneath it could not be explained by natural causation – to account for the tragic consequences of the collapse, they invoked the supernatural mechanism of witchcraft (Evans-Pritchard 1937).

Wild religions not only provide supernatural explanations for misfortune, but in many cases, they also offer solutions. The kinds of solutions that wild religions provide for the prevention and amelioration of misfortune typically take the form of ritual practices, which may be broadly distinguished into four types (Boyer 2019): (1) rituals aimed at managing relationships with spirits, ancestors, and ghosts; (2) shamanic states of trance or possession aimed at healing patients; (3) rituals aimed at warding off or channeling the effects of witchcraft and sorcery; and (4) divinations aimed at diagnosing or predicting human problems. All four ritual types appear to be ubiquitous in human societies, even though organized doctrinal religions and state systems often try to suppress them (Whitehouse 2021b). The reason such rituals are particularly widespread in small-scale, traditional societies appears to be precisely because of the lack of such mechanisms of suppression, at least prior to the spread of states and empires and the organized religions they endorsed.

Wild religions as toolkits

While our evolved psychology may plausibly explain the ubiquity of beliefs in supernatural agents and processes, we also need to explain why such beliefs feature in the toolkits that people deploy when experiencing misfortune. At least part of the explanation seems to lie in the way humans copy each other, especially when the behavior being imitated is causally opaque. Psychologists refer to the copying of causally opaque behavior as "overimitation" (Hoel et al. 2019). Although rare in most other species, including our closest primate relatives, humans overimitate modeled behavior routinely from an early age (Whiten et al. 2009). For example, when children are shown how to open a transparent puzzle box, in which the mechanisms involved can be easily observed and understood, they unsurprisingly copy the method shown to them, but they also copy causally redundant behaviors modeled by the demonstrator – such as tapping the box with a feather – even when the experimenter explicitly tells them not to bother copying any obviously unnecessary steps (Lyons et al. 2007). Derek Lyons and colleagues (2007) attribute this seemingly excessive tendency to overimitate causally opaque behavior to automatic causal encoding – the unconscious tendency to regard all deliberate actions as causally necessary to achieve an end goal. However, a growing body of research suggests that there is another reason why children copy causally opaque behavior – one that could also explain why humans everywhere perform rituals (Whitehouse 2021b). At the core of this research is a distinction between ritual and instrumental stances (Whitehouse 2011, 2012, 2021b).

Much of the socially learned behavior in human societies is causally opaque, at least initially. Even in societies with a simple material culture, one must learn various techniques of food procurement and processing or how to heal wounds or treat fevers without a full understanding of the causal mechanisms involved. This is even more obvious in technologically complex societies, where the internal workings of many everyday objects – from televisions to smartphones – are poorly understood by most users. The way in which such things work may be causally opaque, but we nevertheless observe the procedures necessary, for example, to change channels on a television set or to reboot a phone when the screen is frozen, in the belief that somebody somewhere (e.g., a television engineer or a smartphone designer) understands the inner workings of these devices even if we don't. To think this way is to adopt an *instrumental* stance on social learning. However, humans also routinely copy causally opaque behaviors that are assumed to have no rationale in physical-causal terms – such as local customs, dress codes, and rules of etiquette. When we copy such behaviors, we are adopting a *ritual* stance. In other words, we assume that the behavior is irremediably opaque and it is pointless to seek out a physical-causal rationale for it (Whitehouse 2021b). When we adopt an instrumental stance, our aim is to learn technically useful skills, but when we adopt a ritual stance, our aim is to affiliate with other members of the group. A growing body of empirical research has shown that adopting a ritual stance increases imitative fidelity (Legare et al. 2015) and may be used as a re-inclusion behavior when an ostracism threat is present (Watson-Jones et al. 2014; Watson-Jones, Whitehouse, and Legare 2016).

Humans flexibly flit back and forth between ritual and instrumental stances when deciding whether or how to copy observed behaviors, rather as one might compare objects at different distances through a pair of bifocal spectacles (Jagiello, Heyes, and Whitehouse 2022; Whitehouse 2021b). Actions in particular may be viewed as instrumental in some respects (i.e., strongly oriented to the accomplishment of a material end goal) but ritualistic in other respects (i.e., irremediably causally opaque). An example of this would be a magical ritual – that is, a procedure intended to prevent or ameliorate misfortune but involving steps that cannot even in principle be stipulated in purely physical-causal terms (and hence are regarded as "magic"). This capacity to generate quasi-instrumental rituals (Whitehouse 2021b) would explain the universal tendency of wild religions to adopt ritual techniques as a way of managing misfortune.

The relationship between wild religion and morality

Wild religions and the ritual techniques they utilize clearly do not require moralizing gods. However, that does not mean they are necessarily amoral. It is possible that many of the characteristics associated with wild religions have consequences for the morality of human affairs and even more prominently perhaps for the morality of human relations with gods and ancestors. To explore the relationship between wild religion and moral reasoning, it is necessary to begin with a clear understanding of what morality is and how it is expressed in behavior. A prominent approach to this topic in psychology, discussed also in Jennifer Larson's chapter for this volume (Part 1, Chapter 2), is known as moral foundations theory, which distinguishes five domains: harm/care, fairness/reciprocity, ingroup/loyalty, authority/respect, and purity/sanctity (Haidt and Graham 2009). Although this has proved to be a very fruitful theory, generating a large body of important empirical research (Haidt 2013), here I focus on a more recent effort to differentiate moral domains that is based more systematically on evolutionary thinking and games theoretic modeling – the theory of morality as cooperation (MAC). The MAC theory identifies seven cooperative rules that are deemed morally good everywhere: (1) help your group, (2) care for kin, (3) return favors, (4) be brave, (5) defer to superiors, (6) divide resources fairly, and (7) respect others' property (Curry 2016). Not only is the MAC approach better grounded theoretically, but where the two theories make overlapping predictions, evidence supporting the MAC theory appears to be stronger (Curry, Chesters, and Van Lissa 2019). Importantly, the MAC theory picks out moral domains that have universal salience. Using a representative sample of the world's cultures, it has been shown that the seven forms of cooperation proposed by the MAC theory are judged as morally good in virtually all of them (Curry, Mullins, and Whitehouse 2019). To the extent that the MAC theory formulates a set of basic rules that humans everywhere judge to be good, without any special need for cultural learning or institutional supports, we might describe the seven domains as "wild morality" in much the same way as our list of universal features of reasoning about supernatural agents and forces amount to "wild religion." The question then becomes whether and how wild religion and wild morality are related.

One source of evidence on this topic comes from the study of "great" and "little" traditions in the world religions (Redfield 1955). Great traditions typically thrive among educated urban elites, supported by institutions such as professional priesthoods and sacred scriptures. Such doctrinal traditions are able to depart from the intuitive foundations of religion and morality by postulating highly counterintuitive doctrines and theologies that can be maintained as orthodoxies because of the mnemonic supports provided by routinized teachings, libraries, and systems of formal education (Whitehouse 2004). By contrast, the "little traditions" of relatively uneducated peasant farmers or low-income workers in cities tend to gravitate toward the "wild" end of the spectrum, being grounded more in panhuman intuitions than in the rarefied teachings cultivated via systems of learning in monasteries or theological schools.

Doctrinal and wild dimensions receive varying emphasis from one religious tradition to the next. At one end of the spectrum are traditions mainly emphasizing the pragmatic concerns of wild religion, especially the prevention or amelioration of suffering through the performance of rituals, spells, and the propitiation of supernatural agents. These are among the hallmark features of what Alan Strathern (2019) calls "immanentist" traditions. At the other end are those more oriented to the salvific and eschatological concerns of "transcendentalist" religions. This contrast is quite thoroughly discussed in Larson's chapter (Part I, Chapter 2, this volume). However, to the extent that great and little traditions are interwoven in the world religions, many fall somewhere toward the middle of this spectrum.

To illustrate this, consider the case of Theravada Buddhism in Myanmar (Stanford and Whitehouse 2021). As a "great tradition," Theravada Buddhism exhibits strongly doctrinal characteristics, including a complex body of teachings, for instance, relating to karmic principles, noble truths, pathways to awakening, and meditative practices. However, the "little traditions" practiced by the Burmese laity entail rituals directed to a variety of "wilder" supernatural agents, including spirits, wizards, and demigods, and a wide range of quasi-instrumental (magical) rituals. These two dimensions of Buddhism practiced in Myanmar exhibit distinct patterns of cooperation and moral concern. The practitioners of both evince feelings of loyalty to the group; but whereas those more strongly oriented to the great tradition align themselves with a large, imagined community of fellow believers (Anderson 1991), the followers of the little tradition are more loyal to a local relational network of people they know personally – especially their kin. This is an important difference to note in the moral orientation of wild religions as compared with more cultivated doctrinal traditions. The former unite face-to-face communities of coparticipants, whereas the latter operate on much larger scales. In Myanmar and many other countries where world religions continue to recruit strong followings, great traditions (of doctrinal religion) and little traditions (in wild religion) rub shoulders, often in the spirit of a long-standing modus vivendi. But their contrasting moral orientations have long histories that are instructive to consider. When viewed through the lens of deep history, it becomes clear that it is not only in the scale on which group loyalty is cultivated that the two dimensions of contemporary world religions differ. On the contrary, what we see is a gradual process of domestication of wild religions in which the moral salience of beliefs and practices has expanded in a stepwise fashion. Big gods arrive (if at all) toward the end rather than the beginning of that long and complex process.

The domestication of wild religions in world history

Modern humans have always domesticated wild religions to some extent. For a start, they have continually sculpted in myriad ways our intuitions about supernatural agency, the afterlife, ritual efficacy, intelligent design in nature, and so on, to produce a plethora of locally distinctive ideas about spirits, ancestors, ghosts, witches, and demons. But they have also created a diversity of ritual practices aimed at divining the intentions of those supernatural agents, persuading and coercing them to cooperate, pleading with them and bowing down to them, and feeding and placating them. Some of these beliefs and practices may be regarded as nonfunctional by-products of the way human psychology evolved – a set of magical formulas for warding off misfortune that raise hopes but lack genuine causal efficacy. Nevertheless, at least some of these beliefs and practices – especially when detached from material end goals, becoming merely a matter of local custom and convention – end up serving as identity markers. They become *traditions*, prompting feelings of pride and prosocial commitment as well as feelings of rivalry toward the followers of other traditions. When rituals function in that way they are capable of contributing to the fate of entire religious traditions via processes of cultural group selection (Richerson et al. 2016; Whitehouse 2023).

Since participation in collective rituals is always to some extent an affiliative behavior, the extent to which rituals generate social glue and motivate cooperation among coparticipants has important consequences for the success of their communities in intergroup competition. Any modification of ritual practices that increases the strength of social cohesion is capable of conferring a selective advantage on the groups performing the ritual, for example, by motivating self-sacrifice in war or willingness to favor and trust other members of the group in trading networks. There is compelling evidence that painful initiation rituals contributed to cohesion and violent self-sacrifice in military groups throughout human prehistory and many Indigenous groups "pacified" by colonial administrations in recent centuries (Sosis, Kress, and Boster 2007; Whitehouse 2018). Meanwhile, the development of more routinized rituals likely contributed to the stabilization of larger-scale group identities during the Neolithic transition, by making deviations from cultural norms easier to detect and punish (Whitehouse 2000, 2004, 2021b, Whitehouse et al., 2014).

However, these ways of domesticating wild religion for the purposes of intragroup cooperation and intergroup competition were not defined by beliefs in moralizing supernatural punishment and reward. Rather, wild religion has been domesticated over the course of world history through a gradual process in which different domains of moral concern have come to be incrementally co-opted by religious systems. Big gods appear on the scene relatively late in this process, around the time when religion finally starts to endorse all seven cooperative principles predicted by the MAC theory. This process may be associated with the spread of axiality, culminating in the world religions we know today. The next section briefly reviews that process, drawing on the evidence from history and archaeology.

The evolution of moralizing religion in world history

The domestication of wild religion over the course of world history may be viewed as a multistage process, at least from the perspective of religion's relationship with morality. Wild religion in its purest form is largely utilitarian – a toolkit for managing misfortune – and so it recruits moral concerns only to the extent that it explains disease and suffering as rooted in interpersonal conflicts and jealousies and considers supernatural agents and forces to be manipulable by appeal to moral obligations (e.g., the logic of reciprocity that motivates animal sacrifice or costly acts of devotion). But as a force for moral regulation in human affairs, the first major step in the domestication of wild religion was arguably the manipulation of collective rituals in ways that produced extreme forms of group loyalty. In many small-scale societies, group survival depended on the willingness of warriors to defend the group to the death if necessary. Willingness to fight and die for others does not come easily, and a far more natural response to a deadly outgroup threat is to run away, surrender, or adopt some other strategy that maximizes the chances of individual survival. Yet throughout history, small bands of warriors found ways to stand united in the face of formidable threats, even walking willingly into the jaws of death to protect their groups from annihilation – often with remarkable success (Atran 2016).

The performance of "imagistic" rituals (Whitehouse 1995) involving infrequently performed, emotionally and physically challenging ordeals – such as painful initiation rites (Whitehouse 2006) – would likely have contributed to extreme progroup action and self-sacrifice (Atran and Gómez 2018), by activating such mechanisms as identity fusion (Swann et al. 2012; Whitehouse 2018) and costly signaling (Irons 2001). The psychological processes leading from participation in rituals of this kind to extreme forms of cooperation are now quite well studied (Whitehouse 2021b), helping to deepen our understanding of the likely origins of imagistic practices in human prehistory.

Imagistic practices domesticate wild religion by exploiting the affiliative potential of the ritual stance to an extreme degree. As noted above, participation in irremediably opaque collective behaviors naturally creates distinctive cultural traditions, eliciting ingroup loyalty and outgroup derogation. But when such rituals are rarely performed and emotionally intense (e.g., painful or frightening, as in many forms of hazing and initiation), they become an essential part of autobiographical memory was well as group defining. Numerous studies suggest that such experiences can serve to "fuse" personal and group identities, leading to extreme forms of progroup action (Whitehouse 2018). In this way, imagistic rituals promote group loyalty and bravery – two of the seven principles that the MAC theory predicts will be valued as morally good.

Although imagistic practices and their moral consequences have often left only tantalizing traces in human prehistory, some of the diagnostic features of these kinds of rituals survive in the archaeological record, for example, in the form of painful and dangerous ritual ordeals depicted in wall art or in evidence of feasting events (e.g., Mithen 2004; Whitehouse and Hodder 2010). Moreover, to the extent that imagistic features are detectable in the ethnographic record pertaining to contemporary or recent Indigenous cultures, it is possible to quantify those features and their archaeologically visible material correlates and thereby to estimate the likelihood that such features were present in prehistoric cultures (Gantley, Whitehouse, and Bogaard 2018). Such approaches suggest that imagistic practices among paleolithic foraging bands gradually declined during the rise of agriculture, with the emergence of new ways of domesticating wild religion.

The Neolithic transition arguably heralded a new stage in the evolution of the relationship between religion and morality. A key starting point seems to have been a marked increase in the frequency of collective rituals, enabling societies to spread and grow in size unified by a body of cultural practices standardized through repetition (see, e.g., Whitehouse et al. 2014). If so, the moral principle of loyalty to the group would not have been sustainable with the same levels of intensity and extreme cooperative commitment as may be observed in local warrior cults fused via imagistic practices. As domestic units became increasingly important economically – replacing bands as the core units of production and consumption in early agrarian societies – the twin risks of household failure and declining military cohesion would have made such societies vulnerable to internal collapse and external invasion. Judging by the archaeological importance of burial practices, a common solution seems to have been the development of forms of ancestor worship associated with principles of clanship and descent, providing new ways of enforcing conformism. By virtue of their relative proximity to venerated ancestors, elders may have acquired a privileged position in the management of group affairs. Respect for elders and ancestors can motivate obedient observance of ritual obligations, and this likely contributed to the standardization and spread of religious traditions in early agrarian societies. However, elders could do little to protect their groups from enemy attack. As populations expanded and came into conflict over vital resources, such as cultivable land, warrior leaders rose to prominence.

Some of the big men who established themselves in early agrarian societies may have managed to lay claim to supernatural powers or even divine status, construed as a heritable essence that could be passed on to their sons and heirs. Once their preeminence was institutionalized – for example, in systems of chiefly rank, aristocratic castes and royal lineages – the stage was set for the proliferation of much larger religions, enforced from the top down. Religions in the archaic states added new domains of cooperation to the normative repertoire of worshipers – in particular, deference to authority and respect for property. They did so in a particularly extreme way, legitimating severe forms of inequality, expressed most strikingly in the widespread practice of human sacrifice and the endorsement of elite privilege and wealth (Watts et al. 2016). It is hard to imagine a more graphic demonstration of the power of rulers and their legitimating gods than the extraordinarily bloodthirsty forms of ceremonial killing adopted by the Aztec and Mayan civilizations, such as the extraction of the hearts of live victims (Mignon 1986). And the same elites who presided over such practices in the archaic states around the world were also typically associated with ostentatious displays of wealth – ranging from palatial complexes to luxury goods and symbols of authority made from precious materials (Trigger 2003). Note, however, that religions in the archaic states still did not require the presence of beliefs in moralizing gods to establish complex societies based on principles of centralization and hierarchy.

During the next stage in the evolutionary process, however, the domestication of wild religion took a dramatically new turn with the emergence of what some called "secondary religions" (Assmann 2010) and other "transcendentalisms" (Strathern 2019). As Larson explains (Part I, Chapter 2 of this volume), these concepts refer to partially overlapping features of the fast-spreading doctrinal religions inspired by prophets and messiahs promulgating a vision of rewards for the faithful, often furnishing answers to questions posed more sharply by Axial Age philosophies than by the cosmological systems of the archaic states (Mullins et al. 2018). Axial religions arguably served to unify the otherwise competing cultural groups in multiethnic empires forged through violent processes of conquest, colonization, and absorption (Whitehouse et al. 2019; see also Turchin, Part III, Chapter 5, this volume). Such religions – which included Zoroastrianism and Manichaeism as well as the Abrahamic and Eastern religions that dominate the religious landscape today – extended the relationship between religion and morality further than ever before. For a start, all the Axial religions emphasized the importance of reciprocity and fairness in human affairs to an extent that no earlier religions had done. And they also added big gods to the religious repertoire. As such, moralizing supernatural punishment only became a primary concern in organized religions after, rather than before, the sharpest rises in sociopolitical complexity in world history (Turchin et al. 2023b; Whitehouse et al. 2023).

We see this clearly in the regions of the world painstakingly detailed in Volume Two. Recall that roughly a third of the Natural Geographic Areas (NGAs) covered in the Seshat: Global History Databank and in the chapters that follow were sampled because sociopolitical complexity arose there relatively early compared with other NGAs in the same world region. In such cases, the transition to transcendentalisms was typically preceded by forms of authoritarian religiosity associated with the archaic states. In the case of Egypt, the transition was an endogenous development associated with the emergence of the concept of *ma'at* during the Naqada III period, starting around 3300 BCE (Goebs 2007; see the Egypt narrative in Volume Two).

The same may be said of the Middle Yellow River Valley, where at least some Axial Age characteristics emerged during the first millennium BCE (Clark and Winslett 2011; see the North China narrative in Volume Two). However, in many other of these "early-complexity" NGAs, the transition from authoritarian to axial resulted from the incorporation of small-scale polities into much larger empires and the religions they endorsed. Ancient examples of these engulfing systems include the Achaemenid Empire and its version of Zoroastrianism in the narratives on Susiana, southern Mesopotamia, Sogdiana, and Kachi Plain during the first millennium BCE (see also Skjærvø 2014). As the narratives in Volume Two also show, the same process occurred in more recent times with the European colonization and Christianization of Cuzco Valley (center of the Inca Empire) in the sixteenth century (Betanzos [1880] 1996; D'Altroy 2014; Yaya 2012) and arguably also in regions such as Hawai'i in the nineteenth century, where the process of conversion was endorsed and implemented by Indigenous elites in response to imperial coercive power exerted from without (Fish Kashay 2008; Seaton 1974). In some early-complexity NGAs, by contrast, powerful empires elected to incorporate transcendentalisms rather than have them imposed by invading or colonizing powers, a famous example being the adoption of Christianity by the Roman Empire between 284 CE and 394 CE (Galvao-Sobrinho 1995; see the Latium narrative in Volume Two).

In NGAs where sociopolitical complexity was late to arrive, we commonly observe a leap from simpler forms of religion to full-blown transcendentalisms – bypassing the archaic forms of supernaturally legitimated despotism altogether – via rapid colonization and missionization (Strathern 2023). Examples covered by the narratives in Volume Two include those on the Orokaiva of northeast New Guinea (Iteanu 1990; Schwimmer 1973; Whitehouse 1996), the Iroquois of the Finger Lakes region of upstate New York (Foley [1975] 1996; St. John [1981] 1994), the Akan of the Ghanaian Coast (Ephirim-Donkor 2010), and the A'chik of Garo Hills (Marak 2005) – all of which made the transition from small-scale traditional religions to forms of missionary Christianity during the nineteenth and twentieth centuries. There are exceptions to this in our sample, however. As the narratives show, missionization was resisted or otherwise avoided in some late-complexity NGAs – for example, among the Sakha peoples of the Lena River Valley in eastern Russia (Jochelson [1933] 1997; Popov [1946] 1997; Sauer [1802] 1995; Sieroszewski 1993) and the Chicham- or Shuar-speaking groups in the Lowland Andes (Boster 2003; Descola 1996; Stirling 1938; see the Lowland Andes narrative).

Among those NGAs identified as "in between," the ones in which sociopolitical complexity emerged relatively early or late, many unsurprisingly exhibit a mixture of the patterns observed at the two extremes. Some of these midway NGAs follow the trajectories observed in high-complexity NGAs. For example, like many other West Asian NGAs, Konya Plain transitioned from neo-Hittite religiosity to

Zoroastrianism due to the spread of the Achaemenid Empire around 546 BCE (Dusinberre 2015; see the Anatolia narrative in Volume Two), and the Middle Ganga and Deccan transitioned from archaic forms of immanentism to Buddhism with the spread of the Mauryan Empire in the third century BCE (Johansen 2014; Thapar 2003; see the narrative on North and South India). Paris Basin, meanwhile, followed the same trajectory as Latium, with the Roman religion giving way to Christianity between 284 BCE and 394 CE (Behr 2006; Galvao-Sobrinho 1995; see the Western Europe narrative in Volume Two). Thus, most of the polities in the stratified sample covered in Volume Two and in the Seshat database progressed through the stages described above, and this involved an expansion of the kinds of moral concern that were linked to the religious beliefs and practices in those societies. Whereas in this chapter I emphasize the broadly changing character of religious systems in the evolution of social complexity, the Seshat approach permits us to explore a wide variety of other theoretical dimensions as well, such as the role of advances in military technology emphasized in Peter Turchin's chapter in this volume (Part III, Chapter 5). This is one of the advantages of creating a database that covers a wide range of features that may be causally related to developments in religion and in diverse domains of social life.

Religion, morality, and the future of humanity

Although the world religions today continue to exhibit many axial characteristics, a seismic shift appears to be taking place in the way their moralizing functions are expressed. In some affluent societies, processes of secularization have taken root by choice, while in other regions transformed under the revolutionary banner of communism (most notably the former Soviet Union and Maoist China), organized religions have been systematically suppressed. Flowering in the interstices of these changes, however, have been a great diversity of wild religions – from the persistence of ancestor worship in China and North Korea to beliefs in sorcery, magic, and the evil eye in eastern Europe, and from new age beliefs in affluent Western countries to miraculous healing practices in the globally proselytizing forms of charismatic Christianity. But what will be the future of the relationship between religion and morality? Will there be a further stage, for example, as the need for new forms of international cooperation becomes ever more pressing in the face of global challenges such as the climate crisis, nuclear proliferation, and mass migration?

One thing is for sure: wild religion is here to stay. Every time a child is born, a new bearer of intuitions about the afterlife, supernatural agency, ritual efficacy, and intelligent design is naturally created. But world history shows that these intuitions can be adapted to the needs of the societies in which they occur. In small-scale polities, imagistic practices domesticated wild religions to create warrior cults that allowed the most cohesive groups – championing bravery and localized group loyalty – to win out in competition with less cohesive ones. This mode of religiosity needed to be extensively curtailed and managed in larger-scale societies to make way for religions that favored allegiance to imagined communities, deference to authority, and respect for property. But the ways in which religious and moral intuitions were harnessed in the archaic states were no longer adaptive in the fierce competition between multiethnic empires. Authoritarian religions therefore gave way to axiality and the world religions we know today. But have we now reached a new tipping point in the Anthropocene where the world religions are no longer viable?

Arguably, we now find ourselves on the cusp of a new stage in human history in which our survival depends on whether we can harness our religious and moral intuitions in new ways. Given the destructive power of today's nuclear arsenals, religiously motivated wars are no longer a viable way for empires to spread and flourish. And given the way our economic systems plunder the planet's nonrenewable resources and accelerate the pace of climate change, new forms of cooperation will be needed to avert disaster. Apocalyptic outcomes are, of course, possible, but humanity has so far had an impressive track record of finding solutions to collective-action problems. Whereas much political capital and media attention are invested in international organizations that aim at influencing government domestic policy, the spotlight focuses less on the potential for cooperation across the world's religious communities. This is odd given that most people in the world self-identify as religious and given the cohesive power of religions to motivate cooperation. All the world religions provide scriptural support for stewardship of the earth (Whitehouse 2021a), and all seven forms of cooperation highlighted by the MAC theory are relevant to addressing environmental challenges (Curry et al. 2019). We can therefore imagine the emergence of new forms of global cooperation capable of harnessing our universal religious and moral intuitions in ways that motivate grassroots action on the climate crisis and other global problems, bypassing the parochialism and short-term goals of politicians (Whitehouse 2021b, 2024). Perhaps the next stage in the evolution of religion and morality will be one that places social justice and environmental responsibility more firmly at its core.

References

Anderson, Benedict. 1991. *Imagined Communities: Reflections on the Origin and Spread of Nationalism.* London: Verso Books.

Assmann, Jan. 2010. *The Price of Monotheism.* Translated by R. Savage. Stanford, CA: Stanford University Press. doi: 10.1515/9780804772860.

Atran, Scott. 2016. "The Devoted Actor: Unconditional Commitment and Intractable Conflict across Cultures." *Current Anthropology* 57, no. S13. Accessed February 22, 2024. https://www.journals.uchicago.edu/doi/full/10.1086/685495. doi: 10.1086/685495.

Atran, Scott, and Ángel Gómez. 2018. "What Motivates Devoted Actors to Extreme Sacrifice, Identity Fusion, or Sacred Values?" *Behavioral and Brain Sciences* 41: E193. doi: 10.1017/S0140525X18001565.

Barrett, Justin L. 2004. *Why Would Anyone Believe in God?* Walnut Creek, CA: AltaMira Press.

Baumard, Nicolas, Alexandre Hyafil, Ian Morris, and Pascal Boyer. 2015. "Increased Affluence Explains the Emergence of Ascetic Wisdoms and Moralizing Religions." *Current Biology* 25 (1): 10–15. doi: 10.1016/j.cub.2014.10.063.

Behr, John. 2006. "Gaul." In *The Cambridge History of Christianity*, vol. 1: *Origins to Constantine*, edited by Margaret M. Mitchell and Frances M. Young, 366–79. Cambridge: Cambridge University Press. doi: 10.1017/CHOL9780521812399.022.

Bellah, Robert N. 2011. *Religion in Human Evolution: From the Paleolithic to the Axial Age.* Cambridge, MA: Harvard University Press. doi: 10.4159/harvard.9780674063099.

Bering, Jesse M. 2006. "The Folk Psychology of Souls." *Behavioural and Brain Sciences* 29 (5): 453–62. doi: 10.1017/S0140525X06009101.

Betanzos, Juan de. (1880) 1996. *Narrative of the Incas.* Translated by R. Hamilton and D. Buchanan. Austin, TX: University of Texas Press.

Boster, James S. 2003. "ARUTAM and Culture Change." *Antropológica* 99–100: 165–85. Accessed February 22, 2024. https://biblat.unam.mx/hevila/AntropologicaCaracas/2003/no99-100/11.pdf.

Boyer, Pascal. 1994. *The Naturalness of Religious Ideas: A Cognitive Theory of Religion.* Berkeley, CA: University of California Press. doi: 10.1525/9780520911628.

Boyer, Pascal. 2019. "Informal Religious Activity Outside Hegemonic Religions: Wild Traditions and Their Relevance to Evolutionary Models." *Religion, Brain & Behavior* 10 (4): 459–72. doi: 10.1080/2153599X.2019.1678518.

Boyer, P. 2001. *Religion Explained: The Human Instincts That Fashion Gods, Spirits and Ancestors.* New York: Basic Books.

Clark, Kelly J., and Justin T. Winslett. 2011. "The Evolutionary Psychology of Chinese Religion: Pre-Qin High Gods as Punishers and Rewarders." *Journal of the American Academy of Religion* 79 (4): 928–60. doi: 10.1093/jaarel/lfr018.

Curry, Oliver Scott. 2016. "Morality as Cooperation: A Problem-Centred Approach." In *The Evolution of Morality*, edited by Todd K. Shackelford & Ranald D. Hansen, 27–51. Cham: Springer International. doi: 10.1007/978-3-319-19671-8_2.

Curry, Oliver Scott, Matthew Jones Chesters, and Caspar J. Van Lissa. 2019. "Mapping Morality with a Compass: Testing the Theory of 'Morality-as-Cooperation' with a New Questionnaire." *Journal of Research in Personality* 78: 106–124. doi: 10.1016/j.jrp.2018.10.008.

Curry, Oliver S., Darragh Hare, Cameron Hepburn, Dominic D. P. Johnson, Michael Buhrmester, Harvey Whitehouse, and David W. Macdonald. 2019. "Cooperative Conservation: Seven Ways to Save the World." *Conservation Science and Practice* 2 (1): e123. doi: 10.1111/csp2.123.

Curry, Oliver Scott, Daniel A. Mullins, and Harvey Whitehouse. 2019. "Is It Good to Cooperate? Testing the Theory of Morality-as-Cooperation in 60 Societies." *Current Anthropology* 60 (1). doi: 10.1086/701478.

D'Altroy, Terence N. 2014. *The Incas*. 2nd ed. Chichester: Wiley Blackwell.

Descola, Philippe. 1996. *The Spears of Twilight: Life and Death in the Amazon Jungle*. Translated by Janet Loyd. New York: New Press.

Durkheim, Émile. 1912. *Les Formes élémentaires de la vie religieuse* [The elementary forms of religious life]. Paris: Alcan.

Dusinberre, Elspeth R. M. 2015. *Empire, Authority, and Autonomy in Achaemenid Anatolia*. New York: Cambridge University Press.

Ephirim-Donkor, Anthony. 2010. *African Religion Defined: A Systematic Study of Ancestor Worship among the Akan*. Lanham, MD: Rowman & Littlefield.

Evans-Pritchard, Edward Evan. 1937. *Witchcraft, Oracles and Magic among the Azande*. Oxford: Clarendon Press.

Fish Kashay, Jennifer. 2008. "From Kapus to Christianity: The Disestablishment of the Hawaiian Religion and Chiefly Appropriation of Calvinist Christianity." *Western Historical Quarterly* 39 (1): 17–39. doi: 10.1093/whq/39.1.17.

Foley, Denis. (1975) 1996. *An Ethnohistoric and Ethnographic Analysis of the Iroquois from the Aboriginal Era to the Present Suburban Era*. Accessed March 4, 2024. https://ehrafworldcultures.yale.edu/cultures/nm09/documents/060.

Galvao-Sobrinho, Carlos R. 1995. "Funerary Epigraphy and the Spread of Christianity in the West." *Athenaeum* 83: 431–62.

Gantley, Michael, Harvey Whitehouse, and Amy Bogaard. 2018. "Material Correlates Analysis (MCA): An Innovative Way of Examining Questions in Archaeology Using Ethnographic Data." *Advances in Archaeological Practice* 6 (4): 328–41. doi: 10.1017/aap.2018.33.

Goebs, K. 2007. "Kingship." In *The Egyptian World*, edited by T. Wilkinson, 275–95. New York: Routledge.

Guthrie, Stewart Elliot. 1995. *Faces in the Clouds: A New Theory of religion*. New York: Oxford University Press.

Haidt, Jonathan. 2013. *The Righteous Mind: Why Good People Are Divided by Religion and Politics*. New York: Pantheon Books.

Haidt, Jonathan, and Jesse Graham. 2009. "Planet of the Durkheimians, Where Community, Authority, and Sacredness Are Foundations of Morality." In *Social and Psychological Bases of Ideology and System Justification*, edited by J. T. Jost, A. C. Kay, and H. Thorisdottir, 371–401. Oxford: Oxford University Press. doi: 10.1093/acprof:oso/9780195320916.003.015.

Hoel, Stefanie, Stefanie Keupp, Hannah Schleihauf, Nicola McGuigan, David Buttelmann, and Andrew Whiten. 2019. "'Over-imitation': A Review and Appraisal of a Decade of Research." *Developmental Review* 51: 90–108. doi: 10.1016/j.dr.2018.12.002.

Irons, William. 2001. "Religion as a Hard-to-Fake Sign of Commitment." In *Evolution and the Capacity for Commitment*, edited by Randolph M. Nesse, 290–309. New York: Russell Sage Foundation.

Iteanu, A. 1990. "The Concept of the Person and the Ritual System: An Orokaiva View." *Man* 25 (1): 35. doi: 10.2307/2804108.

Jagiello, Robert, Cecilia Heyes, and Harvey Whitehouse. 2022. "Tradition and Invention: The Bifocal Stance Theory of Cultural Evolution." *Behavioral and Brain Sciences* 45: E249. doi: 10.1017/S0140525X22000383.

Jaspers, Karl. 1948. "The Axial Age of Human History: A Base for the Unity of Mankind." *Commentary* 6: 430. Accessed February 22, 2024. https://www.commentary.org/articles/karl-jaspers/the-axial-age-of-human-historya-base-for-the-unity-of-mankind/.

Jochelson, Waldemar. (1933) 1997. *The Yakut*. Accessed March 5, 2024. https://ehrafworldcultures.yale.edu/cultures/rv02/documents/002.

Johansen, Peter. 2014. "The Politics of Spatial Renovation: Reconfiguring Ritual Practices in Iron Age and Early Historic South India." *Journal of Social Archaeology* 14 (1): 59–86. doi: 10.1177/1469605313515976.

Johnson, Dominic. 2016. *God Is Watching You: How the Fear of God Makes Us Human*. Oxford: Oxford University Press.

Kelemen, Deborah. 2004. "Are Children 'Intuitive Theists'? Reasoning About Purpose and Design in Nature." *Psychological Science* 15 (5): 295–301. doi: 10.1111/j.0956-7976.2004.00672.x.

Legare, Cristine H., Nicole J. Wen, Patricia A. Herrmann, and Harvey Whitehouse. 2015. "Imitative Flexibility and the Development of Cultural Learning." *Cognition* 142: 351–61. doi: 10.1016/j.cognition.2015.05.020.

Lyons, Derek E., Andrew G. Young, and Frank C. Keil. 2007. "The Hidden Structure of Overimitation." *Proceedings of the National Academy of Sciences USA* 104 (50): 19751–6. doi: 10.1073/pnas.0704452104.

Marak, Paulinus R. 2005. *The Garo Tribal Religion: Beliefs and Practices*. New Delhi: Anshah.

McCauley, Robert N. 2011. *Why Religion Is Natural and Science Is Not*. New York: Oxford University Press.

McCauley, Robert N., and E. Thomas Lawson. 2002. *Bringing Ritual to Mind: Psychological Foundations of Cultural Forms*. New York: Cambridge University Press. doi: 10.1017/CBO9780511606410.

McKay, Ryan, and Harvey Whitehouse. 2015. "Religion and Morality." *Psychological Bulletin* 141 (2): 447–73. doi: 10.1037/a0038455.

Mithen, S. 2004. "From Ohalo to Çatalhöyük: The Development of Religiosity during the Early Prehistory of Western Asia, 20,000–7000 BC." In *Theorizing Religions Past: Historical and Archaeological Perspectives*, edited by H. Whitehouse & L. H. Martin, 17–44. Walnut Creek, CA: AltaMira Press.

Mignon, Molly R. 1986. Review of *Ritual Human Sacrifice in Mesoamerica*, by Elizabeth H. Boone, ed., Dumbarton Oaks, Washington, DC, 1984. *American Antiquity* 51 (1): 199–200. doi: 10.2307/280422.

Mullins, Daniel A., Daniel Hoyer, Christina Collins, Thomas Currie, Kevin Feeney, Pieter François, Patrick E Savage, Harvey Whitehouse, and Peter Turchin. 2018. "A Systematic Assessment of the Axial Age Thesis Using Global Comparative Historical Evidence." *American Sociological Review* 83 (3): 596–626. doi: 10.1177/0003122418772567.

Norenzayan, Ara. 2013. *Big Gods: How Religion Transformed Cooperation and Conflict.* Princeton, NJ: Princeton University Press. doi: 10.1515/9781400848324.

Norenzayan, Ara, Azim F. Shariff, Will M. Gervais, Aiyana K. Willard, Rita A. McNamara, Edward Slingerland, and Joseph Henrich. 2016. "The Cultural Evolution of Prosocial Religions." *Behavioral and Brain Sciences* 39. doi: 10.1017/S0140525X14001356.

Popov, A. A. (1946) 1997. Family Life of the Dolgani People. Translated by L. Bromwich. Accessed March 5, 2024. https://ehrafworldcultures.yale.edu/cultures/rv02/documents/057.

Raffield, Ben, Neil Price, and Mark Collard. 2019. "Religious Belief and Cooperation: A View from Viking-Age Scandinavia." *Religion, Brain & Behavior* 9 (1): 2-22. doi: 10.1080/2153599X.2017.1395764.

Redfield, R. 1955. "The Social Organization of Tradition." *The Far Eastern Quarterly* 15 (1): 13-21. doi: 10.2307/2942099.

Richerson, Peter, Ryan Baldini, Adrian V. Bell, Kathryn Demps, Karl Frost, Vicken Hillis, Sarah Mathew, et al. 2016. "Cultural Group Selection Plays an Essential Role in Explaining Human Cooperation: A Sketch of the Evidence." *Behavioral and Brain Sciences* 39: e30. doi: 10.1017/S0140525X1400106X.

Sauer, Martin. (1802) 1995. *An Account of a Geographical and Astronomical Expedition to the Northern Parts of Russia by Commodore Joseph Billings, in the Years 1785-1794.* Accessed March 5, 2024. https://ehrafworldcultures.yale.edu/cultures/rv02/documents/006.

Schloss, Jeffrey P., and Michael J. Murray. 2011. "Evolutionary Accounts of Belief in Supernatural Punishment: A Critical Review." *Religion, Brain & Behavior* 1 (1): 46-99. doi: 10.1080/2153599X.2011.558707.

Schwimmer, Eric G. 1973. *Exchange in the Social Structure of the Orokaiva: Traditional and Emergent Ideologies in the Northern District of Papua.* London: Hurst.

Seaton, S. Lee. 1974. "The Hawaiian Kapu Abolition of 1819." *American Ethnologist* 1 (1): 193-206. doi: 10.1525/ae.1974.1.1.02a00100.

Sieroszewski, Wacław. 1993. *The Yakut: An Experiment in Ethnographic Research.* Moscow: Assotsiatsiia "Rossiiskaia polit. entsiklopediia." Accessed March 5, 2024. https://ehrafworldcultures.yale.edu/cultures/rv02/documents/001.

Skjærvø, Prods Oktor. 2014. "Achaemenid Religion." *Religion Compass* 8 (6): 175-87. doi: 10.1111/rec3.12110.

Sosis, Richard, Howard C. Kress, and James S. Boster. 2007. "Scars for War: Evaluating Alternative Signaling Explanations for Cross-cultural Variance in Ritual Costs." *Evolution and Human Behaviour* 28 (4): 234-47. doi: 10.1016/j.evolhumbehav.2007.02.007.

Stanford, Mark, and Harvey Whitehouse. 2021. "Why Do Great and Little Traditions Coexist in the World's Doctrinal Religions?" *Religion, Brain and Behavior* 11 (3): 312-34. doi: 10.1080/2153599X.2021.1947357.

Stirling, Matthew Williams. 1938. *Historical and Ethnographical Material on the Jivaro Indians.* Washington, DC: Government Printing Office. Accessed March 4, 2024. https://ehrafworldcultures.yale.edu/cultures/sd09/documents/002.

Strathern, Alan. 2019. *Unearthly Powers: Religious and Political Change in World History*. Cambridge: Cambridge University Press. doi: 10.1017/9781108753371.

Strathern, Alan. 2023. "The Emergence of MSP vs. the Spread of Transcendentalist Religion." *Religion, Brain & Behavior* 13 (2): 216–18. doi: 10.1080/2153599X.2022.2065348.

Swann, William B., Jolanda Jetten, Ángel Gómez, Harvey Whitehouse, and Brock Bastian. 2012. "When Group Membership Gets Personal: A Theory of Identity Fusion." *Psychological Review* 119 (3): 441–56. doi: 10.1037/a0028589.

Swanson, G. E. 1960. *The Birth of the Gods: The Origin of Primitive Beliefs*. Ann Arbor, MI: University of Michigan Press. doi: 10.3998/mpub.6484.

Thapar, Romila. 2003. *Early India: From the Origins to AD 1300*. Berkeley, CA: University of California Press.

Trigger, Bruce G. 2003. *Understanding Early Civilizations*. New York: Cambridge University Press. doi: 10.1017/CBO9780511840630.

Turchin, Peter, Harvey Whitehouse, Sergey Gavrilets, Daniel Hoyer, Pieter François, James S. Bennett, Kevin C. Feeney, et al. 2022. "Disentangling the Evolutionary Drivers of Social Complexity: A Comprehensive Test of Hypotheses." *Science Advances* 8 (25). doi: 10.1126/sciadv.abn3517.

Turchin, Peter, Harvey Whitehouse, Jennifer Larson, Enrico Cioni, Jenny Reddish, Daniel Hoyer, Patrick E. Savage, et al. 2023a. "Big Gods and Big Science: Further Reflections on Theory, Data, and Analysis." *Religion, Brain & Behavior* 13 (2) 218–31. doi: 10.1080/2153599X.2022.2065354.

Turchin, Peter, Harvey Whitehouse, Jennifer Larson, Enrico Cioni, Jenny Reddish, Daniel Hoyer, Patrick E. Savage, et al. 2023b. "Explaining the Rise of Moralizing Religions: A Test of Competing Hypotheses Using the Seshat Databank." *Religion, Brain & Behavior* 13 (2) 167–94. doi: 10.1080/2153599X.2022.2065345.

Watson-Jones, Rachel E., Cristine H. Legare, Harvey Whitehouse, and Jennifer Clegg. 2014. "Task-Specific Effects of Ostracism on Imitation of Social Convention in Early Childhood." *Evolution and Human Behavior* 35 (3): 204–210. doi: 10.1016/j.evolhumbehav.2014.01.004.

Watson-Jones, Rachel E., Harvey Whitehouse, and Cristine H. Legare. 2016. "In-group Ostracism Increases High Fidelity Imitation in Early Childhood." *Psychological Science* 27 (1): 34–42. doi: 10.1177/0956797615607205.

Watts, J., S. J. Greenhill, Q. D. Atkinson, T. E. Currie, J. Bulbulia, and R. D. Gray. 2015. "Broad Supernatural Punishment but Not Moralizing High Gods Precede the Evolution of Political Complexity in Austronesia." *Proceedings of the Royal Society B: Biological Sciences* 282 (1804): 2014-556. doi: 10.1098/rspb.2014.2556.

Watts, Joseph, Oliver Sheehan, Quentin D. Atkinson, Joseph Bulbulia, and Russell D. Gray. 2016. "Ritual Human Sacrifice Promoted and Sustained the Evolution of Stratified Societies." *Nature* 532: 228–31. doi: 10.1038/nature17159.

White, Claire. 2021. *An Introduction to the Cognitive Science of Religion: Connecting Evolution, Brain, Cognition, and Culture*. London: Routledge. doi: 10.4324/9781351010979.

Whitehouse, Harvey. 1995. *Inside the Cult: Religious Innovation and Transmission in Papua New Guinea*. Oxford: Oxford University Press. doi: 10.1093/oso/9780198279815.001.0001.

Whitehouse, Harvey. 1996. "Apparitions, Orations, and Rings: Experience of Spirits in Dadul." In *Spirits in Culture, History, and Mind*, edited by A. Howard and J. Mageo, 173-93. New York: Routledge.

Whitehouse, Harvey. 2000. *Arguments and Icons: Divergent Modes of Religiosity*. Oxford: Oxford University Press. doi: 10.1093/oso/9780198234142.001.0001.

Whitehouse, Harvey. 2004. *Modes of Religiosity: A Cognitive Theory of Religious Transmission*. Walnut Creek, CA: AltaMira Press.

Whitehouse, Harvey. 2006. "Rites of Terror: Emotion, Metaphor and Memory in Melanesian Initiation Cults." *Journal of the Royal Anthropological Institute* 2 (4): 703-715. doi: 10.2307/3034304.

Whitehouse, Harvey. 2011. "The Coexistence Problem in Psychology, Anthropology, and Evolutionary Theory." *Human Development* 54 (3): 191-9. doi: 10.1159/000329149.

Whitehouse, Harvey. 2012. "Ritual, Cognition, and Evolution." In *Grounding the Social Sciences in the Cognitive Sciences*, edited by R. Sun. Cambridge, MA: MIT Press. doi: 10.7551/mitpress/8928.003.0015.

Whitehouse, Harvey. 2018. "Dying for the Group: Towards a General Theory of Extreme Self-sacrifice." *Behavioral and Brain Sciences* 41: e192. doi: 10.1017/S0140525X18000249.

Whitehouse, H. 2021a. "From Conflict to COVID: How Shared Experiences Shape Our World and How They Could Improve It." *New England Journal of Public Policy* 33 (2), art. 7. Accessed February 22, 2024. https://scholarworks.umb.edu/nejpp/vol33/iss2/7.

Whitehouse, Harvey. 2021b. *The Ritual Animal: Imitation and Cohesion in the Evolution of Social Complexity*. Oxford: Oxford University Press. doi: 10.1093/oso/9780199646364.001.0001.

Whitehouse, Harvey. 2023. "The Role of Ritual in the Evolution of Social Complexity." In *The Oxford Handbook of Cultural Evolution*, edited by Jamshid J. Tehrani, Jeremy Kendal, and Rachel Kendal. Oxford: Oxford University Press. doi: 10.1093/oxfordhb/9780198869252.013.49.

Whitehouse, Harvey. 2024. *Inheritance: The Evolutionary Origins of the Modern World*. London: Penguin Random House.

Whitehouse, Harvey, Pieter François, Enrico Cioni, Jill Levine, Daniel Hoyer, Jenny Reddish, and Peter Turchin. 2019. "Conclusion: Was There Ever an Axial Age?" In *The Seshat History of the Axial Age*, edited by Daniel Hoyer and Jenny Reddish. Chaplin, CT: Beresta Books. Accessed March 11, 2024. https://static1.squarespace.com/static/548f2ae8e4b068057bfcc7de/t/5f8f4535c7febe08d0d5c435/1603224888007/Conclusion+-+Was+There+Ever+an+Axial+Age+2020.pdf.

Whitehouse, Harvey, Pieter François, Patrick E. Savage, Daniel Hoyer, Kevin C. Feeney, Enrico Cioni, Rosalind Purcell, et al. 2023. "Testing the Big Gods Hypothesis: A Review and 'Retake.'" *Religion, Brain & Behavior* 13 (2): 124-66. doi: 10.1080/2153599X.2022.2074085.

Whitehouse, Harvey, and Ian Hodder. 2010. "Modes of Religiosity at Çatalhöyük." In *Religion in the Emergence of Civilization: Çatalhöyük as a Case Study*, edited by Ian Hodder, 122-45. Cambridge: Cambridge University Press. doi: 10.1017/CBO9780511761416.005.

Whitehouse, Harvey, Camilla Mazzucato, Ian Hodder, and Quentin D. Atkinson. 2014. "Modes of Religiosity and the Evolution of Social Complexity at Çatalhöyük." In *Religion at Work in a Neolithic Society: Vital Matters*, edited by Ian Hodder, 134–55. Cambridge: Cambridge University Press. doi: 10.1017/CBO9781107239043.008.

Whiten Andrew, Nicola McGuigan, Sarah Marshall-Pescini, and Lydia M. Hopper. 2009. "Emulation, Imitation, Over-imitation and the Scope of Culture for Child and Chimpanzee." *Philosophical Transactions of the Royal Society B* 364 (1528): 2417–28. doi: 10.1098/rstb.2009.0069.

Yaya, I. 2012. *The Two Faces of Inca History: Dualism in the Narratives and Cosmology of Ancient Cuzco*. Leiden: Brill. doi: 10.1163/9789004233874.

Chapter 2

Historical Questions
Jennifer Larson

With the exception of afterlife beliefs, moralizing supernatural punishment/reward has rarely been the object of comparative historical study. It is, however, a topic adjacent to many investigations of comparative religion and to the debate over the so-called Axial Age (Hoyer and Reddish 2019). Such discussions often turn on the difficulty of identifying similarities among the religions of the world and on whether terms such as *monotheism* and *transcendence* can be applied across cultures. In order to clarify the terms used in this chapter, I begin with the classification schemes used by Jan Assmann (2010) and Alan Strathern (2019).

Classifying the religions of the world

Following Theo Sundermaier, Assmann distinguishes between "primary" and "secondary" religions. Primary religions are those that "evolve historically over hundreds and thousands of years within a single culture, society and generally also language, with all of which they are inextricably entwined" (Assmann 2010: 1). Examples include the Eurasian polytheisms (e.g., Mesopotamian, Greek, Norse), the Indigenous religions of the American civilizations (e.g., Mayan, Inca, Aztec), and many tribal religions. Secondary religions are those "that owe their existence to an act of revelation and foundation" (Assmann 2010: 1). These traditions react to primary religions, denouncing them as paganism, idolatry, or superstition. Secondary religions are "counterreligions," which (at least initially) adopt an oppositional stance, and in keeping with their claims of revelation, they are also typically religions of the book. Unlike primary religions, they are translocal and (ex)portable.

Applying Assmann's distinction to the category of moralizing religions (defined as those that make interpersonal morality a principal concern), we see that secondary religions dominate the group (e.g., Buddhism, Islam, Christianity, as well as Jainism, Manichaeism, and Zoroastrianism) but that Hinduism is a primary religion (or complex of related primary traditions) that developed into a fully moralizing religion. To the extent that Judaism can be understood to have resulted from reaction against the tradition(s) of people(s) in the southern Levant during the first millennium BCE and later against Greco-Roman polytheism, it is also a secondary religion.

Strathern distinguishes between "immanentist" and "transcendentalist" religions. Immanentist religions represent the default form of human religiosity, and their shared features result from "the inherent characteristics of the evolved mind" (Strathern 2019: 27). These include the immanence of the sacred in the material world, the "promiscuous attribution of personhood" (to ancestors, spirits, deities, etc., whom Strathern calls "metapersons"), a relatively monistic cosmology, and a relatively undifferentiated afterlife. The goal of religious activity in immanentist traditions is to secure health and abundance through reciprocity with metapersons or cultivation of a cosmic status quo, while morality is a set of norms understood to support "the maintenance of successful communal living," and relations with metapersons are "defined by power rather than ethics" (Strathern 2019: 38). The cross-cultural patterns of "wild religion" (Boyer 2020) – discussed by Harvey Whitehouse in the introduction to this volume – are characteristic of immanentist systems, which seek this-worldly prosperity and the avoidance of misfortune. Although immanentisms are rooted in local environments, they are often "translatable" to other immanentist systems, as in the Greek identification of the Egyptian Osiris with Dionysus.

Transcendentalist religions, in contrast, are characterized by an "ontological breach between a transcendent realm and the mundane one" (Strathern 2019: 47). The goal of religious activity is "salvation" from mundane existence, while morality is given a new prominence and reconfigured in terms of a universalizing ethics, especially via codified ethical norms. Transcendentalist religions emphasize individual interiority over group ritual action, claim to offer revealed truths (as opposed to the "errors" of "superstition" and "idolatry" found in other religions), and produce canons, usually written. They are not "translatable" in the manner of Mediterranean polytheisms, but instead produce "universalist creeds fashioned for export as coherent packages" (Strathern 2019: 74).

The immanentist/transcendentalist distinction corresponds fairly well to Assman's primary/secondary terminology, but the emphasis in the two schemes is different: the former is more descriptive of beliefs and practices, while the latter draws attention to a given religion's degree of antiquity and its historical role (if any) in opposing its predecessors. Is there is a distinction between transcendentalist religions and our category of "moralizing religions"? Yes. A moralizing religion is one in which interpersonal morality is the principal concern. Immanentist religions that emphasize interpersonal morality to this degree are unusual but not nonexistent. In Seshat's world sample, ancient Egyptian religion clearly falls into this category.

Historical priority and endogeny of immanentisms

Crucially, Strathern stresses the fact that every transcendentalist religion exists as an unstable synthesis with immanentism; as the default and naturally developing form of human religiosity, immanentist features recur spontaneously unless people are carefully trained to reject them. In Assman's terms, secondary religions are never able to fully purge themselves of the features they criticize in primary religions. The intuition that supernatural power and/or sacredness dwells in places, persons, and objects inevitably persists and resurfaces, stimulating new cycles of transcendentalist reaction and denunciation. For our purposes, one of the key lessons to be drawn from both Assmann and Strathern's accounts is the historical priority of primary/immanentist religions. Endogenous development of immanentist features is the norm in the history of religions. It is not impossible that secondary or transcendentalist religions occurred before the first recorded example, Akhenaten's monotheistic experiment in New Kingdom Egypt, but it seems highly unlikely that they were at all common, particularly given their historical correlation with writing.

Why so many transcendentalist ideas emerged in Eurasia during the first millennium BCE has been the subject of much debate over the phenomenon of "axiality." Transcendentalist movements do not become inevitable at a certain stage of social complexity, as is clear from the absence of transcendentalisms in the precolonial Americas, where both written records and empires were present (see Covey, Part III, Chapter 1, this volume; the Central Andes narrative in Volume Two).[1] Nor is the pattern entirely unidirectional: witness the failure of Buddhism and other secondary religions to supersede the primary traditions of India. Yet Hinduism itself has developed in dialogue with Buddhism. Even Akhenaten's attempt to limit worship to Aten, though swiftly suppressed upon his death, produced a permanent change in the Egyptian religion, as Ramesside theology developed the concept of a hidden Supreme Being (Assmann 2010: 36). Once transcendentalist ideas emerge, they seem to possess remarkable staying power.

In world history, transcendentalist critiques of traditional culture have manifested themselves more broadly than through moralizing religions alone. For example, Platonism and Neoplatonism were arguably never religions, though Plato's thought has transcendentalist features that influenced Hellenistic Judaism as well as early forms of Christianity and Late Antique "pagan" monotheisms. This brings us to another key point: most moralizing religions can be traced to just two sources, Middle Eastern monotheism and the South Asian traditions of dharma and karma. Endogenous development of moralizing religions, with their strong emphasis on supernatural punishment and reward, is rare. Instead, these religions are most often propagated by missionaries, merchants, the ruler's conversion, and conquest.

Much research over the last decade has focused on the potential role of moralizing supernatural punishment and reward (MSP) in "the evolution of the wide-ranging cooperation found in large-scale societies" (e.g., Purzycki et al. 2016). Yet based on the historical record, it is probable that early human religions were of the primary/immanentist type. As described below, these religions lacked high levels of MSP even as they posited cosmic forces and/or metapersons who were highly

---

1   From this point on in the chapter, I cross-reference our World Sample in Volume Two by geographic location, adding the names of cultures where necessary, and chapters in this volume by author.

responsive to human behavior. The behavior of primary interest, however, was ritual action rather than interpersonal harm or altruism.

Morality in primary/immanentist religions

MSP, the phenomenon we are examining in this volume, must be defined etically, that is, from a scientific, outsider's perspective, because we are concerned in this volume with a cross-cultural investigation of how religions attempt to foster prosocial behavior and discourage antisocial behavior. (For a full description of MSP and its various dimensions, see François, "Bridging the Quantitative/Qualitative Divide," Volume Two.) The "moralizing" component of the abbreviation "MSP" refers to interpersonal morality, and thus we are focusing on examples of supernatural punishment and reward for behaviors that affect other people. In practice, however, this aspect of morality is rarely conceptualized separately (Polynesia). Even in moralizing religions, those in which interpersonal ethics is a principal concern, behavior toward metapersons and respect for ritual norms are typically important components of morality. Consequently, blasphemy, sacrilege, or breaking the norms of ritual behavior are expected to draw punishment at least as readily as interpersonal transgressions. The Ten Commandments observed in Judaism and Christianity, for example, combine strictures on antisocial behavior with prohibition of worshiping other gods, making carved images, and blasphemy, together with a requirement for observance of a holy day.

In primary/immanentist religions, this ritual dimension of morality typically takes precedence over interpersonal ethics. It is not that primary religions are amoral. Rather, morality is understood holistically as action that adheres to tradition and supports the received order of things. Emic moral vocabulary in these cultures speaks of concepts such as ancestral custom (e.g., ancient Greek *ta patria*, Roman *mos maiorum*), reverence for parents and gods (*eusebeia, pietas*), and the shame that inhibits wrong behavior (*aidōs, pudor*). Respect for authority is an important virtue, as is reciprocity, both of which are essential in relationships with metapersons (ancestors, spirits, deities). Both responsibility and retribution may be communal, such that a household or a city pays the price for one person's transgression. Finally, the materiality of the sacred in places, persons, and things makes it accessible via ritual; therefore, ritual failure or deviance disrupts the very core of the immanentist endeavor to secure health and prosperity for the community. This is especially the case when human behavior is conceptualized as part of a cosmic balance, such that ritual actions are required to maintain the status quo and deviant behaviors like incest or murder are thought to disrupt this balance, bringing ruin on the community (as with the Iban of Borneo). Evidence of such imbalance may manifest itself in the form of natural prodigies: for instance, both the ancient Romans (Central Italy) and the Tairona (North Colombia) regarded hermaphroditism as a sign of divine displeasure. From an immanentist point of view, even mass human sacrifice may have a moral basis if it is required in order to maintain the natural order and prevent a cosmic catastrophe (Aztecs in the Basin of Mexico; Strathern 2019: 41). These considerations help to explain why primary religions emphasize supernatural punishment for improper behavior toward metapersons, or other forms of ritual deviance. Such failures may be perceived as existential threats to the community, whereas interpersonal transgressions like lying, fraud, theft, and assault are comparatively less serious and less likely to draw supernatural punishment (A'chik of Eastern India).

MSP in primary/immanentist traditions

In many primary/immanentist religions, there appears to be little or no MSP. Surveying the immanentist religions found in the 33 regions of our World Sample, we find 1 with high MSP and 11 with minimal or no MSP, while in 4 cases there is an almost complete lack of information or too much scholarly disagreement to make a judgment (see Table 1). In the other 17 cases, MSP is unquestionably present but is limited in scope, and interpersonal morality is not a principal concern. The most notable geographical pattern is the apparent absence or minimal presence of MSP in several primary religions of the Americas (Covey, Part III, Chapter 1, this volume); of the 8 American religions in our sample, 6 are categorized as having minimal or no MSP, and 2 fall under the category of "not known or scholarly disagreement." It is important to note that records of these cultures before contact with colonialist Europeans are incomplete and suffer from bias, yet the available information does not point to widely distributed or sustained forms of MSP.

Table 1. Levels of MSP in Immanentist Religions in the 33 Regions of Our World Sample

High MSP (Moralizing Religion)	MSP Present but Limited in Scope	MSP Minimal or Absent	Not Known or Scholarly Disagreement
Egypt	Polynesia	Australia (Australian Aborigines)	Basin of Mexico (Aztecs)
	Cambodia	Cahokia (Mississipian culture)	Central and South India
	Crete (Greeks)	Central Andes (Incas)	Inland Niger Delta (Mande)
	Ghanaian Coast (Akan)	Finger Lakes (Haudenosaunee)	North Colombia (Tairona)
	Iceland and Norway (Norse)	Eastern India (A'chik)	

High MSP (Moralizing Religion)	MSP Present but Limited in Scope	MSP Minimal or Absent	Not Known or Scholarly Disagreement
	North India (Vedic culture)	Java	
	Borneo (Iban)	Lowland Andes (Shuar)	
	Anatolia (Hittites)	Mongolia	
	Central Italy (Romans)	Oro Province, Papua New Guinea (Orokaiva)	
	Siberia (Sakha)	Valley of Oaxaca (Zapotec)	
	North China	Yucatán Peninsula and adjacent regions (Maya)	
	Western Europe (Celts)		
	Sogdiana (Indo-Iranians)		
	Mesopotamia (Babylonians)		
	Iran (Elamites)		
	Southern Arabia		
	Japan		

In primary religions that do exhibit some degree of MSP, striking patterns of limitation are noticeable in its deployment. First, metapersons are rarely described as truly omniscient mind readers. Instead, they have an enhanced ability to see and hear what people do. This is a more intuitive and concrete understanding of divine crime detection and one that emphasizes acts over intentions (ancient Greeks in Crete, Hittites in Anatolia). The Akan god Onyakopon, for example, is *Brckyirihuade*, or "the one who knows what is happening in his presence as well as behind his back" (Ghanaian Coast). I contend that many such "omniscient" gods, in fact, can be explained more parsimoniously as all-seeing and all-hearing. Second, scrutiny of moral conduct may be limited to some metapersons, while others are indifferent. In Hawai'i, for example, the *akua*, gods of the state-sponsored religion, were not concerned with interpersonal transgression, but the ancestors (*aumākua*) were (Polynesia). Third, scrutiny and punishment may focus on certain social groups. In early China, for example, Tian and the Mandate of Heaven were concerned especially with the behavior of rulers and their oversight of morality (North China). Fourth, punishment may be reserved for immoral behavior only in certain domains. Among ancient speakers of Indo-European languages, the ethic of reciprocity was expressed through institutions of hospitality supervised by the gods (Crete, Iceland and Norway, Central Italy, North India, and Sogdiana). The murder of a guest in one's home, for example, was an egregious crime expected to draw divine retribution, while many other forms of transgression did not rise to this level.

Another example is the institution of the oath, which seems to have emerged endogenously in many regions of the world (Polynesia, Eastern India, Ghanaian Coast, Mongolia, and other regions mentioned in Volume Two). The very prevalence of oaths as perhaps the most widely attested form of MSP demonstrates a "domain-limited" or hierarchical understanding of moral supervision, in which many antisocial behaviors either fail to rise to the level of cosmic disturbances or are of less interest to metapersons and therefore go unpunished. Furthermore, an oath is a procedure by which individuals "harness" supernatural agents or nonagentic forces to police their own behavior. These agents and forces are not intuitively perceived as fully responsive to bad interpersonal behavior, for if they were fully responsive, oaths would be superfluous (Eastern India). One of the characteristic features of MSP in immanentist religions may be this "harnessing," whereby people devise stratagems to involve reluctant gods in policing behavior. The Akan deity Densu is the most "hot-tempered" in their pantheon and quick to punish injustice, yet he may require repeated prompting before he takes action (Ghanaian Coast). The Greeks inscribed laws on temple walls to place them within the sphere of divine interest, and they made the gods supervisors of the rights of persons freed from slavery (Crete). These strategies, however, evolved slowly and piecemeal, gradually expanding to new domains. Radically different are the kinds of policing found in secondary/transcendentalist religions, where wrongdoers encounter either a natural law of the universe that ensures negative consequences even for minor acts of harm or a mind-reading deity who can detect not only antisocial behavior but also thought crimes, such as "coveting" what one's neighbor has, and is far more self-motivated to punish them.

Naturally developing moral intuitions
The topic of naturally developing moral intuitions has attracted much research in recent years, leading to competing lists of moral domains with pan-human salience (Curry 2016; Curry, Chesters, and Van Lissa 2019; Haidt 2013; Haidt and Joseph 2007). The most often cited domains are returning favors (reciprocity), helping your group (ingroup loyalty), and deference to superiors (respect for authority). Applying these findings to supernatural punishment and reward, we observe that primary/immanentist religions focus on reciprocity and respect for authority, especially as these relate to metapersons, whether they are ancestors, the dead, gods, or animate aspects of the environment. Metapersons are often expected to favor those who bring them offerings by granting them in return prosperity or protection from disaster, and they often require those interacting with them to observe purity measures. While these metapersons may not be moralizing with respect to interpersonal behavior, they are

not amoral, since they themselves conform – at least some of the time – to intuitive expectations about reciprocity (Uruk Period in Mesopotamia). Despite their often fickle natures, the ancient Greek gods were not regarded as completely arbitrary and random actors, for in that case, making offerings would have been useless. In other primary/immanentist religions, moral principles may correspond to a pantheistic cosmos in which failures of respect and reciprocity count as disruptions and draw communal misfortune rather than individualized punishment.

Secondary/transcendentalist religions, on the other hand, react to this state of affairs by drawing attention to interpersonal and individual applications of morality, including individual justice. These religions reflect a stronger focus on the moral domain of harm/care (Haidt 2013), as in the Hindu, Buddhist, and Jain principle of ahimsa, "noninjury," which applies to animals as well as other humans. Perceptions of community and the scope of ingroup loyalty are also affected. As Whitehouse ("Introduction," this volume) notes, these religions encourage alignment with and loyalty to large "imagined communities" of fellow believers. Primary religions as well as immanentist "little traditions" within large secondary religions, meanwhile, emphasize more concrete and intuitive obligations to local communities and especially to kin. On the other hand, secondary/transcendentalist traditions insist upon a variety of nonintuitive moral concepts while simultaneously appealing to higher levels of MSP for their enforcement.

Finally, where MSP exists in primary/immanentist traditions, these tend to be multivocal, with conflicting and evolving claims on questions such as the justice of the gods, what happens to people after they die, and so forth. The unsystematized multivocality found, for example, in ancient Greek culture contrasts with the dogmatic and catechetical thrust of secondary/transcendentalist religions. True, the sacred texts of secondary traditions often display multivocality, yet the canonization process winnows out the most glaring contradictions, and authorities de-emphasize the rest when instructing young people and converts.

Punishment, reward, and the afterlife

According to behavioral economists and psychologists, rewards alone do little to change behavior, and punishments alone are somewhat effective, but a combination of reward and punishment is the most effective (e.g., Andreoni, Harbaugh, and Vesterlund 2003). If MSP has evolved within at least some religions as a way to encourage prosocial behavior, we may hypothesize that in such systems "rewards only" will be very rare, "punishments only" will be present but not predominant, and "a combination of reward and punishment" will be the most common configuration.

The immanentist traditions in our World Sample (see François, "Bridging the Quantitative/Qualitative Divide," Volume Two) reveal no cases of rewards-only MSP. Where MSP is present but interpersonal morality is not a primary concern in the religion, punishment concepts appear to greatly outnumber reward concepts. A combination of rewards and punishments occasionally appears, but rewards tend to consist of generalized this-life benefits, such as prosperity (which may be available in any case to those who properly honor metapersons). Afterlife rewards are not unknown but tend to be limited in scope, as discussed below. Therefore, our sample of immanentist traditions only partially matches our predictions, being biased toward punishment. Transcendentalist religions, however, tend to promise both harsh punishments (as in the Buddhist, Christian, and Islamic versions of Hell) and much-expanded rewards (as in reincarnation to a superior state, nirvana, paradise, or eternal life). This-life punishments and rewards are not absent, but the emphasis is on eschatology. This mix suggests that, other things being equal, these religions should be more effective at incentivizing prosocial behavior. Yet societies use multiple strategies to govern behavior, so it is difficult to separate the effect of MSP from other variables such as peer pressure and law enforcement.

In immanentist religions, as we have seen, MSP is sometimes absent or minimal. Where it is present, it addresses antisocial behavior more than prosocial behavior: that is, it focuses more on punishment of interpersonal transgression than on rewards for active cooperation and altruism. In cases where MSP exists at low levels, it tends to emphasize behavior toward kin, especially fulfilling obligations to parents and avoidance of kin slaying and incest. Among the Sakha people, for example, the matters of concern to the spirits were limited to purity and other ritual requirements, kinship obligations, and oaths (Siberia). Incest was singled out as grounds for punishment among the Iban of Borneo and several other cultures in our sample. Kin-related transgressions were also stressed among immanentist cultures speaking Indo-European languages (Central Italy, Western Europe) and were closely related to belief in the powerful dead. The ancient Greek Erinyes, or Furies, were spirits who administered punishment on behalf of wronged kin, especially parents (Crete).

With respect to transgressions against nonkin, current Seshat data do not specifically distinguish between ingroups and outgroups. Further study of this question is desirable given its relevance to the relationship between MSP and social complexity (for the latter, see Turchin et al. 2018): if MSP drove the transition to larger societies and denser populations, it ought to address behavior toward strangers. In immanentist religions that display MSP, two patterns relevant to strangers are indeed notable. One is the use of the oath backed by divine guarantors or "persuasive analogy" (i.e., magical automatism), which facilitates trade agreements, treaties, testimony in court, and other interactions with strangers. The other is hospitality, a form of reciprocity that may in some cases extend to altruism, as in the offering of food or money to indigent people who are unlikely to return the favor (ancient Greeks in Crete). While hospitality occurs as a fundamental moral value in cultures with little or no MSP (Tiwanaku of the Central Andes, Haudenosaunee of the Finger Lakes), it also became an important focus of MSP in Eurasian immanentist traditions (Romans of Central Italy, Norse of Iceland and Norway, Celts of Western Europe, Vedic religion in North India). In the Eurasian cases, however, MSP appears to have functioned less often to incentivize generosity and more often to punish those who grossly violated the guest–host relationship (e.g., by killing or raping a guest).

Explicit promises of reward for altruism toward strangers are thus relatively rare in immanentist traditions. In ancient Greek religion, kindness toward a stranger was one of the behaviors rewarded with a blessed afterlife, but only for those initiated into the Eleusinian Mysteries and only as late as the fifth century BCE, after a long period of cultural evolution (Crete). In contrast to this piecemeal and circumstantial approach, transcendentalist religions contain universalizing doctrines that, at least hypothetically, expand the ingroup to encompass the stranger, as in Paul's letter to the Galatians (3:28) in the Christian New Testament: "There is neither Jew nor Greek, slave nor free, male nor female, for you are all one in Christ Jesus." In the same letter, "life everlasting" is promised to the new Christians if they do good to everyone but especially to coreligionists (Gal. 6:8–10). The religions of dharma and karma also encourage altruism on a large scale: by the seventh century CE in China, Buddhism led to the establishment of hospitals, kitchens, orphanages, and housing for the elderly (see Stanford on Buddhism, Part II, Chapter 4, this volume; North China).

Many immanentist religions envision an afterlife (whether pleasant or unpleasant) without a moralizing component, where conditions may be general to all (Iban of Borneo, Hittites in Anatolia, Mesopotamia in the first millennium BCE) or based on elite social status (pre-Zoroastrian religion in Sogdiana). Thus, there is no necessary relationship between afterlife concepts and MSP. Quite often, conditions after death are related less to a person's good or bad behavior than to the circumstances of death, such as death in childbirth or battle (Aztec in the Basin of Mexico), dying by one's own hand or as an infant (Iban of Borneo), or death by suicide (Haudenosaunee of the Finger Lakes, Akan of Ghanaian Coast). Reincarnation and/or transmigration may be represented simply as what happens after death, with little or no moralizing component; this seems to have been the case in Druidic religion (Western Europe), in Vedic religion (Das on Hinduism and Stanford on Buddhism, Part II, Chapters 1 and 4, respectively, this volume), and among the A'chik (Eastern India).

Any of these forms of afterlife may acquire a moralizing component through cultural evolution, but often it is not applicable equally to all persons or to all types of transgression. A pattern found in European immanentisms is the reservation of afterlife punishment for those who offended the gods and/or committed the most egregious crimes (Crete in the Archaic Greek period, Iceland and Norway). Once afterlife MSP emerges, however, it has staying power and a meme-like aptitude for cross-cultural transmission. Ancient Mediterranean concepts of afterlife MSP can be traced in the Egyptian Book of the Dead, with its tribunal and weighing of the soul, in ancient Greek teachings of afterlife judges and punishments for impiety, in the torture of the wicked in the Roman underworld, and in the Christian concept of Hell (Central Italy; Czachesz, Part II, Chapter 3, this volume).

Interestingly, every moralizing religion appears to include afterlife MSP in at least some of its historical instantiations, and particularly in pre-modern ones. In transcendentalist religions, afterlife concepts are used as vehicles for universally applicable punishment and reward, with the ultimate reward represented as salvation from death or from other cosmic forces, such as the cycle of rebirth (Strathern 2019: 52). These systems are a better fit for the prediction that MSP will evolve over time to include a combination of punishment and reward, the configuration most likely to enhance social cohesion. At the same time, however, this configuration may be explainable less as a feature that benefits society than one that makes the religious concepts themselves more successful. Unlike this-life punishments and rewards, truth claims about the afterlife are not subject to testing and observation (McCauley and Lawson 2002: 205; Strathern 2019: 226–9).

MSP and causal thinking

The formation of MSP concepts in relation to misfortune tends to be circumstantial and retrospective. That is, rather than anticipating a given misfortune as a result of interpersonal transgression (e.g., all transgressors can expect to be hit by hurricanes), people may conclude only after a misfortune occurs that it is a punishment and attribute the cause to a known transgression (e.g., the hurricane hit because of a certain immoral behavior). Misfortune triggers a search for causes, together with attempts to mitigate the harm through acts of propitiation or restitution. This reasoning backward from the event to a possible cause draws on the common logical fallacy of *post hoc ergo propter hoc*.

A related pattern is the tendency to suspect some hidden transgression behind any striking case of misfortune, especially those misfortunes perceived as the work of metapersons: earthquakes, shipwrecks, crop failures, certain types of illness, sudden unexplained death, and so on. If causal attribution works backward from punishment to (supposed) crime, so that people stricken with illness or accidents are represented as being punished for their transgression, this may work against the social utility of MSP, since the set of unfortunate persons is not objectively congruent with the set of transgressors. If a victim of misfortune is unaware of any transgression, the cause may be sought in the crimes of ancestors and removed by appeasement and purification (Hittites in Anatolia, ancient Greeks in Crete). In other cases, however, potential wrongdoers are warned that their descendants may suffer for their crimes (Altai in Siberia). The common factor in these cases of ancestral fault is an essentialist belief in the transmissibility of moral taint from parent to child, the "family curse."

Beyond the salient cross-cultural patterns, however, the relationship between MSP and misfortune is very culture specific. Illness, for example, may routinely be interpreted as a punishment in some cultures (Hittites in Anatolia) but less often in others (ancient Greeks in Crete, Romans in Central Italy). In contrast to the ad hoc, circumstantial and retrospective causal thinking that is characteristic of immanentism, transcendentalist religions employ prospective thinking and universalizing principles: the sum of all a person's behaviors will be weighed and judged, or will naturally adduce certain effects, leading to blessedness or misery in the afterlife (or sooner).

Despite these divergent modes of thought, techniques for escape from punishment are found in both transcendentalist and immanentist religions. Immanentist versions typically involve offerings of propitiation or appeasement, not different in kind from those made in order to repair ritual faults (Polynesia, Ghanaian Coast). The Roman Catholic sacrament of Confession and Penance is a familiar Western transcendentalist example, and early Christianity included practices such as "second baptism" after repentance (Czachesz, Part II, Chapter 3, this volume). Practitioners of the religions of dharma and karma might intuitively expect to ameliorate the effects of bad intention and acts with good ones – though doctrines vary on this question (Spiro 1982; Stanford on Buddhism, Part II, Chapter 4, this volume). Where metapersons are involved, causal inference draws on social cognition about intentional agency and intuitive expectations about reciprocity. Where nonagentive forces like karma are involved, the process of causal inference must be closer to "naïve physics" (Kubricht, Holyoak, and Lu 2017).

These considerations raise questions about how well MSP, even in moralizing religions, actually worked to incentivize good behavior and reduce antisocial behavior. It is notable that in transcendentalist religions, the drive toward transcendental salvation may at times outpace moralizing concerns, as in the Christian/Pauline concept of "justification by faith," which elevates faith above good works (Czachesz, Part II, Chapter 3, this volume).

MSP and human moral enforcement

The simplest way to enforce moral norms is through reciprocity. In dealing with neighbors, the Early Iron Age Greek poet Hesiod advised, "Give to whoever gives, and do not give to whoever does not give" (*Works and Days*, lines 353-4). In the pre-Hispanic Andes, "networks of mutual reliance" among neighbors and kin withheld benefits like assistance in harvesting crops if reciprocity was absent. Only egregious forms of antisocial behavior, such as rebellion or murder, claimed the attention of the Inca authorities (Central Andes). We have already observed a similar pattern in immanentist traditions with MSP, where the gods and the cosmos react only to egregious transgressions, however, these are defined by a given culture.

In cultures with MSP, the degree of overlap between divine and human justice varies. Haim Shapira (2015) proposes two conceptual models. The first is that of delegation, in which the authority to judge comes from a divine source but the judgment itself is human. The other model is that of participation, where the divine is immanent in the judicial process and the result is regarded as "God's judgment." These two models correspond to different social structures: the delegation model is connected with political authority (elders, rulers, kings), while the participation model is connected with priestly judges and prophecy, as well as procedures using lots or ordeals (e.g., Josh. 7:10–26 [lots], Num. 5:11–31 [ordeal]). Shapira analyzes the Hebrew Bible and Jewish tradition, but this distinction can be usefully applied to some other religions as well. For example, ordeals overseen by local ritual specialists were used by the A'chik (Eastern India) to identify wrongdoers. Ordeals involving fire, water, poison, and combat have been practiced in many cultures, from the Babylonian Code of Hammurabi (to test a woman for adultery) to the mandatory application of ordeals in early medieval England (Kerr, Forsyth, and Plyley 1992). Hugo Mercier (2020) describes oaths, ordeals, and lie detector rituals as procedures that activate intuitions of "immanent justice," equating the misfortune following an oath or failure in the ordeal with guilt.

MSP can thus function independently of human judicial activity, as when people are directly punished through misfortune or a miserable afterlife, or it can function through divinatory processes overseen by human judges.

MSP and complex societies

Could the primary/immanentist version of supernatural reaction to human behavior have contributed to the development of complex societies? How might the focus of human attention on the goal of pleasing metapersons – regardless of their level of moral concern – or maintaining a cosmic balance have supported forms of social cohesion that enabled larger population densities, more levels of social stratification, and other features of complex societies? One possible answer is that the ritual work deemed necessary to support human flourishing in these cultures itself had the effect of increasing social cohesion beyond the kin group. In Greek polytheism, for example, groups at every size and level of society were articulated by ritual, such that admission to ritual participation indicated membership in a family, household, kinship group, ethnic group, tribe, city-state, and/or federal alliance, among many others (Larson 2016). We may speculate that this armature of rituals contributed to the stability of political structures. Since Émile Durkheim, religious ritual has been thought to enhance the group cohesion of participants, but a causal explanation for this effect has been lacking. According to Harvey Whitehouse and Jonathan

Lanman (2014), features of the rituals themselves, such as frequency of performance and use of dysphoric elements, yield either group identity (in the case of "doctrinal ritual") or identity fusion (in the case of "imagistic ritual").

Peter Turchin and colleagues (2023) concluded from analysis of worldwide historical data that moralizing religion, with attendant high levels of MSP, follows rather than precedes the rise of large-scale complex societies, a finding that fits our observations above about the historical priority of immanentisms, with their lower levels of MSP (cf. Whitehouse et al. 2023). Furthermore, Turchin et al. (2023) found that both social complexity and moralizing religion are driven by intense military competition aided by agricultural productivity; pastoralism too exerts a causal effect on MSP. Intense warfare produces strong selective pressure on polities: they must either absorb or be absorbed, destroy or be destroyed (see Turchin, Part III, Chapter 5, this volume). It is easy to see how intense competition leads to large-scale societies as stronger polities conquer weaker ones, but how this process produces moralizing religions is less clear. Perhaps the pressure of intense interpolity competition selects powerfully for what Turchin (2016) calls "ultrasocial" institutions, including religious ones, that strengthen internal cohesion and cooperation. At the psychological level, life-threatening circumstances are believed to increase religiosity levels (Greenberg et al. 2020) and social pressure to adhere to norms (Gelfand et al. 2017). Hence, while high levels of MSP fit well into this picture of selective pressure, the direct mechanism of causality leading specifically to high MSP requires further study.

If we turn from worldwide historical trends to the history of ideas, moralizing religions are related to the much-debated phenomenon of "axiality," which I will define here minimally as a pattern observed in the historical record wherein long-established archaic societies eventually reach a cultural moment in which foundational components of the status quo, such as kinship, political institutions, and ritual, are questioned and devalued (Hoyer and Reddish 2019; Strathern 2019: 23). During an axial moment, immanentist features are attacked and rejected in favor of transcendentalist ones, and there may also be direct critique of social inequality, as in the deprecation of the rich by the Gospel authors in the New Testament (Czachesz, Part II, Chapter 3, this volume). Strathern observes that anxiety about impermanence and awareness of disruptive cultural change were common factors in many instances of axiality. Transcendentalism in its Abrahamic and Indic forms offered the comfort of permanence and unchanging absolutes.

This observation seems to fit the quantitative findings of Turchin et al. (2023) in that the pressures of military competition could clearly engender insecurity and disruption, yet why did this malaise lead to a search for alternatives within larger-scale societies but not in their smaller, less complex predecessors? David Graeber (2011) cites the developments of literacy and coinage, which seem to correlate with axiality. Both involve new forms of cognition in the exercise of abstract concepts. Literacy changes people's perception of their own past, creating a historical past (or many conflicting pasts) in place of the eternal present, while coinage brings new notions of fairness and value, and cross-cultural "translatability." According to Strathern, the key development was the idea that the sacred was not (or not entirely) immanent in the world but somehow beyond it. With this development, salvation became less a matter of health and wealth and more a matter of transcending the world of the senses. According to Assmann, the key development was the concept of false religion. If other people's gods are false, all their cultural practices, including their moral systems, come under suspicion given the way primary religions are fully embedded in their respective cultures. Both new concepts, transcendence and false religion (with its corollary, absolute truth) require more cognitive effort than the familiar and intuitive immanentist world of the indwelling sacred, which accommodates many truths but with little concern for contradiction.

Hybridization, syncretism, and resistance
Regardless of the methods by which transcendentalist, fully moralizing religions spread (through trade, missionary efforts, ruler conversion, or conquest), cultures were not changed overnight: some people resisted conversion, and some features of prior religious systems were retained. The Seshat data include many periods of transition from immanentist to transcendentalist religions. In some much-contested parts of the world, such as Anatolia and Central Asia, changes in the ruling power led to a dizzying succession of different state religions (Anatolia, Sogdiana). In such cases, we must question to what degree the various state religions penetrated the "commoner" population.

Scholarship on religious change in the Hellenistic and Roman Mediterranean emphasizes the agency of conquered and colonized peoples, who accommodated the requirements of the state religion, such as emperor worship, while maintaining their own culture and selectively blending it with Roman traditions. In Roman Gaul, for example, Druidic human sacrifices ended, but the Celtic gods were not neglected (Johnston 2017). Instead of a one-way process, there could be exchange in both directions: for example, the Greek Ptolemaic rulers of Egypt adopted Pharaonic rituals, and the popular deity Sarapis was a hybrid of the Egyptian Osiris-Apis and Greek Hades (Larson 2016: 347; Moyer 2011). These phenomena illustrate the translatability of polytheisms in large-scale societies. What happened, however, when a transcendentalist religion was introduced to peoples with immanentist traditions? Buddhism operated differently from the monotheistic religions. Local gods and other metapersons now functioned within a Buddhist framework and were themselves "converted." Thus, each society that adopted Buddhism produced a distinctive blend of transcendentalism and local immanentist practices (Strathern 2019: 92–7).

The encounter of Christianity and Islam with local immanentisms was more adversarial because of the imperative to denounce the "false" religion and eradicate its rituals. Even in these cases, however, previous religious concepts and practices persisted. A notable pattern is the retention and repurposing of holy places: the Athenian Parthenon (temple of Athena the Virgin) became the Church of Parthenos Maria (Virgin Mary), and sacred springs throughout the Roman Empire became Christian holy wells, in a practice approved by Pope Gregory I (Simpson and Roud 2003). In Islam, the shrine of the Kaaba and Mecca kept the sacred status that they possessed before Muhammad's time. While the cult images at the Kaaba were destroyed, the structure itself and its holy black stone were retained. Another pattern is the survival (or reinvention) of ritual acts such as community processions, circumambulation, and votive offerings. The components of ritual are not arbitrary and random; instead, many recur across religions due to homologies of culture and cognition.

Steadfast resistance to the intrusion of secondary/transcendentalist religions has also been well documented, demonstrating that the meme-like appeal of transcendentalist notions of salvation has its limits (Reddish, Part III, Chapter 4, this volume). Such limits are observable in the record especially when missionaries and colonial authorities have expected Indigenous peoples not only to accept theological dogmas but also to alter fundamental ways of life and patterns of subsistence.

Conclusions

While most cultures do not clearly distinguish between interpersonal and ritual forms of wrongdoing, the implicit assumption in immanentist religions is that ritual offenses are more likely to draw supernatural attention and punishment, or disrupt the cosmic balance. Considering the historical priority and endogeny of immanentisms, as argued above, it is evident that forms of MSP could have arisen as simple expansions of existing beliefs about supernatural punishment for ritual infractions. Cultural evolution of MSP – where MSP occurred at all – might then manifest as a slow, incremental expansion of the behaviors thought to anger metapersons or disrupt the cosmos, the modes of supernatural scrutiny and detection, and/or the groups affected by reward/punishment. Such expansion occurred most notably in Hinduism, which developed into a fully moralizing religion. Cultures vary, however, in the degree to which such expansion occurs over the *longue durée*. In ancient China, for example, MSP seems to have been limited to the relationship between Tian/Heaven and the ruler until the advent of Buddhism, but even the nature of the "Mandate of Heaven" is a matter of debate (North China).

"Axial moments" involve critiques of a culture from within and may introduce radical new forms of causal thinking about justice, producing religions in which interpersonal morality is a primary concern and moral goodness is prioritized over "health and wealth." Whereas the incremental development of MSP in immanentist traditions is implicit and communal, the radical, transcendentalist shift toward universalizing ethics enforced by infallible supernatural powers has often been initiated by vocal individuals who functioned as reformers (Zoroaster, Buddha, Jesus, Mohammad) and whose ideas were committed to writing. Endogenous development of transcendentalisms, with their strong moralizing components, has been rare in world history. Most transcendentalist religions are descended from either Middle Eastern monotheism or the South Asian traditions of dharma and karma. These religions achieved their current dominance through trade, missionary activity, and conquest.

References

Andreoni, James, William Harbaugh, and Lise Vesterlund. 2003. "The Carrot or the Stick: Rewards, Punishments, and Cooperation." *The American Economic Review* 93 (3): 893–902. doi: 10.1257/000282803322157142.

Assmann, Jan. 2010. *The Price of Monotheism*. Translated by R. Savage. Stanford CA: Stanford University Press. doi: 10.1515/9780804772860.

Boyer, Pascal. 2020. "Informal Religious Activity Outside Hegemonic Religions: Wild Traditions and Their Relevance to Evolutionary Models." *Religion, Brain and Behavior* 10 (4): 459–72. doi: 10.1080/2153599X.2019.1678518.

Curry, Oliver Scott. 2016. "Morality as Cooperation: A Problem-Centred Approach." In *The Evolution of Morality*, edited by Todd K. Shackelford and Ranald D. Hansen, 27–51. Cham, Switzerland: Springer International. doi: 10.1007/978-3-319-19671-8_2.

Curry, Oliver Scott, Matthew Jones Chesters, and Caspar J. Van Lissa. 2019. "Mapping Morality with a Compass: Testing the Theory of 'Morality-as-Cooperation' with a New Questionnaire." *Journal of Research in Personality* 78: 106–124. doi: 10.1016/j.jrp.2018.10.008.

Durkheim, Émile. 1915. *The Elementary Forms of Religious Life*. Translated by Joseph Ward Swain. London: Allen & Unwin. doi: 10.1097/00000446-191609000-00024.

Gelfand, Michele J., Jesse R. Harrington, and Joshua Conrad Jackson. 2017. "The Strength of Social Norms Across Human Groups." *Perspectives on Psychological Science* 12 (5): 800–809. doi: 10.1177/1745691617708631.

Graeber, David. 2011. *Debt: The First 5000 Years*. Brooklyn NY: Melville House.

Greenberg, Jeff, Peter J. Helm, Mark J. Landau, and Sheldon Solomon. 2020. "Dwelling Forever in the House of the Lord: On the Terror Management Function of Religion." In *The Science of Religion, Spirituality, and Existentialism*, edited by Kenneth E. Vail and Clay Routledge, 3–20. London: Academic Press. doi: 10.1016/B978-0-12-817204-9.00002-0.

Haidt, Jonathan. 2013. *The Righteous Mind: Why Good People Are Divided by Religion and Politics*. New York: Pantheon Books.

Haidt, Jonathan, and Craig Joseph. 2007. "The Moral Mind: How 5 Sets of Innate Intuitions Guide the Development of Many Culture-Specific Virtues, and Perhaps Even Modules. In

The Innate Mind, Vol. 3, edited by P. Carruthers, S. Laurence, and S. Stich, 367-91. New York: Oxford University Press. doi: 10.1093/acprof:oso/9780195332834.003.0019.

Hoyer, Daniel, and Jenny Reddish, eds. 2019. *Seshat History of the Axial Age*. Chaplin CT: Beresta Books.

Johnston, Andrew 2017. *The Sons of Remus: Identity in Roman Gaul and Spain*. Cambridge MA: Harvard University Press. doi: 10.4159/9780674979352.

Kerr, Margaret H., Richard D. Forsyth, and Michael J. Plyley. 1992. "Cold Water and Hot Iron: Trial by Ordeal in England." *Journal of Interdisciplinary History* 22 (4): 573-95. doi: 10.2307/205237.

Kubricht, James R., Keith J. Holyoak, and Hongjing Lu. 2017. "Intuitive Physics: Current Research and Controversies." *Trends in Cognitive Sciences* 21 (10): 749-59. doi:10.1016/j.tics.2017.06.002.

Larson, Jennifer. 2016. *Understanding Greek Religion: A Cognitive Approach*. New York: Routledge. doi: 10.4324/9781315647012.

McCauley, Robert N., and E. Thomas Lawson. 2002. *Bringing Ritual to Mind: Psychological Foundations of Cultural Forms*. Cambridge: Cambridge University Press. doi: 10.1017/CBO9780511606410.

Mercier, Hugo. 2020. "The Cultural Evolution of Oaths, Ordeals, and Lie Detectors." *Journal of Cognition and Culture* 20 (3-4): 159-87. doi: 10.1163/15685373-12340080.

Moyer, Ian S. 2011. *Egypt and the Limits of Hellenism*. Cambridge: Cambridge University Press. doi: 10.1017/CBO9780511894992.

Purzycki, Benjamin Grant, Coren Apicella, Quentin D. Atkinson, Emma Cohen, Rita Anne McNamara, Aiyana K. Willard, Dimitris Xygalatas, Ara Norenzayan, and Joseph Henrich. 2016. "Moralistic Gods, Supernatural Punishment and the Expansion of Human Sociality." *Nature* 530: 327-30. doi: 10.1038/nature16980.

Shapira, Haim. 2015. "'For the Judgement Is God's': Human Judgment and Divine Justice in the Hebrew Bible and in Jewish Tradition." *Journal of Law and Religion* 27 (2): 273-328. doi: 10.1017/S0748081400000400.

Simpson, Jacqueline, and Steve Roud. 2003. "Pope Gregory's Letter." In *A Dictionary of English Folklore*. Oxford: Oxford University Press. Accessed December 19, 2021. https://www.oxfordreference.com/display/10.1093/oi/authority.20110803100337215.

Spiro, Melford. 1982. *Buddhism and Society: A Great Tradition and Its Burmese Vicissitudes*. 2nd ed. Berkeley CA: University of California Press. doi: 10.1525/9780520341982.

Strathern, Alan. 2019. *Unearthly Powers: Religious and Political Change in World History*. Cambridge: Cambridge University Press. doi: 10.1017/9781108753371.

Turchin, Peter. 2016. *Ultrasociety: How 10,000 Years of War Made Humans the Greatest Cooperators on Earth*. Chaplin CT: Beresta Books.

Turchin, Peter, Thomas E. Currie, Harvey Whitehouse, Charles Spencer, Pieter François, Kevin Feeney, Daniel Mullins, et al. 2018. "Quantitative Historical Analysis Uncovers a Single Dimension of Complexity That Structures Global Variation in Human Social Organization." *Proceedings of the National Academy of Sciences* 115 (2): E144-51. doi: 10.1073/pnas.1708800115.

Turchin, Peter, Harvey Whitehouse, Jennifer Larson, Enrico Cioni, Jenny Reddish, Daniel Hoyer, Patrick E. Savage, et al. 2023. "Explaining the Rise of Moralizing Religions: A Test of

Competing Hypotheses Using the Seshat Databank." *Religion, Brain & Behavior* 13 (2): 167–94. doi: 10.1080/2153599X.2022.2065345.

Whitehouse, Harvey, Pieter François, Patrick E. Savage, Daniel Hoyer, Kevin C. Feeney, Enrico Cioni, Rosalind Purcell, et al. 2023. "Testing the Big Gods Hypothesis with Global Historical Data: A Review and 'Retake.'" *Religion, Brain & Behavior* 13 (2): 124–66. doi: 10.1080/2153599X.2022.2074085.

Whitehouse, Harvey, and Jonathan A. Lanman. 2014. "The Ties That Bind Us: Ritual, Fusion, and Identification." *Current Anthropology* 55 (6): 674–95. doi: 10.1086/678698.

Part II:
Moralizing Religions and Moralizing Supernatural Punishment and Reward

These chapters summarize the essential elements of the major moralizing religions, describe their moralizing supernatural punishment and reward (MSP) features, including trends over time, and offer case studies on MSP dealing with each religion as it functioned in a specific period and cultural context.

Chapter 1

Hinduism
Arunjana Das

Dharma and its karmic and theistic ramifications underlie most of the moralizing supernatural punishment and reward (MSP) systems that developed under the broad purview of Hinduism. These systems, however, go beyond a simple cause-and-effect logic, where certain interpersonal actions incur direct rewards or punishments from agentic or nonagentic forces. At times, what is presented as ritual action around dharma between a person and a deity, with associated supernatural consequences, has at its core a social logic. This logic may comprise, among others, the motivation to achieve certain desired outcomes of interpersonal behavior, such as encouraging group cohesion or identity, or achieving group goals. At other times, several different logics exist at the same time, or new logics emerge that have implications for MSP. As a result, despite dharma being received as the eternal moral law that is unchanging and continuous, communities over centuries have developed a wide spectrum of ways in which they conceive dharma and its implications. This chapter explores the major themes and trends animating MSP in Hinduism, focusing on two cases: (1) the persecuted community of sixteenth- and seventeenth-century Māyāmārā Vaiṣṇavites in Assam, India, and (2) the contemporary Hindutva community in India. While many may rightly question whether Hindutva can count as a part of Hinduism, for the purpose of this chapter, it may be considered as a brand of political Hinduism that continues to play a key role in contemporary Indian politics and may help illumine the various logics relevant to its MSP system.

Introduction

> "Moreover, considering your own dharma, you should not waver. Truly, for a warrior, nothing better exists than a battle fought according to dharma. And if by good fortune, what is gained is an opened door to the celestial world, happy are the warriors, O Pārtha, who obtain such a fight."
> – Bhagavad Gita (chapter II, 31–32. Translation by Graham M. Schweig 2007)

> *"Eka śaraṇa nāma dharma."* (The only dharma is seeking refuge in the name of the Lord.)[1]
> – Maheswar Neog (1963: 23)

---

[1] All translations are mine unless otherwise noted.

In the first quote above, Kṛṣṇa warns Arjuna in the Bhagavad Gita that as a warrior (of the *Kṣatriyaḥ varṇa*), his dharma (duty) or *rāja*-dharma (dharma of the king and warrior) was to fight in a righteous battle; if he were to turn his back on such a battle, he would incur *pāpa* (sin). On the contrary, if he were to die fighting gallantly on the battlefield, he would acquire Heaven. In comparison, in the second quote, a different conception of dharma is presented – a much simpler dharma of bhakti (devotion) to the Lord that carries the supernatural reward of liberation. More importantly, for the purpose of deciphering MSP, this is also a dharma that has a social logic. Irrespective of your *varṇa* – the fourfold social division of Brahmin (priests), Kṣatriyaḥ (kings and warriors), Vaisya (people engaging in various trades), and Ṣudra (those employed as servants or in other occupations that were considered to be lower in the socioeconomic hierarchy) cited in the Ṛgveda – your dharma is one, and it is the same for everyone (*Rig-Veda I* [RV] 1876: 10.90.12). One's dharma is also not affected by one's *āśrama* (religious forms of life that individuals choose voluntarily as a permanent state, i.e., student, householder, hermit, or wandering ascetic), *jāti* (the social group, community, or clan one is born into), class, or any other social divisions.

Dharma is inseparable from its karmic and theistic implications. Transgressing the rules of dharma (the eternal moral law) or going against one's dharma (duty) may destabilize the dharma (cosmic order) of the universe, invite the wrath of a supernatural deity or the *Parama Brahman* (Supreme Spirit, God, or Deity) themselves, or make one the subject of the fruits of one's karma.

Knowing one's dharma is, hence, key to either reaping the supernatural rewards that come with it or avoiding the supernatural punishment that will surely follow if one were to transgress. The views on the ontology and epistemology of dharma in the Hindu canon are, however, nothing short of a cornucopia. For some, dharma is accurate, fixed, and knowable always. For others, it is subjective, knowable only at a certain time, place, and circumstance, or even *sukṣma* (unknowably subtle) at times (Hudson 2013). The related karmic and theistic implications of dharma are equally varied, and from the perspective of MSP, what is offered as a ritual action often has a social logic (Olivelle and Davis 2017). This social motivation and logic may comprise, among others, the desire to achieve certain outcomes of interpersonal behavior, such as encouraging group cohesion or identity, or particular group goals.

This garbing of social logic with ritual logic has been made possible partly because despite the reception of dharma as the eternal moral law that is unchanging and continuous, communities over centuries have developed a wide spectrum of ways in which they conceive dharma and its natural and supernatural implications. These conceptions of dharma sometimes compete and at times contrast with one another. Some of the longest-running intellectual traditions on the science of dharma are the Dharmaśāstra (DhS) texts, which consider what dharma is and how it is to be known. They view dharma in terms of law and conduct in human societies and present an epistemology of dharma that differs from other intellectual traditions, such as the bhakti texts, for example. The overarching message conveyed in the DhS texts is that the epistemology of dharma is scientific and the process and method of knowing dharma are reliable, reproducible, and systematic. When one steps out of this universe, however, one is transported to a bewildering profusion of conceptions of dharma, its epistemology, and its karmic and theistic implications. Another example is that of narrative literature, such as the Purāṇas and the epics. Dharma in these texts is not the accurate, precise, and knowable entity that the DhS texts present it to be (Hudson 2013). It is this tension between how dharma and its associated karmic and theistic implications are conceived in the DhS tradition versus other traditions on dharma that opens up a liminal space for *dhārmic* communities across place and time to contextualize dharma, its ramifications, what it means for them, and hence its MSP.

This chapter explores a few key themes and trends animating this evolution of MSP in Hinduism, focusing on two cases: (1) the persecuted community of Māyāmārā Vaiṣṇavites in medieval Assam, India, and (2) the contemporary Hindutva community in India. While many may question whether Hindutva counts as a part of Hinduism, for the purpose of this chapter, it may rightly be considered as a brand of political Hinduism that continues to play a key role in contemporary Indian politics. The MSP system underlying the cultural milieu of Hindutva promises to be illuminating, especially in exploring a version of the "rally-'round-the-flag" (pun intended) effect that appears in this case.

Political scientist John Mueller (1970: 18) argued that certain intense international events generate a rally-'round-the-flag effect, which tends to give a boost to a president's popularity rating. Although Mueller proposed the definition in looking at popularity levels of American presidents since 1970 in response to international threats or crises, this effect has been explored by political scientists in the context of a wide range of issues – most recently by Sylvia Kritzinger et al. (2021) in terms of how government trust was affected by the perceived threat that the COVID-19 pandemic posed to national health and economic systems and how the government's response to it influenced the public's trust in the government in France and Austria. This term is, however, also applicable in a broader sense to denote the phenomenon of groups rallying around nationalistic goals in response to perceived threats to the nation, such as in the case of Hindutva.

In looking at the evolution of these systems and their adaptation within specific contexts and communities, the lens of systems theory is useful. Seeing religions as complex, adaptive, and dynamic systems (CADS) can account for, to a degree, their spatial and temporal evolution (Cho and Squier 2013). It can also potentially account for the hermeneutical evolution seen in MSP systems within Hinduism and other religious traditions. Hinduism, much like any other religion, displays the characteristics of CADS. It is complex in terms of the many and nonlinear interactions among the various agents, practices, norms, and beliefs. It is adaptive in how it has historically and contemporarily evolved as a response to new circumstances and challenges. It is dynamic in how it has changed over time in terms of new and evolved traditions, their articulations, the accompanying beliefs and practices, hermeneutics, and their application in context-specific ways. And yet it is generally perceived as a continuous, eternal, and unchanging quasi-unitary system of beliefs by its adherents.

Elements of Hindu MSP Systems: Divine Action versus *Karma-Phala*
Dharma, as an epicenter of Hindu systems of MSP, is associated with two key mechanisms through which retribution or reward is experienced by a human for actions toward another human. The first mechanism is through the action of a divine or supernatural being or deity, characterized as *Deva* or *Devi*, or *Parama Brahman*, the Supreme Spirit or God. The second mechanism is through karma, a nonagentic, impersonal force that works automatically based on a logic of *puṇya* (merit) versus *pāpa* (demerit). The totality of one's *puṇya* is weighed against the *pāpa* that one accrues in one's lifetime as the *phala* (fruits) of one's karma, understood as action. Transgressing from one's dharma will incur undesirable consequences (Flood 1996; Krishan 1988, 1997).

Most times, when karma (as action) is aligned with dharma, one accrues *puṇya* as its *phala*. In order to be reborn as a human in the next life, one needs to accrue more *puṇya* than *pāpa* – the underlying assumption in this discourse is that being born as anything other than a human is a subpar result (Sharma 1990). Being reborn, however, is in the larger scheme of things still a subpar result as one is still caught up in *saṃsāra*, the cycle of pain, misery, and suffering, which, in this discourse, is life. To shuffle off the mortal coil of *saṃsāra* altogether for eternity, one needs to accrue a critical mass of *puṇya*. This enables one to achieve *mokṣa* or *mukti* (liberation).

Mukti is also available to humans through the action of a deity who is pleased with them or their actions. For Śaivic communities, this deity is Śiva. For Śākta communities, it is Śakti, available in any of her many incarnations and forms, and for Vaiṣṇava communities, it is Viṣṇu.

Although the basic algorithm of human action and *karma-phala* and divine retribution or reward remains foundational throughout *dhārmic* communities across India, over time, several communities have reinterpreted some of the rules of conduct and introduced new terms, relationships, and hermeneutics or reconceptualized existing ones around this basic algorithm. One of the major motivations behind this variation is the attempt by communities to democratize access to *mukti* by contesting the hegemonic discourse attempted by the Brāhminical minds behind the DhS tradition. This expansion of access to the supernatural reward of *mukti* to groups that were previously excluded from the DhS tradition was accompanied by the flourishing of newer or reconceptualized ways of access that, among other things, rewarded or punished certain interpersonal behaviors.

Religious groups and movements throughout the centuries – from the Jains, Buddhists, and Carvakas to the Tantra authors and proponents of bhakti traditions, such as the Assamese Vaiṣṇava, also known as the Mahāpūruṣiyā – actively contested the ontology and epistemology of dharma advanced by the DhS authors, leading to a spectrum of articulations and conceptualizations of dharma. The next section presents a brief historiographical sketch of key milestones pertinent to the evolution of MSP in Hinduism, including the two communities that constitute the cases for this chapter.[2]

Evolution of dharma conceptualizations and its karmic and theistic consequences

Early conceptualizations of dharma – albeit implicit, some would argue – can be traced back to the period between the early second millennium BCE and 300 BCE, when the four Vedas (Ṛg, Yajur, Atharva, and Sama) are believed to have emerged. The Ṛgveda, dated roughly around the middle of the second millennium BCE, is presented as a precursor of sorts to the corpus of the dharma literature in India, which appeared in the fourth to fifth centuries BCE (Olivelle 2005). It is cited frequently by the authors of the DhS literature, especially its account of creation and the first *puruṣa* (man), Manu, from whose limbs the four *varṇas* are presented to have emerged (RV 1876: 10.90.12).

The period immediately preceding the first century CE marks the emergence of various ascetic religious groups that challenged Brahminic supremacy and the Vedic ideology. Some of these groups, which included Buddhists, Jains, Ajivikas, and Carvakas, began reframing the term *dharma* and using it in their own ideologies. Around this time, the Mauryan Empire began consolidating its territory in the Indian subcontinent, reaching the zenith of its rule over the country. Emperor Aśoka, the grandson of Chandragupta Maurya, converted to Buddhism and employed the term *dharma* to propagate an ideology of nonviolence, compassion, and justice (Olivelle and Davis 2017). As a response to these challenges to the Vedic ideology from both emerging religious ascetic sects and usage of the term by Aśoka in his imperial ideology, the first few DhS appeared, which sought to co-opt the term and to reclaim it from reframing by these groups (Olivelle and Davis 2017). They did so in ways that not only sought to solidify Brahminic supremacy but also attempted to lay

---

2 Please note that I do not claim to present a comprehensive look into this evolution; the chapter merely gives a selective picture, focusing on the emergence of MSP as related to the major traditions, such as Śaivic, Śākta, and Vaiṣṇava, and concluding with the example of a type of contemporary political Hinduism in the form of Hindutva.

down dharma-*pramāṇas* (i.e., the epistemology of dharma) and the secondary rules of dharma (Lingat and Derrett 1973). Secondary rules of law denote how primary rules of law are founded and decided – while primary rules can be seen as duty conferring, secondary rules are those that provide power (Hart 1961). In other words, the secondary rules decide who gets to make the primary rules of law.

The DhS tradition is founded upon *varṇāśrama* dharma, which divides human society into four *varṇas* and four *āśramas*. As per the DhS tradition, *varṇas* are social classes of people who are born with an inner propensity (*svabhāva*) that is determinative of the activities (karma), occupation (*svakarma*), and duty (*svadharma*) of each class (Aktor 2018). The tradition prescribes ritual logics that pervade almost every area of human life, from areas that are as personal as morning ablutions to those that are more public, such as rules and governance around the monarchy and jurisprudence (*vyavahāra*) (Rocher 2003). *Varṇāśrama* dharma puts Brahmins at the top of the ritual and social hierarchy. At the bottom are Śudras and those who are *avarṇa* (i.e., without a *varṇa*) – who are outside of the *varṇa* system and below the lowest rungs of it, excluded from a range of ritual, and hence social, functions and spaces. Interpersonal behavior is guided to a great degree by the logic of the *varṇāśrama* system, which the DhS authors attribute to the earliest of the Vedas, the Ṛgveda. Transgressions of these prescribed rules require expiation in the form of *prāyascit* (repentance) to nullify the karmic demerit accrued through these transgressions. This can take the form of ritual offerings of material objects to a deity or sacrificial rituals (Lingat and Derrett 1973).

There is also *sādhāraṇa* dharma, or a common dharma that is applicable to all – for example, respecting elders, protecting the innocent, and so on (Lingat and Derrett 1973). There are often times when one's *svadharma*, or duty, may compete with *sādhāraṇa* dharma – the scene in the Bhagavad Gita where Arjuna takes counsel from Kṛṣṇa being a classic case of competing dharmas.

A competing set of dharma literature emerged during this time that presented a fundamentally different view of dharma and in a structure that was alien to the DhS – the narrative form, for example, the dharma epics, such as the Mahābhārata and the Rāmāyaṇa, and the Purāṇic literature. While the DhS emphasized the clarity, precision, and knowability of dharma, the epics and Purāṇic literature emphasized the *sukṣma*, or subtle, nature of dharma (Hudson 2013). This Purāṇic literature went on to contribute to the formation of some of the competing communities, such as the Śākta and Śaiva sects, which drew from this set of literature and added to it from local traditions and lore. Several new texts associated with the Śaiva and Śākta traditions appeared during this period advancing their own ideology of dharma and its karmic and theistic implications.

New Vaiṣṇava sects also formed around the country as part of the pan-India bhakti movement. One such sect was the community of Mahāpuruśia dharma in

Assam in Northeast India, founded by the fifteenth-century spiritual teacher and social reformer Śrīmanta Śankardeva.[3] This community sought to challenge aspects of the traditional Vedic dharma conceptualizations and the hegemonic discourse regarding Brahmin supremacy in Indian society. Śankardeva drew from the Bhagavad Gita, the Bhāgavata Purāṇa, and other elements of the Hindu canon to redefine dharma as *"eka śaraṇa nāma dharma"* (The only dharma is seeking refuge in the name of the Lord) in *Kali yuga* (Bhuyan 2008; Neog 1980; Phukan 2017). *Kali yuga* is the last of the four yuga, or time periods, which are *Satya, Tretā, Dwāpar*, and *Kali*. The Hindu understanding of time and soteriology states that with each *yuga* there is progressive moral decline of humankind and an erosion of dharma. Thus, achieving *mokṣa* in each yuga calls for different tools – what worked in *Satya yuga* may not work in *Kali yuga*.

From the late nineteenth to the early twentieth centuries, with the emergence of the anticolonial freedom movement in India, a new brand of political Hinduism appeared in the form of Hindutva – which means literally the state of being Hindu or the sense of Hindu-ness (Bhatt 2020; Jaffrelot 2009; Sharma 2011). The community very effectively synthesizes various theological doctrines and draws from a range of sources to propagate a discourse that has been used towards achieving group goals, such as rallying round the flag, metaphorically and literally. MSP is an integral part of this discourse.

Understanding Hindu MSP through CADS: The emerging *kamala* (lotus) as a metaphor

One way of understanding the evolution of conceptualizations of dharma and the hermeneutics around it is through the lens of CADS. It provides the scholar of dharma the means to understand how the seemingly continuous, eternal, and unchanging tradition of dharma as moral law could have a wide variety of conceptualizations across time and space.

It would be helpful to take a step back and consider the category of religion itself. Religions also manifest as CADS (Cho and Squier 2013). First, they are systems in the sense that they comprise sets of elements that work together through interconnected networks, processes, and structures toward a telos. While a religious studies scholar, such as Richard Sosis (2019), views the telos of a religious system to be social cohesion, cooperation, or coordination, a theologian will likely view these as collateral effects of a religious system, the *telos* being salvation or liberation of the soul, or unity with the Brahman and the universe, depending on the religious system the theologian is rooted in.

---

3   I was born, raised, and socialized within this community.

Second, religions are complex. It is challenging to provide a complete definition or account of a religion in terms of explaining all its features and many possible components – such as myth, narratives, texts, traditions, institutions, doctrine, hierarchy, supernatural agents, and a meaning system, among others – which interact with one another in nonlinear, and sometimes unpredictable, ways to give rise to various phenomena, patterns, structures, events, and behavior that we may understand to be religious in nature.

Third, religions are not static: they are dynamic and evolve spatially and temporally. Religions such as Christianity or Hinduism may appear unitary – a theologian would argue that the truth inherent in religion is indeed unitary and eternal, dharma being an example – but their expression and practice have evolved geographically and over time. Finally, religions are adaptive. They respond to new circumstances and realities. For example, the religious discourse around civil rights has evolved over time in America along racial, gender, and sexual identities, among others. Such an evolution can be seen in other circumstances as well, such as peace and war.

Agents play a role in how religious systems evolve. They interact with the various elements and structures of these systems in a fashion that is mutually constitutive; that is, just as systems constrain or enable the actions of agents, the latter also contest the system and contribute to its evolution (Giddens 1984). Systems also interact with one another and can mutually influence one another.

This mutually interactive and constitutive process gives rise over a period of time to certain properties, known as emergent properties in systems theories. These properties cannot be explained in terms of a simple two-way interaction between two system elements but are results of the complex and mutually constitutive process among agents and system elements (Sosis 2019).

The many conceptualizations of dharma and the associated karmic and theistic implications can be seen as emergent properties of Hindu religious systems. It is helpful to think of the *kamala* (the Indian lotus, *Nelumbo nucifera*) as a metaphor for this process of evolution – just as every *kamala* that flowers from the same riverbed can differ slightly in shape, size, and even color depending on several different internal and external (environmental) factors, the MSP systems that emerge in various contexts may differ on account of these very contexts, although they share the same riverbed of dharma and its karmic and theistic implications. Additionally, just as each *kamala* may develop many different petals, each MSP system may also develop subcomponents that are derived from the foundational riverbed of dharma.

In the sections that follow, we will look at two examples of this emergence as manifested in the MSP systems underlying the two cases selected for this chapter. In the first case, the MSP system underlying Māyāmarā Vaiṣṇavite theology includes a few key themes with several subthemes, such as Guru, *nāma*, bhakti, *bhakat* (disciple), and *Deva*. In the second case, the MSP system underlying Hindutva theology includes the following key themes: *Rāma-Rājya, sāmājik samarasatā* (social harmony), *sevā* (service), *dharma-rakṣā* (the protection, preservation, and upholding of Hindu dharma), karma, and *karma-phala*. One thing to note is that in both cases, MSP works at two levels. The first is direct cause and effect (e.g., karma); the second level is a more complex derivative, wherein social logic underlies ritual action and related MSP.

Case I: Role of *nāma* dharma and guru *mahimā* in social cohesion and group identity in the medieval Māyāmārā Vaiṣṇavite community

In the backdrop of the fourteenth- and fifteenth-century pan-India bhakti movement, the spiritual and social reformer, litterateur, and poet Srīmanta Śaṅkardeva and his disciple Mādhavadeva proposed the *Eka-śaraṇa-nāma-dharma* tradition (Barua 2013; Neog 1977). Drawing from the Bhāgavata Purāṇa, they not only offered a revolutionary way of obtaining *mukti* but also attempted to encourage social cohesion in a society that was divided along rigid lines of caste and class (Neog 1998). Also known as Śaraniā or Mahāpuruśiyā dharma, in a society where most of the underprivileged and lower classes were either unlettered or did not have access to religious texts written in Sanskrit, the teachings propagated by the two reformers sought to democratize access to *mukti* through *nāma*, worship of the Lord through songs, as the only way and dharma (Datta 1996; Neog 1980).

The tenets and implications of *nāma* dharma are found in the scriptural texts written by Śaṅkardeva, Mādhavadeva, and the many spiritual descendants who came after them, including Aniruddhadeva, the founder of the Māyāmārā Vaiṣṇavite community, a subsect founded as part of the larger Assamese Vaiṣṇavite movement (Das 2013; Nath 2014).

The MSP around *nāma* dharma works on three levels. The first level is the world of the texts, where *nāma* is presented as the great equalizer that democratizes access to bhakti and *mukti*. In *Kali yuga*, it is *Hari nāma* (singing the name of the Lord) that is the only dharma, the only cleanser of all sins, and the only tool to break free from the bonds of karma ("Bhakti Maṅgal Ghoṣa" [BMG] 2020: 5).[4] The second level is the world behind the texts, that is, the context in which the texts were written – the socioeconomic and political forces that were operative at the time in Assamese society that especially affected the Māyāmārā Vaiṣṇavite community. The third level is the world in front of the texts, that is, how the texts were received within and outside the community.[5]

---

4   The text was originally written in old Assamese and Vrajawali. The verses quoted in this book have been translated into English by me, Assamese being my native tongue.
5   In thinking through these three worlds as they relate to the text, and vice versa, the approach taken by me draws inspiration from the hermeneutical approach of Martin Heidegger and Friedrich

The world of the texts is very much connected to the world behind the texts. In a highly ritualistic society with stringent functions and roles prescribed in terms of caste and class, where animal and sometimes human sacrifices to various local and mainstream gods and goddesses were rife, proposing *nāma* dharma as the only dharma brought about a spiritual revolution of sorts. There are two supernatural rewards that are presented as the effects of engaging in *nāma* dharma, bhakti and *mukti*, where the latter is presented as a collateral effect rather than the one to aspire for (BMG 2020: 29). In other words, a disciple should engage in *nāma* dharma to acquire the inner state of bhakti rather than with the objective of attaining *mukti*. When one engages in *nāma* dharma thusly, one's *pāpa*, the accumulated karmic demerit, is completely washed away, and *mukti* is assured (BMG 2020: 28). *Nāma* dharma even has the potential to free one from the bondage of karma (BMG 2020: 5) In other words, for one who regularly engages in *nāma* dharma, karmic prescriptions (karma as action) are neutralized and the algorithm of *puṇya* versus *pāpa* does not apply any more. This reevaluation of dharma and karma contests the MSP systems propagated in *varṇāśrama*, Śaiva, and Śākta dharmas.

The revolution brought about by the proponents of *nāma* dharma was not only spiritual in nature but also social (Borah 2016; Nath 2003; Saikia 1998). Although *nāma* is presented in the text as a ritual action between a person and a deity, Lord Viṣṇu, there was a social logic underlying it aimed at addressing the deeper societal ills resulting from strict adherence to caste and class functions. *Nāma* made *mukti* available to all irrespective of caste, class, and literacy level. At a time when most of the masses in the region were unlettered – let alone fluent in written Sanskrit, the language of the DhS – *nāma* presented a simpler and more accessible route to *mukti* for everyone (Goswami 2003). There are explicit references in the texts that claim that bhakti and *nāma* are for all (BMG 2020: 406–407, 804–805). The text refers to the creation story associated with the four *varṇas* cited in the Ṛgveda and argues that irrespective of one's *varṇa*, if one does not know Viṣṇu and does not worship him, one acquires *doṣa* (sin) (BMG 2020: 197–8). There are no specific supernatural punishments prescribed in the texts for those who discriminate *bhakta* (disciples) on the basis of *varṇa*, in *nāma* dharma, but the supernatural reward of *mukti* is certainly withheld from them. In addition, related ritual actions such as *Satsaṅga* (literally meaning "company of pious people" or in this context "company of other disciples"; BMG 2020: 696–716) were prescribed, and ritual spaces called *nāmaghara* (house of *nāma*) and *śatra* were created with the specific purpose of regular communal gathering for *nāma* (Das 2013; Rahman 2015). In effect, although *nāma* is presented as a ritual action conducted in ritual spaces, it is also very much a social

---

Schleiermacher. This hermeneutical approach may, however, not always be appropriate or adequate when reading texts from non-European contexts.

action conducted in a social space, thereby incentivizing the blurring of caste and class boundaries and encouraging social cohesion.

It is in the world in front of the texts (the third level) that we begin to find MSP trends that were more specific to the Māyāmarā community. During the lifetime of Śankardeva and Mādhavadeva, the precepts of Assamese Vaiṣṇavism were founded upon the texts written by these two reformers. After their death, however, a chasm emerged, leading to four divisions: the Brahma, Puruṣa, Nikā, and Kāla *saṃhati* (sects). Of these, the Kala *saṃhati* went the furthest in attempting to implement the egalitarian vision of Śankardeva and Mādhavadeva. After their death, while not every *saṃhati* rejected the contestation of *varṇāṣrama* dharma by *nāma* dharma, only the Kāla *saṃhati*, and within it the Māyāmarā community, truly embraced this notion in word and practice (Neog 1980). Sri Sri Aniruddhadeva, the founder of the community, actively sought to reach out to groups that were underprivileged, unlettered, and marginalized and ignored by the other sects (Ahmed 2003). The descendants of Aniruddhadeva who accepted headship of the Māyāmarā sect continued in this egalitarian tradition, to the point of having Śudra spiritual heads initiate Brahmin disciples into the community – a first in the history of Vaiṣṇavism in the region and perhaps the country (Neog 1982). The Guru in this community, hence, is very dear to the disciples and considered the very embodiment of the divine (BMG 2020: 127). The Guru is indispensable on the path to bhakti, and the inner state of bhakti cannot be attained if one is not under the tutelage of a Guru (BMG 2020: 6–8; "Geet Śāstra" 2020: 2).

The *mahimā* (wonder, glory, and awe) associated with a Deva or a Guru is presented as a quasi-agentic force that has the potential for meting out rewards and punishments. Although the subsects in the other *saṃhati* also believed this, it was especially the case with the Māyāmarā community. While the social logic underlying *nāma* dharma serves to incentivize social cohesion, the logic underlying Guru *mahimā* rewards or punishes behavior toward the Guru or the ritually sacred scriptures, which include the written corpus of the two cofounders and Aniruddhadeva.

The Guru's *mahimā* rewards devotion and respect to the Guru, the ritual texts, and the action prescribed in the texts. It may also act in a punitive way when there are transgressions of the prescribed ritual action between a person and a deity, including those with an underlying social logic. One example of this is the religious restriction on access to one of the key texts of the community, the *Nij-Śāstra*, which is open only to selected members in the community who have gone through a prescribed ritual process of *śarana* (ritualistic initiation into the religious community) and *bhajan* (a ritualistic process of receiving a senior status in the community) (Gohain 2003). The text is not available to the general public and is kept fiercely guarded by the community (Baruah 2003). Members believe that anyone who seeks access to the *Nij-Śāstra* through devious means and/or with evil intentions will meet with supernatural retribution associated with the *mahimā* of the Guru.[6]

The term *Nij* means one's own. For a community practicing an egalitarian message, a text that overtly functions to delineate what is theirs may also serve to reinforce group identity and encourage group cohesion at a time when members of the community were widely marginalized by other Vaiṣṇava communities and disenfranchised by the then monarchy. The supernatural retribution that Guru *mahimā* may bring to those who disrespect the precepts around the śāstra serves the overt function of incentivizing conformance both inside and outside the community and deterring transgressions, but it also reinforces communal identity and belongingness.[7]

There are other, more overtly interpersonal transgressions that may invite the punitive action of Guru *mahimā* or the wrath of Deva, such as *beybhicāra*, *pāpa*, and *aparādha* (Konwar 2003). *Beybhicāra* are great transgressions that bring high karmic demerit. There are four *beybhicāra* described in the texts: (1) Guru-*beybhicāra*: disloyalty or disrespect to the Guru; (2) Deva-*beybhicāra*: disloyalty or disrespect to Deva; (3) *phala beybhicāra*: attachment to things other than bhakti and *mukti*; and (4) bhakti *beybhicāra*: harboring or practicing devotion toward other gods (BMG 2020: 307; Konwar 2003).

Along with the four *beybhicāra*, there are five great *pāpa*, actions that will bring equal karmic demerit as *beybhicāra* (or even greater): (1) murder of a Brahman, (2) killing of a cow, (3) murder of a Guru, (4) having inappropriate relations with the wife of a Guru (*Guru-patni gaman*), and (5) stealing (*cauurya*) (BMG 2020: 205; Konwar 2003).

In addition, there are *aparādha*, actions that bring karmic demerit but to a lesser degree: for example, partaking in liquor, engaging in adultery, or what is perceived as licentious behavior, and debauchery. Righting the wrong of these *aparādha* requires *prāyascita* (repentance). Engaging in *prāyascita* can neutralize the karmic demerit accrued through the *aparādha* (BMG 2020: 714; Konwar 2003).

A key phenomenon observed in the Māyāmārā community is the hermeneutical pivot of *Guru-ṛna* (debt to the Guru).[8] On account of its egalitarian message and practice, the community soon won wide popular appeal among the masses, especially the underprivileged classes.[9] At a time when several other śatras (sects), fearing per-

---

[6] This is based on oral lore associated with the Nij-Śāstra gathered through my background interviews with community members.

[7] This is a hypothesis proposed by me based on secondary sources and background interviews with community members.

[8] This is based on my background interviews with community members.

[9] The egalitarianism, however, was more visible in the case of castes and classes than in gender. Although women enjoyed a few more liberties in this community compared with other Vaiṣṇava communities in the then Assam, they were still restricted access to a range of spiritual functions,

secution from the monarchy and intending to gain royal patronage, aligned themselves with the monarchy, the Māyāmarā *satra* remained independent and refused royal patronage (Gogoi 2015; Gogoi and Gogoi 2020). This not only brought the *satra* squarely in the crosshairs, both figuratively and literally, of the Ahom monarchs but also complicated its relationships with the other *satras* as the latter began to ostracize it to the point of taking up arms against it. The Ahom monarchy soon began viewing it as a political rival and threat and started a systematic exercise of economic, social, and religious persecution bordering on extermination. Generations of Ahom kings persecuted the community – several of the *Mahantas* and *Gosains*, spiritual heads of the community, were either exiled or assassinated by the Ahom monarchy (Hazarika 1999; "Tungkhungia Buranji" 1932). The brutal persecution of the community members and killings of the spiritual heads reached a critical mass in the late eighteenth century when disciples of the sect rose up in arms to avenge the murders of their spiritual heads in what is popularly known as the Māyāmarā rebellion (Borah 1983). Their slogan was "*mori jau, maari jau, Guru'r ṛn xudhi jau*" ("We will kill or be killed, but we will repay the *ṛna*, debt, to the Guru") (Baruah 2003: VI).

Combined with this persecution, over a period of 50 years, a range of socioeconomic and political factors influenced an emerging hermeneutic in this community, that of *Guru-ṛna*. Whereas *nāma* dharma functioned on an individual metaphysical level and a disciple was free of karmic obligations if he or she were to engage in *nāma* dharma, repaying the Guru's debt became a companion karmic obligation to *nāma* dharma. When the Guru, as an embodiment of the Divine itself, opened *nāma* dharma as the only rudder for the celestial boat of life, the disciples automatically incurred a moral loan that needed to be repaid. In this discourse, one way of repaying this moral loan that the Guru's *mahimā* instilled in a disciple was to avenge the Guru's humiliation and murder by taking up arms against the tyrannical monarchy.

Case II: Role of sevā and sāmājik samarasatā in the "rally-'round-the-bhagwā-dhwaja" (saffron flag) effect in contemporary Hindutva

"*Sāmājik samarasatā se āyegā Rāma-Rājya.*" (*Rāma-Rājya* will arise from social harmony.)

– Vijaya Shankara Tiwari (2022: 4)[10]

---

spaces, and rituals. Some of these restrictions continue in contemporary times. In general, in Assamese Vaisnavism, ritual functions are highly gendered (see Bora 2018).

10   The translation from Hindi to English was done by me.

The Hindutva discourse presents *Rāma-Rājya* as the telos of India's theo-ethical universe (Udayakumar 2005). *Rāma-Rājya* is a socio-ethical imaginary, a utopic vision of the future where Indian society will resemble again the Satya Yuga when Lord Rāma was king and dharma – understood both as cosmic order and societal and individual righteousness – was at its zenith (Sarkar 1996). This metaphysical framework has long been in use in Indian politics and was also used by Mahatma Gandhi during India's anticolonial struggle for independence. The utopian future, as per this framework, presently manifests only territorially as *Rāma-Janambhumi* (the birthplace of Lord Rāma), the territory bound by the nation-state of India (Vishva Hindu Parishad [VHP] n.d.-a). In other words, while *Rāma-Janambhumi* is the past and the present of the country, *Rāma-Rājya* is the future. This future is not only the telos of the Indian nation-state but also a reward that comprises spiritual and societal goods. But this reward cannot be harvested unless Hindus expressively strive for certain intermediate goals and actions, such as sāmājik samarasatā, dharma-rakṣā, and sevā.[11]

The goal of social harmony is evidently geared toward prosociality, but it is directed toward creating a Hindu society. In other words, the social logic underlying *sāmājik samarasatā* seeks to reframe or rather provide an addendum to the DhS conceptualization of *varṇāśrama* dharma in the service of achieving a Hindu nation. Presenting untouchability as a custom foreign to Hinduism and brought to the country by the British colonizers and Muslim invaders, it overlooks the explicit position that the DhS tradition adopts in generally associating permanent ritual pollution with Śudras and *avarṇas* and their exclusion from several ritual spaces and functions. Regarding *sāmājik samarasatā*, the VHP, a Hindu nationalist organization in India, says,

> Temples and other places were always open to everyone in the country, irrespective of caste and class. There is a need for a campaign to bring back social harmony in the country. ... the Vishwa Hindu parishad was founded to protect Hindu Dharma, ... and to bring back social harmony in the country. It is now ready to bring this social revolution. (Tiwari 2022: 5)

The hegemonic and normative discourse that the DhS tradition attempts to promote regarding the ritually and socially superior position of the Brahman and Kṣatriyaḥ *varṇas* and the marginalization and disenfranchisement of the Śudras and the *avarṇas* remains a moral hot potato that the Hindutva universe would

---

11 In this discourse, Hindu dharma is conceptualized in terms of both religion and the moral law of the universe. The VHP (n.d.-b) notes on its website regarding protecting Hindu dharma, "The objective of the VHP is to organize – consolidate the Hindu society and to serve – protect the Hindu Dharma."

prefer to chuck into a black hole. Instead, the community argues that being born in India makes one automatically Hindu and, hence, pure. Every part of nature – the land, trees, air, animals, rocks, and mountains – in India is pure simply by virtue of being a part of this pure land. Hence, no Hindu can be impure. Hindus, however, need to maintain this purity by following the Hindu *paddhati* (way of life). The VHP notes in its newsletter,

> Every Hindu is pure. Being born in a Hindu family implies that all kinds of class and caste distinctions have been erased. … Following the Hindu paddhati (way) of life purifies a person. A Hindu cannot be achut or tyajya. (Tiwari 2022: 5)

Thus, if there is a group boundary that Hindutva leaders emphasize in their discourses, it is that of being a Hindu, irrespective of caste, class, or *jāti*.[12] Therefore, one Hindu should not look down upon another Hindu – each Hindu is equally pure as the other simply by virtue of being born in the pure Motherland of India, Bharata Mata, the incarnation of the goddess Durga herself. It is only this kind of social harmony that will bring the reward of *Rāma-Rājya* (Tiwari 2022, 4).

Sharing the legacy of Rāma and being future recipients of the inheritance of *Rāma-Rājya*, however, also puts a *dhārmic* obligation on every Hindu – that of *dharma-rakṣā*, that is, to protect and preserve the Hindu dharma, especially against "foreign" entities, such as Christian missionaries, Muslim invaders, British colonizers, and Muslim-majority countries accused of persecuting Hindus. In this discourse, Hindu dharma needs to be fought for, protected, and preserved from these foreign threats; this need is presented as urgent and to be addressed using violence if called for.[13]

Dharma-rakṣā is an intermediate goal, but it also comprises actions taken toward reaching that goal. *Dharma-rakṣā* as a group goal has three specific rewards: theo-political, ethical, and cosmic. First, protecting Hindu dharma will ensure that Hinduism as a religion and India as a nation are preserved. Being able to maintain the territory of India as the Motherland and *Rāma-Janambhumi* is, hence, contingent upon the continuation of Hindu dharma (Rashtriya Swayamsevak Sangh [RSS] 2020 – a Hindu nationalist organization in India). Second, the eternal supernatural reward of *Rāma-Rajya* cannot be realized if Lord Rāma's way of life, that is, dharma

---

12 It does not follow, however, that this is also found empirically in Hindutva practice.
13 "Khoon kharaba hona hai tho ek baar ho jane do" (If blood must be shed, let it be shed once and for all). Leading up to the demolition of the Babri Masjid in Ayodhya on December 6, 1992, Sadhvi Rithambhara, the founder of Durga Vahini, the female wing of the VHP, and a vocal Hindutva proponent with thousands of followers in the community, famously called openly for bloodshed in a public speech that was played over and over again in households in North India (see Prasannan and Mukerji 2017).

as the eternal moral law, ceases to exist. Third, for dharma as the cosmic order of the universe to be preserved, the future continuation of Hindu dharma, as a religion and a way of life, itself is key. In other words, these material (in the form of the nation and its culture), spiritual and social (in the form of *Rāma-Rajya*), and moral and cosmic (in the form of moral law and cosmic order) rewards become group goals, to attain which in the future requires human action in the present. From the perspective of MSP, the threat of the withholding of the reward of *Rāma-Rajya* is a punishment in itself, which will cease the Hindu way of life and effectively destroy the Hindu nation.

The logic underlying *dharma-rakṣā* is, hence, very much social, but it is geared toward rallying the group around its goal of building a nation only for Hindus, or rather Hindus who subscribe to the ideals of Hindutva as prescribed by the group. While it engenders prosociality within the group, it fosters antisocial behavior toward those who remain outside the group.

The clearest example of prosociality, however, is exemplified in the discourse on the notion of *sevā* (service). The Rashtra Sevika Samiti, the female wing of the RSS, defines *sewā* on its website:

> "Service" means to pay respect to the needs of other people. "Rashtra Sevika Samiti" is inherent in the name of "service" in this organization of women. The service woman has a permanent value and natural quality. The service also has special significance in the work-plan of the Samiti. The service of the national service, the people living here, the animals, birds, trees, mountains, rivers, the sea etc., all the components of the creation of the work is to protect. Enlighten the spirit of the nation, its way of life, and the culture of culture. (Rashtra Sevika Samiti n.d.)[14]

The RSS, the VHP, and the Rashtra Sevika Samiti engage in several service projects nationally, and to some degree internationally through Sewa International, among others.[15]

There are two different logics underlying the discourse presented regarding *sewā*. First is the karmic logic of doing good to others to accrue *puṇya*. In this universe, each Hindu will have a different lived experience based on their karmic wallet – a human's wealth, strength, fame, family, and relationships are a result of karmic merit from a past life. Similarly, disease, ill fortune, poverty, and other material

---

14 See also https://www.rashtriyasewabharati.org/.
15 Sewa's connection to Hindutva ideology and concerns about how the funds raised were funneled into Hinduization programs have been highlighted by a few investigative reports (Sabrang Communications Private Limited, Mumbai, India, and The South Asia Citizens Web, France 2002; see also Pahwa 2021).

afflictions are a result of karmic demerit. Those who are more fortunate in this life as a result of this karmic algorithm can accrue even more *puṇya* if they are kind and helpful toward those who are poor, suffering, and less fortunate. *Sewā* is a means of helping the less fortunate in this life and accruing *puṇya* in this life.

The second logic – the unstated one – involves a mixture of political, social, and ritual logics based on achieving group goals around proselytism and recruitment, that is, the goal of religious conversion through, and as, development and welfare politics; this has been increasingly the case since the 1990s (Bhattacharjee 2016; Chidambaram 2012). *Sewā* is an effective means of proselytizing Hindutva among those who have not yet converted to its ideals through patronage, especially the marginalized groups of people known as Adivasis (Banerjee 2012; *Hindustan Times* 2015). It also creates liminal spaces to reach out to groups that cannot be accessed through mainstream, male-dominated channels – for example, families and women, through women's empowerment and employment schemes (Kovacs 2004). It is also a way to "reverse" conversions under their "*ghar wāpsī*" (homecoming) program (*Hindustan Times* 2015).

While the first logic of prosociality engendering *puṇya* is used as a motivation for group members, and potentially nonmembers, to participate in *sewā*, it is also a mechanism to realize the second logic of achieving the group goal of spreading Hindutva through proselytization, recruitment (and *ghar wāpsī* of converts), development politics, and patronage, ultimately contributing to the rally-'round-the-flag effect – or rather, in this case, "rally 'round the *Bhagwā Dhwaja*" (the saffron flag as a symbol of Hindutva).

Conclusion

The logics of what one may call Hindu MSP are guided by varying conceptions of dharma and its karmic and theistic implications among communities. Adopting a systems theory approach helps us understand how a tradition believed to be eternal, continuous, and unchanging gave rise to two different MSP systems in two different contexts, exemplified by the two case studies explored in this chapter. Although the particular elements of the two MSP systems look different, they are united by a few key commonalities that may offer a framework to look at MSP systems in other contexts.

First, what may appear as ritual logic in Hinduism may have an underlying social logic. In the case of *nāma* dharma, we find that *nāma* as a prescribed ritual act between a person and a deity comes with a few qualifiers that serve a social function. It incentivizes social cohesion by democratizing access to bhakti and *mukti* – both supernatural rewards. Being a prescribed group activity conducted in an appointed ritual communal space (*nāmaghara*), it also encourages group and communal identity.

Second, there may be logics that are obviously social but on closer inspection are a mixture of intertwined ritual, social, and political logics that may interact with one another. We see this in the Hindutva case, where the obviously social logic of social harmony leading to *Rāma-Rajya* reveals an underlying layer of what one can call a ritual-political logic – revising the category of Hindu to include Hindutva and defining social harmony in terms of this category in the service of group goals. Similarly, the simple social logic of *sewā* being associated with *puṇya* serves as a complement to an equally, if not more, important ritual-political and social logic of expanding the purview of Hindutva and the "rally-'round-the-*Bhagwā-Dhwaja*" effect in both metaphorical and literal ways.

Third – and related to the second point above – complex interaction of sociopolitical and economic forces over time can create new logics, for example, revision of the category of Hindu. We also find the emergence of new logics in the Māyāmārā Vaiṣṇava community, where the conception of *Guru-ṛn* emerged as a direct result of this complex interaction.

Understanding this process of how complex societies use a combination of logics, how new logics emerge over time, and what their implications are for the societies themselves could provide opportunities for future study.

References

Primary sources

"Bhakti Mangal Ghoṣa." 2020. In *Sri Sri Aniruddhadeva Rachanavali* [Compilations of works by Sri Sri Aniruddhadeva], edited by Dambarudhar Nath. Guwahati: Assam Prakashan Parishad.

"Geet Śastra." 2020. In *Sri Sri Aniruddhadeva Rachanavali* [Compilations of works by Sri Sri Aniruddhadeva], edited by Dambarudhar Nath. Guwahati: Assam Prakashan Parishad.

Rig-Veda I. 1876. Edited and translated by Hermann Grassmann. Leipzig: F. A. Brockhaus.

"Tungkhungia Buranji." 1932. In *A Chronicle of Tunkhungia Kings of Assam*, edited by Surya Kumar Bhuyan. Guwahati: Department of Historical and Antiquarian Studies.

Secondary sources

Ahmed, Minamuddin. 2003. "Sri Sri Aniruddhadeva and Social Formation in Upper Assam." In *Life and Teachings of Sri Sri Aniruddhadeva*, edited by Swarnalata Baruah, 103–113. Dibrugarh: Dibrugarh University.

Aktor, Mikael. 2018. "Social Classes: Varṇa." In *Hindu Law: A New History of Dharmaśāstra*, edited by Patrick Olivelle and Donald R. Davis, 60–77. Oxford: Oxford University Press. doi: 10.1093/oso/9780198702603.003.0005.

Banerjee, Sikata. 2012. *Make Me a Man!: Masculinity, Hinduism, and Nationalism in India*. New York: SUNY Press.

Barua, Archana. 2013. "Mahapurush Sankaradeva and the Bhakti Renaissance in Assam in Light of the Phenomenology of Religious Experience." *Prajñā Vihāra: Journal of Philosophy and Religion* 14 (1–2). Accessed March 14, 2024. http://www.assumptionjournal.au.edu/index.php/PrajnaVihara/article/view/768/684.

Baruah, Swarnalata, ed. 2003. *Life and Teachings of Sri Sri Aniruddhadeva*. Dibrugarh: Dibrugarh University.

Bhatt, Chetan. 2020. *Hindu Nationalism: Origins, Ideologies and Modern Myths*. London: Routledge. doi: 10.4324/9781003085553.

Bhattacharjee, Malini. 2016. "Seva, Hindutva, and the Politics of Post-Earthquake Relief and Reconstruction in Rural Kutch." *Asian Ethnology* 75 (1): 75–104. Accessed March 24, 2024. file:///C:/Users/91984/Downloads/Asian%20Ethnology%2075-1%202016,%2075-104,%20Bhattacharjee,%20Malini.pdf.

Bhuyan, Abhijit. 2008. "Sankardeva and Neo-Vaishnavism in Assam." *Ishani* 2 (3).

Bora, Simashree. 2018. "Gendered Devotion in Neo-Vaishnavism: Women, Monks and Sattras of Majuli, Assam." *Indian Journal of Gender Studies* 25 (3): 331–50. doi: 10.1177/0971521518785665.

Borah, Dhrubajyoti. 1983. *Moamoria Gana Abhuyuthan*. [The Moamoria/Mayamara public rebellion]. 1st ed. Nalbari: Journal Emporium.

Borah, Rinku. 2016. "The Neo-vaishnavism of Srimanta Sankaradeva: A Great Socio-cultural Revolution in Assam." *MSSV Journal of Humanities and Social Sciences* 1 (1). Accessed March 14, 2024. https://mssv.ac.in/media-library/uploads/iSbAV355wd7CriGmaPS24lZEoX-1yZwpLdRwjc3Qg.pdf.

Cho, Francisca, and Richard King Squier. 2013. "Religion as a Complex and Dynamic System." *Journal of the American Academy of Religion* 81 (2): 357–98. doi: 10.1093/jaarel/lft016.

Chidambaram, Soundarya. 2012. "The 'Right' Kind of Welfare in South India's Urban Slums: Seva vs. Patronage and the Success of Hindu Nationalist Organizations." *Asian Survey* 52 (2): 298–320. doi: 10.1525/as.2012.52.2.298.

Das Anjan. 2013. "Bhakti Movement, Srimanta Sankardeva and Satra Institution of Assam." Social Science Research Network. Accessed March 14, 2024. https://deliverypdf.ssrn.com/delivery.php?ID=348094069068099095116083125112001024022087061054024018026093000006065029028031107106002063005047108007015085098076087071119016046053082082007100064089066102005122030095085017074112114089083083110064109064096122004-126095084000127071102086088002029101119&EXT=pdf&INDEX=TRUE.

Datta, Birendranath. 1996. "Sankaradeva and the Tribals of North-East India." In *Essays on Sankardeva*, edited by Ranjit Kumar Dev Goswami, 205–208. Guwahati: Forum for Sankaradeva Studies.

Flood, Gavin. 1996. *An Introduction to Hinduism*. Cambridge: Cambridge University Press.

Giddens, Anthony. 1984. *The Constitution of Society*. Cambridge: Polity Press.

Gogoi, Biswadip. 2015. "The Matak, Mayamara Sect and Moamaria Revolt: A Brief Revisit." *Integrated Journal of Social Sciences* 2 (1): 23–7.

Gogoi, Khogen, and Monjit Gogoi. 2020. "Understanding the Society and Culture of Mayamara Satras of Assam in 18th Century: A Historical Analysis." *Solid State Technology* 63 (6): 8691–703.

Gohain, Birendra K. 2003. "Nij-Śāstra: An Introduction." In *Life and Teachings of Sri Sri Aniruddhadeva*, edited by Swarnalata Baruah, 140–48. Dibrugarh: Dibrugarh University.

Goswami, Gokulendra Narayana Deva. 2003. "Place of the Depressed Classes in Sri Sri Aniruddhadeva's Bhakti Mangal Ghosa." In *Life and Teachings of Sri Sri Aniruddhadeva*, edited by Swarnalata Baruah, 149–56. Dibrugarh: Dibrugarh University.

Hart, Herbert Lionel Adolphus. 1961. *The Concept of Law*. Oxford: Clarendon Press.

Hazarika, Annie. 1999. *Axomor Itihasat Sri Sri Aniruddhadeva aru Mayamara Vaisnava Sampradaya* [Sri Sri Aniruddhadeva and the Māyāmarā Vaiṣṇava Community in the history of Assam]. Guwahati: Lawyers Book Stall.

Hindustan Times. 2015. "RSS to Launch New Projects for Tribals." April 12, 2015. Accessed March 1, 2024. https://www.hindustantimes.com/india/rss-to-launch-new-projects-for-tribals/story-CgLJuGXFkqq1JkyvZ25qlK.html.

Hudson, Emily T. 2013. *Disorienting Dharma: Ethics and the Aesthetics of Suffering in the Mahabharata*. New York: Oxford University Press. doi: 10.1093/acprof:oso/9780199860760.001.0001.

Jaffrelot, Christophe, ed. 2009. *Hindu Nationalism: A Reader*. Princeton, NJ: Princeton University Press. doi: 10.2307/j.ctt7s415.

Konwar, Bhaba Kanta. 2003. "A Critical Appraisal of the Bhakti Mangal Ghosa." In *Life and Teachings of Sri Sri Aniruddhadeva*, edited by Swarnalata Baruah, 118–139. Dibrugarh: Dibrugarh University.

Kovacs, Anja. 2004. "You Don't Understand, We Are at War! Refashioning Durga in the Service of Hindu Nationalism." *Contemporary South Asia* 13 (4): 373–88. doi: 10.1080/09584930500070597.

Krishan, Y. 1988. "The Vedic Origins of the Doctrine of Karma." *South Asian Studies* 4 (1): 51–55. doi: 10.1080/02666030.1988.9628366.

Krishan, Yuvraj. 1997. *The Doctrine of Karma: Its Origin and Development in Brāhmaṇical, Buddhist, and Jaina Traditions*. New Delhi: Bharatiya Vidya Bhavan.

Kritzinger, Sylvia, Martial Foucault, Romain Lachat, Julia Partheymüller, Carolina Plescia, and Sylvain Brouard. 2021. "'Rally Round the flag': The COVID-19 Crisis and Trust in the National Government." *West European Politics* 44 (5-6): 1205–231. doi: 10.1080/01402382.2021.1925017.

Lingat, Robert, and John Duncan Martin Derrett. 1973. *The Classical Law of India*. Berkeley, CA: University of California Press.

Mueller, John E. 1970. "Presidential Popularity from Truman to Johnson1." *American Political Science Review* 64 (1): 18–34. doi: 10.2307/1955610.

Nath, Dambarudhar. 2003. "Social Background of the Neo-Vaiṣṇavite Movement in Assam: A Case Study on the Māyāmarā Vaiṣṇavism of Sri Sri Aniruddhadeva." In *Life and Teachings of Sri Sri Aniruddhadeva*, edited by Swarnalata Baruah, 157–166. Dibrugarh: Dibrugarh University.

Nath, Dambarudhar. 2014. "Cult, Ideology and Conflict: The 'Māyāmarā' Vaishnavism and Social Conflict in 18th Century Assam." *Proceedings of the Indian History Congress* 75, 351–7.

Neog, D. 1963. *Jagat-Guru Śaṅkardew*. Nagaon: Srimanta Sankardeva Sangha.

Neog, Maheswar. 1977. "The Bhakti Cycle of Assamese Lyrics: Bargits and After." In *Bargit of Mahapurush Shree Shankardeb*, 1–22.

Neog, Maheswar. 1980. *Early History of the Vaiṣṇava Faith and Movement in Assam: Śaṅkaradeva and His Times*. New Delhi: Motilal Banarsidass.

Neog, Maheswar. 1982. *Socio-political Events in Assam Leading to the Militancy of the Māyāmariyā Vaiṣṇavas*. Kolkata: Centre for Studies in Social Sciences.

Neog, Maheswar. 1998. "The Contribution of the Sankardeva Movement to the Culture and Civilisation of India." Guwahati: Forum for Sankardeva Studies.

Olivelle, Patrick, ed. 2005. "VII. Explorations in the Early History of Dharmasastra." In *Between the Empires: Society in India 300 BCE to 400 CE*, 1000–1023. New York: Oxford University Press.

Olivelle, Patrick, and Donald R. Davis, eds. 2017. *Hindu Law: A New History of Dharmaśāstra*. New York: Oxford University Press.

Pahwa, Nitish. 2021. "COVID Relief Donations Are Supporting a Project to 'Hinduize' India: Why are Twitter, Microsoft, and Google Promoting a Charity with Ties to Right-Wing Nationalism?" Slate.com, June 8, 2021. Accessed March 28, 2022. https://slate.com/news-and-politics/2021/06/covid-india-charity-sewa-hindu-nationalism.html.

Phukan, Bimal. 2017. *Srimanta Sankaradeva: Vaishnava Saint of Assam*. Bloomington, IN: Partridge India. Accessed March 15, 2024. https://www.google.co.in/books/edition/Srimanta_Sankaradeva_Vaishnava_Saint_of/GDc-DgAAQBAJ?hl=en&gbpv=1&printsec=frontcover.

Prasannan, R., and Debashish Mukerjee. 2017. "ARCHIVAL: Ground Report of Babri Masjid Demolition." December 6, 2017. Accessed March 18, 2024. https://www.theweek.in/news/india/from-the-archives-ground-report-babri-masjid-demolition.html.

Rahman, Mehjabeen Suraiya. 2015. "Role of Satra & Namghar in the Evolution of Genesis of Assamese Identity." *International Journal of Social Sciences and Management* 2 (2): 108–113. doi: 10.3126/ijssm.v2i2.12143.

Rashtra Sevika Samiti. n.d. "Seva." Accessed March 18, 2024. https://sevikasamiti.org/Seva.

Rashtriya Swayamsevak Sangh. 2020. "ABKM Resolution: The Construction of Mandir at Ram Janmasthan a Symbol of National Pride." March 14, 2020. Accessed April 5, 2024. https://www.rss.org//Encyc/2020/3/16/ABKM-Resolution-THE-CONSTRUCTION-OF-MANDIR-AT-RAM-JANMASTHAN-A-SYMBOL-OF-NATIONAL-PRIDE.html.

Rocher, Ludo. 2003. "The Dharmaśāstras." In *The Blackwell Companion to Hinduism*, edited by Gavin Flood, 102–115. New York: Blackwell. doi: 10.1002/9780470998694.ch5.

Sabrang Communications Private Limited, Mumbai, India, and The South Asia Citizens Web, France. 2002. "The Foreign Exchange of Hate: IDRF and the American Funding of Hindutva." November 20, 2002. Accessed March 28, 2022. https://www.sabrang.com/hnfund/sacw/downloads/sabrang_sacw.pdf.

Saikia, Purnananda. 1998. *Sankaradeva: A Revolutionary Reformer*. Accessed March 12, 2024. http://www.atributetosankaradeva.org/revolutionary_reformer.pdf. (Reproduced from *Sankaradeva: Studies in Culture*, edited by Bhaba Prasad Chaliha. Nagaon: Srimanta Sankardeva Sangha.)

Sarkar, Sumit. 1996. "Indian Nationalism and the Politics of Hindutva." In *Contesting the Nation: Religion, Community, and the Politics of Democracy in India*, edited by David Ludden, 270–93. Philadelphia, PA: University of Pennsylvania Press.

Schweig, Graham M, trans. 2007. *Bhagavad Gītā: The Beloved Lord's Secret Love Song*. San Francisco: Harper.

Sharma, Arvind. 1990. "Karma and Reincarnation in Advaita Vedānta." *Journal of Indian Philosophy* 18: 219–36. doi: 10.1007/BF00190312.

Sharma, Jyotirmaya. 2011. *Hindutva: Exploring the Idea of Hindu Nationalism*. New Delhi: Penguin Books.

Sosis, Richard. 2019."The Building Blocks of Religious Systems: Approaching Religion as a Complex Adaptive System." In *Evolution, Development and Complexity: Multiscale Evolutionary Models of Complex Adaptive Systems*, edited by Georgi Yordanov Georgiev, John M. Smart, Claudio L. Flores Martinez, and Michael E. Price, 421–49. Cham: Springer. doi: 10.1007/978-3-030-00075-2_19.

Tiwari, Vijaya Shankara. 2022. *Hindu Viswa Newsletter*, February 1–15, 2022.

Udayakumar, S. P. 2005. *Presenting the Past: Anxious History and Ancient Future in Hindutva India*. Westport, CT: Greenwood.

Vishva Hindu Parishad. n.d.-a "FAQ – Shri Ram Janmabhoomi Movement." Accessed March 14, 2024. https://vhp.org/faq/1/.

Vishva Hindu Parishad. n.d.-b "Introduction." Accessed March 18, 2024. https://vhp.org/introduction/.

Chapter 2

Rabbinical Judaism

Tamás Biró

Judaism is often conceived in the Western world by general lay opinion as the first highly moralizing religion, which conferred morality to its sister religions: God gave the Ten Commandments to Moses; hence, Judaism was born, whence grew Christianity and Islam. Add to it the popular preconception about the Hebrew Bible's most moralizing God, vengefully and violently enforcing the Law, a picture based on many biblical stories as well as on descriptive verses comparable to these:[1]

> ... for I the Lord your God am a jealous God, punishing children for the iniquity of parents to the third and the fourth generation of those who reject me. (Exod. 20:5 = Deut. 5:9)

> A jealous and avenging God is the Lord; the Lord is avenging and wrathful; the Lord takes vengeance on his adversaries and prolongs it against his enemies. (Nah. 1:2)

> O Lord, you God of vengeance, you God of vengeance, shine forth! Rise up, O judge of the earth; give to the proud what they deserve! ... He will repay them for their iniquity, and wipe them out for their wickedness; the Lord our God will wipe them out. (Ps. 94:1-2, 23)

The story is not so simple, however. The Hebrew Bible (Old Testament)[2] and its ethical system, centered around a divinity with a complex character, are the products of long development (Jokiranta, Part III, Chapter 3, this volume). Rather than focusing on that development, this chapter presents the various subsequent stages that led to Rabbinical Judaism, as we know it nowadays, and the role of moralizing supernatural punishment and reward (MSP) therein.

---

1 New Revised Standard Version [NRSV], Updated Edition.
2 The term Hebrew Bible is the neutral term used to denote the books contained in the Jewish scriptures (the Tanakh), that is, the Old Testament according to the Protestant canon. In this chapter, the terms Bible and biblical shall always refer – unless otherwise noted – to the Hebrew Bible, excluding the New Testament.

What is Rabbinical Judaism?

The religion(s) of the Israelites in earlier biblical times, which it would be anachronistic to call Judaism, underwent many stages. A critical study of the biblical texts often unveils contradictory views and conflicting positions. Observing these contradictions enables the modern scholar to reconstruct the complex history of the texts and of the religious and ethical systems underlying them. In contrast, observing them has always posed great challenges to theologians of all denominations, who aimed at developing a consistent ethical system – and in line with contemporaneous moral values, at that – that could arguably be derived from the Scriptures.

The term *Jew* (Hebrew *yehudi*, Greek *Ioudaios*, originally meaning "Judean, from the province of Judea") only slowly acquired the meaning we are familiar with (Boyarin 2019). Following the Babylonian exile (sixth century BCE), a loose spectrum of Yahwistic cults could be observed from Elephantine, in the south of Egypt, through Judea and Samaria to Mesopotamia. We shall use the label *Judaization* to describe the process by which a new ethnic and religious identity gradually emerged in the Persian and Hellenistic periods, in Palestine and in the Diaspora.[3] In a parallel development, for most, Jerusalem and its Temple would become the sole center of the cult, except for the Samaritans, who would reject the centrality of Jerusalem (John 4:20) and would preserve, up to this day, a separate Israelite but non-Jewish religion.

Besides the temples, a second focus of these Yahwistic cults in the Persian and Hellenistic periods was a growing body of literature: the Law (i.e., the Torah, or Pentateuch, or the Five Books of Moses), as well as prophetic, poetic, and historical books and more recent pieces of literature. Much later, some of them would be known as "books of the Bible" (depending on the various canons). The many-centuries-long editorial work on the Pentateuch reached its final stage probably in the Persian period, creating a text – still quite fluid – that would serve as the central pillar of both Judaism and Samaritanism. In these communities, this process of *Torahization* (Petersen 2022) would become a key survival strategy after the destruction of their temples by the Romans in 70 CE and by the Hasmonean king John Hyrcanus I around 111 BCE, respectively (Bourgel 2016). Besides the Jewish and Samaritan versions of the Torah, further books acquired varying levels of religious significance, especially in Judaism.

The second major step toward what we know nowadays as Judaism was *rabbinization* (McDowell, Naiweld, and Stökl Ben Ezra 2021). Even while construing

---

3   Karel van der Toorn (2019) describes how the Israelite community in Elephantine acquired a nascent Jewish identity in the fifth century BCE (cf. Van der Toorn 2019: 142 for a summary). At that point, in the Persian period, Samarians (not yet Samaritans) were still included in the Aramaic term yĕhûdāyēʾ, the meaning of which had recently shifted from "Judahites" to "Jews." Van der Toorn also emphasizes that the Elephantine community adopted a Diaspora identity relative to the religious centers and authorities in either Judea or Samaria.

it differently, various heirs of the Israelite tradition – e.g., Samaritans, Qumranites, and Christians – preserved a "temple-like" cult, with priests, altars, and/or (symbolic or real) sacrifices, such as the Eucharist in Christianity and the Passover sacrifice in Samaritanism.[4] In contrast, following the destruction of the second Jerusalem temple in 70 CE, an originally small and peripheral circle of scholars, known as the rabbis, possibly related to the predestruction faction of the Pharisees (Cohen 1984; Rosen-Zvi 2020), gradually developed a novel form of Judaism. Downplaying the role of the priestly classes (the Kohanim of Aaronic descent and the Levites), associated to a now defunct form of the cult, this new group presented themselves as the true holders of the tradition originating from Mount Sinai (cf. Mishnah Avot 1).

They advanced two innovative assertions: first, that Moses received not only the Ten Commandments at Sinai but the whole Torah, from Genesis 1 to Deuteronomy 34, and second, that Moses also received the Oral Law (*tora she-be-al-pe*, or Oral Torah), a body of instructions and explanations on the Written Law (*tora she-bikhtav*, or Written Torah). An unbroken chain of transmission connected *Moshe rabbenu* ("Moses, our master," literally, "our rabbi" – observe the rabbinization of the past) to the rabbis of the Roman period. Therefore, they claimed to possess the true interpretation of the Pentateuch, *pace* Samaritans, Christians, Gnostics, latter Karaites, and followers of any other nonrabbinic[5] forms of Judaism. Moreover, they argued that the whole (written) Torah is divine and perfect as it was composed by God himself, not by Moses – and prior to the creation of the world, as its blueprint, at that.[6] Therefore, each and every linguistic minutia of the text carries some message – such as details of the Jewish legal system (*halakhah*), especially for those following in the footsteps of the second-century sage Rabbi Akiva, or esoteric information for adherents of the Late Antique and medieval Jewish mysticism (Kabbalah).

After the Hebrew Bible was canonized by the early second century CE, the oral lore of the rabbis formed the basis of rabbinic literature. The latter includes several genres. Targums are Aramaic translations of biblical books. Midrash collections on various books of the Hebrew Bible contain exegetical and homiletic traditions

---

4   For the role of priests and Levites in Qumran, refer to Balázs Tamási (2022: 109).
5   The word "rabbinic" covers two, less defined terms, referring to (1) Late Antique rabbinic culture (e.g., rabbinic literature, rabbinic circles) and (2) medieval and modern rabbis.
6   Compare, for example, Gen. Rabba 1:1 and 1:4, Lev. Rabba 19:1, Mishnah Avot 3:14, and b Ned 39b on the Torah as a tool for the creation. Note that this theologically correct version has coexisted in Judaism with the traditional and more intuitive narrative about the Torah being dictated by God and written down by Moses during the 40 years of wandering in the wilderness. The rabbis in the Babylonian Talmud (B. Bat. 14b–15a) discussed the question of who wrote the last sentences of Deuteronomy about the death of Moses. Did God dictate them to Moses, who noted them down with tears as a prophecy, or was it Joshua, following the death of Moses? However, this question is irrelevant for the theologically correct narrative about God giving the entire Torah to Moses on Sinai. Yet not many seem to have raised theological objections to this famous passage in the Talmud.

organized according to the structure of the biblical text. The Mishnah, compiled by Rabbi Judah ha-Nasi at the beginning of the third century, is a collection of primarily legal traditions organized thematically. A similar collection, the Tosefta, is a "supplementary" collection compiled a few decades later. The Palestinian Talmud and the Babylonian Talmud contain the discussions of subsequent generations of rabbis in Palestine and in Mesopotamia, respectively. The starting point of a discussion is a paragraph of the Mishnah, but then the discourse can move on to other topics, while biblical verses are frequently quoted and analyzed as proof texts. *Halakhah* refers to rabbinic material of legal nature, and *aggadah* to everything else (primarily narratives but also ethics, folklore, science, etc.).

After Torahization and Judaization, followed by rabbinization, the third step toward what can be called "mainstream Rabbinical Judaism" was *Babylonization* (Lavee 2014: 85).[7] While the literary activity of the rabbinic circles was quite widespread in the Late Antique and early medieval periods, it was the Babylonian Talmud that became the focal point, and even the symbol, of subsequent Judaism (Wimpfheimer 2018: 8, 103–104). In turn, medieval rabbinic literature, taking the Babylonian Talmud as its starting point, culminated in the Shulhan Arukh, the law code of Joseph Caro, in the sixteenth century. While the Karaites rejected rabbinization (or "de-rabbinized" themselves) in the early Middle Ages and the Yemenite Jewry might have been affected somewhat less by Babylonization, it is safe to state that "mainstream Rabbinical Judaism" (since the late medieval and early modern period) is the product of these three stages. Modern developments should be covered in a separate study.

MSP in Torahized Early Judaism

Anders Klostergaard Petersen (2022: 345) argues that different forms of late Second Temple Judaism "filled different niches in the cultural landscape," which they adapted to or changed considerably. These different forms of Torahized Judaism (and Samaritanism) developed various interpretations of the Torah, which "instantiates ideals of Israelite/Judaic religion to be instilled on the members of the group by setting up a *reward and punishment system* [emphasis added] aimed to enforce the ideals."

Furthermore, Petersen underscores that the Torah should not be seen as a reflection of the reality in the Second Temple period but rather as a theoretical construction: a "legacy of the fathers" or as "expressing ideals" but not a "constitution and official legal foundation." Reality, in fact, would be determined by age-old routines, as well as by Persian, Hellenistic, and Roman law and customs. It would take centuries

---

7   Sacha Stern (2001, 2019) employs the Jewish calendar to show how religious authority moved from the Land of Israel to Babylonia in the last centuries of the first millennium CE.

of legal and exegetical discourse in Rabbinical Judaism and its alternatives to harmonize the text of the Pentateuch – sometimes vague or blurred, sometimes underdetermined or impractical, and sometimes even self-contradictory[8] – with reality, with actual legal and ritual practices.

However, the key moral ideals of the Torah, the prophets, and further books on their way to canonization (remember, no Bible yet!) were already ostensible in prerabbinic Judaism (Early Judaism, Late Second Temple Judaism, or "Common Judaism"). The reward and punishment system enforcing them originated in Deuteronomic theology (see Jokiranta, Part III, Chapter 3, this volume), most clearly appearing in Deuteronomy 11:

> So if you faithfully obey the commands I am giving you today – to love the Lord your God and to serve him with all your heart and with all your soul – then I will send rain on your land in its season, both autumn and spring rains, so that you may gather in your grain, new wine and olive oil. I will provide grass in the fields for your cattle, and you will eat and be satisfied. Be careful, or you will be enticed to turn away and worship other gods and bow down to them. Then the Lord's anger will burn against you, and he will shut up the heavens so that it will not rain, and the ground will yield no produce, and you will soon perish from the good land the Lord is giving you. Fix these words of mine in your hearts and minds; tie them as symbols on your hands and bind them on your foreheads. Teach them to your children, talking about them when you sit at home and when you walk along the road, when you lie down and when you get up. Write them on the doorframes of your houses and on your gates, so that your days and the days of your children may be many in the land the Lord swore to give your ancestors, as many as the days that the heavens are above the earth. (Deut. 11:13–21)[9]

Deuteronomistic history (Joshua, Judges, 1–2 Samuel, and 1–2 Kings) developed a pattern of reward and punishment as an interpretation of the annals of Israel (Collins 2018: 188), culminating in the Babylonian exile, as already foreseen in Deuteronomy 11:17: "Then the Lord's anger will burn against you, … and you will soon perish from the good land the Lord is giving you." Importantly, here the reward only depended on Israel's faithfulness to their God, and the punishment only ensued from their worshiping other divinities.

---

8   To give a single example, in the Covenant Code a male slave is released after six years of servitude (Exod. 21:2–11) but not a female slave (Exod. 21:7), whereas the Deuteronomic Code extends this law to female slaves (Deut. 15:12).
9   NRSV, Updated Edition.

Yet in the prophets' messages, the exile would also become a consequence of moral misdeeds, besides infidelity to God. Following are a few examples from various periods, from Hosea, referring to the fall of the Northern Kingdom in the eighth century, to Zechariah, addressing those returning from the Babylonian exile (late sixth century):

The Lord has a charge to bring against Judah; he will punish Jacob according to his ways and repay him according to his deeds. … But you must return to your God; maintain love and justice, and wait for your God always. The merchant uses dishonest scales and loves to defraud. Ephraim boasts, "I am very rich; I have become wealthy. With all my wealth they will not find in me any iniquity or sin." … But Ephraim has aroused his bitter anger; his Lord will leave on him the guilt of his bloodshed and will repay him for his contempt. (Hos. 12:2–6, 8–14)

Therefore, my people go into exile for lack of knowledge; their nobles are dying of hunger, and their multitude is parched with thirst. … But the Lord of hosts is exalted by justice, and the Holy God shows himself holy by righteousness. (Isa. 5:13–16)

Will the Lord be pleased with thousands of rams, with ten thousands of rivers of oil? Shall I give my firstborn for my transgression, the fruit of my body for the sin of my soul? He has told you, O mortal, what is good, and what does the Lord require of you but to do justice and to love kindness and to walk humbly with your God? (Mic. 6:7–8)

If you really change your ways and your actions and deal with each other justly, if you do not oppress the foreigner, the fatherless or the widow and do not shed innocent blood in this place, and if you do not follow other gods to your own harm, then I will let you live in this place, in the land I gave your ancestors for ever and ever. (Jer. 7:5–7)

The word of the Lord came to Zechariah, saying: "Thus says the Lord of hosts: Render true judgments, show kindness and mercy to one another; do not oppress the widow, the orphan, the alien, or the poor; and do not devise evil in your hearts against one another. But they refused to listen and turned a stubborn shoulder and stopped their ears in order not to hear. They made their hearts adamant in order not to hear the law and the words that the Lord of hosts had sent by his spirit through the former prophets. Therefore, great wrath came from the Lord of hosts. Just as, when I called, they would not hear, so, when they called, I would not hear, says the Lord of hosts, and I scattered them with a whirlwind among all the nations that they had not known. Thus, the land they left was desolate, so that no one went to and fro, and a pleasant land was made desolate." (Zech. 7:8–14)

In turn, by the time of the emergence of Early Judaism, the theology of the Deuteronomist was transformed into a theology of punishment and reward that depended on Israel's behavior toward God and humans alike. The canon surfacing at the center of religion washed away the differences in the perspectives taken by various biblical authors, homogenizing their worldviews. (Entertaining a single mental theology is conspicuous even today when people refer to "*the* Bible saying" such and such.) Torahization emphasized the Law, of which the Yahwistic cult was only a subfield. Therefore, even if in the original context Israel strayed far from God by following worthless idols (cf. Jer. 2:5), the latter phrase would be put in parentheses or read symbolically, and Israel's infidelity was now understood as a broader disloyalty to the Torah. Moses' Law contained both ceremonial and social precepts, and the two sets of commandments (*mitzvot*; sing. *mitzvah*) were considered equally important. At the pinnacle of this transformation, the second-century sage Rabbi Akiva singled out "You shall love your neighbor as yourself" (Lev. 19:18) as the most fundamental principle in the Torah (Sifra Kedoshim 4:12).

Extending the Deuteronomist's theology, the Babylonian Talmud (b Yoma 9b) suggests that the First Temple in Jerusalem was destroyed because of idol worship, forbidden sexual relations, and bloodshed, proposing creative readings of biblical verses to prove that each of them happened in the last days of the First Temple. Based on the Tosefta (t Menahot 13:4), it continues by conceiving an MSP system concerned with interpersonal behavior:

> However, the Second Temple – [in whose days people] were busy with Torah [study], with commandments, and with acts of kindness – why was it destroyed? Because of wanton hatred. [This comes to] teach you that wanton hatred is equivalent to the three [most severe] transgressions [taken together]: idol worship, forbidden sexual relations and bloodshed. (b Yoma 9b)

According to the Jewish tradition, each of the two tablets of the Ten Commandments contained five commandments, the first five pertaining to the relationship "between man and God" (*bein adam le-maqom*), and the last five to the relationship "between man and his fellow" (*bein adam le-havero*) (Greenberg, Rothkoff, and Kadosh 2007). Already, Philo of Alexandria had noted,

> And after this commandment relating to the seventh day he gives the fifth, which concerns the honour to be paid to parents, giving it a position on the

confines of the two tables of five commandments each; for being the concluding one of the first table, in which the most sacred duties to the Deity are enjoined, it has also some connection with the second table which comprehends the obligations towards our fellow creatures. (De decalogo 22 [106])

To sum up, social and sacramental laws were considered to be strongly intertwined. The Deuteronomist's system of supernatural punishment and reward, originally focused on the monopoly of a single deity, was applied by the period of Early Judaism to the whole spectrum of Torah law. This spectrum ranged from prosocial behavior and ethics to civil, criminal, and ceremonial legislation. The prophets' voice contrasting cult with God's message (1Sam. 15:22; Jer. 6:19–20) was (and has been) replaced in Judaism by adherence to the Torah law by interweaving ritual and ethical norms. Keep in mind, moreover, that *Torah* does not refer only to the specific words and sentences in the Pentateuch; it is rather "a symbol of divine legislation and moral justice [invoked regularly by people] without knowing the specifics of the commandments themselves" (Wimpfheimer 2018: 3[10]).

It was in the context of this revised, moralistic theology that the above paragraph from Deuteronomy 11 made it into Jewish liturgy. It was added to the Shema (Deut. 6:4–9) as its second portion, certainly not later than the second century CE (Mishnah Berakhot 2:2). The Mishnah also relates that all three portions of the Shema had been recited in the Jerusalem Temple, preceded by the Decalogue (m Tamid 5:1), even though the Ten Commandments would not be read outside the Temple service, so that heretics "shall not say that only these [the Ten Commandments] were given to Moses on Mount Sinai" (y Ber 1, 3c; cf. Idelsohn [1932] 1995: 91). While the historical value of the Mishnah, compiled in the early third century CE, for reconstructing the liturgy in the pre-70 CE Jerusalem Temple has long been a matter of debate, it is noteworthy that the Nash papyrus, usually dated as early as the second century BCE, also contained the Decalogue together with (the first portion of) the Shema (Greenberg 2007). The Ten Commandments continued to be recited in some synagogues for more than a millennium, and elsewhere the first two portions of the Shema were interpreted as a paraphrase of the Decalogue (Idelsohn [1932] 1995]: 91–2). Many prayer books even today have the Ten Commandments at the end of the morning prayer for private recitation.

Thus emerged a daily ritual: the reading of the three portions of the Shema in the morning and in the evening. It included and later alluded to the Decalogue and

---

10 Wimpfheimer, in fact, discusses the symbolic use of the Ten Commandments and the American Constitution, contrasting their "symbolic meaning" to their "essential meaning" (literal meaning, original content) and to their "enhanced meaning" (reception). Subsequently, he applies this model to the Babylonian Talmud. I am confident he would not oppose the use of his framework to the various registers of the Torah.

also to all other commandments of God. Thus, the sentence "Keep these words that I am commanding you today in your heart" (Deut. 6:6; see also Deut. 11:13) was not understood in its contextual sense as referring to Moses' farewell address before the Israelites crossed the Jordan but as referring to the entire Torah – as if God were speaking on Mount Sinai and not Moses 40 years later. Similarly, the second section of the Shema, Deuteronomy 11:13–21, was recognized as containing rewards and punishments for obeying or disobeying the words of God in general. The ritual usage of the text permitted not paying attention to the words themselves and forgetting their original sense, the Deuteronomic theology. The ritual, instead, reinforced the MSP system for the broad spectrum of Torah law.

Hence, the Shema, a text recited twice each day, ideally in a synagogue, became a prototypical example of a "doctrinal ritual" early on. Conforming to the proposal of Harvey Whitehouse (2021: 125), this standardized ritual probably contributed to group formation, to the emergence of a broad social reality sometimes referred to as Synagogal Judaism or Common Judaism. Here, we enter shaky ground, however. We hardly know anything about the social conditions and the lived religion in nonelitist, nonpartisan Late Antique Judaism, let alone about the mechanisms by which a specific ritual contributed to group formation.

Much has been speculated based on the interpretation of texts and archeological finds, but only few solid data are available. Recent scholarship (for an overview, refer to the helpful articles in McDowell, Naiweld, and Stökl Ben Ezra 2021; Schwartz and Weiss 2012; and the references therein) envisions a loose network of Jewish communities in Palestine, and elsewhere in the Roman Empire and beyond, organized around synagogues but also embedded in the local (non-Jewish) environment, as reflected, for instance, by the Pauline epistles. Before 70 CE, these communities must have maintained some connections with Jerusalem, including occasional pilgrimages to the Temple (depending on one's economic prosperity, geographic location, and religious conviction) and the sharing of ideas, texts, and practices. At the same time, these communities were also open to non-Jewish ideas and practices, not always keeping the borders of Judaism clear-cut, as best seen by their receptiveness to Christianity as well as by the pagan motifs on Late Antique synagogue mosaics.

The local synagogues – where the liturgy most probably focused on biblical texts – successfully replaced the Jerusalem Temple, with its priests and sacrifices, as the center of religious activities even before 70 CE. Run by the local community, lay people, some of whom might have been wealthier and some of whom might have been more knowledgeable, they were not under the authority of the rabbinic circles, even after 70 CE. Some of these communities were absorbed by Christianity and later by Islam; a handful of them might have formed the basis of Karaism and other Jewish sects in the eighth to tenth century (Bacher 1895); but many of them remained "just plain Jewish." The rabbinization of these latter communities took several centuries. As José Costa puts it, "Rabbinization [of Judaism] seems to have consisted essentially in the rabbinization of the synagogues (and in the 'synagogalization' of the rabbis)" (McDowell, Naiweld, and Stökl Ben Ezra 2021: 112–113).

Despite the lack of sources, I conjecture that this form of nonrabbinic or pre-rabbinic "Synagogal Judaism" was strongly Judaized and Torahized. Judaization consisted of a (Diaspora) Jewish identity and of some ties to Jerusalem and its Temple, or to the memory thereof. Torahization consisted of a central role for the Pentateuch in their liturgy, and of an MSP system derived therefrom. The system of supernatural punishment and reward promoted certain forms of prosocial and ritual behaviors, and itself was promoted by the liturgy in the synagogue. The fates of the two Jerusalem Temples provided additional proof of the MSP system postulated in this culture.

Case study 1: Rabbinical Judaism as reflected in the Mishnah

The first axiom of Rabbinical Judaism, as explained earlier, is that Moses received the entire written Torah as well as its explanation, the Oral Torah, from God on Mount Sinai. The Pentateuch is the blueprint of creation, not "simply" a human text written under divine inspiration. It must be read, expounded, and implemented literally, that is, letter by letter. Referring to it as a *symbol* of Judaism; using it for ritual, liturgical purposes; cherry-picking certain passages; or reading it allegorically will not suffice. The rabbis opted for a very close reading of the biblical text, but then, they were willing to read the text in creative ways for it to fit their needs.

The rabbis, in this respect the heirs of the Pharisees (Acts 23:6–8), believed in the resurrection of the dead. They posited a *world to come* (*olam ha-ba*): the righteous shall "have a share in the world to come," whereas the wicked shall not. Note that this concept is temporal, unlike the spatial concept of Heaven and Hell in other traditions. Interestingly, the ancient Israelite notion of *Sheol*, a dark abode in the netherworld for good and bad, underwent significant changes in the late Second Temple period, distinguishing between the fate of the righteous and the fate of the wicked: the Garden of Eden and the *Gehinnom* (Greek *Gehenna*) (Hartman et al. 2007). The biblical word *Sheol* was simply understood as "grave" by the rabbis,[11] whereas the latter two concepts did not feature prominently in subsequent rabbinic cosmology: appearing sporadically in the *aggadic* (nonlegal) passages, they rather belonged to the interface of theology and folklore.

In contrast, the notion of having a share in the world to come was employed by the rabbis in the Mishnah as a tool to enforce certain basic articles of faith:

---

11 Refer to Marcus Jastrow (1903: 1505).

All of Israel [the Jewish people] has a share in the world to come, as it is stated: "Your people shall all be righteous; they shall possess the land forever. They are the shoot that I planted, the work of my hands, so that I might be glorified." (Isa. 60:21). And these are those who have no share in the world to come: one who says the resurrection of the dead is not derived from the Torah; and one who says the Torah did not originate from Heaven; and an Epicurean. Rabbi Akiva says: Also one who reads apocryphal literature, and one who whispers invocations over a wound saying: "I will not bring upon you any of the diseases that I brought upon the Egyptians, for I am the Lord who heals you" (Exodus 15:26). Abba Shaul says: also one who pronounces the Tetragram with its letters. (m Sanh 10:1)

Observe how the rabbis in the Mishnah (mainly late first to early third century CE) threatened with losing their share in the world to come those who would not accept the rabbis' authority and who misused the Torah – for instance, those reading the wrong books, those pronouncing the text incorrectly, those misinterpreting it, and those employing it for magical purposes. Most interestingly, the rabbis included those who maintained that the Pentateuch does not mention the resurrection of the dead (only the prophetic books do) and who rejected the rabbis' creative eisegeses. Additionally, an *epikores* (Epicurean) is also denied the world to come. This term, with a complex history, might have referred to one rejecting God's involvement in worldly matters, that is, a divine MSP system.

Thus, having a share in the world to come is employed here as a reward and punishment system to maintain – in fact, to establish – a society with a rabbinic authority that advocates a specific reward and punishment system. With the Jewish people dispersed in the Roman and Sasanian Empires, and without the political means to ostracize heretics, the long process of rabbinization in the first millennium CE could not have taken place without efficient tools. I conjecture that the above MSP system could have been such a device.

Beyond the maintenance of rabbinic authority, however, having a share in the world to come, or losing it, is too crude a concept to regulate behavior; it should rather be viewed as a rhetorical tool in the Rabbinical literature. The passage above begins with a very strong statement, a radical reading of a verse from Isaiah, and it is followed by contradictory statements. Even if we read the second part as listing exceptions, we do not get a sufficiently fine-grained MSP system that directly influences everyday human behavior.

A more refined system is introduced in a different passage of the Mishnah, where prosocial behavior suddenly takes over theology:

> These are the commandments that have no measure:[12] the corners of the field, the first-fruits, pilgrimage, righteous deeds, and Torah study. The following are the commandments for which one enjoys the usufruct in this world, while the capital remains for them in the world to come: honoring one's father and mother, righteous deeds, making peace between a person and their fellow, whereas Torah study [weighs] as much as them all. (m Peah 1:1)

The opening paragraph of the Mishnah tractate on *peah*, the laws on leaving the corners of one's field unharvested (Lev. 19:9 and 23:22), and on other gifts for the poor, understandably focuses on social and interpersonal issues. It suggests that we all harvest "credits" for fulfilling the commandments and performing good deeds in our lifetime. Some of these credits depend on passing some threshold, while other deeds earn you "recognitions" independently of the measure of your deed. Moreover, you can make use of these credits either in this world or in the world to come. Yet some deeds are so precious that you can safely enjoy their "interest" in this world while saving the "principal" for the world to come. Finally, Torah study – the number one value of the rabbis – is so much treasured that its credits equal the credits earned for all the other commandments taken together. Elsewhere in the Talmud (b BB 9a), rav Asi says, "Charity is equal to all other mitzvot combined." Since these are *aggadic* (non-*halakhic*) statements, the apparent contradiction does not pose any problem as long as the ethical values conveyed – the prominence of Torah study and charity – are compatible.

This section of the Mishnah is recited every morning as the first study passage from the Oral Torah. Hence, ritualization has ensured the interiorization of this credit-based MSP system. The life of the follower of Rabbinical Judaism is indeed a constant pursuit of merits (Hebrew *zekhut*) and avoidance of dishonors.

Should a person's own merits not suffice to ensure their goals (a good life, health, prosperity, a share in the world to come, etc.), they can even refer God to the merits of their righteous forefathers, such as Abraham, Isaac, and Jacob, since God promises in the Decalogue to show "steadfast love to the thousandth generation of those who love me and keep my commandment" (Exod. 20:6 = Deut. 5:10). The merits of the martyrs are also sometimes referred to, for instance, in the *Avinu malkenu* supplication on High Holidays. Taking a step toward popular religion (still endorsed by many rabbis), praying at the grave of a righteous person would benefit the supplicant, because the righteous person's merits will contribute to their own.

---

12 Certain commandments have "measures" (defined by the Oral Torah, according to rabbinic lore) that specify the minimal amount needed to fulfill a mitzvah, or the threshold beyond which a prohibition is punishable. Yet in the listed cases, any small amount will suffice to fulfill the commandment.

Apropos, the extension of the system of supernatural punishment and reward beyond the worldly life also provides a quick answer to the apparent injustice present in our world. While we all have vices and virtues, the righteous who suffer in this world will only take virtues to the world to come, whereas the wicked, consuming all their virtues in this world, will have none left for the world to come.

The High Holidays, Rosh Hashanah and Yom Kippur, highlight the MSP system on a yearly basis. Based on some statements in the Mishnah, Late Antique and medieval Judaism developed a picture of God judging the destiny of each individual based on their deeds in the previous year and writing their names either in the Book of Life, or in the Book of Death. The decision made on Rosh Hashanah is sealed on Yom Kippur. Therefore, the month of Elul, before Rosh Hashanah, as well as the 10 days between (and including) these holidays are especially apt for repentance (*teshuvah*). The famous medieval poem (eleventh to twelfth century) from Germany *Unetanneh Tokef* most dramatically describes God's verdict on these days. Its closing words, however, provide relief: "But repentance, prayer, and charity mitigate the severity of the decree." The heaviness of these days, the long prayers with cantorial performances, and the 25-hours-long fast on Yom Kippur (not eating and not drinking at all) culminating with the sound of the shofar turn these days into a very intense experience.[13] A set of imagistic rituals, they possibly pave the way for a "fusion mechanism" with local and global Jewries as the larger communities (Whitehouse 2021: 104).[14]

At the same time, the Mishnah emphasizes that divine atonement is granted only for sins that concern commandments on the relationship between man and God (*bein adam le-maqom*); but in the case of sins between humans (*bein adam le-havero*), one must first seek forgiveness from one's fellow human (m Yoma 8, 9), which obviously should also involve the fixing of any damage caused. Hence, the MSP system does enforce prosocial behavior and excludes workarounds.

Moreover, one must always make *teshuvah*, not only on or just before the High Holidays. "Repent one day before your death," said Rabbi Eliezer famously; yet, you cannot know when you will die (m Avot 2:10, and the commentary of Ovadiah of Bertinoro, based on Avot de-Rabbi Natan). Thus, the MSP system works all the year round, even if a certain period of the year is particularly dedicated to it. From a ritual frequency perspective, a noteworthy development is the introduction of the monthly Yom Kippur Katan (minor day of atonement) in some communities since the sixteenth century.

---

13   See also Tamás Biró (2013b: 129).
14   The question ought to be analyzed more carefully, including empirical studies. For a different approach to Jewish rituals, leading to a somewhat different conclusion, refer to Biró (2013a, 2013b).

To sum up, Rabbinical Judaism – as reflected in its earliest source, the Mishnah – views the Torah as God's law book. Often, a worldly court of rabbis had to adjudge cases, and therefore, an elaborate legal system of civil law, family law, and even criminal law was developed in the Rabbinical literature (including the Mishnah, the Babylonian Talmud, medieval codices, and rabbinic responsa, among others). There are other cases, however, that are handled by the "heavenly court." You can never know how many points you earn with a good deed and how many you lose with a wrong deed. Still, a supernatural punishment and reward system is constantly monitoring you. As Rabbi Judah Ha-Nasi, the compiler of the Mishnah, puts it in the tractate Avot, a special, nonlegalistic section, often called in English "The Ethics of the Fathers,"

> Be careful with light commandments as with grave ones, as you cannot know the reward for the fulfillment of the commandments. Reckon the loss of a commandment against the reward, and the gain of a transgression against the loss. Look at three points to avoid transgression, and know what is there above you: an eye that sees, an ear that hears, and all your deeds are written in a book. (m Avot 2:1)

Case study 2: *Tikun olam*

The expression *Tikkun olam* (repairing the world) is pervasive nowadays, referring to "Jewish responsibility for the welfare of society at large" (Blidstein 1995: 5). There is a joke that when the American president arrived in Israel, before starting his speech, he quietly asked his translator how to say "*Tikkun olam*" in Hebrew – that is, the expression is so ubiquitous that the president was not aware of its Jewish origin.[15] This expression has a long history, and it has undergone many semantic shifts (Cooper 2013; Rosenthal 2005).

Rather than exploring the possible meanings of this elusive expression in Late Antique Rabbinical and liturgical sources, we turn to Isaac Luria (1534–1572), often referred to as the Arizal, the most influential sixteenth-century mystic in Safed. Although the product of a rabbinized and Babylonized Jewry, Jewish mysticism (Kabbalah) from the twelfth and thirteenth centuries onward also had its roots in neoplatonism, Gnosticism, and Late Antique Jewish mysticism in Palestine. Lurianic Kabbalah in the sixteenth century concerns us most here because many of its concepts, thoughts, and practices were adopted in subsequent centuries by popular movements, such as Shabbateanism, Frankism, and Hasidism. Unlike earlier mystical and philosophical works read by only a selected few, Luria's system of thought

---

15 More than a joke, Levi Cooper (2013: 19–20) discusses President Barack Obama using this term several times.

had a significant impact on the socio-religious life of many Jewish communities in the last few centuries.

Lurianic Kabbalah proposed an absolutely novel doctrine of emanation and creation (Scholem 2007: 641–8 offers a much more precise and detailed description). It all began with the *Tzimtzum*, the "contraction" of the *Ein-Sof* (the Infinite), which provided space for worlds and ontological events. Next followed the "breaking of the vessels," a cosmic catastrophe: the light emanating struck the vessels of the lower *Sefirot* (emanations), with pieces and sparks scattering and falling down, and the dark forces of evil took on substance (*kelippot*, shells or husks). All subsequent processes of creation are the beginning of the *Tikkun*, the "reparation," the restoration of the original creation. Moreover, Man is designed to complete this *Tikkun*, separating the holy sparks from the *kelippot* and redeeming and lifting them on high, back to their origin.

Already in earlier kabbalistic works, such as the Zohar, performing the mitzvot had cosmic significance (Rosenthal 2005: 223). So in Luria's system,

> Israel has been dispersed in the Diaspora to gather the holy sparks and return them to heaven via Torah and righteous deeds. Since humanity created the problem of sin through Adam's sin, it is up to humanity to repair that sin via deeds. (as recorded by Haim Vital; see Rosenthal 2005: 226)

Therefore, the cosmic catastrophe ("breaking of the vessels"), humanity's catastrophe (Adam's sin), and the catastrophe of the Jewish people (the exile) are coalesced, and performing the mitzvot of the Torah is the remedy for all of them. If transgressing God's commandments leads to exile, according Deuteronomy 11, then undoing the exile can be achieved by fulfilling God's will. The gathering of the exiled people and the coming of the Messiah (their precise order being a matter of conflict between the religious Zionists and the anti-Zionists) will be followed by the resurrection of the dead and then by the world to come, a world of spiritual existence; thus, the three original catastrophes will be undone in reverse order. In popular versions of the Lurianic Kabbalah, Israel's mission is to repair the world by performing the commandments and thereby hastening the coming of the Messiah.

The notion that performing mitzvot contributes to repairing the world also entered the liturgy of those communities, groups, and movements that were amenable to mysticism. For instance, the commandment in the Pentateuch to count 49 days from Passover to Shavuot, the Feast of the Weeks (Lev. 23:15; Deut. 16:9), called *sefirat ha-omer* (counting the omer) is easily associated with the seven lower *Sefirot*. Therefore, the following passage is recited by many each day from Passover to Shavuot, after counting the omer:

Master of the universe, You commanded us through Moses, Your servant, to count Omer Count in order to cleanse us from our encrustations of evil [*kelippa*] and from our contaminations, as You have written in Your Torah: "You are to count from the morrow of the rest day ..." (Lev 23:15–16) so that the souls of Your people Israel be cleansed of their contamination. Therefore, may it be Your will, Hashem, our God, and the God of our forefathers, that in the merit [*zekhut*] of the Omer Count that I have counted today, may there be corrected [or repaired, *yetukkan*] whatever blemish I have caused in the Sefirah [name of the sefirah appropriate for the day]. May I be cleansed and sanctified with the holiness of Above, and through this may abundant bounty flow in all the worlds. And may it correct [or repair, *letakken*] our lives, spirits, and souls from all sediment and blemish; may it cleanse us and sanctify us with your exalted holiness. Amen. Selah![16]

In this new form of Judaism, infused with mysticism, the credits (merits, *zekhut*) one earns for fulfilling the commandments have an enhanced role. They are used not only to "buy yourself" divine reward in this world or in the world to come but also to "repair," to correct your soul and the entire creation in a metaphysical dimension. Sins cause sediment and blemish to the *Sefirot*, but good deeds cleanse them. The reward is not simply your own share in the world to come but the redemption of the entire world.

Twentieth-century Reform rabbis Emil Fackenheim and Eugene Borowitz (Rosenthal 2005: 235) and educator Shlomo Bardin (Cooper 2013: 17) were among the first to employ the term *tikkun olam* in a novel sense in the United States in the mid-twentieth century. Originally proposed as a theological answer to the Holocaust (Krasner 2013: 62), this mixture of Jewish and social values resonated very well since the 1960s with left-wing ideologies among the American Jewry, including the progressive streams (Reform and Reconstructionist Judaism) and the heirs of Bundism, the former Yiddish-speaking secular socialist movement. It was soon adopted by Conservative Jews and later even by the modern Orthodox Jews (Shatz, Waxman, and Diament 1997). As Jonathan Krasner (2013: 62) observes, "By the end of the twentieth century, tikkun olam was widely acknowledged as a central Jewish tenet and even as a rationale for Jewish survival."

The Lurianic usage and the modern usage of the expression share the same logic: the Jewish community/nation/people have an obligation toward the well-being of the entire world, and the good deeds of each individual fix some of the world's imperfections. Members of the community are rewarded by the conviction that their deeds are small but significant contributions toward a better future. At the same

---

16 From Nosson Scherman (1997: 285).

time, inaction leads to guilt about letting the world deteriorate, which is a kind of psychological pressure, and punishment.

Needless to say, the messianic visions of a sixteenth-century mystic differ enormously from the visions of a postmodern left-wing utopist. They would also disagree on what counts as a good deed. Should you hasten the coming of the Messiah by keeping Shabbat (the Sabbath) and leaving the lights on, or should you save the Earth by saving electricity? Should you slaughter animals according to the traditional rules of kashrut, or should you stun the animals beforehand? Should you observe the *shmitah* years (the Sabbath of the Land), exactly every seventh year, as prescribed by the Torah and the rabbis, or is it preferable to apply crop rotation with the newest agricultural technologies?

And yet in both cases, it is culturally postulated that an individual's actions are part and parcel of a joint enterprise by the larger (postulated) community. Given the strong link between joint attention and social cognition (Mundy 2018), it is reasonable to hypothesize that such actions will reinforce the individual's sense of belonging to the community.

As a sequel of the *Haskalah* (the Jewish Enlightenment), Abraham Geiger (1810–1874), the intellectual founder of Reform Judaism in Germany, equated Judaism with universal monotheism and ethics (Batnitzky 2011: 36–9). Moses Bloch (1815–1909), a conservative Talmudist and the first director of the Rabbinical Seminary in Budapest, wrote a long treatise, organized according to the structure of Maimonides's *Mishneh Torah*, explaining the universal moral values and motives behind each and every subfield of Jewish law (Bloch 1886). In this approach, unnoticed by the larger public, *halakhah* is not a goal but a necessary and sufficient means to achieve a universal moral ideal.

One wonders why Bloch's (1886) work did not boost religious observance among Hungarian Jews, why both concepts of *tikkun olam* were more successful in creating a proactive community than Bloch's reference to universal moral ideas. It turns out that it is not enough to propose a pleasant philosophy. You must also find cognitively adequate techniques to align people behind your cause. Probably Bloch's readers were not convinced that observing the traditional mitzvot would bring about a modern, enlightened, and moralistic version of the universal messianic vision: "The Lord will become king over all the earth; on that day the Lord will be one and his name one" (Zech. 14:9).

Summary

A famous teaching of Antigonos of Sokho in the Mishnah (Avot 1:3) states,

> Do not be like the slaves who serve the master in order to receive a reward. Rather be like slaves who serve the master not in order to receive a reward. And let the fear of Heaven be upon you.

This very influential quote summarizes the threefold attitude of Rabbinical Judaism toward God. The primary task of a Jew in this world is to serve the Heavenly Master, whose orders are known from the Torah: from the text of the Pentateuch as expounded by the rabbis. The best way of doing so is by serving Him out of love: *li-shmah, le-shem shamayim* (i.e., "for the sake of heaven"). Yet, should a person not have the right disposition, a system of rewards as well as a system of threats ("the fear of Heaven") are also in place to enforce the divine will.

While the rabbis have always emphasized the value of performing the mitzvot out of love for God, we have seen that several institutions have been in place for two millennia to support the MSP system in Judaism, the origins of which are thoroughly *nomian* (legalistic) (Hayes 2017: 2). Indeed, what forced Jews to adhere to *halakhah*, the Jewish law? Certainly not philosophical considerations, as demonstrated by the lack of impact of Bloch's proposal. According to a famous dictum attributed to Ahad Ha'am, the most prominent representative of cultural Zionism, "More than the Jewish people have kept Shabbat, Shabbat has kept them." Yet, what mechanisms ensured that Jews would keep Shabbat, without which Jewish identity could not have been maintained? Moreover, what motives urged wealthy, and not so wealthy, Jews in all periods of history to invite the poor to their Shabbat tables and Passover Seder nights (the first night of Passover), to support charity organizations, and to ransom fellow Jews on the slave market? What motivated them to care for the sick, the foreigner, the orphan, the widow, and the dead – which is said to be the greatest of all mitzvot since the dead cannot return your good deed?

Social pressure is certainly one answer. At times, law enforcement measures were also available to the community. Another reason is the MSP system of Rabbinical Judaism, which emphasizes the collection of merits for performing mitzvot: either by the individual, who will have a share in the world to come, or by the entire world, which is awaiting redemption by the Messiah. Transgressions have the opposite effect.

In this chapter, special emphasis has been placed on liturgy as it is the most easily analyzed aspect of religion that has an impact on a social scale. Moreover, key structures of the liturgy probably preceded the rabbinization of Judaism. We have observed how Deuteronomy 11 recited twice a day and Mishnah Peah 1:1 recited upon awakening might have contributed to the interiorization of an MSP system. Deuteronomy 11, the second portion of the Shema, highlights *kabbalat ol mitzvot* (acceptance of the commandments), whereas Peah 1:1 promises that credits are valued both in this world and in the world to come. Historical events, such as the destruction of the two Jerusalem Temples, have also been interpreted within this framework by the liturgy: "… because of our sins we were exiled from our country" is recited several times a year in the Musaf prayer for festivals.[17]

Future work should focus on the different channels through which a postulated system of supernatural punishment and reward is communicated to and interiorized by the larger Jewish population. Such channels might include pre-modern education (what did a *melamed* [religious teacher] say to the pupils in a *heder* [elementary Jewish school], and how?) and synagogues (what did a rabbi preach?) in pre-modern times. Ideas in philosophical, *halakhic*, and mystical works might also have reached, directly or indirectly, a larger audience. Only by looking at all those data together can we reconstruct the mechanisms by which a postulated system of punishment and reward contributed to the stability of Jewish communities, to the social cohesion of Jewries in an ever-changing Diaspora in Late Antique, medieval, early modern, and recent history.

References

Bacher, Wilhelm. 1895. "Qirqisani, the Karaite, and His Work on Jewish Sects." *The Jewish Quarterly Review* 7 (4): 687–710. doi: org/10.2307/1449971.

Batnitzky, Leora. 2011. *How Judaism Became a Religion: An Introduction to Modern Jewish Thought*. Princeton, NJ: Princeton University Press. doi: 10.1515/9781400839711.

Biró, Tamás. 2013a. "Is Judaism Boring? On the Lack of Counterintuitive Agents in Jewish Rituals." In *Mind, Morality and Magic: Cognitive Science Approaches in Biblical Studies*, edited by István Czachesz and Risto Uro, 120–143. Bristol, CT: Acumen.

Biró, Tamás. 2013b. "When Judaism Became Boring: The McCauley-Lawson Theory, Emotions and Judaism." In *Judaism and Emotion: Texts, Performance, Experience*, edited by Sarah Ross, Gabriel Levy, and Soham Al-Suadi, 123–51. New York: Peter Lang.

Blidstein, Gerald J. 1995. "Tikkun Olam" [Repairing the world]. *Tradition: A Journal of Orthodox Jewish Thought* 29 (2): 5–43.

Bloch, Moses. 1886. *Die Ethik in der Halacha* [Ethics in the Halakhah]. In *Jahresbericht des Landes-Rabbinerschule in Budapest für das Schuljahr 1885–86* [Yearbook of the rabbinical seminary in Budapest for the academic year 1885–1886]. Budapest: Athenaeum.

Bourgel, Jonathan. 2016. "The Destruction of the Samaritan Temple by John Hyrcanus: A Reconsideration." *Journal of Biblical Literature* 135 (3): 505–523. doi: 10.1353/jbl.2016.0032.

Boyarin, Daniel. 2019. *Judaism: The Genealogy of a Modern Notion*. New Brunswick: Rutgers University Press. doi: 10.2307/j.ctt2111gsh.

---

17 See, for example, S. Singer (1990: 646). A separate study would be needed to analyze all the occurrences of this statement in Jewish culture and to demonstrate how deeply it is engrained in Judaism. Regarding Judaism's perspective on history, the classic work is still Yosef Hayim Yerushalmi's (1982) Zakhor: Jewish History and Jewish Memory (several editions).

Cohen, Shaye J. D. 1984. "The Significance of Yavneh: Pharisees, Rabbis, and the End of Jewish Sectarianism." *Hebrew Union College Annual* 55: 27–53.

Collins, John J. 2018. *Introduction to the Hebrew Bible and Deutero-Canonical Books.* 3rd ed. Minneapolis, MN: Fortress Press. doi: 10.2307/j.ctt1w6tbx5.

Cooper, Levi. 2013. "The Assimilation of Tikkun Olam." *Jewish Political Studies Review* 25 (3/4): 10–42.

Greenberg, Moshe. 2007. "Nash Papyrus." In *Encyclopaedia Judaica*, vol. 14, edited by Michael Berenbaum and Fred Skolnik, 783–4. 2nd ed. New York: Macmillan Reference USA.

Greenberg, Moshe, Aaron Rothkoff, and David Kadosh. 2007. "Decalogue." In *Encyclopaedia Judaica*, vol. 5, edited by Michael Berenbaum and Fred Skolnik, 520–26. 2nd ed. New York: Macmillan Reference USA.

Hartman, Louis F., Joseph Gedaliah Klausner, Gershom Scholem, and Haïm Z'ew Hirschberg. 2007. "Eschatology." In *Encyclopaedia Judaica*, vol. 6, edited by Michael Berenbaum and Fred Skolnik, 489–504. 2nd ed. New York: Macmillan Reference USA.

Hayes, Christine. 2017. "Can We Even Speak of 'Judaism and Law'?" In *The Cambridge Companion to Judaism and Law*, edited by Christine Hayes, 1–16. New York: Cambridge University Press. doi: 10.1017/9781139565974.001.

Idelsohn, Abraham Zebi. (1932) 1995. *Jewish Liturgy and Its Development.* New York: Dover.

Jastrow, Marcus. 1903. *A Dictionary of the Targumim, Talmud Bavli, Talmud Yerushalmi and Midrashic Literature.* London: Luzac.

Krasner, Jonathan. 2013. "The Place of Tikkun Olam in American Jewish Life." *Jewish Political Studies Review* 25 (3/4): 59–98.

Lavee, Moshe. 2014. "No Boundaries for the Construction of Boundaries: The Babylonian Talmud's Emphasis on Demarcation of Identity." In *Rabbinic Traditions between Palestine and Babylonia*, edited by Ronit Nikolsky and Tal Ilan, 84–116. Leiden: Brill. doi: 10.1163/9789004277311_004

McDowell, Gavin, Ron Naiweld, and Daniel Stökl Ben Ezra, eds. 2021. *Diversity and Rabbinization: Jewish Texts and Societies between 400 and 1000 CE.* Cambridge: Open Book. doi: 10.11647/obp.0219.

Mundy, Peter. 2018. "A Review of Joint Attention and Social-Cognitive Brain Systems in Typical Development and Autism Spectrum Disorder." *European Journal of Neuroscience* 47 (6): 497–514. doi: 10.1111/ejn.13720.

Petersen, Anders Klostergaard. 2022. "From Torah to Torahization: A Biocultural Evolutionary Perspective." In *Torah: Functions, Meanings, and Diverse Manifestations in Early Judaism and Christianity*, edited by William Zurawski Schniedewind, Jason S. Boccaccini, and Gabriele Boccaccini, 343–66. Atlanta, GA: SBL Press. doi: 10.2307/j.ctv2cw0sj7.22.

Rosenthal, Gilbert S. 2005. "*Tikkun haOlam*: The Metamorphosis of a Concept." *The Journal of Religion* 85 (2): 214–40. doi: 10.1086/427314.

Rosen-Zvi, Ishay. 2020. "Early Judaism and Rabbinic Judaism." In *Early Judaism and Its Modern Interpreters*, edited by Matthias Henze and Rodney A. Werline, 489–518. 2nd ed. Atlanta, GA: SBL Press. doi: 10.2307/j.ctv1bd4n9z.26.

Scherman, Nosson. 1997. *The Complete Artscroll Siddur (Nusach Ashkenaz)*. Rahway, NJ: Mesorah.

Scholem, Gershom. 2007. "Kabbalah." In *Encyclopaedia Judaica*, vol. 11, edited by Michael Berenbaum and Fred Skolnik, 586–692. 2nd ed. New York: Macmillan Reference USA.

Schwartz, Daniel R., and Zeev Weiss, eds. 2012. *Was 70 CE a Watershed in Jewish History? On Jews and Judaism before and after the Destruction of the Second Temple*. Leiden: Brill. doi: 10.1163/9789004217447.

Shatz, David, Chaim I. Waxman, and Nathan J. Diament, eds. 1997. *Tikkun Olam: Social Responsibility in Jewish Thought and Law*. Northvale, NJ: Jason Aronson.

Singer, S., trans. 1990. *The Authorised Daily Prayer Book of the United Hebrew Congregations of the Commonwealth of the British Commonwealth of Nations*. Centenary ed.

Stern, Sacha. 2001. *Calendar and Community: A History of the Jewish Calendar, 2nd Century BCE–10th Century CE*. Oxford: Oxford University Press.

Stern, Sacha. 2019. *The Jewish Calendar Controversy of 921/2 CE*. Leiden: Brill. doi: 10.1163/9789004388673.

Tamási, Balázs. 2022. "Levi, Levites and Worship in Qumran." In *Understanding Texts in Early Judaism: Studies on Biblical, Qumranic, Deuterocanonical and Cognate Literature in Memory of Géza Xeravits*, edited by József Zsengellér, 107–117. Berlin: Walter de Gruyter. doi: 10.1515/9783110768534-007.

Van der Toorn, Karel. 2019. *Becoming Diaspora Jews: Behind the Story of Elephantine*. New Haven, CT: Yale University Press. doi: 10.12987/yale/9780300243512.001.0001.

Whitehouse, Harvey. 2021. *The Ritual Animal: Imitation and Cohesion in the Evolution of Social Complexity*. Oxford: Oxford University Press. doi: 10.1093/oso/9780199646364.001.0001.

Wimpfheimer, Barry Scott. 2018. *The Talmud: A Biography*. Princeton, NJ: Princeton University Press.

Yerushalmi, Yosef Hayim. 1982. *Zakhor: Jewish History and Jewish Memory*. Seattle, WA: University of Washington Press.

Chapter 3

Christianity
István Czachesz

In several Western European democracies, more than a third of the population believe in Heaven, as shown by the latest World Values Survey (WWS 2020), including Norway (34%), the United Kingdom (35.2%), and Finland (33.9%). The percentage is considerably higher in culturally Roman Catholic and Eastern Orthodox nations, as well as the United States (66.9%). Belief in Hell is almost as widespread in these countries as belief in Heaven. The lowest values in the West are reported in Denmark, where still 17.8% believe in Heaven and 9.4% in Hell. Moreover, although longitudinal data are sparse, they show varying trends but no overall decline since the 1980s. The persistence of afterlife beliefs after centuries of secularization suggests that belief in Hell and Heaven is firmly ingrained in Christian cultures. This chapter looks at the origins and history of postmortem rewards and punishments in Christianity, focusing especially on their connection with moral behavior.

Moralizing supernatural punishment and reward in the earliest Christianity

Christianity emerged in the Roman Empire in the first and second centuries CE as a branch of ancient Judaism (Horrell 2004), negotiating its place among Jewish religious factions and other ancient cults for several centuries before becoming the dominant religion of the late Roman Empire. Jesus of Nazareth, who lived in the Roman province of Judea (and neighboring territories, such as the vassal kingdom of Herod Antipas) in the first decades of the first century CE can be thought of as both the founder and a cultic figure of Christianity.

All four gospels (biographical narratives about Jesus) in the New Testament mention the appearance of John the Baptizer (or John the Baptist) before Jesus. John was a prophetic character who urged his listeners to repent and produce good "fruits" (a biblical metaphor for good behavior) so as to escape God's imminent punishment (Luke 3:8–9; Matt. 3:7–10). It is notable that John addresses the religious perfectionists (Pharisees) and aristocratic elites (Sadducees) of contemporary Jewish society, in particular, which indicates social critique rather than (or in addition to) individual moral chastisement. In other parts of the gospels, Jesus himself warns Jewish leaders that they will not be admitted into the "kingdom of heaven" (Matt. 23).

Another group of sayings promises the poor, meek, and persecuted that they will be rewarded in Heaven (Matt. 5:1–12; Luke 6:20–23), while warning the rich that they will "mourn and weep" (Luke 6:24–5). Jesus also talks about a poor man by the name Lazarus who is taken to Abraham's bosom (a Jewish conceptualization of Heaven; Bock 2008: 1368–70) immediately after he dies, while the rich man at whose gate Lazarus spent his days is taken to the underworld (Greek *Hades*) to be tormented (Luke 16:19–31). The gospel sayings about the postmortem fate of the rich and the poor (a typical concern of the Gospel of Luke) is reminiscent of the Greek idea of the reversal of fates in the afterlife. For example, the satirist Lucian of Samosata (c. 125 CE to c. 180 CE) depicts the powerful of this world toiling in lowly occupations in the afterlife (Menippus 17; Czachesz 2012: 14–15).

Why are the rich punished in the afterlife? First, one may argue that the rich man is punished for ignoring poor Lazarus; however, this is not stated in the narrative. Another gospel story about a rich young man (Matt. 19:16–24; Luke 18:18–30) seems to suggest that the possessions of the man rather than his lack of charity prevent him from entering the kingdom of Heaven, although there is some room for the latter interpretation as well. Second, scholars argue that economic gain was viewed with suspicion in the ancient Mediterranean world as it implied taking advantage of others (Esler 2004: 18) and violating the solidarity of the free (male) citizenry (Morris, Saller, and Scheidel 2013: 11). Thus, it can be surmised that for this reason some of the gospel sayings attack the accumulation of wealth. Third, the advertising of poverty as an ideal could reflect the actual poverty of the Christ followers, and the prospect of a postmortem reversal of fates could help them cope with poverty. In sum, allowing for a range of possible interpretations of the relevant passages, the postmortem punishment of the rich envisioned in the gospels can be understood as moralizing supernatural punishment and reward (MSP) only with limitations.

Other gospel sayings associate day-to-day morality more directly with divine rewards and punishments. A prominent example is the reinterpretation of ancient Jewish legal tradition (from the Hebrew Bible and its Greek translation), as found in the Sermon on the Mount (Matt. 5:21–48). For example, the scope of the commandment against murder (Exod. 20:13) is expanded in such a way that saying, "You fool" to one's "brother or sister" makes one liable to the "fiery Geenna." Similarly, the commandment against adultery (Exod. 20:14) implies, in this reading, that looking at a woman with lust destines one to *Geenna*. Even more shocking, if possible, is the suggested recipe to prevent such adultery of the heart: it is better to "tear out" one's eye than causing the entire body to suffer in the afterlife. The latter advice is immediately followed by the recommendation to cut off one's hand to avoid sinful behavior. The encouragement of cruel self-mutilation suggests that the respective sayings were not meant as ethical guidelines in a literal sense. Perhaps, a small group of fanatics might have attempted to live by such rules, but the rules were certainly not suitable to foster large-scale social cooperation. One explanation of the "Antitheses" (so called because they contrast the Jewish law with a new, radical morality) is that they prove the impossibility of abiding by God's laws consistently.

Yet another group of gospel sayings describes "two ways" that lead to salvation and damnation, respectively:

> Enter through the narrow gate, for the gate is wide and the road is easy that leads to destruction, and there are many who take it. For the gate is narrow and the road is hard that leads to life, and there are few who find it. (Matt. 7:13–14)

Other gospel passages elaborate on what the above alternatives mean in concrete terms. For example, Jesus describes the last judgment as the Son of Man (a mythological character in contemporary Jewish tradition, referring to Jesus himself in this passage) sitting on his throne and separating the "sheep" (standing on his right) from the "goats" (standing on his left) (Matt. 25:31–46). Jesus explains that anyone who helped the hungry and thirsty, welcomed the stranger, clothed the naked, nursed the sick, and visited the prisoners, in fact, did those things to Jesus himself and hence will inherit the "kingdom (of heaven)" and go on to eternal life. Anyone who failed to do so, in contrast, is destined to eternal punishment by the devil and his angels.

The teaching of the two ways plays an important role in the *Teaching of the Twelve Apostles* (commonly referred to as Didache), a Christian writing usually dated to the late first century CE. The text (Didache 1–6) describes "two paths, one of life and one of death," and enumerates a series of virtues and vices. It is notable that postmortem rewards and punishments are not mentioned in the Didache, at least not in the preserved form of the text (Aldridge 1999). Scholars argued that the doctrine of the two ways was derived from Judaism and was characteristic of early Jewish Christianity (Sandt and Flusser 2002), that is, Christians who remained loyal to their Jewish roots (Horrell 2004). The Letter of James, a New Testament writing of uncertain authorship and date, also draws on the two-ways tradition (Sandt 2007) and warns that "judgment will be without mercy to anyone who has shown no mercy" (James 2:13).

A different kind of divine punishment is hinted at in the Gospel of John. When Jesus meets a man on the road who has been blind since birth (John 9:1–12), Jesus' disciples assume that either the man or his parents must have sinned to cause this blindness, an idea that Jesus rejects. The interpretation of illness as the consequence of sin is not unique to this story. In another healing story from the same gospel, Jesus warns the healed patient not to commit sin any more so that "nothing worse" happens to him (John 5:14). The apostle Paul, whose work we will discuss in more detail later, expresses the belief that not treating the body of Christ (i.e., the bread of the Lord's Supper) with respect made members of the congregation ill (1 Cor. 11:29–30). The Acts of Barnabas, a late antique legend about the Christianization of the island of Cyprus, suggests that an earthquake demolished a stadium hosting a pagan festival after the apostle "rebuked" the place, killing and wounding "many" (Acts of Barnabas 19). The demolishing of pagan buildings by earthquake occurs as a literary motif in other Late Antique Christian texts as well (Czachesz 2017: 125–8; Poplutz 2017: 989–91). Although such examples are interesting and deserve further investigation, I am not treating the conception of illness and catastrophic events as divine punishment in more detail in this chapter since it does not play a major role in the moral universe of historical Christianity. For example, while modern stereotypes of the Middle Ages might make us believe that mental illness was widely considered to be divine punishment in that era, a critical assessment of the sources (Kroll and Bachrach 2005) demonstrates that this was at best a marginal view.

In sum, MSP is mentioned in the gospels (in sayings attributed to Jesus) and other Christian writings in the first century CE in connection with selected virtues and vices. In some cases, it is not clear whether moral admonitions imply postmortem consequences. Alternatively, sins could be seen to cause illness and even death, a concept that seems persistent, albeit marginal, in the Christian tradition. After the Christian ideas of Heaven and Hell developed in the second century CE, they dominated the discourse on divine rewards and punishments.

Heaven and Hell

The cultures of the ancient Mediterranean world and the ancient Near East had varying concepts about the afterlife and the places associated with it. The image of the afterlife in Christianity has been influenced by at least two major cultural traditions (Bremmer 2003): (1) that of ancient Greece and its reinterpretation in the Hellenistic world and (2) that of ancient Judaism with its own complex history. Judaism, on its part, absorbed influences from Babylonia, Persia, and Hellenism. The classical Jewish notion of the afterlife was Sheol, a place in which the deceased live as shadows. Starting from the second century BCE, we know of Jewish notions of a final judgment and postmortem rewards in Heaven and punishments in Hell (Bauckham 1998: 49–80), which different Jewish groups accepted to varying degrees.

In the gospels, Jesus mentions the places of postmortem rewards and punishments rather passingly. The word *Geenna* is probably derived from the name of a valley near Jerusalem (Valley of Hinnom), where human sacrifice took place in ancient times, according to tradition. The gospels refer to *Geenna* as a fiery place of postmortem punishment. The Gospel of Luke mentions Hades, which is the usual Greek word for the underworld. The rich man in the Lazarus story is taken to Hades to be tortured immediately after he dies, without an intervening period or a day of judgment. The same story describes postmortem reward (Heaven) as being with the Jewish patriarch Abraham. The place of postmortem reward is frequently referred to as the "kingdom of heaven" or "paradise" (Luke 23:43). The kingdom of Heaven, however, is not clearly described as a place above and beyond Earth. Together with the "the kingdom" and "the kingdom of God," it is also associated with a better world, the presence of God's rule on earth, or the restored kingdom of ancient Israel (Duling 1992).

Among the New Testament writings, the Book of Revelation offers the most detailed description of postmortem rewards and punishments. This text, presented as a first-person account by "John," identified as "Christ's servant," is varyingly dated to the late first or early second century CE and belongs to the genre of apocalyptic literature. In a primary sense, apocalyptic texts describe visions of Heaven and Hell, including mythological figures and events, and often make predictions about the historical future. Some apocalyptic texts, including the Book of Revelation, also talk about the end of times and a final judgment. The Book of Revelation (chapters 4-14) gives a detailed account of Christian saints and martyrs participating in a heavenly worship liturgy, which apparently takes place in the seer's present time. God sits on a throne, Christ appears as a lamb, and there is mention of various positive and negative mythological characters, objects, and events. Correlating the story with historical and nonhistorical realities has fueled speculation since antiquity.

Most important for our purposes is the scene of the final judgment (unfolding gradually from Rev. 14). The saints and martyrs who are already with God are joined by the dead, who are raised to participate in the judgment. A new earth and a new Heaven are created as places of eternal bliss, with the heavenly Jerusalem as their center (Rev. 21). The place of punishment, in contrast, is described rather parsimoniously as a lake "burning with fire and sulfur" (Rev. 21:8, cf. 19:20, 20:15). Whereas life in Heaven is supposed to continue forever (Rev. 22:5), the punishment of the condemned is only identified as a "second death" (Rev. 21:8). A brief list of sinners is given with the mention of the fiery lake: "the cowardly, the faithless, the polluted, the murderers, the sexually immoral, the sorcerers, the idolaters, and all liars" (Rev. 21:8). Matters are complicated by the repeated mention of "the book of life" (Rev. 3:5, 13:8, etc.), which contains the names of people destined for the heavenly Jerusalem; conversely, not being recorded in the book leads to a second death in the lake of fire. How names become recorded in the book of life is unclear. At some point, we learn that the names were entered "from the foundation of the world" (Rev. 13:8), but another passage suggests that the book records people's "works" (Rev. 20:12). The text also mentions eternal punishment, outside the context of the final judgment: the worshipers of "the beast and its image" (possibly referring to the cult of the Roman emperors) are going to be tormented with fire and sulfur "for ever and ever" (Rev. 14:9-11).

The Apocalypse of Peter, written in the first half of the second century CE, is the earliest known Christian text providing a systematic account of postmortem rewards and punishments (Bremmer and Czachesz 2003). It describes Heaven as a sunny, lush garden with flowers, spices, plants, and incorruptible fruit. The good scent of the garden is so intense that even spectators of the vision can smell it. A ray goes forth from the faces of the righteous inhabiting Heaven, like the ray of the sun; their raiment shines; their bodies are whiter than snow and "redder than any rose," such that the narrator is not able "to declare their beauty"; their hair is curling and flourishing and falls comely about their faces and shoulders "like a garland woven of nard and various flowers or like a rainbow in the air."

The Ethiopic text of *The Apocalypse of Peter* (discussing Heaven in the final part of the writing) speaks about intense, crystal-like shining, compares the heads and bodies of the righteous to roses and their hair to a rainbow in the water, and describes "a crown of nard woven from fair flowers" on their shoulders. The text goes on to describe Hell, which receives more attention than Heaven. Sins are punished in specific ways, often with a recognizable connection between the sin and the punishment. People who blasphemed against "the way of righteousness" are hanged from the tongue and burnt by fire. Other sinners are hanged from different body parts, such as the hair or legs. Women who conceived children outside marriage and procured an abortion are made to sit in a pool of discharge and excrement, with their eyes burned by flames coming from their children. As for parents who committed infanticide, flesh-eating animals come forth from the mothers' rotten milk and torment the parents. Those who persecuted and gave over "the righteous ones" have to sit in a dark place, they are burned waist high and tortured by evil spirits, and their innards are eaten by worms. Various other sinners are made to sit in burning mud and bodily discharges, such as blood, pus, and excrement. Those who blasphemed and spoke ill of "the way of righteousness" bite their lips and get fiery rods in their eyes. False witnesses bite their tongues and have burning flames in their mouths. They who trusted their riches, did not have mercy on orphans and widows, and were ignorant of God's commandments wear rags and are driven on sharp and fiery stones. Men who behaved like women and women who had intercourse with other women endlessly throw themselves into an abyss. Men and women whose sin is unspecified hit each other with fiery rods. Those who did not obey their parents slip down from a fiery place repeatedly; they are also hanged and tormented by flesh-eating birds. Slaves who did not obey their masters chew their tongues and are burned in eternal fire. They who did charity and regarded themselves righteous are blind and deaf, pushing one another other onto live coal.

The text's attention to sexual behavior is obvious; taking the whole catalog into consideration, the writing appears to protect the traditional system of the ancient Mediterranean household. Also remarkable is the inclusion of the persecutors of Christianity. While the existence of persecutions in the second century CE has been called into question recently (Moss 2014), their mention in *The Apocalypse of Peter* suggests otherwise. The list is anything but comprehensive, singling out only some behaviors considered punishable in the afterlife. Conspicuously absent are rules for prosocial behavior toward the ingroup (or punishments for the breach of such rules), which would make sense in an emerging and possibly persecuted religious movement. Given the impressionistic approach of the text, it was most likely not intended (and could not possibly serve efficiently) to outsource moral policing to MSP.

The Apocalypse of Peter offers the earliest portrait of the afterlife as we know it from medieval art (such as Gothic churches and Hieronymus Bosch's altarpieces) and literature (such as Dante's *Divine Comedy*). The *Apocalypse of Paul* (*Visio Pauli*), dated to the fourth century CE (Czachesz 2012: 35), probably drew on the *Apocalypse of Peter*. The list of sins changed somewhat, and we meet in Hell, among others, corrupt Christian leaders as well as churchgoers gossiping or falling asleep during worship service. The imagery of Heaven and Hell survived the Middle Ages and remains persistent, to varying degrees, in modern, secular societies. Studies on the cognitive aspects of afterlife imagery show how it engages evolved cognitive systems, which contributes to its continuing appeal (Czachesz 2012: 157–80; Närhi 2014).

Who goes to Hell?

As we have seen, the first 100 years of Christian tradition produced two different concepts of postmortem punishments: (1) perishing in a cataclysmic event (and being excluded from Heaven) and (2) languishing forever in a place of eternal torment. The latter option became more widespread probably for cognitive reasons. Insofar as we think of postmortem punishment in terms of "costs" projected into the future, eternal torment possibly weighed more than instant annihilation. Let us look into the question of why people were believed to face such punishments.

The first group of candidates are non-Christians. The Book of Revelation and *The Apocalypse of Peter* single out especially the persecutors of the Christ followers. Since admission to Heaven is contingent on membership in the Christian community (see also Paul's writings, e.g., Rom. 5:9; 1 Thess. 1:10, 5:9), non-Christians are excluded by implication. Tertullian of Carthage (c. 155–c. 225), writing toward the end of the second century CE, appears to take pleasure in the thought of pagans tormented in Hell (*The Shows* 30, Tertullian 1887b: 91). This raised questions about the fate of Jews and pagans who lived before Jesus and thus had no chance to become his followers. Of course, Christianity inherited the Jewish Heaven, together with the heroes of the Jewish religion who were thought to be there already, such as Abraham. Socrates was a revered figure in early Christian circles (Döring 1979), which makes it unlikely that he was thought to be in Hell; Dante eventually pictured him and other great pagan philosophers in Purgatory (cleansing fire, a kind of waiting room for Heaven). The first known "universalist" was Origen of Alexandria (c. 185–c. 254), writing in the early third century CE, who proposed that punishments were remedial and ultimately everyone was bound for Heaven (*On First Principles* 1.6.2–3, 2.10.1, Origen 1973:70–3).

How does such an idea of postmortem punishments work as MSP? In the original context of early Christianity before the fourth century CE, membership in the Christ movement was voluntary, and leaving the group was easy (in practical terms). Thus, convincing outsiders of the prospect of God's immanent judgment could be an effective recruitment tool. This was John the Baptist's message and Paul's rhetoric in Athens (as presented in Acts 17:31). The weakness of the strategy is that one needs to accept the idea of MSP first to be motivated to convert and it prevents people from leaving only as long as they maintain that belief. Indeed, most of the members of Paul's Athenian audience remain unconvinced (Acts 17:32–4). The dynamics is entirely different, however, when it comes to exclusion of group members. If the believer is convinced that exclusion deprives them of postmortem rewards and destines them for postmortem punishment, they will be willing to accrue considerable costs to retain membership.

Loss of membership in the Christian assembly seems to have been a serious issue. Any other private religion allowed members to have multiple affiliations, and such religions were seen as viable alternatives (and additions) to each other. However, Christianity inherited an exclusivist ideal from Judaism: multiple membership was not tolerated and was understood to exclude one from postmortem rewards (like the fate believed to be destined for "worshippers of the beast"). Thus, being excluded from a Christian group left one in a desperate situation. Moreover, from the earliest years, there was an ambition to maintain high moral standards in the Christian assemblies, possibly inherited from Pharisaic Judaism, as evidenced by sayings such as "Be perfect, therefore, as your heavenly Father is perfect" (Matt. 5:48). Moral transgressions could ultimately lead to expulsion from the group – also referred to as giving the unrepentant sinner over to Satan (1 Cor. 5:5; Satan is the evil mythological antagonist of postexilic Judaism).

This takes us to the second domain of application of postmortem punishment: retaliation for particular sins. What exactly were the sins that Christians worried about? A straightforward answer would be that Christians simply borrowed the laws (and their oral interpretation) of contemporary Judaism. That this was not exactly the case is suggested by gospel passages that criticize Jewish laws and practices as either misguided (e.g., Mark 7:1–23) or not radical enough (e.g., the Matthean Antitheses, Matt. 5:21–48). There are vice lists in various letters of the New Testament, which Wayne Meeks (1995: 68) has ordered alphabetically, starting with "abusive language" and ending with "wickedness." These vice lists have been identified as Hellenistic in nature. The lengthy moral instructions in Paul's letters, the Didache, and other sources (Meeks 1995: 66–90) suggest an ongoing engagement with moral rules in Christian groups. While it appears that Christians had (or at least strived toward) a strict moral code from the beginning, postmortem punishments are mentioned only in some cases. Paul does not mention the punishment of specific sins in the afterlife; however, in connection with some sins, he warns that "those who do such things will not inherit the kingdom of God" (Gal. 5:19-21; also 1 Cor. 6:9-10; Eph. 5:3-5).

It is logical to conclude that the actual and immediate cost of sinful behavior was not torture in the afterlife but souring one's relationship with the group and risking expulsion. What we understand from the sources is that group members admonished each other (e.g., Matt. 18:15; 2 Thess. 3:15; 2 Tim. 4:2), as well as developing practices of forgiveness and restoration (Fitzgerald 2009). Even excommunicated members could be readmitted through a new process of candidacy, culminating in a second baptism (Fitzgerald 2009: 797). Tertullian writes about the communal ritual of penance, in which repentant sinners undertake a series of symbolic actions, kneel before the elders of the congregation, and ask all members to "join their embassy of supplication [before God]" (*On Repentance* 9, Tertullian 1887a: 664). The inclusion of the masses in the Church from the fourth century CE posed new challenges, and the concept of justification took center stage.

Justification and penance

The six authentic letters of the apostle Paul are the earliest Christian documents, written in the 40s and 50s CE. When Paul discusses resurrection and divine judgment (e.g., 1 Cor. 15; Rom. 2:5-10), his main focus is on "eternal life" with Christ rather than eternal punishment. His key term is *justification*.

> For I am not ashamed of the gospel; it is God's saving power for everyone who believes, for the Jew first and also for the Greek. For in it the righteousness of God is revealed through faith for faith, as it is written, "The one who is righteous will live by faith." (Rom. 1:16-17, New Revised Standard Version Updated Edition)

The words *just* (and the derivative *justify*) and *righteous* (and the derivative *righteousness*) represent different forms of the same Greek root (*dikaios*, just or righteous). The "gospel" in this passage does not (yet) mean a biographical writing about Jesus; rather, it means the "good news" that the death and the resurrection of Jesus Christ from the dead provide an opportunity for his followers to attain salvation. Salvation, in turn, can be understood simply as avoiding God's wrath and participating in eternal life. How all of this exactly plays out according to Paul (e.g., as spelled out in subsequent chapters of the Letter to the Romans) is beyond the scope of this chapter. A key concept he often uses is "the law," that is, the body of divine laws in the Old Testament (possibly including their oral interpretations). While Paul expresses varying positions on the law, his general argument (in passages such as

Rom. 3:9, 23) is that everyone falls short by the standard of the law; thus, no one can achieve salvation simply by striving to do good deeds. Paul goes as far as condemning the ambition to achieve salvation by keeping the law (e.g., Gal. 3:10–12), as it is impossible in principle.

As we have seen, Pauline Christianity (at least in the words of its leader) is in direct conflict with contemporary ideas of MSP. Paul's thoughts on justification served as points of reference for later theologians. In the fifth century CE, Augustine of Hippo (354–430) argued that although humans possess free will, this is compromised so badly that they are "not able not to sin" (Latin *non posse non peccare*). It is the grace of God that brings salvation (through Christ), which Augustine understood as healing, liberation, or forgiveness, alternatively (McGrath 2013: 70). Augustine was reacting to Pelagius (active 390–418), a native of Britain, who asserted the human ability to perform good deeds and earn salvation by merit. Although the problem was debated back and forth during the Middle Ages, Augustine's idea of justification by grace prevailed and formed the foundation of both Catholic and Protestant teachings.

It is not coincidental that the concept of justification by grace became the official doctrine of the Church at the beginning of the fifth century. Until that point, Christians were composed of (relatively) small communities with members who joined the religion (and remained members in case they were born in Christian families) voluntarily, often accepting social alienation and even violent death (martyrdom). Christians, in general, upheld high moral standards and helped one another to live up to them. That situation changed considerably after Christianity became the official religion of the Roman Empire (in 380 CE) and other religions faced increasing societal and political confrontation. The demography of the Church changed from overwhelmingly urban to mostly rural, probably with overall lower educational and literacy levels. They were often converted by social pressure and even violence.

Unlike the Greek and Roman religions, Christianity had moral aspects tightly integrated into its religious framework. It was not easy to convey that novel model (and the related practices), developed in the context of an elitist movement, to the mass membership of the post-Constantinian Church. The new system can be summarized in this way: humans commit all kinds of sins, which destines them for eternal punishment in Hell; humans lack the power to perfect themselves so they can escape eternal punishment; God offers a way out of sin (and its consequences), but humans have to accept His offer; God's grace works through the practices of the Church, which believers have to follow to escape Hell.

The representations of vices, the final judgment, and eternal punishment in medieval art were educating churchgoers about sin and its consequences. A particular understanding of vices was based on the concept of "the seven deadly sins," which caught the popular imagination and generated rich literature and iconography (Barringer 1988). Rooted in the early monastic tradition and more properly called the "capital sins" (lust, gluttony, greed, sloth, wrath, envy, and pride – with variations), they identified the character traits and habits that underlie specific sinful actions; as such, they helped with self-examination and penance (Voll and Kenel 2003). The practice of penance itself was transformed considerably: from the Celtic Church, the habit of confessing one's sins to a priest privately spread to the rest of Europe. In the fully developed form of the sacrament of penance, the priest announces the absolution of sins immediately after the confession (Dallen 2003).

Penance plays a key role in Eastern Orthodox practice as well (McGuckin 2011: 300–306). The Orthodox Church developed the concept of "theosis" (deification) (Bouteneff 2010), which lacks the forensic aspect of "justification," and its focus on Jesus' sacrifice, and concentrates instead on Christ's victory over death and the inner perfection of the believer (McGuckin 2011: 198–204). According to the Orthodox tradition, Christ destroyed Hell, but people are re-creating it for themselves (Alfeyev 2010: 113–15). While the Orthodox Church does not accept the notion of Purgatory, it maintains that anyone can be rescued from Hell by the prayers of the living.

The Protestant Reformation of the sixteenth century was a complex sociological and theological process, with involved philosophical discussions of Augustine's concept of justification. Here, we are more concerned with the institutional aspect of the Reformation. In the medieval system, as we noted above, the Church assumed a mediating role between God and the Christian masses. Martin Luther (1483–1546) revolted against such mediation and the corruption that came with it. Consequently, private confession and penance disappeared from Protestant Christianity. The Reformers certainly recognized the potential negative implications of the doctrinal and institutional changes they introduced. In the Heidelberg Catechism, an important educational document of the Swiss branch of the Reformation initiated by John Calvin (1509–1564), we read the following question about justification by grace: "But does not this doctrine make men careless and profane?" (Q64). The Catechism suggests that "it is impossible that those, who are implanted into Christ by a true faith, should not bring forth fruits of thankfulness."

The dust had barely settled after the Reformation and the ensuing religious wars when the Enlightenment started to erode the medieval worldview. Meanwhile, Protestant orthodoxy elaborated on the theological heritage of the Reformation. Liberal Christianity, in turn, tried to maintain the Christian institutions as guardians of morality while downplaying the mythological apparatus behind them. As a response to both Protestant orthodoxy and liberalism, new groups emerged that emphasized personal piety and high moral standards. Heaven and Hell played important roles, especially in the North American revivals (Butler 1991). In these movements, the prospects of postmortem rewards and punishments increased the perceived reward of membership as well as the perceived cost of defection (cf. Launonen 2022), much as in earliest Christianity. The continued emphasis on afterlife beliefs probably contributes to the global expansion of evangelicalism. It needs to be noted, however, that evangelicals are embracing universalist concepts of Hell in increasing numbers (MacDonald 2012).

Conclusion

Christianity was one of the ancient religions that promised a favorable lot in the afterlife. During the first to fourth century CE, Christian communities were based on self-dedication, mutual support, and practices of moral repair. Hell was thought to be a threat for those outside the movement, and belief in postmortem rewards and punishments could boost group morale. After Christianity gained religious and political domination, the emphasis shifted to institutional practices, and avoiding eternal (or temporary in the case of Purgatory) punishment in the afterlife was contingent on the practice of penance. A fundamental tenet of Christianity is that Christ's salvation both transforms the believer in this life and saves them from eternal punishment. Christian traditions hold different theological accounts and popular conceptualizations of how exactly this happens and what supernatural punishment means at all. Generally speaking, insofar as MSP plays a role in the Christian ethos, it incentivizes religious attendance and practice rather than simply inducing fear of Hell to avoid it by good behavior. Finally, the cognitive appeal of Heaven and Hell boosted the prevalence of MSP in Christian populations (as well as assumedly in other cultures), irrespective of its possibly adaptive role in cultural evolution.

References

Aldridge, Robert E. 1999. "The Lost Ending of the Didache." *Vigiliae Christianae* 53 (1): 1–15. doi: 10.1163/157007299X00118.

Alfeyev, Bishop Hilarion. 2010. "Eschatology." In *The Cambridge Companion to Orthodox Christian Theology*, edited by Mary B. Cunningham and Elizabeth Theokritoff, 107–120. Cambridge: Cambridge University Press. doi: 10.1017/CCOL9780521864848.008.

Barringer, Robert. 1988. "Seven Deadly Sins." In *Dictionary of the Middle Ages*, vol. 11, edited by Joseph R. Strayer, 211–2. New York: Charles Scribner's Sons.

Bauckham, Richard. 1998. *The Fate of the Dead: Studies on the Jewish and Christian Apocalypses.* Leiden: Brill. doi: 10.1163/9789004267411.

Bock, Darrell L. 2008. *Luke 9:51–24:53*. Grand Rapids, MI: Baker Academic.

Bouteneff, Peter. 2010. "Christ and Salvation." In *The Cambridge Companion to Orthodox Christian Theology*, edited by Mary B. Cunningham and Elizabeth Theokritoff, 93–106. Cambridge: Cambridge University Press. doi: 10.1017/CCOL9780521864848.007.

Bremmer, Jan N. 2003. "The Apocalypse of Peter: Greek or Jewish?" In *The Apocalypse of Peter*, edited by Jan N. Bremmer and István Czachesz, 1–16. Leuven: Peeters.

Bremmer, Jan N., and Czachesz, István, eds. 2003. *The Apocalypse of Peter*. Leuven: Peeters.

Butler, Jonathan M. 1991. *Softly and Tenderly Jesus is Calling: Heaven and Hell in American Revivalism, 1870–1920*. Brooklyn, NY: Carlson

Czachesz, István. 2012. *The Grotesque Body in Early Christian Discourse: Hell, Scatology, and Metamorphosis*. Sheffield: Equinox.

Czachesz, István. 2017. *Cognitive Science and the New Testament: A New Approach to Early Christian Research*. Oxford: Oxford University Press. doi: 10.1093/acprof:oso/9780198779865.001.0001.

Dallen, J. 2003. "Penance, Sacrament of." In *New Catholic Encyclopedia*, vol. 11, edited by Thomas Carson and Joann Cerrito, 66–71. Detroit, MI: Thomson/Gale.

Döring, Klaus. 1979. *Exemplum Socratis: Studien zur Sokratesnachwirkung in der kynisch-stoischen Popularphilosophie der frühen Kaiserzeit und im frühen Christentum* [The example of Socrates: Studies on the reception of Socrates in the Cynic and Stoic popular philosophy of the Early Imperial Period and in early Christianity]. Wiesbaden: F. Steiner.

Duling, Dennis C. 1992. "Kingdom of God, Kingdom of Heaven." In *The Anchor Bible Dictionary*, vol. 4, edited by David Noel Freedman, 56–69. Garden City, NY: Doubleday. doi: 10.5040/9780300261905-103.

Esler, Philip F. 2004. "The Mediterranean Context of Early Christianity." In *The Early Christian World*, vol. 1, edited by Philip F. Esler, 2–25. London: Routledge.

Fitzgerald, Allan D., OSA. 2009. "Penance." In *The Oxford Handbook of Early Christian Studies*, edited by Susan Ashbrook Harvey and David G. Hunter, 786–807. Oxford: Oxford University Press. doi: 10.1093/oxfordhb/9780199271566.003.0039.

Horrell, David G. 2004. "Early Jewish Christianity." In *The Early Christian World*, vol. 1, edited by Philip F. Esler, 136–67. London: Routledge.

Kroll, Jerome, and Bernard Bachrach. 2005. "Sin and Mental Illness in the Middle Ages." *Psychological Medicine* 14 (3) 507–514. doi: 10.1017/S0033291700015105.

Launonen, Lari. 2022. "Hell and the Cultural Evolution of Christianity." *Theology and Science* 20 (2): 193–208. doi: 10.1080/14746700.2022.2051251.

MacDonald, Gregory. 2012. *The Evangelical Universalist*. 2nd ed. Eugene, OR: Cascade Books.

McGrath, Alister E. 2013. *Historical Theology: An Introduction to the History of Christian Thought*. Chichester: Wiley-Blackwell.

McGuckin, John Anthony. 2011. *The Orthodox Church: An Introduction to Its History, Doctrine and Spiritual Culture*. Oxford: Wiley-Blackwell.

Meeks, Wayne A. 1995. *Origins of Christian Morality: First Two Centuries*. New Haven, CT: Yale University Press.

Morris, Ian, Richard P. Saller, and Walter Scheidel. 2013. "Introduction." In *The Cambridge Economic History of the Greco-Roman World*, edited by Walter Scheidel, Ian Morris, and Richard P. Saller, 1–12. Cambridge: Cambridge University Press. doi: 10.1017/CHOL9780521780537.002.

Moss, Candida R. 2014. *The Myth of Persecution*. New York: Harper Collins.

Närhi, Jani. 2014. "Counterintuitiveness of Hell and Paradise in the Apocalypses of Paul and Peter." *Literature & Theology* 28 (3): 270–83. doi: 10.1093/litthe/fru020.

Origen. 1973. *On First Principles*. Translated by George William Butterworth. Gloucester, MA: Peter Smith.

Poplutz, Uta. 2017. "Gottloser Wettlauf in die Zerstörung (Barnabas Lässt Ein Stadion Einstürzen): ActBarn 19" [Ungodly race to destruction (Barnabas makes a stadium to collapse)]. In *Kompendium der Frühchristlichen Wundererzählungen. Band 2: Die Wunder der Apostel* [Compendium of early Christian miracle stories, Vol. 2: The miracles of the apostles], edited by Ruben Zimmermann, István Czachesz, Bernd Kollmann, Susanne Luther, Annette Merz, and Tobias Nicklas, 984–92. Gütersloh: Gütersloher Verlagshaus.

Sandt, Huub van de. 2007. "James 4,1-4 in the Light of the Jewish Two Ways Tradition 3,1-6." *Biblica* 88 (1): 38–63.

Sandt, Huub van de, and David Flusser. 2002. *The Didache: Its Jewish Sources and Its Place in Early Judaism and Christianity*. Assen: Royal Van Gorcum; Minneapolis, MN: Fortress Press.

Tertullian. 1887a. *On Repentance*. Translated by S. Thelwall. In *The Ante-Nicene Fathers*, vol. 3: *Latin Christianity: Its Founder, Tertullian*, edited by A. Roberts and J. Donaldson, 657–68. Buffalo, NY: Christian Literature.

Tertullian. 1887b. *The Shows or De Spectaculis*. Translated by S. Thelwall. In *The Ante-Nicene Fathers*, vol. 3: *Latin Christianity: Its Founder, Tertullian*, edited by A. Roberts and J. Donaldson, 79–91. Buffalo, NY: Christian Literature.

Voll, U., and A. Kenel. 2003. "Deadly Sins." In *New Catholic Encyclopedia*, vol. 4, edited by Thomas Carson and Joann Cerrito, 565–7. Detroit, MI: Thomson/Gale.

World Values Survey. 2020. "WVS Wave 7, 2014–2020." https://www.worldvaluessurvey.org/WVSContents.jsp.

CHAPTER 4

Buddhism
Mark Stanford

Originating in India between the sixth and fourth centuries BCE (Fogelin 2003), Buddhism inherited much of the cosmological outlook of the Vedic religion that preceded it, including belief in reincarnation. It radically reimagined Vedic views of morality, holding that individual destiny, including in future reincarnations, was the result of the moral character of one's previous actions. Buddhist doctrines were maintained and transmitted by the monkhood (*sangha*), which took up residence in monasteries and maintained temple complexes for lay use. There, monks and nuns studied texts that centered around nirvana, escape from the cycle of rebirth through intellectual and esoteric means. Meanwhile, laypeople remained largely concerned not with nirvana but with the cultivation of merit, or good karma, to ensure a better reincarnation.

Indian Buddhism subdivided early on into myriad schools, based on differing monastic regulations and interpretations of scripture. Three of these would form the major currents of world Buddhism down to the present. Theravada Buddhism thrived in Sri Lanka and spread from there to what are now Burma, Thailand, Cambodia, and Laos. Mahayana Buddhism spread from India to East Asia via trade routes through Central Asia and took root in China, Japan, and Korea. Vajrayana, an offshoot of Mahayana that emphasized esoteric practices, found followings throughout East Asia, becoming dominant primarily in Tibet. All of these would become effectively extinct in India after the 13th century, supplanted by Hinduism and Islam.

In all cases, Buddhism commingled with preexisting religions rather than replacing them. In Southeast Asia, Theravada incorporated local spirit cults, recasting them within a Buddhist cosmology. In China, Buddhists initially framed their beliefs in Confucian and Daoist terms but met with successive waves of repression by regimes that viewed them as representatives of a foreign religion. Japanese and Tibetan Buddhism combined with local spirit worship in ways paralleling similar trends in Theravada.

Much of Buddhist historiography has tended to read pre-modern Buddhism through a modern lens. Since the 19th century, attempts have been made to recast Buddhism, based on literal readings of scripture, as concerned mainly with meditative practices to achieve enlightenment (Gombrich and Obeyesekere 1988; McMahan 2009). This has been compounded by an overriding scriptural focus in scholarship (Hallisey and Hansen 1996), especially on early Buddhism, which can now be corrected by the growing archaeological evidence (Fogelin 2015). In fact, pre-modern laypeople had limited access to texts and abstruse metaphysics. Most practitioners likely experienced Buddhism as predominantly concerned not with asceticism but with the management of karma.

Moralizing supernatural punishment and reward in Buddhism

Indeed, karma is the principle on which most moralizing supernatural punishment and reward (MSP) in Buddhism is based. According to doctrine, intentional actions plant a "seed" that bears their moral valence. At some future time, whether in this life or the following one or more reincarnations, this seed bears karmic "fruit," bringing about outcomes that are good or bad to the extent the action was good or bad. The moral valence of actions may be judged by their conformity with Buddhist ethics, which includes the five precepts (prohibitions on killing, theft, "sexual misconduct," lying, and intoxication); a set of special rules for monks and nuns (the *Vinaya*); and injunctions such as making charitable donations (*dana*). Good or bad karma made in this lifetime is referred to as "merit" or "demerit," respectively, and making donations, especially to the *sangha* (Buddhist monastic order or community), is a particularly effective form of merit making. Because one cannot know the extent of karma accumulated from previous lives, living morally cannot guarantee positive outcomes; it is, nonetheless, the best way to increase their likelihood.

Central to Buddhist notions of karma is a rich cosmology of heavens, hells, and other realms, populated by a pantheon of supernatural agents (Mahathero 2018). While some karmic effects can be felt in this lifetime, the most salient effects are to be expected in realms inhabited in lifetimes to come (Gombrich 1975). The worst realms are hells, populated by demons, who subject victims to gruesome, protracted torments until they die and are reborn elsewhere. Above the hells are other realms of suffering: rebirth as an animal as punishment for acts of delusion or as a hungry ghost (*peta*) as punishment for avariciousness. Better than these is rebirth as a human. The best realms are the heavens, where those with excellent merit may be reborn as gods (*devas*) and live in bliss until they too die and are reborn elsewhere.

While the key doctrinal role of the agents who populate these realms is to act as an example of the outcomes that await practitioners depending on their behavior (Saddhatissa 1997: 10), many agents also interact with humans in this lifetime. Many Buddhists throughout history have feared attack by demons or ghosts, or enlisted the protection of gods. But some have pointed to a tension between karma and supernatural intervention (Spiro 1970: 155). If destiny is determined by past actions, how can a malevolent supernatural agent cause further harm? And what could be the purpose of appealing to a supernatural agent for help if karma cannot be changed?

One answer is that the actions of supernatural agents are also the product of human karma. The demons who populate hells must punish in accordance with the demands of karma; were they to punish overzealously, their own karma would suffer (Gombrich 1975). Similarly, ghosts and spirits who attack people in this lifetime can only do so to the extent that their victims' karma allows it. Those who live morally are less vulnerable to supernatural harm. While punishing supernatural agents are a fearsome incentive to cultivate merit, they are merely vehicles of karmic punishment; in the absence of such agents, punishment would simply come in another form.

A final aspect of karma is the concept of merit transfer. Through ritual and meditative practices, it is possible to share merit with less fortunate beings, such as ghosts or those suffering in hell. Although karma is entirely self-made, early Buddhism and Theravada overcame this by claiming that a meritorious act could give recipients the opportunity to make their own merit through a sincere endorsement of the act (Pemaratana 2013). Mahayana merit transfer was more expansive, allowing for deities to transfer merit to humans, thus saving them.

Merit transfer is relevant to MSP for two principal reasons. First, the ability to receive merit from others mitigated the punitive effects of karma to some extent in some societies. Second, merit transfer is itself a meritorious activity and is often achieved through prosocial acts such as donations in the name of the merit recipient; thus, in some cases, it may be considered a further inducement to MSP.

These key features – karma, the cosmology of heavens and hells, the karmic nature of supernatural intervention, and merit transfer – were present in early Indian Buddhism and continued throughout pre-modern Buddhism. As Theravada left India and became established in Sri Lanka and Southeast Asia, it maintained most of this framework in the classical form, adding to the pantheon of supernatural agents but continuing to interpret their actions through the lens of karma. Mahayana altered the doctrine far more, providing a new set of deities who offered the possibility of salvation from karmic consequences. However, except in the most radical of Mahayanist sects, the core elements of the karma doctrine remained much the same.

Case study: Early Indian Buddhism (third century BCE to first century CE)

The concept of karma, and much of the accompanying cosmology, formed part of Indian religion prior to Buddhism. However, Buddhism introduced several radical innovations in the understanding of MSP. Karma was reimagined from the particularistic ethic of a caste society to a universalistic morality more suited to an emerging merchant class. It came to be understood solely as pertaining to intentional actions, thus only to morally relevant behavior. It became possible to cultivate merit, including through donations to the *sangha*. Gods, demons, and spirits were brought within the karmic frame of reference: not only was their state determined by their karma, but the punishments and rewards they could bestow depended on the karma of the recipients, thus moralizing the role of supernatural agents. Finally, the Buddha became an object of veneration, perhaps capable of cleansing sins and offering divine protection.

Early Vedic references to karma did not apply to action in general but only to correct performance of rituals by the priestly caste. Later, in the Upanishads, karma became "ethicized" (Obeyesekere 2002). That is, it began to refer more widely to moral and immoral behavior. It was still largely understood, however, as pertaining to particularistic obligations that differed depending on one's caste. Buddhism and Jainism introduced a key innovation by reframing karma in universalistic moral terms. This new karma applied neither to correct performance of rituals nor to fulfilment of specific caste obligations but to universal ethical principles (Appleton 2014: 65). Good and bad actions were now taken to produce desirable and undesirable fruits, respectively, either in this lifetime or in a future one. Unlike Jainism, Buddhism made the further modification that karma resulted only from intentional acts (McDermott 1980: 181). Involuntarily harmful actions had no karmic consequences.

In the context of caste society, this was a radical change. While karma continued to provide an explanation for inequalities such as caste, it now affirmed free will and the potential for everyone, regardless of caste, to make their own future karma through present action (Akira 1990: 188). This new karma doctrine was a radically hopeful one, promising that even the lowliest might better their lot through adherence to universalistic moral injunctions (Gombrich 2006: 80). It is no surprise that Buddhism initially appealed largely to urbanites in the newly developing cities in the Gangetic Plain, and to an emerging merchant class, who spread the religion along trade routes and likely found the new universalistic ethic a useful underpinning for cooperation with like-minded fellow merchants (Thapar 2002).

Moreover, religious participation offered the promise of actively improving one's future not only by avoiding immoral behavior but also by engaging in merit making. Buddhist monasteries typically included a stupa, where laypeople and monastics performed both individual and communal rituals (Fogelin 2003). The most common ritual was circumambulation of the stupa, believed in itself to generate merit. Communal rituals included monastic sermons to laypeople, which revolved largely around morality and its karmic consequences, with scarcely any mention of nirvana (Gombrich 2006: 76). Most importantly, stupas provided a means of accumulating merit through donations to maintain the stupa and the associated monastery. The largest donors, apart from merchants, were monastics themselves, who were often drawn from wealthy backgrounds (Fogelin 2003). Thus, contrary to the mythological image of the early *sangha* as composed of wandering ascetics in pursuit of nirvana, it seems likely that the primary concern of Indian Buddhists was the pursuit of merit (Matthews 1986: 125). As in later Buddhism, the most effective way to pursue merit appears to have been through donations to the *sangha*.

This raises the question of whether the karmic benefits of such donations can be considered a form of MSP. On the one hand, these rewards are not given in return for generalized prosociality but for donations to a religious institution. On the other, such donations are not sacrifices to a supernatural agent; they often go toward supporting the livelihood of monks, and the intention behind them is to aid others by supporting the spread of the religion. Moreover, the *sangha* has historically employed the proceeds of donations to perform a variety of socially and economically beneficial roles. As early as the late centuries BCE, these included management and provision of water for the community and management and improvement of agricultural land; later, this would extend to services such as banking, medicine, education, and child care (Shaw 2011, 2013). Thus, the supernatural reward for donations to the *sangha* was perceived as a reward for prosocial behavior, which did in fact often have prosocial consequences.

Merit making also presents the potential to attenuate the effects of bad karma through good deeds. Early Buddhist thought contains opposing views on this subject. Scripture held that this was impossible; all deeds must bear fruit at some point in the future, and to commit a good deed could delay but not remove the effects of a bad one. However, some schools, such as the Sarvastavadins and Theravadins, held that repentance immediately following an immoral act could remove its karmic force (McDermott 1980). Despite doctrine to the contrary, many laypeople throughout history have gravitated toward the belief that good karma can cancel out bad (Spiro 1970: 119). Certainly in later Indian Buddhism, there are accounts of individuals washing away sins by ritually washing Buddha images (Fogelin 2015: 213). Whether such practices prevailed in the early centuries is less clear. Regardless, throughout the history of Indian Buddhism, it is likely that at least some practitioners saw the cancelling out of bad karma as possible.

The cosmology of heavens and hells described above was already present in India before Buddhism, and was shared by both Buddhism and Jainism. From early times, practitioners were exposed to a body of stories describing in detail the realms in which one might find oneself as a result of moral and immoral actions (Appleton 2014: 49). The existence of gods, demons, and spirits was not negated, but the effects of their actions on humans were reinterpreted as the result of humans' own karma.

One example of this is the concept of "spells" (*dharani*) (Spiro 1970: 157). These incantations consist of passages from sutras. When recited, they have the power to enlist the protection or material aid of gods. But they have no effect when recited by the immoral; bad karma renders incantations impotent (Rhys Davids 2017: 219). This may be seen as an indirect form of MSP. If one acts morally, one may avail of magical protection from gods; if one acts immorally, such protection disappears.

Another agent is the Buddha himself. In early Buddhism, doctrine treated the Buddha as having ceased to exist as a conscious presence after his death. However, his relics were buried in key stupas, with other stupas recapitulating these in symbolic form. Circumambulation was rendered more effective by the Buddha's physical presence and constituted an act of worship (Fogelin 2015: 25). He is described in scripture not as an ordinary man but as a superhuman being, with a range of distinct, godlike physical characteristics (Mahathero 2018). While it is impossible to be sure to what extent early laity saw him as a god capable of punishing or rewarding them, many Buddhists today perceive him in this way (Berniūnas, Dranseika, and Tserendamba 2020; Purzycki and Holland 2019; Stanford and Jong 2019). We may tentatively posit that such a view was likely to have been extant among at least some of the laity in the early centuries too.

In summary, MSP in early Indian Buddhism centered around a radical reimagining of the doctrine of karma. Those who acted morally, especially by making substantial donations to the *sangha*, could expect rewards in this lifetime, reincarnation on a better plane, or both. Those who acted immorally could expect misfortune in this lifetime and the torments of hell or at least a worse human or animal existence in the next. Meanwhile, ghosts, demons, and spirits might attack those who have accumulated bad karma, while the assistance of gods and perhaps the Buddha himself might be secured by those who have cultivated good karma. Early Buddhism thus succeeded in recasting even divine intervention as the result of individual morality.

Postclassical developments

The Theravada world

Theravada MSP does not represent a radical departure from early Buddhism. Unlike Mahayana, Theravada preserves the early canonical description of the Buddha as having existed in a physical realm and passed out of existence; neither he nor his disciples can intervene to save followers from their karma. However, all Theravada societies integrated local "little traditions" of spirit worship and possession into their cosmology and practice. They thus augmented the classical cosmology with still more supernatural agents.

The doctrinal Theravada view of karma is thoroughly psychological. Intentional acts create mental contents, which persist into the future and eventually manifest themselves as correspondingly good or bad outcomes (McDermott 1980). At each moment, the state of the mind is determined by its contents in the previous moment. This explains why unintentional acts cannot have karmic consequences; karma arises from mental causes. The mechanism that determines rebirth is therefore the state of the mind at the moment of death. Those whose minds are riddled with attachments and aversions as a result of bad actions are reborn in an undesirable state. To purify the mind, one must behave morally and perform merit-making activities, such as donations to the *sangha* (Egge 2002: 46). So long as these are performed with the right intentions, the mind is purified, and chances of a better rebirth are increased.

Merit making continued to be central to the practice of Theravada. In the early centuries in Sri Lanka, this was the principal concern of the laity, and the most popular sutras were those concerning the degrees of merit that could be earned through different forms of giving (Rahula 1956: 254–63). Royal and wealthy families kept "merit books," in which they recorded good works, including lists of temples and pagodas constructed by kings and ministers. While many monks pursued the higher goal of nirvana, this appears to have been all but absent from the minds of the laity. Instead, merit making offered better outcomes not only in the next life but also in this one, and violent kings engaged in merit making to erase their sins. Less wealthy followers expressed devotion to the *sangha* through smaller gifts and by virtue of their underlying intention, could expect no less promising a karmic reward. Similar patterns were found throughout the Theravada world.

Unlike in India, where Buddhism began as a religion of an urban merchant class, in the Theravada world, it became a religion of peasant societies (Gombrich 2006: 143). Moreover, while in East Asia, imperial polities with Confucian roots inflected Mahayana morality with values favoring loyalty to the emperor and social harmony, Theravada polities were more loosely structured, taking the form of "mandalas," in which subjects had few moral obligations to the king (Tambiah 2013). Theravada kings were typically seen as semidivine beings worthy of respect and fear, but their legitimacy derived from their ability to protect and expand the Buddhist religion (Gombrich 2006: 142; Walton 2016). A few thinkers saw royal legislation as emanating ultimately from the Buddha, and therefore compliance with laws as intrinsically meritorious (Huxley 1995). But an alternative attitude, which may have been more widespread among commoners, was to see monarchs as a distant inconvenience, whose interference might be likened to a natural disaster (Lammerts 2018). In general, Theravada conceptions of MSP thus continued to revolve mainly around interpersonal conduct and obligations to the *sangha*.

Similarly, although monasteries continued to engage in economic activity, such as acting as landlords and bankers (Gombrich 2006: 162), it is less clear, unlike in the Mahayana world, to what extent they provided welfare and social services, tending instead toward the renunciate ideal of detachment from society (Rahula 1956: 192). But monasteries did provide some crucial services. In particular, until the modern era, they were the sole providers of religious and secular education and ensured an unusually high level of literacy (Silber 1995: 91). Monks provided counseling and mediated in interpersonal disputes, as well as performing life cycle rituals. Theravada societies developed a custom of universal temporary ordination of boys, and monasteries often operated orphanages or boarding schools. This, combined with the flexibility of allowing ordinations of variable lengths, meant that monasteries could function as a social safety net: the poor, elderly, and infirm could be ordained for periods of time and live from the proceeds of donations. Thus, donations to Theravada monasteries not only helped long-term members of the *sangha* but had wider prosocial benefits too.

Canonical supernatural agents continued to play an active role. In Sri Lanka, the workings of the universe, including karma, were effected by a hierarchy of gods, each level subdelegating authority originally delegated by the Buddha (Gombrich 2006: 142). This hierarchy mirrored the political structure of the kingdom. In Burma, *devas* were seen as guardians of Buddhist doctrine and were sometimes believed not only to monitor humans but also to throw stones down from heaven on those who misbehaved. Once a year, at the time of the Burmese New Year festival, the king of the gods, Sakka, would descend from the heavens in his chariot, soar over the land, and compile a written record of the wrongdoings and good deeds of every human (Nyunt 2005: 18). In Thailand, *devas* became a high form of guardian spirits, capable of protecting only those who adhered to Buddhist morality (Esterik 1982). While punishment or reward remained the consequence of karma, the gods thus functioned as its handmaidens.

Divine intervention was not always morally inflected. The Sri Lankan pantheon incorporated a larger number of Hindu gods as well as gods corresponding to the planets. In exchange for worldly assistance, followers could make vows to these gods, promising to make an offering or carry out a meritorious act. While some gods were concerned with morality and would only help those who upheld it, others were indifferent and responded only to sacrificial offerings (Goomasekera 2006).

Theravada societies further added a range of local, nondoctrinal spirits to their pantheons. These spirits, often guardians of a particular village, household, field, or lineage, were not concerned with Buddhist morality (Spiro 1978; Tambiah 1970). Instead, they would punish or refuse to protect those who failed to propitiate them properly. Often this entailed collective sacrificial obligations on the part of a village or household, and the cults around these spirits may have fostered the sorts of local and particularistic moral sensibilities that doctrinal Buddhism overlooked (Stanford and Whitehouse 2021). However, most such spirits were not overtly concerned with policing interpersonal conduct.

When these spirits were not propitiated, or were otherwise dissatisfied, they could act to cause harm to humans, for example, through disease or an accident. Typically, Theravadins would offer a multicausal explanation for such events: misfortune was simultaneously the result of bad karma and having failed to propitiate a spirit (Engel and Engel 2010). This was also the case in involuntary spirit possessions; malevolent spirits could only enter into the impure minds of those who had accumulated bad karma or failed to adhere to Buddhist doctrine (Spiro 1978: 253). Thus, the actions of ostensibly amoral agents too were integrated into karma doctrine.

The Mahayana world

The various forms of Mahayana, and its Vajrayana offshoots, which became dominant in East Asia, introduced key changes in MSP. Mahayana transformed the Buddha into a present supernatural agent or force and allowed for the simultaneous presence of large numbers of Buddhas and bodhisattvas, who possessed salvific power to redeem those with bad karma and in some cases ensure their rebirth on a heavenly plane. The inevitability of karmic consequence was weakened by the sanctioning of practices such as confession, which could attenuate the effects of immoral action. However, a strong emphasis on merit making and avoidance of bad karma through morality persisted.

Mahayana understandings of the nature of the Buddha came to have profound implications for MSP. While early Buddhism held that the Buddha was a physical being, who ceased to exist after his death, Mahayana claimed that he was but a manifestation of a universal Buddha nature, which existed in all beings. This Buddha nature not only allowed for the simultaneous coexistence of many Buddhas but also engendered the potential for any individual to become a bodhisattva – that is, one who has reached the point of being able to achieve enlightenment but has instead remained to help others on their spiritual path. The bodhisattva ideal was central to Mahayana religiosity, exhorting practitioners to demonstrate compassion and strive for the merit and enlightenment of other beings. Many took a bodhisattva vow, an inherently meritorious act comprising a solemn commitment to strive to become a bodhisattva for the benefit of others.

According to scripture, bodhisattvas possessed both superhuman powers and limitless compassion. They thus became the object of appeals to overcome karmic destiny. This power to interfere with the effects of karma was rooted in early Mahayana texts, which claimed that certain religious acts, such as confession, repetition of a mantra, or recitation of a sutra, could have this effect (Attwood 2014). This extended to a range of purificatory practices in later Mahayana (Ghose 2007). However, these practices did not override karma beliefs; some Mahayana thinkers denied that it was even possible to nullify karma (Ch'en 1972: 111). In practice, merit making and avoidance of bad karma continued to be highly salient in most Mahayana societies, and the presence and prominence of purification rituals varied widely (McGuire 2014: 15).

The power of bodhisattvas led to a proliferation of cults. In China bodhisattva cults revolved around four key figures: Wenshu, Dizang, Puxian, and Guanyin (Avaloketisvara). These beings could grant protection and favor, in this lifetime and the next. Like the *devas* of early Buddhism and Theravada, they responded to the recitation of spells, as well as other rituals, including repentance and confession. Each bodhisattva specialized in certain areas of concern, and while each had their own elaborate cult, practitioners could, depending on their needs, engage in the devotional practices of more than one such cult. Accordingly, many iconographic depictions combine multiple bodhisattvas, each one representing their respective areas of specialization. While many devotional practices lacked a clear moral character, others required uprightness. Puxian, in particular, protected and rewarded only those who upheld the scriptures and practiced continual repentance for sins (Heller 2014: 226).

As in the Theravada world, Mahayana societies incorporated a variety of local spirits into their pantheons. In Japan, spirits known as *kami*, which often guarded particular localities and could be propitiated in exchange for protection or to avoid their wrath, continued to be venerated, and in many cases, they were reimagined as bodhisattvas (Deal and Ruppert 2015: 150–51). In Tibet, shamanic practices around Bon deities continued, and they were similarly recast as Buddhas or bodhisattvas (Kvaerne 1995).

Mahayana cosmology included also the presence of many Buddhas, who, like bodhisattvas, took on deity-like characteristics, able to intervene to aid and protect petitioners. Particularly salient were those Buddhas who dwelt in so-called Pure Lands, realms resembling heavens but populated by Buddhas instead of *devas*. Devotion to one such Buddha gave rise to Pure Land Buddhism, which originated in Indian Mahayana but developed particularly in Tang dynasty China. This revolves around Amitabha, a Buddha who lives in the Pure Land of Sukhavati (Weinstein 1987: 66). Rebirth in Sukhavati guarantees not only bliss but also eventual progression to enlightenment. Texts suggest that this rebirth can be achieved only by the grace of Amitabha, which is granted to the faithful and may be secured through recitation of Amitabha's name or other devotional practices. Anyone, good or evil, may enter Sukhavati provided they perform these practices properly.

In one branch of Japanese Pure Land Buddhism, karma beliefs experienced perhaps their most dramatic shift. The Shinran school introduced a fatalistic belief that individual actions are predetermined by karma. It is useless to modify one's behavior; one might as well murder and steal because all behavior is predetermined and there is no hope of changing one's destiny. Instead, salvation must be sought through Amitabha's intervention. This is achieved by declaring faith in Amitabha, through recitation of a single phrase, the *nembutsu*. Thus, in Shinran doctrine, karma ceased to be a force of MSP, serving instead only to explain present circumstances (Kawamura 1986).

Nevertheless, karma continued to be a powerful motivating force throughout Mahayana history. The proliferation of devotional and magical means to circumvent karma tended to form an amalgam with karma beliefs, in which practitioners strove for a better reincarnation through a combination of ethical, devotional, and esoteric acts (McGuire 2014: 10–16). Like the merit books in Sri Lanka, we find "morality books" in China, setting out the karmic consequences, even as quantitative points, of a range of daily actions and providing ledgers where readers could track their karmic progress (Brokaw 1987). And in Japan, didactic stories emphasized the inevitability of karmic retribution, not only in the next life but immediately in this one – even for those who would ultimately achieve rebirth in the Pure Land (Deal and Ruppert 2015: 66–67). Meanwhile, devotion to bodhisattvas accompanied merit making through donations, even construed sometimes as direct donations to the poor or infirm (Deal and Ruppert 2015: 88). The continued patronage of monastic institutions throughout the Mahayana world serves as further evidence that merit making was highly salient (Ch'en 1972: 295; Deal and Ruppert 2015: 50).

Case study: Tang dynasty China (609–907 CE)

The Tang dynasty represents the high water mark of Chinese Buddhism. By that time, Buddhism had achieved elite acceptance and imperial patronage and was widely diffused among the populace. Scholastic orders flourished, enriched by contact with India and Southeast Asia. Nevertheless, Buddhism continued to compete with Confucianism and Daoism and frequently came under attack for undermining particularistic Confucian morality. This culminated in the Great Persecution of 845 CE, which dealt a blow from which Chinese Buddhism never fully recovered.

Upon arrival in China, karma beliefs met with, and overlaid, preexisting MSP beliefs. Prior Chinese religion had no place for reincarnation; moral punishment instead came from heaven and was inflicted on individuals in this lifetime, on their descendants, or on society collectively (Jan 1986). Karma beliefs challenged this by holding that reincarnation allows all punishment to accrue to the individual, while explaining why this often fails to occur within one lifetime (Ch'en 1972: 70). These beliefs clashed with Confucian ideas, and universalistic karmic morality was seen as undermining loyalty to kin, especially one's father and the emperor (Ch'en 1972: 215). As a result, hybrid understandings arose. For example, karmic punishment might take the form of punishment of one's descendants, with the proviso that the descendants too have bad karma that must be worked out.

By the time of the Tang, Chinese concepts of karma had reached an accommodation with Confucian values (Smith 1993). Buddhist scriptures emphasizing the value of filial piety were emphasized, such that the moral code more closely resembled older Chinese norms (Xing 2016). Merit transfer was greatly extended and could now be employed to aid deceased ancestors in the next life (Kohn 1998). The functions of ancestor worship were thereby facilitated within a karmic worldview.

Depictions of heavens and hells were extraordinarily vivid and reinforced the consequences of behavior. Paintings of hells were common, especially on temple walls; they were seen as having a powerful motivational effect (Teiser 2006: 126–7). To existing hells, Tang dynasty Buddhists added a further layer: a "purgatory," in which the dead would be kept for several years between death and rebirth. This consisted of a labyrinthine structure containing up to 10 courts as well as torture chambers. Judges – the 10 Yama kings – sat in the courts, and the morality of the dead was evaluated sequentially by each. They were then subjected to gruesome tortures as punishment. This purgatory allowed the living to aid their relatives through offerings to the judges; but it also rendered karma more visceral in what was a heavily bureaucratized society (Teiser 1994: 5).

The Tang saw the growth of an unprecedented monastic economy, driven by both elite endowments and donations from commoners. Merit making remained a paramount concern, as evidenced by the construction of a vast number of pagodas and temples. Monasteries engaged in economic activities touching on virtually every aspect of life. They operated water mills, provided irrigation, acted as landowners – often employing an enslaved workforce – and provided banking services, facilitating the birth of an embryonic form of capitalism. Many engaged in charity, operating alms houses, hospitals, and refuges for the elderly and the disabled, as well as public works, such as building roads and bridges, digging wells, or planting trees (Ch'en 1972: 295). It has been argued that the individualistic nature of karma in early Buddhism was incompatible with the Chinese ethical tradition, which was historically concerned with governing interpersonal conduct to promote the welfare of society (Kohn 1998; Mollier 2014). Monasteries bridged the gap between these concerns, allowing individuals to make merit through donations, which would be used for the wider good of society (Smith 1993).

Devotion to the bodhisattva Dizang flourished during the Tang. Dizang was associated with the afterlife and could render assistance to deceased ancestors, including saving those suffering in hells. Such assistance could be secured through practices such as making Dizang images (Ng 2007). But the making of these images, and the temple construction of which they were often a part, equally served the purpose of merit making, for both oneself and one's ancestors. While previous meritorious action may not have been necessary to enlist the aid of this bodhisattva, such acts were considered to belong to the overall calculus of merit making.

Yet amoral means of making merit or erasing sins were also popular. Magical objects, such as pillars inscribed with spells, held the power to erase karma, without any effort on the part of those who came into their presence (Copp 2012: 93). Not only donations but also sacrifices, including even self-mutilation or self-immolation, could be directed at relics in exchange for merit.

Pure Land Buddhism also flourished in this period, especially among commoners. At first glance, the doctrine that a blissful rebirth can be achieved simply through faith in Amitabha might seem to render karma ineffective. But Pure Land was not a distinct school; devotion to Amitabha was integrated into wider Buddhist religiosity rather than negating it (Sharf 2002). Practitioners continued to prioritize moral behavior and merit making while simultaneously venerating Amitabha and aspiring either to rebirth in the Pure Land or the securing of such rebirth for their deceased ancestors (Yu 2014).

In sum, Buddhism under the Tang illustrates both the continuing motivational power of karma and the complex ways in which supernatural agents and magical practices could subvert karmic destiny. Rather than dividing neatly into schools, Tang Buddhism represented an admixture of beliefs and practices, in which those who aspired to salvation by bodhisattvas or Buddhas nevertheless engaged in merit making and strove to adhere to the precepts (Poceski 2014: 54). They were reminded to do so by graphic depictions of the hells and purgatory that awaited them otherwise and by their obligation to attempt to save deceased ancestors from such a fate. However, meritorious behavior was not always prosocial; critics of Buddhism claimed that vast resources were wasted on the pursuit of merit through the construction of images and sites with no social value (Weinstein 1987: 64–65). Such criticisms contributed to the persecution of Buddhists in 845 CE, which brought an end to the golden era of Tang Buddhism.

Conclusion

This brief account raises several points relevant to MSP. First, throughout Buddhist history, the impersonal force of karma has exerted its power through personified supernatural agents. Moreover, these agents vary across contexts – from the Yama kings of Chinese purgatory to the Sri Lankan divine bureaucracy. Unlike punitive gods elsewhere, these agents mostly lack discretion; karma uses them as an instrument of its inevitable consequences. Their ubiquity suggests that personified agents of MSP may be more cognitively optimal than an abstract force. Such agents can terrify, inspire hope, and relieve; their stories are compelling and easy to transmit. Karma provides a doctrinal framework for these stories, but without them, it might not enjoy the same transmission advantages.

A second point is whether merit accrued from merit making can be considered a form of MSP. While some merit was made through donations to charity, the bulk always resulted from donations to the *sangha*. Donations were intended to help monks or to help humanity by spreading Buddhism, and the *sangha* often used donations to provide social services. Undoubtedly, donations underpinned the spread of Buddhism and were therefore a form of ingroup-directed prosociality. Nonetheless, many merit-making activities, such as circumambulation, have no obvious prosocial aspect; and while merit transfer is intended to help the dead or other supernatural agents, we might instead consider it a form of sacrifice. For Buddhists, all forms of merit making constitute moral activity; but whether they actually direct aid toward other humans varies widely.

A final point is the widespread presence of nonmoralizing methods of counteracting karma. Whether through bodhisattvas or spells, Buddhists everywhere have found ways of attempting to mitigate past immoral actions. Even where doctrinally a good moral history is necessary for supernatural help, this may not always function as MSP. Because one's karma from past lives is unknowable, it is always possible that even if one behaves badly in this lifetime, one has enough previous good karma to render interventions effective. Regardless, even where methods of mitigating karma became popular, these seem to have augmented karmic motivation rather than displacing it.

In sum, pre-modern Buddhism was eminently concerned with MSP. The primary force in this was karma, an impersonal mechanism instantiating universalistic moral proscriptions, as well as primarily ingroup-directed charitable injunctions. The effects of karma were embodied in pantheons of supernatural agents inhabiting graphically terrifying or tantalizing realms. Buddhists everywhere grappled with ways to mitigate karma, including at times through the direct intervention of supernatural agents. But the underlying motivational force of karma is a unifying thread throughout pre-modern Buddhist history.

References

Akira, Hirakawa. 1990. *A History of Indian Buddhism: From Sakyamuni to Early Mahayana*. Honolulu, HI: University of Hawai'i Press. doi: 10.1515/9780824890636.

Appleton, Naomi. 2014. *Narrating Karma and Rebirth: Buddhist and Jain Multi-Life Stories*. Cambridge: Cambridge University Press. doi: 10.1017/CBO9781139523998.

Attwood, Jayarava. 2014. "Escaping the Inescapable: Changes in Buddhist Karma." *Journal of Buddhist Ethics* 21: 493–525.

Berniūnas, Renatas, Vilius Dranseika, and Delgermend Tserendamba. 2020. "Between Karma and Buddha: Prosocial Behavior among Mongolians in an Anonymous Economic Game." *International Journal for the Psychology of Religion* 30 (2): 142–60. doi: 10.1080/10508619.2019.1696497.

Brokaw, Cynthia. 1987. "Yüan Huang (1533–1606) and *The Ledgers of Merit and Demerit*." *Harvard Journal of Asiatic Studies* 47 (1): 137–95. doi: 10.2307/2719160.

Ch'en, Kenneth. 1972. *Buddhism in China: A Historical Survey*. Princeton, NJ: Princeton University Press.

Copp, Paul. 2012. "Chinese Religion in the Sui and Tang Dynasties." In *The Wiley-Blackwell Companion to Chinese Religions*, edited by Randall L. Nadeau, 75–98. Chichester: Blackwell. doi: 10.1002/9781444361995.ch4.

Deal, William E., and Brian Ruppert. 2015. *A Cultural History of Japanese Buddhism*. Hoboken, NJ: Wiley Blackwell.

Egge, James R. 2002. *Religious Giving and the Invention of Karma in Theravada Buddhism*. Abingdon: Routledge.

Engel, David M., and Jaruwan S. Engel. 2010. *Tort, Custom, and Karma: Globalization and Legal Consciousness in Thailand*. Stanford, CA: Stanford University Press.

EsterikPenny. 1982. "Interpreting a Cosmology: Guardian Spirits in Thai Buddhism." *Anthropos*, no. 77: 1–15.

Fogelin, Lars. 2003. "Ritual and Presentation in Early Buddhist Religious Architecture." *Asian Perspectives* 42 (1): 129–54. doi: 10.1353/asi.2003.0021.

Fogelin, Lars. 2015. *An Archaeological History of Indian Buddhism*. Oxford: Oxford University Press. doi: 10.1093/acprof:oso/9780199948215.001.0001.

Ghose, Lynken. 2007. "Karma and the Possibility of Purification: An Ethical and Psychological Analysis of the Doctrine of Karma in Buddhism." *Journal of Religious Ethics* 35 (2): 259–90. doi: 10.1111/j.1467-9795.2007.00306.x.

Gombrich, Richard F. 1975. "Buddhist Karma and Social Control." *Comparative Studies in Society and History* 17 (2): 212–20. doi: 10.1017/S0010417500007751.

Gombrich, Richard F. 2006. *Theravada Buddhism: A Social History from Ancient Benares to Modern Colombo*. London: Routledge. doi: 10.4324/9780203130254.

Gombrich, Richard F., and Gananath Obeyesekere. 1988. *Buddhism Transformed: Religious Change in Sri Lanka*. Princeton, NJ: Princeton University Press. doi: 10.1515/9780691226859.

Goomasekera, Sunil. 2006. "Bara: Buddhist Vows at Kataragama." In *Dealing with Deities: The Ritual Vow in South Asia*, edited by Selva J. Raj and William P. Harman, 107–28. Albany, NY: SUNY Press.

Hallisey, Charles, and Anne Hansen. 1996. "Narrative, Sub-ethics, and the Moral Life: Some Evidence from Theravāda Buddhism." *Journal of Religious Ethics* 24 (2): 305–27.

Heller, Natasha. 2014. "Bodhisattva Cults in Chinese Buddhism." In *The Wiley Blackwell Companion to East and Inner Asian Buddhism*, edited by Mario Poceski, 221–38. Hoboken, NJ: Wiley Blackwell. doi: 10.1002/9781118610398.ch11.

Huxley, Andrew. 1995. "Buddhism and the Law: The View from Mandalay." *Journal of the International Association of Buddhist Studies* 18 (1): 47–96.

Jan, Yun-Hua. 1986. "The Chinese Understanding and Assimilation of Karma Doctrine." In *Karma and Rebirth: Post Classical Developments*, edited by Ronald W. Neufeldt, 145–68. New Delhi: Sri Satguru.

Kawamura, Leslie S. 1986. "Shinran's View of Karma." In *Karma and Rebirth: Post Classical Developments*, edited by Ronald W. Neufeldt, 191–202. New Delhi: Sri Satguru.

Kohn, Livia. 1998. "Steal Holy Food and Come Back as a Viper: Conceptions of Karma and Rebirth in Medieval Daoism." *Early Medieval China* 1: 1–48. doi: 10.1179/152991098788220432.

Kvaerne, Per. 1995. *The Bon Religion of Tibet: The Iconography of a Living Tradition*. London: Serindia.

Lammerts, Christian D. 2018. *Buddhist Law in Burma: A History of Dhammasattha Texts and Jurisprudence, 1250–1850*. Honolulu, HI: University of Hawai'i Press.

Mahathero, Punnadhammo. 2018. *The Buddhist Cosmos: A Comprehensive Suvey of the Early Buddhist Worldview, According to Theravāda and Sarvāstivāda Sources*.

Matthews, Bruce. 1986. "Post-classical Developments in the Concepts of Karma and Rebirth in Theravada Buddhism." In *Karma and Rebirth: Post Classical Developments*, edited by Ronald W. Neufeldt, 123–44. New Delhi: Sri Satguru.

McDermott, James P. 1980. "Karma and Rebirth in Early Buddhism." In *Karma and Rebirth in Classical Indian Traditions*, edited by Wendy Doniger O'Flaherty, 165–92. London: University of California Press.

McGuire, Beverley Foulks. 2014. *Living Karma: The Religious Practices of Ouyi Zhixu*. New York: Columbia University Press. doi: 10.7312/columbia/9780231168021.001.0001.

McMahan, David L. 2009. *The Making of Buddhist Modernism*. Oxford: Oxford University Press. doi: 10.1093/acprof:oso/9780195183276.001.0001.

Mollier, Christine. 2014. "Karma and the Bonds of Kinship in Medieval Daoism: Reconciling the Irreconcilable." In *India in the Chinese Imagination: Myth, Religion and Thought*, edited by John Kieschnick and Meir Shahar, 171–81. Philadelphia, PA: University of Pennsylvania Press. doi: 10.9783/9780812208924.171.

Ng, Zhiru. 2007. *The Making of a Savior Bodhisattva: Dizang in Medieval China*. Honolulu, HI: University of Hawai'i Press.

Nyunt, Khin Maung. 2005. *Myanmar Traditional Monthly Festivals*. Yangon: Innwa.

Obeyesekere, Gananath. 2002. *Imagining Karma: Ethical Transformation in Amerindian, Buddhist and Greek Rebirth*. London: University of California Press. doi: 10.9783/9780812208924.171.

Pemaratana, Soorakkulame. 2013. "Evolution of the Theravada Buddhist Idea of 'Merit-Transference' to the Dead, and Its Role in Sri Lankan Buddhist Culture." *Buddhist Studies Review* 30 (1): 89–112. doi: 10.1558/bsrv.v30i1.89.

Poceski, Mario. 2014. "Buddhism in Chinese History." In *The Wiley Blackwell Companion to East and Inner Asian Buddhism*, edited by Mario Poceski, 40–62. Hoboken, NJ: Wiley Blackwell. doi: 10.1002/9781118610398.

Purzycki, Benjamin Grant, and Edward C. Holland. 2019. "Buddha as a God: An Empirical Assessment." *Method and Theory in the Study of Religion* 31 (4–5): 347–75. doi: 10.1163/15700682-12341453.

Rahula, Walpola. 1956. *History of Buddhism in Ceylon: The Anuradhapura Period*. Colombo: M. D. Gunasena.

Rhys Davids, Thomas William. 2017. *The Milinda Panha: The Questions of King Milinda*. Altenmunster: Jazzybee.

Saddhatissa, Hammalawa. 1997. *Buddhist Ethics*. Somerville, MA: Wisdom.

Sharf, Robert H. 2002. *On Pure Land Buddhism and Ch'an/Pure Land Syncretism in Medieval China*. T'oung Pao 88 (4): 282–331. doi: 10.1163/156853202100368398.

Shaw, Julia. 2011. "Monasteries, Monasticism, and Patronage in Ancient India: Mawasa, a Recently Documented Hilltop Buddhist Complex in the Sanchi Area of Madhya Pradesh." *South Asian Studies* 27 (2): 111–30. doi: 10.1080/02666030.2011.614409.

Shaw, Julia. 2013. "Archaeologies of Buddhist Propagation in Ancient India: 'Ritual' and 'Practical' Models of Religious Change." *World Archaeology* 45 (1): 83–108. doi: 10.1080/00438243.2013.778132.

Silber, Ilana Friedrich. 1995. *Virtuosity, Charisma, and Social Order: A Comparative Sociological Study of Monasticism and Theravada Buddhism and Medieval Catholicism.* Cambridge: Cambridge University Press. doi: 10.1017/CBO9780511520846.

Smith, Richard J. 1993. "Buddhism and the 'Great Persecution' in China." In *Critical Moments in Religious History*, edited by Kenneth Keulman, 59-76. Macon: Mercer University Press.

Spiro, Melford E. 1970. *Buddhism and Society: A Great Tradition and Its Burmese Vicissitudes.* New York: Harper & Row.

Spiro, Melford E. 1978. *Burmese Supernaturalism.* Philadelphia, PA: Prentice Hall.

Stanford, Mark, and Jonathan Jong. 2019. "Beyond Buddhism and Animism: A Psychometric Test of the Structure of Burmese Theravada Buddhism." *Plos One* 14 (12): e0226414. doi: 10.1371/journal.pone.0226414.

Stanford, Mark, and Harvey Whitehouse. 2021. "Why Do Great and Little Traditions Co-exist in the World's Doctrinal Religions?" *Religion, Brain & Behavior* 11 (3): 312-34. doi: 10.1080/2153599X.2021.1947357.

Tambiah, Stanley. 1970. *Buddhism and Spirit Cults in North-East Thailand.* Cambridge: Cambridge University Press.

Tambiah, Stanley. 2013. "The Galactic Polity in Southeast Asia." *HAU: Journal of Ethnographic Theory* 3 (3). doi: 10.14318/hau3.3.033.

Teiser, Stephen F. 1994. *The Scripture on the Ten Kings and the Making of Purgatory in Medieval Chinese Buddhism.* Honolulu, HI: University of Hawai'i Press. doi: 10.1515/9780824846541.

Teiser, Stephen F. 2006. *Reinventing the Wheel: Paintings of Rebirth in Medieval Buddhist Temples.* London: University of Washington Press.

Thapar, Romila. 2002. *Early India: From the Origins to AD 1300.* London: Allen Lane.

Walton, Matthew J. 2016. *Buddhism, Politics and Political Thought in Myanmar.* Cambridge: Cambridge University Press. doi: 10.1017/9781316659144.

Weinstein, Stanley. 1987. *Buddhism under the T'ang.* Cambridge: Cambridge University Press.

Xing, Guang. 2016. "The Teaching and Practice of Filial Piety in Buddhism." *Journal of Law and Religion* 31 (2): 212-26. doi: 10.1017/jlr.2016.20.

Yu, Jimmy. 2014. "Pure Land Devotion in East Asia." In *The Wiley Blackwell Companion to East and Inner Asian Buddhism*, edited by Mario Poceski, 201-220. Hoboken, NJ: Wiley Blackwell. doi: 10.1002/9781118610398.ch10.

Chapter 5

Manichaeism
Paul C. Dilley

Manichaeism, perhaps uniquely among the moralizing religions, incorporated into its doctrine and practice teachings about both a personal rebirth and a final judgment, followed by a cataclysmic end to the current world. Both scenarios of rebirth and judgment were expressed as moralizing supernatural punishment and reward (MSP) for acting in conformity with the ethical standards of the religion, which included both interpersonal behavior and behavior toward animals and plants, all based on the logic of freeing light particles that have been trapped in the material world. Behavioral expectations differed substantially for the elect, who were the leaders of the Manichaean community, and for the catechumens who supported them.[1]

For all humans, divine judgment would occur after death, and, theoretically, could continue for the same individual through a series of rebirths until the final judgment, when Jesus would separate the light particles of sufficiently virtuous Manichaeans from the darkness. While the light would ascend to the Kingdom of Light to spend eternity with the Father, the remaining light particles, those of the wicked as well as non-Manichaeans, would be forever encased in a prison. Manichaeans also embraced a notion of Heaven and Hell – in part through appeal to multiple other religious traditions – which floated ambiguously between immediate postmortem judgment and the final divine consummation.

Introduction to Manichaeism

Manichaeism has long held a central position in the history of religions. It was founded by Mani (216 CE to c. 277 CE), a visionary, teacher, and writer active in third-century Sasanian Mesopotamia who attracted a broad following of disciples and eventually gained the support of Shah Shapur I. He founded communities across the Sasanian Empire and promoted missionary work in the Roman Mediterranean to the west and Central and South Asia to the east. Mani had been raised in a baptizing group known as the Elchasites, where he probably became familiar with the Jewish Bible in Aramaic translation as well as early Christian texts in Aramaic, including the Diatessaron or another Gospel harmony, though it is unlikely that he engaged extensively with the writings of Paul until he left this community. At some

---

1 Manichaean catechumens are frequently referred to in modern scholarship as "auditors," the Latin term that was used by Augustine, among others.

point Mani became familiar with other religious traditions of Sasanian Iran and its environs, including Zoroastrianism, some aspects of which he developed within his teachings, and Buddhism, with which he likely became familiar during his travels to India (Dilley 2020).

The most salient feature of the Manichaean community's structure was the division of adherents into two major classes: the auditors, known as "catechumens" in Greek and Coptic texts, and the elect. The elect were governed by the three seals: (1) of the mouth (apparently signifying avoidance of harmful perceptions from the senses activated in the head); (2) of the heart (apparently signifying avoidance of harmful thoughts and desires); (3) and of the hand (apparently signifying avoidance of harmful activities) (BeDuhn 2000: 33–40). Although the precise symbolic meaning of these three seals is uncertain and may not have been standardized, the elect were also known for the requirement of strict celibacy, as reproduction prolonged the entrapment of light particles; the rejection of permanent possessions in favor of itinerant preaching; and the avoidance of wine and flesh, which was thought to be particularly impure, as well as the harvesting of any kind of food, which brought injury to the light within plants. As a result, the elect depended on the catechumens to provide them with food, which occurred as part of a daily ritual meal. Because of their pure way of life, the elect were thought to purify the light trapped in certain vegetables through their alimentary processes (BeDuhn 2000: 126–62) and then to release this light through the singing of hymns after the meal.

In addition to presiding at these daily meals, the elect presumably were responsible for the teaching of the catechumens, as well as the recruitment and training of other elect. They also directed the ritual life of the community during the weekly meetings on the Sunday sabbath, when the auditors gathered for readings and the singing of psalms; the Monday liturgy, by contrast, was centered on the elect, during which they fasted, refrained from activities such as the copying of texts, and repented of their sins, as evidenced by the elaborate confessionals preserved in Turfan and Dunhuang (Sundermann [1999] 2012b). While the elect surely participated on both Sundays and Mondays, it remains uncertain whether or not the catechumens participated on Mondays, and the exact context and day of their own confession is not known. There was also an annual series of four or five two-day festivals in honor of martyrs, both mythological and historical, marked by fasting and vigils. Mani's own imprisonment and death at the hands of the Sasanian emperor Bahram I was commemorated over 27 days, during a month of fasting, after which the Bema festival, the culmination of the liturgical year, was celebrated. This certainly involved a solemn element, including the tearful confession of sins, and the empty throne might have symbolized the coming of Jesus for the last judgment.

Some Manichaean sources and polemical texts mention "10 commandments" incumbent on the catechumens (and presumably also the elect), although it is unclear whether these had a single, widespread formulation. The only extant full account of these is by the Abbasid bibliographer Ibn an-Nadim: "renouncing the worship of idols; renouncing the telling of lies; renouncing avarice; renouncing killing; renouncing adultery; renouncing stealing; the teaching of defects; magic; the holding of two opinions about the faith; neglect; and lassitude in action" (from *Kitāb Fihrist*, trans. Dodge 1970: 789; for other, partial lists, see the discussion in BeDuhn 2000: 53–6). Manichaean catechumens had the opportunity to offset any harm they did to the light through, for example, the giving of alms (e.g., food offerings) for the daily ritual meal of the elect, as well as other ways of supporting the community. For example, according to chapter 80 of the Kephalaion, a doctrinal compendium preserved in Coptic, catechumens were responsible for fasting on "The Lord's Day" (Sunday); prayer to the sun and the moon, the two great cosmic vessels of light back to the Kingdom of Light; and almsgiving, which also included recruiting a child or a family member to train as an elect and other forms of donation (Gardner 1995).

Mani's teachings on postmortem rewards and punishments

The elect and the auditors thus had a two-tiered system of behavioral expectations, although there was substantial overlap. Similarly, MSP in Manichaeism was a multitiered system of rewards and punishments, in which distinctions were connected to these differing codes. Manichaeans considered two separate scenarios for individual judgment: (1) that which would occur immediately after death and (2) the complicated apocalyptic drama that would occur at the end of time. In the following section, I will consider all these contexts. Like all reconstructions of Manichaean teaching, this overview must be considered tentative, given the fragmentary sources; nor should we assume perfect consistency among Manichaean writings given their multiple languages and cultural contexts, from Spain to Central Asia. Indeed, Mani himself may have developed his teachings over multiple decades of promulgating his message.

According to an-Nadim, the *Shaburagan*, Mani's writing in Middle Persian dedicated to the Sasanian emperor Shapur I, described the three forms of postmortem judgment:

> These are the three paths apportioned for the souls of humans. One of them leads to paradise (lit. "the gardens") and they (who travel on it) are the elect. The second leads (back) to the world and (its) terrors, and they (who travel on it) observe the religion and provide assistance to the elect. The third leads to *jahannam* (i.e. hell) and they (who travel on it) are the wicked people. (an-Nadim in *Kitāb Fihrist*, trans. Reeves 2011: 101)

We will consider each of these in turn.

The salvation of the elect

As the leaders of the Manichaean community, the elect, who were also called "the righteous," were expected to observe strict standards of renunciation and behavioral codes, they were in turn believed to enjoy immediate postmortem salvation for their light souls. There were seven stages of ascent, during which the soul journeys through the material world, in which light particles and divine beings are still enmeshed, following the elaborate structures of Manichaean cosmogony and cosmology (Richter 1998). During the first stage, at or immediately after the time of death, the light-soul separates itself from the deceased material body; it is endangered by demons but also greeted by helpers from the light realm, for example, an image of the individual's twin, a virgin of light, or Mani himself, sometimes accompanied by three angels. The soul (or at least the soul of virtuous Manichaeans) is presented with victory symbols, such as a wreath of light. It then ascends to the Judge, who resides in the upper atmosphere and judges all souls according to their deeds. If the elect soul has lived righteously, it is allowed to ascend upward through the cosmos, through the standard path of light particles: past the column of glory to the "ships" of the moon and the sun, eventually reaching the doorstep of the Kingdom of Light (Kósa 2016).

Reincarnation

Others, both Manichaean catechumens and non-Manichaeans, have their light-souls recycled and return to the world to begin anew the struggle with the darkness. The usual term for this process in Greek is *metaggismos* (undergoing change), which is often translated as reincarnation, a term that I use here, as the Manichaean concept does indeed encompass the assumption of a new body. The exact relation of Manichaean *metaggismos* to the concept of reincarnation in South Asian religions, including Buddhism, needs further investigation. And in any case, its precise mechanisms also remain obscure. Mani's canonical work *Treasure of Life* seems to have covered "how they [catechumens] shall be released and purified; each one of them in accordance with his deeds and his contribution to the church" (cf. Kephalaion 91, Gardner 1995: 238). In Kephalaion 92, a catechumen asks Mani why there is no depiction of reincarnation in his *Picture Book*; Mani responds that the possible paths are too many to illustrate but assures his audience that the end result of reincarnation will be ascent to the light, which is the destiny of the righteous elect. So a virtuous catechumen could hope to get reincarnated as an elect and eventually achieve salvation upon death. Reincarnation for sinners, however, is a demotion, for example, in the form of animals, who were thought to be primarily creatures of darkness rather than light. It is unclear in the extant sources whether "negative" reincarnations can be reversed, though presumably "positive" ones could be ruined by failure to follow the commandments.

The end of the world

The second scenario of postmortem judgment is apocalyptic/eschatological, which occurs at the end of the struggle between the light and the darkness (for an overview, see Sundermann [1998] 2012a). The prophethood of Mani, who was seen as the last of a succession of earlier prophets, their "seal," marks the beginning of the end of the world. As in Christianity, the end times were thought to be presaged by a period in which the community is persecuted, as occurred following the arrest and death of Mani. The *Sermon on the Great War*, composed by Mani's disciple Koustaios – which is extant in Coptic translation though fragmentary – gives a sense of the period leading up to the end times. Persecution leads to a great war, in which the righteous suffer, but the survivors enjoy the reign of a king who brings justice and supports the Manichaean community; this golden age is broken by the arrival of the Antichrist and other false prophets (Gardner and Lieu 2004: 220–26). The final judgment is then inaugurated by a heavenly figure known as Jesus the Splendor, or Xradesahryazd (God of the World of Wisdom) in the Middle Persian *Shaburagan*, which contains the most extensive account of this stage and is closely related to the eschatological section in the Gospel of Matthew chapters 25 and 26 (Baker-Brian 2011: 28).

In particular, Jesus the Splendor separates the righteous from sinners, making this an important locus of MSP teaching, and non-Manichaeans from Manichaeans. The judgment itself seems to echo the tripartite division of the fate of souls after death but in a slightly more finalized manner: the just elect ascend immediately to the New Paradise, while sinners are condemned to hell, and the rest enjoy another Reign of Righteousness on earth, that is, as catechumens whose eventual salvation is assured. This too comes to an end as the various emanations of the Kingdom of Light, who had been holding up the world by their presence during the slow escape of the light, abandon the cosmos, literally causing the heavens to fall and start a great cataclysmic fire. The remnant of light that is still redeemable is collected in the Last Statue, which is transported to the New Paradise, while the unredeemable portion is condemned to the Bolos, or prison, which was crafted for the denizens of the Kingdom of Darkness, including human sinners (and, presumably, non-Manichaeans, that is, members of "sects").

Heaven and Hell

Mani also drew upon other religious traditions to emphasize that earlier prophets across cultures, whom he considered his direct predecessors and characterized as apostles of light, also taught about heavenly reward and the eternal punishments of hell. In one extended passage from volume 2 of the *Kephalaia*, he notes how Zarades (who was sent to Persia), Bouddas (sent to India), the mysterious Aurentes/Kebellos (sent to "The East"), an unidentified apostle (sent to Parthia), as well as various antediluvian patriarchs, such as Adam and Enoch, were all taken up to Heaven and down to Hell and bore witness to their followers about the existence of both realms as a motivation for obeying their teaching:

> They returned, they came to this place again. And when they came, they spoke. They bore witness about the land of light and hell, that they exist. They did that which was entrusted to them by God. Those, then, who became disciples of them: they did good deeds; they came forth from their body and they went to the land of light, the city of the well favored. Their testimony exists in their writings. (2Ke 423,27–424,5: Gardner, BeDuhn, and Dilley 2018)

Mani then appeals to his own experience of rapture, on the model of those of the previous apostles:

> I myself, whom you are looking at: I went to the land of light. Indeed, I have seen the land of light with my own eyes, the way that it exists. Again, I have [seen] hell with my eyes, the way that it exists. (2Ke 424,7–10: Gardner, BeDuhn, and Dilley 2018)

Mani situates his claims to visionary experience, which allows him to act as a witness of Heaven and Hell, within a chain of earlier apostles who made similar otherworldly journeys and used the experience to gain followers who practiced their teachings and thus ascended to Heaven. His personal revelation of the structure of Heaven is confirmed in his *Picture Book*, where he is portrayed many times gazing at various parts of the complex structure of the cosmos as he imagined it (Gulácsi 2015: 478–81). Exactly the same claim was made by Mani's rival Kartir, a Zoroastrian mobed who gradually rose to prominence at the court of Shapur and his successors and was later involved in Mani's arrest and death: in a Middle Persian inscription he recounts how he requested a sign and received a vision that "there is a heaven and there is a hell, and he who is virtuous goes forth to heaven and he who is sinful is cast into hell" (Kartir, inscription 37, MacKenzie 1989: 61). He then goes on to list aspects of his ascent that demonstrate further significant connections to the Manichaeans. Kartir and Mani both drew on postmortem rewards and punishment in the competition for imperial patronage to demonstrate the importance of following their teachings. Indeed, multiple communities in the Sasanian Empire followed closely related teachings on Heaven and Hell, as demonstrated by the many shared motifs across Late Antique Greco-Roman, Jewish, Christian, Mandaean, Manichaean, Zoroastrian, and Buddhist texts on the afterlife (Dilley 2014).

It is also quite possible that Manichaeans meditated on descriptions of postmortem punishment in order to cultivate a habit of observing the community's precepts.

A fragment of a Manichaean writing in Parthian (M 6020) contains an extensive discussion of the sufferings that sinners will feel:

> Time and again they cut off his ears, and time and again they hack his tongue into slices, and in the same manner they cut all his limbs. And time and again they pour molten copper into his mouth and give him glowing-hot iron to eat and drive iron nails into his ears – who can wholly describe the wicked, horrible distress and suffering which that unfortunate unbeliever who soils the pure religion must undergo. (Henning 1965: 31–3, with slight modifications from Sims-Williams 2009)

This homiletic description of punishment is striking for its visual nature and may have in fact corresponded to illustrations in Mani's *Picture Book*, which, as we have seen, included the three kinds of postmortem judgments. The process of reincarnation as a result of sin also seems to have been presented in a highly evocative way: a polemical source describes a "punishment-fits-the-crime" logic that is also seen in contemporary accounts of hell: reapers of barley find themselves as barley; the rich find themselves as beggars (*Acts of Archelaus* 9). Thus, Manichaeans had written/oral and visual resources for individual meditation on MSP. While there is no explicit evidence for this practice, a related cognitive discipline known as the fear of God, which developed as a Christian ascetic practice in the third and fourth centuries, involved meditation on the last judgment in terms very similar to those presented in M 6020 (Dilley 2017: 148–85; Dilley 2019).

Case study: psalms and memorial services for the dead

The psalms to Jesus, which are preserved in the Coptic Manichaean *Psalm Book*, concern the hour of death and assume the voice of the soul at the hour of death, which calls out to Jesus (and Mani) for help:

> Come to me, Lord Jesus, stand with me in the hour [of my] need. ... I beg thee, Lord Mani, give [me] quickly the reward of my faith and my prayers and my fastings and my alms that I gave in thy name. Let the three angels come forth before me and give me now my garland, the robe, and my prize, according to thy true promises which thou didst promise to them that have believed in thee. (Psalm CCLXVII, Allberry 1938).

The speaker, presumably a catechumen because of the mention of alms, reminds Jesus of his good deeds, which are deserving of reward, and requests the presence of the divine escorts and prizes that will ensure a favorable postmortem judgment.

The psalms to Jesus might have been spoken by living Manichaeans as a kind of *memento mori* and as a motivation to follow the commandments. But what if they were recited at a service on behalf of somebody else? Any catechumen, apparently, could hope for immediate salvation if a commemorative liturgy was held after their death in which the elect and others prayed for their departed light-soul and alms were offered by their family members. This memorial service for the dead is discussed in Kephalaion 115 (Gardner 1995: 276–84), a lengthy chapter that begins with an unnamed catechumen asking Mani the following question:

> Tell me: The entreaty and the prayer by which [the] saints pray, beseeching for [someone; do they help] him any? How is it [beneficial] for him; or [else does it help] him not? For we have heard from you [just so, that] each one shall receive retribution according to his deeds. (Gardner 1995: 277)

Mani's long response confirms that if the elect ("the saints") faithfully request aid for a departed catechumen, it will be granted to them, just as during the creation of the world, when the various emanations of the Kingdom of Light requested aid from the Father for the salvation of light particles, this aid was granted them.

Siegfried Richter (1998) hypothesizes that another group of Coptic psalms, the psalms of Heracleides, were recited at these ceremonies on behalf of the deceased. Like the psalms to Jesus, the psalms of Heracleides also emphasize the good deeds of the deceased, but they chronicle the stages of ascent *after* the soul is separated from the body and assume a positive outcome of salvation. The soul, which once again speaks in the first person, celebrates and narrates its journey upward to the Land of Light:

> The seven fearful demons [probably a reference to the planets] have passed away [from me], their foul hands empty of my blood, their heart also laden with grief and sorrow because they were not able to trap me in the nets of lust, for I have never been a slave of iniquity that works outrage. Oh Savior, o Son of God, [take] me unto thee quickly, wash me in the dews of the Column of Glory. (Psalm CCLXXXII, Allberry 1938: 103)

In a sense, these psalms express the intended result of the ritual, namely a successful ascent to the New Paradise. And these psalms are relentlessly positive, emphasizing the positive actions of the light soul as it ascends, regardless of the personal identity or history of the deceased being commemorated.

Conclusion

Manichaean teachings about the afterlife and MSP featured a curious, perhaps unique dichotomy between immediate salvation or eventual damnation, on the one hand, and the light soul's temporary reincarnation(s) before the ultimate resolution of its fate. This corresponded precisely to the dichotomy between the elect and the catechumens in the Manichaean community hierarchy. In some sense, the dual track of postmortem punishment was a means of resolving the potential tension between the two offices: the possibility of gradual progress, even if across lifetimes, authorized catechumens to maintain somewhat more "worldly" lifestyles, including bearing children and raising a family, while still holding out the hope of eventual salvation. But there was also an ongoing question about the possibility for catechumens too to enjoy immediate salvation, if not through their own merits at least by those of the elect who led memorial services on their behalf. This ambiguity points as well to a fundamental tension of the catechumen status: despite their efforts to live according to the 10 commandments and other moral codes, including regular prayer, fasting, and almsgiving, they were not rewarded with heavenly rest after death; instead, they had to hold on to the hope that their light-selves, reincarnated into another body, would eventually reach the goal of salvation.

References

Allberry, C. R. C. 1938. *A Manichaean Psalm-Book, Part II.* Stuttgart: Kohlhammer.

Baker-Brian, Nicholas. 2011. *Manichaeism: An Ancient Faith Rediscovered.* London: T&T Clark.

BeDuhn, Jason. 2000. *The Manichaean Body: In Discipline and Ritual.* Baltimore, MD: Johns Hopkins University Press.

Dilley, Paul C. 2014. "'Hell Exists, and We Have Seen the Place Where It Is': Rapture and Religious Competition in Sasanian Iran." In *Mani at the Court of the Persian Kings: Studies on the Chester Beatty Kephalaia Codex,* edited by Iain Gardner, Jason BeDuhn, and Paul C. Dilley, 211–46. Leiden: Brill. doi: 10.1163/9789004282629_009.

Dilley, Paul C. 2017. *Monasteries and the Care of Souls in Late Antique Christianity: Cognition and Discipline.* Cambridge: Cambridge University Press. doi: 10.1017/9781316875094.

Dilley, Paul C. 2019. "Theory of Mind from Athens to Augustine: Divine Omniscience and the Fear of God." In *The Routledge Handbook of Classics and Cognitive Theory,* edited by Peter Meineck, William Michael Short, and Jennifer Devereaux, 270–78. London: Routledge. doi: 10.4324/9781315691398-17.

Dilley, Paul C. 2020. "Conflict and Cultural Transmission along the Iranian-Roman Contact Zone: The Manichaean Law of Zarades." In *Quand les dualistes polémiquaient: Zoroastriens et manichéens* [When the dualists polemicized. Zoroastrians and Manichaeans], edited by Flavia Ruani and Mihaela Timus, 173–8. Leuven: Peeters. doi: 10.2307/j.ctv1q26vfv.13.

Dodge, Bayard. 1970. *The Fihrist of al-Nadim: A Tenth-Century Survey of Muslim Culture.* 2 vols. New York: Columbia University Press.

Gardner, Iain. 1995. *The Kephalaia of the Teacher*. Leiden: Brill. doi: 10.1163/9789004328914.

Gardner, Iain, Jason BeDuhn, and Paul C. Dilley. 2018. *The Chapters of the Wisdom of My Lord Mani, Part III: Pages 343–442 (Chapters 321–347)*. Leiden: Brill. doi: 10.1163/9789004363403_003.

Gardner, Iain, and Samuel N. C. Lieu. 2004. *Manichaean Texts from the Roman Empire*. Cambridge: Cambridge University Press. doi: 10.1017/CBO9780511616891.

Gulácsi, Zsuzsanna. 2015. *Mani's Pictures: The Didactic Images of the Manichaeans from Sasanian Mesopotamia to Uygur Central Asia in Tang-Ming China*. Leiden: Brill. doi: 10.1163/9789004308947.

Henning, W. B. 1965. "A Grain of Mustard." *AION* 50: 29–47.

Kósa, Gábor. 2016. "The Manichaean 'New Paradise' in Text and Image." *Studies on the History of Exchange Relations in the East Asian World* 13: 27–113.

MacKenzie, D. N. 1989. "Kerdir's Inscription." In *The Sasanian Rock Reliefs at Naqsh-I Rustam*, edited by G. Herrmann, 35–62. Berlin: D. Reimer.

Reeves, John C. 2011. *Prolegomena to a History of Islamicate Manichaeism*. Sheffield: Equinox. doi: 10.1558/isbn.9781845538514.

Richter, Sebastian. 1998. *Die Aufstiegspsalmen des Herakleides. Untersuchungen zum Seelenaufstieg und zur Seelenmesse bei den Manichäern* [The ascension psalms of Heracleides: Investigations into the ascension of the soul and the soul mass among the Manichaeans]. Wiesbaden: Reichert.

Sims-Williams, Nicholas. 2009. "The Bactrian Fragment in Manichaean Script (m1224)." In *Literarische Stoffe und ihre Gestaltung in mitteliranischer Zeit: Kolloquium anlässlich des 70. Geburtstages von Werner Sundermann* [Literary materials and their design in the middle Iranian period: Colloquium on the occasion of Werner Sundermann's 70th birthday], edited by Desmond Durkin-Meisterernst, Christiane Reck, and Dieter Weber, 245–68. Wiesbaden: Reichert.

Sundermann, Werner. (1998) 2012a. "Eschatology II. Manichaean Eschatology." In *Encyclopedia Iranica*, edited by Ehsan Yarshater. Accessed February 10, 2024. https://iranicaonline.org/articles/eschatology-ii.

Sundermann, Werner. (1999) 2012b. "Festivals II. Manichaean." In *Encyclopedia Iranica*, edited by Ehsan Yarshater. Accessed February 10, 2024. https://www.iranicaonline.org/articles/festivals-ii.

CHAPTER 6

Islam
Aria Nakissa[1]

This chapter explains the central role of moralizing supernatural punishment and reward (MSP) in Islam. The chapter is divided into three sections. The first section offers a brief overview of Islamic history. The second section discusses basic Islamic theological, moral, and legal doctrines, situating them in relation to religious trends in the Late Antique world. The third section discusses the many different forms of Islam that have developed over the course of history, providing two illustrative case studies. The first case study examines the Middle East during the classical period (900–1200 CE). The second examines pre-modern Muslim Southeast Asia (1200–1800 CE).

Overview of Islamic history

Islam emerged in the Arabian peninsula during the seventh century CE. At that time, Arabia was located between two powerful empires. To the west was the Byzantine Empire, which encompassed Southeast Europe, the Levant, Egypt, and coastal North Africa. To the east was the Sasanian Empire, which encompassed Persia and Mesopotamia. Both empires were characterized by strong states, large-scale agriculture, developed urban centers, and ancient religious traditions. The official religion of the Byzantine Empire was Christianity. The empire's population was predominantly Christian, although there existed a Jewish minority. The official religion of the Sasanian Empire was Zoroastrianism. The empire's population was predominantly Zoroastrian, although there were also significant Jewish, Christian, and Manichaean minorities. As we will see, Islam endorses many doctrines shared by Judaism, Christianity, Zoroastrianism, and Manichaeism.

In the seventh century, the major central area in the Arabian peninsula was populated by Arab tribes, who made their living through pastoralism, caravan trading, and raiding. In this area, there were few urban centers, no state, and little agriculture. For hundreds of years, Arabs (and closely related peoples) had been converting to Judaism and Christianity (e.g., Nabateans, Ghassanids, Ḥimyarites). Jewish and Christian communities were concentrated on the northern and southern fringes of the peninsula, although some were scattered in the central region. Prior to the rise of Islam, many Jews and Christians had come to regard the Arabs as descendants

---

[1] Aria Nakissa is a lecturer in the Faculty of Islamic Studies and Faculty of Social Sciences, Indonesian International Islamic University.

of the prophet/patriarch Abraham (Ibrāhīm) through his son Ishmael (Ismāʿīl) (Goudarzi 2019: 457–62; Hughes 2017: 38–43).

In the seventh century, most Arabs embraced a polytheistic religiosity, which also acknowledged a Supreme Creator God known as Allāh. The primary religious site of the pre-Islamic Arabs was a cube-shaped building known as the Kaʿba. Located in the city of Makka, the Kaʿba was dedicated first to the worship of Allāh and second to the worship of other lesser gods (e.g., Hubal, Manāt, al-Lāt, al-ʿUzzā). There was no idol to represent Allāh as He was conceived of as transcending forms (Peters 1994: 27). Nevertheless, the lesser gods were represented in the form of idols, and such idols were housed within the Kaʿba (Peters 1994: 19–29). At the same time, like many other pre-modern polytheisms (e.g., Egyptian, Greco-Roman, Hindu), Arab polytheism developed a monotheistic minority current. Proponents of this current were known as *ḥanīfs*. *Ḥanīfs* believed that *Allāh* was the only god and attributed this teaching to Abraham (De Blois 2002: 16–25; Stroumsa 2015: 16–17, 155–8).

Muḥammad (570–632 CE) was an Arabian merchant born in the city of Makka. He was inclined toward *ḥanīf* teachings. At 40 years of age, he began to have visions and other religious experiences. He considered these to be divine revelations from Allāh transmitted by the angel Gabriel (Jibrīl). In these revelations, Allāh affirmed that Abraham had rejected polytheism/idolatry and built the Kaʿba (along with Ishmael) as a site for monotheistic worship. Allāh appointed Muḥammad as His last prophet and ordered him to preach Abrahamic monotheism (*tawḥīd*), and related religious doctrines, to all the world. Muḥammad took up this task for the next two decades until his death in 632. During this period, he built a large community of religious believers. He also established a sizable theocratic state in western Arabia, centered in the city of Madina (350 km north of Makka). Shortly before his death, Muḥammad succeeded in conquering Makka and cleansing the Kaʿba of idols.

Following Muḥammad's death, the early Muslims continued to build on his conquests, annexing all of the Sasanian lands and most of the Byzantine lands. By 750 CE, Muslims had built a theocratic empire extending from Spain and Morocco in the west to Central Asia and North India in the east. Between 750 and 1500, the expansion continued more slowly through a mixture of conquest, missionary work, and contact with Muslim traders. Through missionary work and trade, Islam spread along the Silk Road, Indian Ocean, and Trans-Saharan trade routes. These developments produced five major geographical regions with populations that were largely or almost entirely Muslim before 1800: (1) the Middle East and North Africa, (2) Sub-Saharan East and West Africa, (3) Central Asia, (4) South Asia, and (5) Southeast Asia. Significant Muslim populations also existed in other regions like Southeast Europe and Western China.

During the modern period, Western countries have accumulated enormous political, economic, and social power. This process has gone hand in hand with a precipitous decline in the power of Muslim countries. The era of Muslim conquests came to an end around 1700 with the failed Ottoman siege of Vienna and the death of the Indian Mughal emperor Aurangzeb. Between the late eighteenth century and the mid-twentieth century, modernizing European empires (i.e., British, French, Dutch, and Russian) established control over almost all regions with significant Muslim populations. Most Muslim countries were granted formal political independence following World War II. Nevertheless, they resemble other countries in the Global South in that they are comparatively weak and exist in a world dominated by the Global North (especially the West).

At present, there are 1.8 billion Muslims, which amounts to 24% of the total global population (Lipka 2017). This makes Islam the world's second largest religion in terms of adherents.

Basic Islamic teaching

Over the past two decades, it has become standard for scholars to situate basic Islamic teachings in relationship to the world of late antiquity (Al-Azmeh, 2014; Anthony 2020; Crone 2015, 2016; El-Badawi, 2014; Hoyland 2015; Hughes 2017; Reynolds 2010; Salaymeh 2016; Stroumsa 2015). This world encompasses the linked Middle Eastern and Mediterranean regions (i.e., regions dominated by the Byzantine and Sasanian Empires). Temporally, it extends from the third to eighth century CE. The Late Antique world is marked by a series of major religious developments culminating in the rise of Islam.

Prior to the rise of Islam, the major religions of the Late Antique world were Judaism, Christianity, Zoroastrianism, and Manichaeism. These religions shared (more or less) a basic set of religious teachings. Seven of these teachings became central to Islam. They are also important for understanding MSP in an Islamic context. Let us consider these teachings one at a time.

First, Late Antique religions affirm the existence of one Supreme Being or God (El/Yahweh, Ahura Mazda). Such religions recognize other lesser spirit beings as well. Some of these aid God in promoting morality (e.g., *yazatas*, angels), while others may oppose God and morality (e.g., *daevas*, demons). Late Antique religions can be considered monotheistic, although this monotheism is often somewhat complex (e.g., Christian trinitarianism, Zoroastrian dualism).

Islam endorses a simple and straightforward monotheism. It affirms the existence of one God, called Allāh, who is omniscient (*al-'Alīm*) and omnipotent (*al-Qādir*). He created the universe ex nihilo (*al-Khāliq*) and controls everything within it.

Allāh demands moral behavior from human beings, using reward (*thawāb*) and punishment (*'iqāb*) to encourage this behavior (Lange 2016; Nakissa 2020; Rustomji 2010). In this world, Allāh dispenses rewards like health, fertility, and material goods. He dispenses punishments like plagues, military losses, and natural disasters

(Nakissa 2020: 1109–111). However, as we will see shortly, Allāh's most important rewards and punishments are dispensed in the afterlife.

The fact that Allāh is omniscient and omnipotent makes Him a very effective agent for implementing MSP. Since He knows everything, He can keep track of every moral and immoral act, no matter how small. His unlimited power ensures that He can dispense proper rewards and punishments for these acts. For instance, He is capable of imposing deserved punishment on the mightiest individuals and communities (e.g., Pharaoh, the people of Thamūd, the Quraysh) (see Qur'ān 7:73–9, 79:24). The Qur'ān, Islam's chief scriptural text, states: "Whether you conceal what is in your hearts or reveal it, Allāh knows it. He knows about whatever is in the heavens and the earth. And Allāh has power to do all things" (Qur'ān 3:29).

Second, Late Antique religions hold that God usually communicates His teachings through revelation given to prophets or messengers/apostles (e.g., Moses, Zoroaster, Paul, Mani), although it may also be given to others (e.g., the Talmudic sages). Islam acknowledges a particular line of prophets that encompasses Jewish and Christian figures. Thus, Adam, Noah, Abraham, Ishmael, Moses, and David are considered to be prophets, as is Jesus (who is considered to be a prophet rather than God). Islam also acknowledges Arab prophets outside the Jewish and Christian traditions, such as Hūd, Ṣāliḥ, and Shuʿayb (Wheeler 2006).

Third, Late Antique religions hold that divine revelation is preserved in the form of scriptural texts (e.g., the Avesta, Hebrew Bible, New Testament, Manichaean Heptateuch). As noted above, in Islam, the primary scriptural text is the Qur'ān. It is held that Muḥammad continuously received bits of revelation (waḥī) during the roughly 20-year period of his prophetic mission. The Qur'ān collects together these bits of revelation and is about 600 pages in length. Muslims equate the text of the Qur'ān with the literal words of God. The content of the Qur'ān is somewhat heterogeneous. However, it centers on three primary topics: (1) teachings on theological doctrine, (2) teachings on proper moral norms, and (3) stories of past prophets. Scriptural texts like the Avesta, Hebrew Bible, and New Testament were produced by communities and gradually evolved over long periods of time (e.g., over 500 years in the case of the Hebrew Bible). By contrast, the Qur'ān that we have today may be ascribed to Muḥammad and was canonized within about two decades of his death (Sadeghi and Goudarzi 2012; Sinai 2017; Van Putten 2019).

Islam acknowledges a second type of scriptural text after the Qur'ān, known as ḥadīth reports. Muslims hold that not all of the divine revelation received by Muḥammad is contained in the Qur'ān. Muḥammad conveyed some of this revelation through his statements (e.g., "Men may not wear gold") and some of it through his actions (e.g., Muḥammad's prayer provides a model for Muslims on how to pray). Ḥadīth reports are accounts of Muḥammad's statements and actions (sunna). Between the late eighth and early tenth centuries, Muslim scholars produced large authoritative compilations of ḥadīth reports (e.g., al-Muwatta', Saḥīḥ al-Bukhārī, Saḥīḥ Muslim). Western scholars recognize that many ḥadīth reports cannot, in fact, be reliably traced back to Muḥammad. Rather, they represent the views of religious authorities who lived during the first century or two following Muḥammad's death. In other words, ḥadīth reports blend together views actually articulated by Muḥammad with views of very early religious authorities (see Brown 2009; Motzki 2002; Reinhart 2010).

Islam is emphatic that divine revelation ends with Muḥammad, who is referred to in the Qur'ān (33:40) as the "seal of the prophets" (khātam al-nabiyyīn). This means that Muḥammad's teachings form a definitive doctrine and may not be altered. Compared with other religions (e.g., Judaism, Christianity, Hinduism, Buddhism), Islamic theological doctrines and worship practices are remarkably standardized and stable over time, and can largely be traced to Muḥammad.

Prophets and scriptural texts are important components of the MSP framework in Islam. Allāh uses prophets to inform humans that they must follow particular moral norms and that He will reward and punish them for their behavior. Scriptural texts preserve these prophetic teachings for later generations. Through scripture, later generations acquire knowledge about the moral norms they must follow and the consequences of their actions.

Fourth, Late Antique religions endorse a set of norms. In some cases, these norms regulate large areas of human life and may described as "divine law." Classical examples of divine law include Hindu law (dharma), Jewish law (Torah), and Zoroastrian law (Davis 2010; Licari 2019; Macuch 2015). In Islam, divine law is known as Sharī'a (Emon and Ahmed 2018; Hallaq 2009; Nakissa 2019; Schacht 1982). Sharī'a norms are derived from Islamic scriptural texts (i.e., the Qur'ān and ḥadīth reports). In Islam, it has also traditionally been held that authentic knowledge is gradually lost over time. Hence, those who lived closest to the time of Muḥammad are considered the most knowledgeable about his teachings. Much of this knowledge has not been passed on to later generations (e.g., many ḥadīth reports have been forgotten). Because the earliest Muslim generations are the most knowledgeable, later Muslims should defer to their interpretations of scriptural texts (i.e., taqlīd). Special emphasis is placed on deference to the Muslim generations (salaf) who lived during the first two centuries or so following Muḥammad's death. This being the case, Sharī'a norms are actually based on scriptural texts and on interpretations of these texts attributed to the early Muslims. The interpretive efforts (i.e., ijtihād) of early Muslim scholars led them to produce comprehensive systems of Sharī'a doctrine (madhhabs). Four of these scholars are particularly important: Abū Ḥanīfa (d. 767), Mālik (d. 795), al-Shāfi'ī (d. 820), and Ibn Ḥanbal (d. 855). All later Muslims are expected to defer to the systems attributed to these scholars. In terms of their content and principles, however, these systems do not differ significantly from one another.

Understanding MSP in Islam requires an adequate grasp of the Sharī'a. The Sharī'a specifies which moral norms Muslims must follow if they wish to win rewards from Allāh and avoid His punishments. However, the Sharī'a is quite complex and contains many different types of norms.

The core of the Sharī'a is understood to consist in norms of worship (*'ibāda*). The most important of these norms are the five daily prayers (*ṣalāh*), fasting during the month of Ramadan (*ṣawm*), annual payment of alms (*zakāh*), and pilgrimage to Makka once in a lifetime (*ḥajj*).

Muslim worship is tied to a particular understanding of Allāh. Allāh is kind (*al-Raḥmān*), and He is responsible for creating all of the benefits (*ni'am*) that humans enjoy in life – including their food, health, and shelter. Islam associates benefit giving with specific emotional and moral consequences. Thus, when one individual gives another a benefit, the benefit receiver should feel love for the benefit giver and express gratitude. The benefit receiver also has a moral obligation to reciprocate by seeking to please the benefit giver. As receivers of countless benefits from Allāh, humans should feel love for Allāh, express gratitude to Allāh, and strive to please Allāh. In Muslim worship, believers are commanded to reflect on the benefits they have received from Allāh while expressing their love and gratitude to Him (see Hallaq 2009: 225–38; Nakissa 2022).

Similar to Jewish, Zoroastrian, and Hindu law, many Sharī'a norms are partially or primarily concerned with ritual purity (*ṭahāra*) (Katz 2002; Nakissa 2022). This is especially true with respect to worship, which frequently has ritual purity as one of its conditions (e.g., ablution is required for the five daily prayers and for key parts of the pilgrimage).

Apart from norms of worship, there are Sharī'a norms for regulating diet, hygiene, dress, gender roles, sexuality, marriage, family life, inheritance, trusts, commercial transactions, contracts, torts, criminal punishment, judicial procedure, governance, and warfare (Katz 2002; Hallaq 2009; Peters 2005; Tucker 1998).

Many Sharī'a norms concern relationships between Muslims and the relationship of the Muslim community with other communities. Hence, numerous Sharī'a norms are designed to strengthen and preserve marital relationships (e.g., penalizing adultery), familial relationships (e.g., the obligation to care for elderly parents), an individual's relationship with God (e.g., daily worship), and relationships between Muslims as a community (e.g., charity and mutual military defense). Sharī'a norms encourage general altruism toward Muslims. Matters are more complex with respect to non-Muslims (*kuffār*). The Sharī'a encourages honesty, fairness in commercial transactions, and basic kindness when dealing with individual non-Muslims. At the same time, non-Muslim communities are seen as largely hostile competing groups, which must be confronted in keeping with considerations of realpolitik. Muslims are to grant basic rights (e.g., protection of life and property) to non-Muslim communities with whom they have treaty relations (*'aqd al-dhimma, ṣulḥ*). Such treaties ideally (though not necessarily) affirm Muslim political domination. In the absence of treaty relations, it is assumed that Muslim and non-Muslim communities are in a state of war (i.e., non-Muslim lands are *Dār al-Ḥarb*) (see Afsaruddin 2022; Hallaq 2009: 324–41; Nakissa 2022).

Religious scholars hold that the aim of enforcing Sharī'a norms is not simply to ensure proper behavior. It is also to mold people's beliefs, emotions, and character traits (*akhlāq*). Hence, scriptural texts insist that Muslims believe in God (*īmān*), love God (*ḥubb*), and fear God (*taqwā*), while possessing character traits such as humility (*khuḍū'*), generosity (*karam*), and patience (*ṣabr*). Sharī'a norms are understood to foster proper beliefs, emotions, and character traits. Religious scholars often theorize this process using ideas associated with Aristotelian virtue ethics (Mahmood 2005; Nakissa 2019).

Islam contains specific guidelines for the enforcement of Sharī'a norms. Hence, Muslims are obliged to (1) follow Sharī'a norms in their own lives, (2) shun and criticize other individuals for violating Sharī'a norms, and (3) establish a state that legally enforces Sharī'a norms in society (*al-amr bi-l-ma'rūf wa-l-nahī 'an al-munkar*) (Cook 2004; Stilt and Saraçoğlu 2018).

Fifth, in the Late Antique world, religion was closely associated with politics, empire building, and war. Judaism and the Hebrew Bible provided precedents for the view that religion legitimates wars of conquest and empire building (Firestone 2012; Jenkins 2011). Christianity and Zoroastrianism were understood to sanction empires (i.e., Byzantine, Sasanian), and the wars of conquest waged by these empires (Corey and Charles 2012; Fowden 1993; Kolbaba 1998; McDonough 2013). In Christianity and Islam, large-scale conquests operated as a means of facilitating universal missionary work. Islam explicitly approved of conquest (i.e., jihād) for this purpose (Afsaruddin 2022; Hallaq 2009: 324–41; Nakissa 2022), whereas Christian positions on this matter were complex and contradictory, and shifted over time (Corey and Charles 2012; Jenkins 2011; Kolbaba 1998).

Notably, in Islam, conquest does not merely aim at facilitating missionary work (in a narrow sense). The Sharī'a is understood to embody morality – especially in the sense of justice (*'adl*) and the protection of legitimate rights (*huqūq*). The Muslim ruler (*imām*) ideally wages wars to establish Sharī'a in his lands and throughout the world. In this way, he propagates proper morality and justice across the globe. Wars of this kind form part of Islam's MSP framework. Hence, Allāh is not merely concerned with enforcing morality within the Muslim community. Rather, He sanctions war as a means of ensuring that morality is enforced everywhere. A parallel can be found in contemporary Western discourse on universal human rights. Such discourse often posits that military force is a legitimate means of establishing and maintaining human rights norms throughout the world.

Sixth, Late Antique religions hold that there is an afterlife and that an individual's fate depends on their moral behavior. Those who have lived a morally good life experience great pleasure in Heaven, while those who have lived a morally bad life experience great pain in Hell. Variants of this basic idea have a place in Judaism, Christianity, Zoroastrianism, and Manichaeism, as well as Islam. In Islam, afterlife doctrine is laid out in the Qur'ān and the ḥadīth reports. According to this doctrine, individuals begin to experience a state of pleasure or pain immediately after they die as they are placed in the grave (e.g., bad people are tormented in the grave by angels). Then, all humans are resurrected bodily at the end of time (*Yawm al-Qiyāma*). It is believed that angels monitor humans throughout their lives and keep a record of their deeds, no matter how insignificant. Humans are confronted with this record upon their resurrection. Addressing this matter, the Qur'ān (99:6–8) states, "On that Day, people will come forward in separate groups to be shown their deeds. Whoever has done an atom's weight of good will see it, but whoever has done an atom's weight of evil will see that" (Abdel Haleem 2004: 431). The record is then presented to Allāh, and He issues a judgment, with the help of a scale of justice (*mīzān*). Allāh takes account of a person's deeds, alongside their beliefs and moral character (*akhlāq*) (e.g., humility, generosity, love of God, fear of God). A person who lacks belief in Islam is condemned to an eternity in Hell (at least if that person had lived after the coming of Muḥammad and heard his message). As for those who believe in Islam, there are two possibilities. If a person's good deeds and moral character outweigh their bad deeds and faults, the person is immediately granted Heaven for eternity. If matters are otherwise, the person is sent to Hell for a period of time to suffer and is then granted Heaven for eternity. In Islam, Heaven is conceptualized as a garden paradise (*janna*), wherein an individual may enjoy all types of pleasures, including sensual pleasures (e.g., fine foods, mansions, sex with beautiful virgins) (Gunther and Lawson 2017; Rustomji 2010). However, it is widely held that the highest pleasure consists in spending time with Allāh (who is beloved by believers). Hell (*jahannam*) is conceptualized as a pit filled with burning fire (*nār*), in which individuals are tortured in a graphic manner (e.g., their skin is scorched by the flames, they are made to drink festering water) (Lange 2016). The level of pleasure or pain experienced in the afterlife is proportional to one's deeds on earth (i.e., morally better people have more extensive pleasures in Heaven, and morally worse people have more severe punishments in Hell).

Seventh, Late Antique religions hold that the ordinary world will come to an end, marking the final triumph of the forces of moral good over the forces of moral evil. In Judaism and Christianity, understandings of the end times center on the notion of a messiah. Similar ideas are found in Islam. Islamic doctrines about end times are largely based on ḥadīth reports, which are often unclear and seemingly contradictory. Many such doctrines cannot be reliably traced to Muḥammad, although they became widespread in the first two centuries after his death (Damir-Geilsdorf and Franke 2015; Saritoprak 2003; Stowasser 2004). The most basic and commonly accepted Islamic eschatological claims can be described as follows. As humans approach the end times, evil will become increasingly prevalent in the world (e.g., promiscuity, alcohol drinking), the teachings of Islam will be forgotten and abandoned, and fear-inducing natural events will occur (e.g., earthquakes, the sun rising from the west). Eventually a one-eyed false messiah (*al-masīḥ al-dajjāl*) will arise and win followers by performing miracle-like acts. For a short period, he will rule over the world, encourage evil, and work to destroy what remains of the Islamic religion. Subsequently, the true messiah will return and kill the false messiah. The true messiah is identified with Jesus, who is understood to be a prophet supportive of Islam. A righteous descendant of Muḥammad (known as the mahdī) will also help in the fight against the false messiah. Following the defeat of the false messiah, there will be a short period of righteousness, peace, and justice on earth. Allāh will then end the world and resurrect the dead for judgment.

These beliefs can be situated in relationship to Islam's MSP framework. Hence, in the end times, Allāh uses the messiah and the mahdī to overcome and permanently destroy all those who side with the forces of moral evil.

Diverse historical forms of Islam

Islam took diverse forms over the course of its history. The three most important types of diversity were generated by sectarianism, mysticism, and religious-cultural syncretism.

First, we will consider sectarianism. In Islam, there are three primary sects: Sunnis, Shiites, and Kharijites (Andani 2016a, 2016b; Haider 2014; Hoffman 2012; Schmidtke 2016). Throughout history, a large majority of Muslims have been Sunnis. Shiites have been a significant minority, whereas Kharijites have been much fewer in number. Today, Sunnis are 87% to 90% of the global Muslim population, Shiites are 10% to 13%, while Kharijites are less than 1% (Pew Research Center 2011). The analysis of Islam presented thus far has centered on the Sunni view.

The splintering of the Muslim community into sects was initially driven by conflicts, during the first 30 years after Muḥammad's death, over who should rule the Muslim community. These conflicts had a limited impact on Sunni and Kharijite doctrines but greatly impacted Shiite doctrines (see Andani 2016a, 2016b; Haider 2014). The Shiites held that the imām (i.e., ruler/leader) of the Muslims should be a close blood descendant of Muḥammad (typically through the line of ʿAlī and Fāṭima). Most Shiites also came to believe that imāms had special access to hidden forms of divine knowledge and were uniquely guided by God. This divine knowledge and guidance became the basis for new teachings on theology and Sharīʿa norms. Furthermore, Shiites disagreed over which of Muḥammad's descendants should be the imām, leading them to break up into subsects. The Twelver Shiites are by far the largest of these subsects. They developed between the seventh and tenth centuries. With a few exceptions, Twelver Shiites endorse theological doctrines and understandings of the Sharīʿa that resemble those of Sunnis. By contrast, Ismaili Shiites endorse teachings that radically differ from Sunnism. These teachings entail the abrogation and fundamental reinterpretation of much of the Sharīʿa.

There is much more that can be said about the three sects as they admit of some internal diversity. For instance, not only do Sunnis recognize a number of schools of Sharīʿa doctrine (Ḥanafīs, Mālikīs, Shāfiʿīs, Ḥanbalīs), they also recognize a number of schools of theological doctrine (Ashʿarīs, Māturīdīs, Ahl al-Ḥadīth) (Schmidtke 2016; Winter 2008). Nevertheless, no Islamic sect departs from the general pattern associated with Late Antique religions. All sects hold that there exists one God; that God communicates His teachings to certain humans (e.g., prophets, imāms); that these teachings are preserved in divine scripture (e.g., Qurʾān, ḥadīth reports, sayings of imāms); that God endorses a system of norms; and that there is a Heaven where people are recompensed for their good moral behavior as well as a Hell where people are punished for wrongdoing.

A second type of diversity in Islamic history pertains to mysticism (Sufism) (Green 2012; Karamustafa 1994; Schimmel 1975; Trimingham 1998). Sufi movements began to emerge in the ninth and tenth centuries and subsequently became central to Muslim religiosity. Sufis are Muslims who seek direct religious experiences and associated forms of knowledge (e.g., *maʿrifa, ilhām, fanāʾ*). Such experiences may take the form of visions, dreams, or a mystic/void experience. Different groups of Sufis (e.g., Rifāʿiyya, Qādiriyya, Shādhiliyya, Mawlawiyya, Bektāshiyya, Naqsbandiyya, Chishtiyya) developed various methods for inducing the desired religious experiences (see Trimingham 1998: 166–217). These methods included worship, moral righteousness, asceticism, bodily movements, ingestion of intoxicants, music, and so on. Generally speaking, Sufi groups can be arrayed on a spectrum. At one end are Sufis who emphasized adherence to orthodox Sunni Islam (i.e., those who valued sobriety [*ṣaḥw*]) (Mojaddedi 2003). They introduced techniques for inducing religious experiences that did not obviously violate Sharīʿa norms. At the other end were Sufis who admitted that Sharīʿa norms could be useful to common people. However, they legitimated abandonment of these norms when doing so facilitated religious experiences (i.e., they valued drunkenness [*sukr*]) (Karamustafa 1994; Mojaddedi 2003). These nonorthodox Sufis were often exceptionally open to adopting beliefs and practices from other cultural and religious traditions (e.g., Christianity, Hinduism), especially if they facilitated religious experiences. Consequently, nonorthodox Sufism encouraged cultural and religious syncretism. Both orthodox and nonorthodox forms of Sufism became very influential in the pre-modern Muslim world. Nevertheless, even nonorthodox Sufis did not break from the general pattern of Late Antique religiosity.

A third type of diversity pertains to religious-cultural syncretism. In every region that Islam entered, it came to be blended with local religious and cultural traditions. These traditions were referred to as ʿādah (custom, or general culture) and in some cases as adab (etiquette, or high culture). There were different reactions to such blending. Here, it is possible to identify two general approaches, which may be called the "orthodox approach" and the "nonorthodox syncretic approach." The orthodox approach rejected adopting non-Islamic religious practices. However, it accepted local cultural practices on the condition that they did not violate Sharīʿa norms. For instance, an individual could adopt the local dress as long as it did not violate Sharīʿa norms against exposing particular parts of the body (e.g., upper thighs for both sexes, hair for females). The nonorthodox syncretic approach is different. Those who embraced this approach considered themselves Muslims because they acknowledged Islam as a source of truth and moral guidance. However, they continued to regard some portion of their local religious and cultural traditions as additional sources of truth and moral guidance. On this view, local traditions could legitimate some beliefs and norms that are contrary to orthodox Islam.

In any Muslim society, some people gravitated more toward the orthodox approach, while others preferred the nonorthodox syncretic approach. The balance between these approaches differed by region. Hence, the orthodox approach was comparatively strong in lands conquered early in Islamic history, such as the Middle East, North Africa, and parts of Central and South Asia. However, the nonorthodox syncretic approach was comparatively strong in other, more peripheral lands, including Sub-Saharan Africa, Southeast Asia, Western China, and Southeast Europe.

I will now illustrate the diversity of Islam with two case studies. In these studies, I give special attention to the question of whether, and to what extent, Islamic teachings were actually followed in particular Muslim societies. In other words, were MSP-related Islamic doctrines merely preserved in the books of a scholarly elite? Or did they actually shape behavior in society at large? If they did shape social behavior, what concrete institutional mechanisms were involved?

The Middle East in the classical period

The formative period in Islamic history begins with the emergence of Islam in the seventh century. It ends with highly systematized and stable legal and theological doctrines in the tenth century. The classical period runs from the tenth century until the thirteenth century, when the Muslim world was politically and culturally transformed by the Mongol invasions (see Berkey 2003: 111–258; Lapidus 2014: 92–268).

In the classical period, the Middle East was an influential hub of religious and cultural activity (e.g., Arabic and Persian adab). Compared with other regions, it was relatively wealthy and urban, and had a large population. The most important cities in the Middle East were located in Iraq, Iran, the Levant, and Egypt. The region was sustained by widespread agriculture and long-distance trade. By the classical period, most of the populations in the Middle East had converted to Sunni Islam, although there remained significant Shiite, Christian, and Jewish minorities.

Life in the classical Middle East was characterized by particular institutions (Berkey 1992; Lapidus 2014: 92–268). Many institutions were religious in character and were overseen by religious scholars ('ulamā') of different ranks. Support for institutions (e.g., building maintenance, stipends for religious scholars) came from endowments (*awqāf*) as well as charitable donations. Major religious institutions included mosques, *kuttābs*, *madrasas*, and *khānaqāhs*. The mosque (*masjid*) served as a place of worship (especially the five daily prayers) and also communicated basic religious knowledge to the masses through sermons and public lessons. The *kuttāb* was an elementary school that taught memorization of the Qur'ān, everyday religious norms, and basic literacy in Arabic. The *madrasa* was a type of college that offered more advanced education (Berkey 1992; Ephrat 2000). The core *madrasa* curriculum focused on religious subjects and the teaching of Arabic, although some instruction was also offered in history, philosophy, science, and mathematics. The *khānaqāh* was a Sufi center, with spaces for worship, residential accommodations, and shrines dedicated to dead Sufi masters (Green 2012; Trimingham 1998).

The classical Middle East also had characteristic political and legal institutions (Crone 2004; El-Hibri 2021). Generally speaking, ultimate political power was in the hands of a ruler (sulṭān/imām) drawn from the military aristocracy. The ruler was responsible for promoting Islam by funding religious institutions and enforcing Sharī'a norms. The ruler was likewise responsible for promoting the general material interests (*maṣāliḥ*) of the populace. This meant guaranteeing public safety, defending the borders, ensuring the basic functioning of the economy (e.g., food production, long-distance trade), and undertaking necessary building projects (e.g., roads, hospitals, fortresses). Religious scholars held that Islam endorsed promoting the general material interests of the people. They also acknowledged that Sharī'a norms, operating alone, were not always sufficient to promote these interests. Hence, the ruler was entitled to introduce additional regulations to achieve these ends (*al-siyāsa al-sharī'iyya*). These could take the form of new regulations (*qānūns*) or official endorsements of existing customary law ('*ādah*). In theory, additional regulations were never supposed to conflict with the Sharī'a. However, in practice, significant conflict did occur, and additional regulations frequently overrode the Sharī'a. The ultimate result was a dualistic legal system that consisted in some significant portion of the Sharī'a and also some additional regulations. This dualistic system was applied through three institutions. First, the ruler appointed Muslim religious scholars as judges in Sharī'a courts. Second, the ruler, his governors, and his bureaucrats ran a system of tribunals (*maẓālim*), which supplemented the Sharīʿa courts and focused on applying additional, non-Sharīʿa regulations (Fadel 2018; Hallaq 2009: 51–5, 159–222; Tillier 2018). Third, the ruler appointed individuals to enforce public morality (*ḥisba*) (Stilt and Saraçoğlu 2018). These individuals punished open transgression of Sharīʿa norms (e.g., in matters of dress, sex, worship) and prevented fraud in marketplace transactions.

In the Jewish, Christian, and Islamic traditions, religion has always exerted some influence over political and legal institutions. In the Islamic case, this level of influence was especially high (Fadel 2018). In the classical Middle East, Sharīʿa norms concerning ritual worship, dress, diet, and family life were enforced by society at large, with the backing of the courts. Sharīʿa norms concerning commercial transactions were frequently but partially applied by the courts. Norms on criminal punishment, governance, and war were sometimes applied but frequently ignored by the courts. Nevertheless, this situation reflects a type of maximum in Islamic history. Most Muslim societies were less orthodox, and applied the Sharīʿa to a lesser extent, than Middle Eastern societies during the classical period. Classical Middle Eastern societies provided an influential model for other Muslim societies throughout history.

Pre-modern Southeast Asia

The history of Islam in pre-modern Southeast Asia runs from about the thirteenth century to the eighteenth century (see Aljunied 2022: especially 13–87; Lapidus 2014: 432–46; Riddell 2001: 101–167). It can be explained as follows.

Large empires with sizable tax bases can provide patronage for education, research, writing, literature, art, and architecture. These activities generally take place in cities, where it is possible to gather together the needed personnel, financial resources, and materials. Cities backed by imperial patronage frequently become influential hubs of cultural and religious production. In the pre-modern period, many such hubs could be found in the Middle East, India, and China. However, they were lacking in Southeast Asia. This region had a small population and little urbanization, due in part to tropical diseases and the land being unfit for intensive agriculture. Natural barriers also prevented the unification of peoples into major empires. Lacking its own hubs, Southeast Asia was highly receptive to adoption of cultural and religious trends from elsewhere. Here, the Indian Ocean trade played a crucial role.

For over 2,000 years, Indian Ocean trade routes have carried goods and ideas across Eurasia. Indian Ocean trade routes link the southern coast of China with Southeast Asia, Southeast Asia with coastal India, and coastal India with the Middle East and East Africa. From the first centuries of the common era to the fifteenth century, Hindu and Buddhist religious traditions spread through trade routes from

India to Southeast Asia. These traditions merged in a syncretic manner with local traditions that were animistic and polytheistic.

Southeast Asia witnessed the emergence of some notable, but modestly sized, Hindu and/or Buddhist kingdoms between the ninth and fourteenth centuries CE (e.g., Pagan, Angkor, Ayutthaya, Srivijaya, Majapahit) (Andaya and Andaya 2015). In the thirteenth century, northern India was conquered by Muslims. Whereas in the past, Indian traders and religious scholars had carried Hindu and Buddhist traditions from India to Southeast Asia, now they carried Islamic traditions. Beginning in the thirteenth century, Southeast Asia began to experience a wave of Islamicization. This wave was concentrated in "Island Southeast Asia," including lands that are now a part of Malaysia, Indonesia, and the Philippines. By the sixteenth century, Islam had become the dominant religion in many of these lands. Nevertheless, these lands were home to numerous ethnic groups with distinctive customs and languages (e.g., Javanese, Minangkabau, Bugis). These ethnic groups had already integrated their local cultural and religious traditions with elements of Hinduism and Buddhism. Islam was now added to this mixture, producing a highly syncretic version of the religion. For instance, mosques were built in the style of Hindu temples, pre-Islamic deities were worshiped (e.g., Ratu Kidul), and alternative forms of gender and family life were maintained (e.g., matrilineality among the Minangkabau, the five-gender system of the Bugis) (Formichi 2020: 43–74; Ricklefs 2006). Some Southeast Asians promoted a more orthodox brand of Islam. They were opposed, however, by a larger population of nonorthodox Muslims, many of whom were also inclined toward nonorthodox versions of Sufism (Riddell 2001: 101–138; Ricklefs 2006).

The Islamicization of Southeast Asia involved the proliferation of mosques and madrasas (*pesantren*). However, these were not as abundant, as architecturally impressive, or as well-endowed as those found in the Middle East. These institutions were staffed by religious scholars of humble rank. Students who desired higher-level religious studies traveled to destinations in the Middle East (e.g., Makka, Cairo). Owing to the dearth of eminent indigenous religious scholars, efforts were made to import foreign scholars from places like the Middle East and India.

From the thirteenth century into the modern period, modestly sized Islamic kingdoms were established in Islamicized areas of Southeast Asia (e.g., the sultanates of Samudera Pasai, Melaka, and Mataram). Rulers (from the military aristocracy) patronized the teaching and preaching of religious scholars and appointed them as high-ranking political counselors and judges. Nevertheless, generally speaking, there was no developed system of Islamic courts like that found in the Middle East. Law in the region was heavily based on custom (*adat*) and decrees from the ruler, and these norms often ran contrary to Sharīʿa norms. That being said, religious scholars cooperated with the ruler and local aristocrats to promote and enforce some portion of Sharīʿa norms (Hadi 2004: 147–83; Hallaq 2009: 388–9). Sharīʿa norms were followed to a large extent in the realms of ritual worship, dress, diet, and family life. To a lesser, but still significant, extent, they shaped the ruler's policies on criminal punishment, governance, and warfare (see Formichi 2020: 43–74; Hadi 2004: 147–83; Yakin 2015).

Conclusion

Compared with other pre-modern religious traditions, Islamic doctrine was highly stable and standardized. Although Islam took many diverse historical forms, it never broke from the general pattern of Late Antique religiosity, in which MSP had a central place. Islamic religious norms (i.e., Sharī'a norms) were not merely preserved in books, but rather, Muslim societies actually applied them to a significant extent throughout history. This commitment to the application of religious norms was likely motivated, in large part, by the prospect of supernatural rewards and punishments.

References

Abdel Haleem, M. A. S. 2004. *The Qur'an: A New Translation.* Oxford: Oxford University Press.

Afsaruddin, Asma. 2022. *Jihad: What Everyone Needs to Know.* Oxford: Oxford University Press. doi: 10.1093/wentk/9780190647315.001.0001.

Al-Azmeh, Aziz. 2014. *The Emergence of Islam in Late Antiquity: Allāh and His People.* Cambridge: Cambridge University Press. doi: 10.1017/CBO9781139410854.

Aljunied, Khairudin, ed. 2022. *Routledge Handbook of Islam in Southeast Asia.* New York: Routledge. doi: 10.4324/9780429275449.

Andani, Khalil. 2016a. "A Survey of Ismaili Studies Part 1: Early Ismailism and Fatimid Ismailism." *Religion Compass* 10 (8): 191–206. doi: 10.1111/rec3.12205.

Andani, Khalil. 2016b. "A Survey of Ismaili Studies Part 2: Post-Fatimid and Modern Ismailism." *Religion Compass* 10 (11): 269–82. doi: 10.1111/rec3.12222.

Andaya, Barbara Watson, and Leonard Andaya. 2015. *A History of Early Modern Southeast Asia, 1400–1839.* Cambridge: Cambridge University Press. doi: 10.1017/CBO9781139051323.

Anthony, Sean. 2020. *Muhammad and the Empires of Faith: The Making of the Prophet of Islam.* Berkeley, CA: University of California Press. doi: 10.1525/9780520974524.

Berkey, Jonathan. 1992. *The Transmission of Knowledge in Medieval Cairo: A Social History of Islamic Education.* Princeton, NJ: Princeton University Press. doi: 10.1515/9781400862580.

Berkey, Jonathan. 2003. *The Formation of Islam: Religion and Society in the Near East, 600–1800.* Cambridge: Cambridge University Press. doi: 10.1017/CBO9780511817861.

Brown, Jonathan. 2009. *Hadith: Muhammad's Legacy in the Medieval and Modern World.* Oxford: Oneworld.

Cook, Michael. 2004. *Commanding the Right and Forbidding the Wrong in Islamic Thought.* Cambridge: Cambridge University Press.

Corey, David, and J. Daryl Charles. 2012. *The Just War Tradition: An Introduction*. Wilmington, DE: ISI Books.

Crone, Patricia. 2004. *God's Rule – Government and Islam: Six Centuries of Medieval Islamic Political Thought*. New York: Columbia University Press.

Crone, Patricia. 2015. "Jewish Christianity and the Qur'ān (Part One)." *Journal of Near Eastern Studies* 74 (2): 225–53. doi: 10.1086/682212.

Crone, Patricia. 2016. "Jewish Christianity and the Qur'ān (Part Two)." *Journal of Near Eastern Studies* 75 (1): 1–21. doi: 10.1086/684957.

Damir-Geilsdorf, Sabine, and Lisa Franke. 2015. "Narrative Reconfigurations of Islamic Eschatological Signs: The Portents of the 'Hour' in Grey Literature and on the Internet." *Archiv Orientalni* 83: 411–37. doi: 10.47979/aror.j.83.3.411-437.

Davis, Donald R. 2010. *The Spirit of Hindu Law*. Cambridge: Cambridge University Press. doi: 10.1017/CBO9780511674754.

De Blois, François. 2002. "Nasrānī (Ναζωραιος) and ḥanīf (εθνικός): Studies on the Religious Vocabulary of Christianity and of Islam." *Bulletin of the School of Oriental and African Studies* 65 (1): 1–30. doi: 10.1017/S0041977X02000010.

El-Badawi, Emran Iqbal. 2014. *The Qur'ān and the Aramaic Gospel Traditions*. New York: Routledge. doi: 10.4324/9781315855981.

El-Hibri, Tayeb. 2021. *The Abbasid Caliphate: A History*. Cambridge: Cambridge University Press. doi: 10.1017/9781316869567.

Emon, Anver, and Rumee Ahmed. 2018. *The Oxford Handbook of Islamic Law*. Oxford: Oxford University Press.

Ephrat, Daphna. 2000. *A Learned Society in a Period of Transition*. Albany, NY: SUNY Press.

Fadel, Mohammad. 2018. "Al-Qaḍi." In *The Oxford Handbook of Islamic Law*, edited by Anver Emon and Rumee Ahmed, 301–326. Oxford: Oxford University Press.

Firestone, Reuven. 2012. *Holy War in Judaism: The Fall and Rise of a Controversial Idea*. Oxford: Oxford University Press. doi: 10.1093/acprof:oso/9780199860302.001.0001.

Formichi, Chiara. 2020. *Islam and Asia*. Cambridge: Cambridge University Press. doi: 10.1017/9781316226803.

Fowden, Garth. 1993. *Empire to Commonwealth: Consequences of Monotheism in Late Antiquity*. Princeton, NJ: Princeton University Press. doi: 10.1515/9781400844241.

Goudarzi, Mohsen. 2019. "The Ascent of Ishmael: Genealogy, Covenant, and Identity in Early Islam." *Arabica* 66 (5): 415–84. doi: 10.1163/15700585-12341543.

Green, Nile. 2012. *Sufism: A Global History*. Malden, MA: Wiley-Blackwell.

Gunther, Sebastian, and Todd Lawson. 2017. *Roads to Paradise: Eschatology and Concepts of the Hereafter in Islam*, vol. 1. Leiden: Brill. doi: 10.1163/9789004333154_002.

Hadi, Amirul. 2004. *Islam and State in Sumatra: A Study of Seventeenth-Century Aceh*. Leiden: Brill. doi: 10.1163/9789047402046.

Haider, Najam. 2014. *Shī'ī Islam: An Introduction*. Cambridge: Cambridge University Press.

Hallaq, Wael. 2009. *Sharīʿa: Theory, Practice, Transformation.* Cambridge: Cambridge University Press.

Hoffman, Valerie. 2012. *The Essentials of Ibāḍī Islam.* Syracuse, NY: Syracuse University Press.

Hoyland, Robert. 2015. *In God's Path: The Arab Conquests and the Creation of an Islamic Empire.* Oxford: Oxford University Press.

Hughes, Aaron. 2017. *Shared Identities: Medieval and Modern Imaginings of Judeo-Islam.* New York: Oxford University Press.

Jenkins, Philip. 2011. *Laying Down the Sword.* New York: HarperCollins.

Karamustafa, Ahmet. 1994. *God's Unruly Friends.* Salt Lake City, UT: University of Utah Press.

Katz, Marion. 2002. *Body of Text: The Emergence of the Sunni Law of Ritual Purity.* Albany, NY: SUNY Press.

Kolbaba, Tia M. 1998. "Fighting for Christianity: Holy War in the Byzantine Empire." *Byzantion* 68 (1): 194–221.

Lange, Christian, ed. 2016. *Locating Hell in Islamic Traditions.* Leiden: Brill. doi: 10.1163/9789004301368.

Lapidus, Ira. 2014. *A History of Islamic Societies.* 3rd ed. Cambridge: Cambridge University Press. doi: 10.1017/CBO9781139048828.

Licari, François-Xavier Licari. 2019. *An Introduction to Jewish Law.* Cambridge: Cambridge University Press. doi: 10.1017/9781108379878.

Lipka, Michael. 2017. "Muslims and Islam: Key Findings in the U.S. and around the World." Washington, DC: Pew Research Center. August, 9, 2017. Accessed February 26, 2022. https://www.pewresearch.org/fact-tank/2017/08/09/muslims-and-islam-key-findings-in-the-u-s-and-around-the-world/.

Macuch, Maria. 2015. "Law in Pre-modern Zoroastrianism." In *The Wiley Blackwell Companion to Zoroastrianism,* edited by Michael Stausbergand and Yuhan Sohrab Dinshaw Vevaina, 289–98. Malden, MA: Wiley Blackwell. doi: 10.1002/9781118785539.ch17.

Mahmood, Saba. 2005. *The Politics of Piety.* Princeton, NJ: Princeton University Press.

McDonough, Scott. 2013. "Military and Society in Sasanian Iran." In *The Oxford Handbook of Warfare in the Classical World,* edited by Brian Campbell and Lawrence A. Tritle, 569–622. Oxford: Oxford University Press. doi: 10.1093/oxfordhb/9780195304657.013.0031.

Mojaddedi, Jawid. 2003. "Getting Drunk with Abū Yazīd or Staying Sober with Junayd: The Creation of a Popular Typology of Sufism." *Bulletin of the School of Oriental and African Studies* 66 (1): 1–13. doi: 10.1017/S0041977X03000016.

Motzki, Harald. 2002. *The Origins of Islamic Jurisprudence.* Leiden: Brill. doi: 10.1163/9789004491533.

Nakissa, Aria. 2019. *The Anthropology of Islamic Law: Education, Ethics, and Legal Interpretation at Egypt's al-Azhar.* Oxford: Oxford University Press. doi: 10.1093/oso/9780190932886.001.0001.

Nakissa, Aria. 2020. "The Cognitive Science of Religion and Islamic Theology: An Analysis Based on the Works of al-Ghazālī." *Journal of the American Academy of Religion* 88 (4): 1087–120. doi: 10.1093/jaarel/lfaa059.

Nakissa, Aria. 2022. "Islam and the Cognitive Study of Colonialism: The Case of Religious and Educational Reform at Egypt's al-Azhar." *Journal of Global History* 17 (3): 394–417. doi: 10.1017/S1740022821000267.

Peters, F. E. 1994. *The Hajj: The Muslim Pilgrimage to Mecca and the Holy Places.* Princeton, NJ: Princeton University Press. doi: 10.1515/9780691225142.

Peters, Rudolph. 2005. *Crime and Punishment in Islamic Law.* Cambridge: Cambridge University Press.

Pew Research Center. 2011. "Sunni and Shia Muslims." January 27, 2011. Accessed February 27, 2022. https://www.pewforum.org/2011/01/27/future-of-the-global-muslim-population-sunni-and-shia/.

Reinhart, Kevin. 2010. Juynbolliana, Gradualism, the Big Bang, and Ḥadīth Study in the Twenty-first Century. *Journal of the American Oriental Society* 130 (3): 413–44.

Reynolds, Gabriel Said. 2010. *The Quran and Its Biblical Subtext.* New York: Routledge. doi: 10.4324/9780203856451.

Ricklefs. M. C. 2006. *Mystic Synthesis in Java: A History of Islamization from the Fourteenth to the Early Nineteenth Centuries.* Norwalk, CT: EastBridge.

Riddell, Peter. 2001. *Islam and the Malay-Indonesian World.* Honolulu, HI: University of Hawai'i Press.

Rustomji, Nerina. 2010. "Early Views of Paradise in Islam." *Religion Compass* 4 (3): 166–75. doi: 10.1111/j.1749-8171.2009.00199.x.

Sadeghi, Behnam, and Mohsen Goudarzi. 2012. "Ṣanʿāʾ1 and the Origins of the Qurʾān." *Der Islam* 87 (1–2): 1–129. doi: 10.1515/islam-2011-0025.

Salaymeh, Lena. 2016. *The Beginnings of Islamic Law: Late Antique Islamicate Legal Traditions.* Cambridge: Cambridge University Press. doi: 10.1017/9781316459485.

Saritoprak, Zeki. 2003. "The Legend of al-Dajjal (Antichrist): The Personification of Evil in the Islamic Tradition." *The Muslim World* 93 (2): 291–307. doi: 10.1111/1478-1913.00024.

Schacht, Joseph. 1982. *An Introduction to Islamic Law.* Oxford: Clarendon Press.

Schimmel, Annemarie. 1975. *Mystical Dimensions of Islam.* Chapel Hill, NC: University of North Carolina Press.

Schmidtke, Sabine, ed. 2016. *The Oxford Handbook of Islamic Theology.* Oxford: Oxford University Press.

Sinai, Nicolai. 2017. *The Qurʾan: A Historical-Critical Introduction.* Edinburgh: Edinburgh University Press.

Stilt, Kristen, and M. Safa Saraçoğlu. 2018. "Hisba and Muhtasib." In *The Oxford Handbook of Islamic Law,* edited by Anver Emon and Rumee Ahmed, 327–56. Oxford: Oxford University Press. doi: 10.1093/oxfordhb/9780199679010.013.9.

Stowasser, Barbara Freyer. 2004. "The End Is Near: Minor and Major Signs of the Hour in Islamic Texts and Contexts." In *Apocalypse and Violence,* edited by Abbas Amanat and John J. Collins, 45–67. New Haven, CT: Yale Center for International and Area Studies.

Stroumsa, Guy. 2015. *The Making of the Abrahamic Religions in Late Antiquity.* Oxford: Oxford University Press. doi: 10.1093/acprof:oso/9780198738862.001.0001.

Tillier, Mathieu. 2018. "The Mazalim in Historiography." In *The Oxford Handbook of Islamic Law,* edited by Anver Emon and Rumee Ahmed, 357–84. Oxford: Oxford University Press.

Trimingham, J. Spencer. 1998. *The Sufi Orders in Islam.* Oxford: Oxford University Press. doi: 10.1093/oso/9780195120585.001.0001.

Tucker, Judith. 1998. *In the House of the Law: Gender and Islamic Law in Ottoman Syria and Palestine.* Berkeley, CA: University of California Press. doi: 10.1525/9780520925380.

Van Putten, Marijn. 2019. "'The Grace of God' as Evidence for a Written Uthmanic Archetype: The Importance of Shared Orthographic Idiosyncrasies." *Bulletin of the School of Oriental and African Studies* 82 (2): 271–88. doi: 10.1017/S0041977X19000338.

Wheeler, Brannon. 2006. "Arab Prophets of the Qur'an and Bible." *Journal of Qur,anic Studies* 8 (2): 24–57. doi: 10.3366/jqs.2006.8.2.24.

Winter, Tim, ed. 2008. *Cambridge Companion to Islamic Theology.* Cambridge: Cambridge University Press. doi: 10.1017/CCOL9780521780582.

Yakin, Ayang Utriza. 2015. "The Register of the Qadi Court 'Kiyahi Pĕqih Najmuddin' of the Sultanate of Banten, 1754–1756 CE." *Studia Islamika* 22 (3): 443–86. doi: 10.15408/sdi.v22i3.2354.

Part III:
Comparative and Analytical Perspectives

CHAPTER 1

Evolutionary Approaches to Moralizing Supernatural Punishment and Reward Beliefs in the Americas
R. Alan Covey

Beliefs in moralizing supernatural punishment and reward (MSP) are widespread across the Americas, from Muslims in Detroit to Mayan Catholics in the Guatemalan highlands, to the Jewish community of Buenos Aires. The contemporary prevalence of such beliefs is intimately tied to the spread of Abrahamic religions and the adoption of Christian elements into Indigenous belief systems, a centuries-long process that raises questions about how today's beliefs compare with precontact Indigenous religions. Such questions are significant because cross-cultural analyses of prehistoric religious evolution use ethnographically documented Native American beliefs. Recent evolutionary scholarship often makes only selective observations intended to illustrate a general model (e.g., Norenzayan 2013) or bypasses the ethnographic corpus entirely in favor of field experiments in communities that are considered to reflect prehistoric social evolution, despite the obvious evidence of Abrahamic influences (e.g., Lang et al. 2019).[1]

Current evolutionary approaches seek to move beyond general, group-level religious classifications, but in doing so, they evince a problematic assumption that previous cross-cultural studies have accurately reconstructed a global trajectory of religious evolution that can be elaborated without critical reanalysis (e.g., Norenzayan and Shariff 2008). Such confidence is unwarranted, and this chapter uses Native American societies to illustrate persistent problems in the holocultural study of prehistoric religious evolution. A discussion of sampling flaws and unrealistic representations of the ethnographic present reveals patterns in the Americas that challenge global models for the evolution of moralizing religions. Descriptions of contact-era complex societies indicate that MSP beliefs were absent or not well developed, suggesting that such beliefs did not coevolve with sociopolitical complexity in the precontact Americas.

Cross-cultural studies of moralizing religion
Most evolutionary studies of prehistoric religion use the ethnological databases that George Peter Murdock began to compile in the 1930s. Murdock was instrumental

---

1   The Evolution of Religion and Morality Project sample includes Cachoeira, whose "local god" is the Candomblé god, a diasporic African deity; Marajó, whose local god is Virgin Mary; and Huatasani, where many participants identified Catholic saints as local supernatural entities (Purzycki et al. 2022: 43).

in designing the Cross-Cultural Survey, an attempt to organize ethnographic information for theoretically informed quantitative analysis (Murdock 1940). He spent years tweaking and expanding his cross-cultural database, attempting to build a detailed and representative ethnological sample. After Murdock (1949) presented data from 250 cultures in his book *Social Structure*, critics questioned the representativeness of his global sample. Meanwhile, quantitative social scientists (e.g., Naroll 1961) addressed Galton's Problem – the effect of sampling multiple closely-related cultures – debating whether it was preferable to compile the largest possible sample (for statistical strength) or to select a global sample that limited the effects of cultural diffusion and shared histories.

Murdock responded by compiling the World Ethnographic Sample (WES), a "carefully selected sample of all the cultures known to history and ethnography" (Murdock 1957: 664). Rejecting a random sample, he sought instead to subdivide major world regions geographically, selecting consistent sample sizes in each, to represent the full range of human diversity. Of his 565 cultures, 110 came from North America and 77 from South America, where Murdock had struggled previously to assemble detailed ethnographic literature. The WES did not code religious beliefs, but Guy Swanson (1960) used it for sampling in his study of religious evolution. As social scientists like Swanson began to conduct quantitative research using the WES, Murdock continued to make modifications to it.

From 1962 to 1967, Murdock published, corrected, and expanded data from 1,170 cultures in the Ethnographic Atlas (EA), a compilation designed for computerized analysis. The EA was not a representative sample but presented a consistently coded record of "all the societies with adequate ethnographic coverage" (Murdock 1967: 109).[2] Drawing on Swanson's (1960: 56–7) study of religious evolution, the EA contained a variable (34) for belief in a "high god": "a spiritual being who is believed to have created all reality and/or to be its ultimate governor, even though his sole act was to create other spirits who, in turn, created or control the natural world" (Murdock 1967: 160). This variable could be coded as "absent or not reported" (Absent), "present but otiose or not concerned with human affairs" (Otiose), "present and active in human affairs but not offering positive support to human morality" (Present/Nonmoralizing), or "present, active, and specifically supportive of human morality" (Moralizing). The coding structure could not assess moral oversight not performed by a high god.

Soon after completing the first version of the EA, Murdock published the Standard Cross-Cultural Sample (SCCS) with Douglas White. The SCCS comprised 186 well-described ethnographic cultures, purposively structured across geographical areas to avoid Galton's Problem, and "pinpointed" specific times and subgroups

---

2   The present analysis uses data from the 1999 version of the EA, as compiled by Kirby et al. (2016).

(Murdock and White 1969). The SCCS was presented as a robust data set that could be used to assess multiple variables associated with cultural change, including religion. The SCCS employed the same "high gods" coding as the EA, to which subsequent researchers have added religion-based codes. Although questions have been raised about data quality (Rohner, Berg, and Rohner 1982), the SCCS has become the most commonly used database for cross-cultural research.

The sample of 65 cultures from the Americas selected for the SCCS overrepresents less-complex societies relative to other regions.[3] Native American groups represent 58% (n = 46) of the "stateless societies" in the SCCS but less than 10% of the "large states" (2/34), one of which is modern Haiti. By contrast, half (14/28) of the selected circum-Mediterranean cultures were "large states," with just one "stateless society" included. Murdock understood the problem of regionally biased sampling, having critiqued a 1915 study for overpopulating its category of "lower hunters" with Australian cases while overrepresenting "upper hunters" with North American examples, "so that their generalizations … were actually only corrupted regional generalizations" (Murdock 1968: 305). The geographic sampling of the SCCS produced similar effects, representing the Americas as less evolved and modern than the circum-Mediterranean region.

Given that the Americas contributed so many examples of the "earliest" forms of human social organization, some issues of chronology in the SCCS should be noted. Murdock and White dated most of their cultures to 1851–1950, "the heyday of professional anthropology" (Murdock and White 1969: 341). The vast majority of Native American ethnographic samples from that time were acephalous societies with fewer than 100 members. By contrast, all accounts of Indigenous societies with two or more levels of jurisdiction beyond the local community dated to before 1850.[4] For studying the evolution of moralizing beliefs in the Americas, early ethnohistoric literature provided the only descriptions from complex societies.

Additionally, Murdock and White manipulated the dates assigned to some cultures, backdating published ethnographic literature "to avoid insofar as is possible the acculturative effects of contacts with Europeans" (Murdock and White 1969: 340). In North America, they "reconstructed" dates for at least 15 cultures, so as to present a "pristine" ethnographic present prior to missionization, territorial displacement, epidemic disease, resource degradation, and forced resettlement (Table 1). It should be noted that even the modified 19th-century dates came long after first contact for most groups, and the ethnographic record reflects centuries of Indigenous cultural responses.

Table 1. Some Reconstructed Dates for North American Societies

---

[3] This count includes two Afro-descendant societies (Haitians and Saramacca).
[4] The Afro-descendant population of Haiti is excluded here.

Group	Reconstructed Date	Reference	Description
Kaska	1900	Honigmann (1954)	"Just prior to intensive missionization"
Eyak	1890	Birket-Smith and De Laguna (1938)	"Prior to full acculturation"
Pomo	1850	Gifford (1923), Barrett (1908), Loeb (1926)	"Prior to the inrush of European settlers"
Yokuts	1850	Gayton (1945)	"Prior to the influx of settlers following the gold rush"
Gros Ventre	1880	Flannery, Cooper (1953–1957)	"Shortly prior to missionization and the disappearance of the buffalo"
Hidatsa	1836	Bowers (1948), Matthews (1877)	"Prior to depopulation in a severe smallpox epidemic"
Creek	1800	Swanton (1922)	"Prior to Tecumseh's rebellion and removal to Oklahoma"
Chiricahua	1870	Opler (1947)	"Immediately prior to the reservation period"

Source. SCCS.

Native Americans and religious evolution

Despite significant sampling flaws, Native Americans have been part of the global cross-cultural study of religious evolution since the 1960s. When the SCCS appeared, neo-evolutionary interpretations were well established in anthropology, and influential new work on religious evolution was emerging (Bellah 1964; Wallace 1966). Neo-evolutionism built on anthropological and sociological studies of "primitive religions" that debated how the environment, culture, and psychology influenced religious development (e.g., Lowie 1936). Other fields already promoted evolutionary schemas in which their own beliefs figured as the most evolved (Ellwood 1923) or fittest (Mathews 1911), and many Western academics portrayed the distance between their own "modern" religion and the "primitive" and "archaic" beliefs that they studied as reflecting different stages of a universal evolutionary trajectory.

In 1960, Swanson published a cross-cultural study of 50 cultures randomly selected from the different regions of Murdock's WES. Overall, he identified 19 cases of belief in a "high god" (Swanson 1960: 65), which he treated as evidence of monotheistic beliefs (Swanson 1960: 56), although many groups worshiped high gods who were inactive or uninterested in human morality.[5] In fact, Swanson only designated six

---

[5] In the Americas, Swanson (1960: 216) coded nine samples as Absent, three as Otiose, two as Present/Nonmoralizing, and just two (Cuna and Yahgan) as Moralizing.

cultures as Moralizing (Swanson 1960: 216). Despite the significant number of ambiguous and contradictory cases in his sample, he argued for a correlation between political hierarchy and belief in a high god, although not necessarily a moralizing one (see Peregrine 1996: 89).

Following Swanson's study, other researchers turned to Murdock's global data sets to test other associations. Gerhard Lenski and Jean Lenski (1974: 106) used the EA to link intensive agriculture and pastoralism with moralizing beliefs, while Ralph Underhill (1975) employed it to evaluate associations with economic complexity. More recent analyses have utilized SCCS data to assess the association between moralizing gods and subsistence practices, population sizes, and environmental conditions (e.g., Dow 2006; Johnson 2005; Peoples and Marlowe 2012; Roes 1995; Sanderson and Roberts 2008; Simpson 1984; Snarey 1996). Such studies employed EA data less frequently, often in tandem with SCCS data (e.g., Botero et al. 2014; Roes 1993; Roes and Raymond 2003). Although most cross-cultural studies of religious evolution differentiate Moralizing codes from other beliefs, there is often an assumption that high gods tend to monitor human morality.

Some researchers have expressed concern that the religious beliefs coded in the SCCS and EA are not as culturally pristine as was once assumed. John Snarey evaluated the impact of Christian and Muslim missionaries, concluding that 61% ($n = 113$) of SCCS societies were studied after missionary work had commenced, making them "more likely than premissionized societies to posit a Supreme Deity who was active in human affairs" (Snarey 1996: 92). Other studies (e.g., Johnson 2005; Roes and Raymond 2003) addressed religious influence using a variable (713) that distinguishes "classical" religions (Christianity, Islam, Hinduism, Buddhism) from "preclassical" and "mixed" practices (see Whyte 1978 for the original code). In the Americas, where precontact "classical" religions were absent, a quarter of the SCCS cultures (8/32) were coded as "mixed," reflecting religious diffusion before the ethnographic present. More recently, William Divale and Albert Seda's (2000) "modernization" codes included variables for the presence/absence of Changes in Native Religion (1836) and Introduction of Foreign Religion (1837). Kathryn Kirby and colleagues (2016) mapped 32 cases of Indigenous religious change and 46 examples of introduced foreign religions in the Americas. Although the utility of this coding is questionable – the precontact Inca and Aztec empires are coded as Present for both variables – it is consistent with a growing acknowledgment that many Indigenous religions coded in the SCCS reflect diffusion of Abrahamic beliefs.

For the nine Native American cases coded as Moralizing in the SCCS, the cited authorities acknowledge extensive Western contacts prior to anthropological study

(Table 2).⁶ Although some downplay the diffusion of moralizing beliefs, at least six Moralizing religions reflect Christian influences. The Gros Ventre and Yahgan provide the best evidence of precontact moralizing beliefs, but they were egalitarian hunter-gatherers, contradicting scholarly claims of an association between moralizing gods and agrarian hierarchies.⁷

Table 2. External Influences on Moralizing Beliefs in the Americas

Culture	Cited Authorities	High God	Comments
Gros Ventre	Flannery, Cooper	Supreme Being	Missionaries arrived in the 1840s; ethnographers thought that "the Supreme Being concept is tied intimately into ... a ritual which itself is obviously aboriginal, with only the faintest traces, if any, of Christian infiltration" (Cooper, in Flannery and Cooper 1953: 9).⁸
Papago	Underhill, Lumholtz	Earth Maker	Missionaries arrived in the late 1600s. No ethnographic mention of a moralizing high god, although "many still pray to the sun, which they call father" (Lumholtz 1912: 356–7).
Sierra Popoluca	Foster	Dios (Christian God)	"Superimposed upon, or rather integrated with these aboriginal beliefs are many Christian concepts. The Popoluca recognizes *Dios* as supreme, the creator of the world and all the peoples in it" (Foster 1945: 185).
Quiche	Bunzel, Schultz-Jena	God	"The most striking feature of these invocations is the inclusion of God, Christ, and the saints among the diversified forces of nature, divine law, and the masters of human activities" (Bunzel 1952: 265).

---

6   As Table 2 demonstrates, Moralizing is applied to cases where a noncreator provides moral oversight (Yahgan, Aymara, Papago) and where the high god is not engaged with humans (Miskito).

7   Swanson (1960: 71–72) dismissed the Yahgan as a "negative case" because the early authority believed in "primitive monotheism."

8   For the closely related Arapaho, Kroeber (1907: 313) noted the recognition of the Christian God, called Hixtcābā-nih'ançan, a figure identical to the Gros Ventre Supreme Being, Ixtcibəni :həhat.

Culture	Cited Authorities	High God	Comments
Miskito	Conzemius	Wan-Aisa	"Nowadays both tribes believe in the existence of a Supreme Deity. ... This conception has probably been borrowed from Christianity. ... He does not appear to worry a great deal about the individual being. ... He lives so far away from earth that it is impossible to enter into relations with Him" (Conzemius 1932: 126).
Cuna	Nordenskiöld, Wafer, Stout	Dieu (God)	Cuna contacts began in the early 1500s. The Christian god is a creator and a moral punisher: "C'est Dieu qui a tout qui punit les pécheurs" [It is God who has everything who punishes sinners] (Nordenskiöld 1929: 148).
Warrau	Turrado Moreno, Wilbert	Unclear	"A belief in a supreme being has been reported. Competent students doubt whether this is an original *Warrau* belief, but no details are known" (Kirchhoff 1948: 879).
Aymara	Tschopik	God/Christ and Virgin Mary	Despite Spanish colonization, "Catholicism has attained no more than nominal acceptance among the Chucuito Aymara" (Tschopik 1951: 147). The Christian God is recognized as a high god with no active interest in human life (Tschopik 1951: 190); some lesser spirits care about human morality.
Yahgan	Gusinde, Bridges, Lothrop	Watauinewa	This high god is not a creator but the controller of the environment and food supply, and punisher of wickedness (Lothrop 1928: 172).

Source. SCCS.

The more comprehensive ethnographic sample in the EA contains similar interpretive and sampling flaws, with even less support for precontact Moralizing beliefs in the Americas, where cases coded as Absent (56.1%) are twice as prevalent as in other world regions (27.2%). Only 10.5% of Native American societies in the EA were coded as Moralizing, one third of the proportion seen elsewhere (31.8%). Although these figures could be associated with the overrepresentation of "simple" societies from the Americas, the significant differences between the Americas and other world regions – and between the proportions of different "high gods" codes in the EA and SCCS – raise doubts about the general models developed from the ethnological databases. Moralizing beliefs are comparatively rare in the Americas, and their distribution does not support an association with sociopolitical complexity.

Given the acknowledged impact of missionary work on ethnographic populations, it is not surprising that when all the religious beliefs recorded in the EA are subdivided by reported date, 20th-century samples have a larger proportion of cultures with Moralizing beliefs than earlier periods (Table 3).[9]

Table 3. Temporal Dimensions of Religious Beliefs in the EA

Date	Absent	Otiose	Present, Morally Inactive	Present, Morally Active	Total
Before 1850	18 (40%)	18 (40%)	3 (7%)	6 (13%)	45
1850–1899	90 (48.4%)	54 (29.0%)	6 (3.2%)	36 (19.4%)	186
1900–1949	123 (29.9%)	146 (35.4%)	30 (7.3%)	113 (27.4%)	412
1950–	46 (34.8%)	40 (30.3%)	3 (2.3%)	43 (32.6%)	132
Total	277 (35.7%)	258 (33.3%)	42 (5.4%)	198 (25.5%)	775

The EA contains more pre-1850s cultures from the Americas ($n = 26$) than from all the other world regions combined ($n = 19$). That sample included a very low percentage of Absent codes (15%, or 4/26), with 16 societies (64%) coded as Otiose and 3 (12%) as Present/Nonmoralizing. Just three early groups from the Americas had Moralizing beliefs: Hasinai (1770), Shawnee (1820), and Fox (1830); all were back dated using 20th-century sources. Prior to those "reconstructed" dates, the Hasinai had experienced missionization efforts and other cultural disruptions (Hickerson 1996), and the Shawnee had interacted with the neighboring Moravian missionaries and embraced the revitalization movement of the prophet Tenskwatawa (Edmunds 1983). The Fox tribe had also engaged with French Jesuits well before their migration to the American Midwest, and ethnographers considered their belief in a "great manitou" to reflect European influence (Jones 1939: 13). Overall, the earliest recorded Native American cultures in the EA suggest widespread belief in inactive and/or nonmoralizing supernatural beings, including in complex societies, such as circum-Caribbean chiefdoms (e.g., Taíno [Otiose], Muisca [Absent], and Natchez [Otiose]) and the Aztec (Present/Nonmoralizing) and Inca (Otiose) empires. The sampling flaws and coding limitations of the EA and SCCS render them ineffectual for developing better models of the development and pre-modern spread of moralizing beliefs.

Recent approaches to moralizing religions

Twentieth-century cross-cultural studies of the origins of "high god" beliefs used sociological theorists (Émile Durkheim, Karl Marx, and Max Weber) to develop

---

[9] The SCCS also shows temporal patterning, with nearly half of all cases collected after 1950 (47%, or 14/30) coded as having moralizing "high god" beliefs.

research hypotheses. Since then, evolutionary scholarship in biology, psychology, and anthropology has emphasized the development of human morality, altruism, and prosociality, synthesizing the quantitative results of holocultural analyses with new experiments and fieldwork. A prominent general model emerging from this scholarship is Ara Norenzayan's (2013: 4) "Big Gods Hypothesis," which argued that moralizing religions developed in early agricultural communities in Southwest Asia to facilitate the social dynamics of larger communities. From there, "the *Big Gods* of prosocial religions proliferated in the last 12,000 years of the Holocene period through cultural diffusion, population expansions, and conquest" (Norenzayan 2013: 8). Norenzayan's claim of a single early Holocene origin of moralizing religions contrasts with previous cross-cultural studies and with the ethnological databases, which coded the Babylonian, Egyptian, and Roman polities as Absent for a moralizing high god. Historians and scholars of religious history have criticized Norenzayan's model for its overall lack of evidence (e.g., Thomassen 2014).

In response, Norenzayan acknowledged that the coevolution of complexity and religious prosociality "could be different in different places and historical periods," but he leaned into long-standing assumptions of a relationship between complex societies and moralizing beliefs, insisting that the gods of chiefdoms "are more powerful and moralizing than those of foragers, but not as powerful as full-fledged Big Gods of states and empires" (Norenzayan 2015: 330). Instead of attempting an independent analysis of archaeological or early historical evidence, Norenzayan and his colleagues continued to repeat without evidence that "prosocial religions" spread globally since the start of the Holocene (e.g., Norenzayan et al. 2016; Purzycki et al. 2016: abstract). Their psychological field tests involving "culturally diverse" participants continued to cite flawed holocultural studies to support the baseline assumption that social complexity is associated with moralizing "high god" beliefs. Although they were often critical of the midcentury ethnological compilations, their research built on unfounded claims that came directly from those sources.

In recent years, scholars working with the Seshat Global History Databank have pursued the question of moralizing religions using direct evidence from history (and to a more limited extent, archaeology) to bypass the problems arising from treating the modern ethnological data as representative of human antiquity. The Seshat scholarship also acknowledges the limitations of the coding established by Swanson and Murdock, developing the concept of *moralizing supernatural punishment and reward* as an alternative to the presence/absence of high gods with moralizing concerns. Where possible, the Seshat database records variables related to whether MSP was a primary concern for supernatural entities and whether or not punishments were "certain and predictable," applied across regions and social hierarchies, and/or imposed on the living or in the afterlife. The seven variables developed to measure

MSP capture 16 possible belief categories, measurable across three different social levels (rulers, elites, and commoners).

MSP in complex societies in the contact-era Americas

Agriculture and complex societies developed in three different regions in the Americas (Central Andes, Mesoamerica, and Eastern Woodlands), offering significant ways to move beyond flawed holocultural representations by using direct evidence of MSP beliefs. By looking at the earliest recorded descriptions of the most complex contact period societies, it is also possible to assess the evolutionary assumptions of Norenzayan and other researchers. The present discussion emphasizes early Spanish contact and colonization across the Americas, beginning with the chiefdoms of the Caribbean before moving to Mesoamerica and the Andes.[10] The earliest eyewitness accounts of religious life in those regions came soon after the arrival of the first Spaniards (1490s–1530s), recorded by *conquistadores*, friars, and Spanish officials. Primary sources reflect the literary goals and cultural values of the European writers, but they offer valuable first-hand information about contact period practices.

Caribbean

Accounts of the earliest European voyages describe some religious practices in the chiefdoms of the Greater Antilles. On Hispaniola, chiefs (*caciques*) maintained special buildings outside their villages that housed powerful carved objects called *cemis*. Elites interacted with these by snorting a hallucinogenic snuff to alter their consciousness (Columbus, 1969, Second Voyage), suggesting that many *cemis* were not actively engaged with the everyday world where humans lived. Different *caciques* claimed to have the most powerful *cemis*, and Christopher Columbus described how they rigged the statues to function as a sort of ventriloquist's doll, convincing ordinary people that the figures spoke to them. In addition to *cemis*, the people of Hispaniola venerated sacred stones that helped to ensure crop fertility, guarantee rainfall, and facilitate childbirth.

The Jeronymite Ramón Pané ([c. 1498] 1999) claimed that the people of Hispaniola believed in an invisible and eternal god and his mother, although his account does not specify their role in human life. José Arrom (1980: 35) describes this "generous Sustaining Being" as "peaceful and kind," translating his most common titles as "Spirit of Cassava and the Sea," "Being without Male Ancestor," and "Lord Cassava Giver." While the Caribbean peoples recognized an entity that ensured abundant sustenance on land and in water, Pané ([c. 1498] 1999, chapter 15) identified *cemis* as the most important sacred beings in human communities. Some were ancestral

---

10 Subsequent work could include less well-documented Spanish contact areas, regions of early French and English colonization, and prehistoric archaeological evidence.

bones, and others were made of wood or stone. These powerful objects were discovered in wild places and brought to human settlements, and some had to be bound to keep them from returning to the wild forest. Pané distinguishes between those that spoke and those that governed agriculture, rainfall, and wind patterns. Sick people would bring a shaman (*bohuti*) to ingest hallucinogens and consult the *cemi* about the cause of the sickness. *Cemis* did not always give accurate advice to healers, and they were sometimes said to engage in what might be construed as morally unconstrained behavior – for example, the *cemi* Corocote began to sleep with the women of the man who possessed him (Pané [c. 1498] 1999, chapter 21). A female *cemi* called Guabancex was feared for causing house-destroying hurricanes and unleashing floodwaters in the mountain valleys when she was angered.

The early Caribbean chiefdoms did not believe in supernatural beings whose primary interest was human morality. Although powerful *cemis* could create natural disasters, they could also be consulted in healing ceremonies and community festivities to ensure fertility and rainfall. *Caciques* had a closer relationship with *cemis*, but it was framed in terms of maintaining or restoring health and fertility, rather than moralizing punishment. The earliest descriptions suggest an absence of MSP in the Caribbean, which was settled by maize-farming chiefdoms. This is consistent with the EA coding for the Taíno belief in "otiose" gods.

Mesoamerica

Eyewitness descriptions of Mesoamerica remarked on the urban states and marketplaces of that region. They recognized the existence of full-time priests and of religious texts, which had developed among multiple linguistic groups. Scholarly reconstructions of Late Postclassic Mesoamerican religions often rely heavily on descriptions written decades later by Catholic religious men (e.g. Sahagún [1577] (2021); Landa), as well as colonial Indigenous sources (e.g., Popul Vuh, Chilam Balam). These sources reflect active missionary efforts to promulgate Christian doctrine, as well as Indigenous conversion and syncretism in the years following first contact (Farriss 2018). The present discussion focuses instead on the cursory descriptions of early eyewitnesses, as well as recent interpretations of surviving Postclassic texts.

Lowland Maya

Eyewitness accounts of Lowland Maya polities stated that local rulers lived close to well-built and ornately furnished temples that housed images made of stone, gold, and wood. Elite people made daily offerings of incense in those buildings and performed auto-sacrifices that involved bloodletting (e.g., Cortés, [1519] 2001: 163, First Letter). They frequently offered human sacrifices in temples to make their petitions to the gods more favorable. Gabrielle Vail's (2000: 142–3) analysis of Postclassic Maya codices proposed that large numbers of Mayan deities were "members of overlapping complexes or clusters," of which the most important were (1) maize, (2) flowers/fertility/life force, (3) the earth, (4) creation/celestial continuity, and (5) war/sacrifice/death. A central emphasis of royal ritual action was to conduct rituals and make offerings to ensure rainfall and agricultural fertility. The calendrical organization of everyday and ritual time highlighted the ritual role of elites in maintaining cosmic continuity across temporal cycles. Although the religious practices of Mayan speakers incorporated important elements of Christian theology during the colonial period, the portrayal of supernatural beings and their relationship to the human world does not support the conclusion that MSP was an important element in their cosmological function. To the extent that Classic Maya iconography reflects later values, moral authority was apparently associated with the ruling elite, who maintained relationships with supernatural beings who were not strictly moral, and who used temporal power to reinforce the behavior of their subjects (Scherer et al. 2018).

Nahua
While advancing toward Tenochtitlán, Hernán Cortés ([1519] 2001, Second Letter) noted temples that housed sacred figures in major urban centers, as well as shrines at mountain passes and other natural landmarks. In the Mexica capital, Cortés visited vast religious precincts staffed by full-time priests, who supervised elite youths until their marriages. Priests wore special vestments, a contrast with the Maya lowlands, where rulers performed the principal sacrifices. The bodies of high-ranking leaders were also found in Tenochtitlán's temple complexes, along with large numbers of images fashioned from wood and stone and other materials. The Spaniards understood that each "idol" had a specific domain in the human world, such as wars and harvests (Cortés [1519] 2001: 262, Second Letter). When Cortés cast down some of these to replace them with Catholic icons, the Mexica ruler warned him that the people would be provoked to rise up,

> as they believed that these idols gave them all their temporal goods, and, in allowing them to be ill-treated, they would be angered, and give nothing, and would take away all the fruits of the soil, and cause the people to die of want. (Cortés [1519] 2001: 261, Second Letter)

The Spaniards understood that elite priests went to the Nahua sacred images, making sacrifices that helped to sustain human endeavors. If those beings kept a watch on how humans treated one another, the Spaniards were unaware of such beliefs. It should be noted that Cortés frequently mentioned punishment in his letters, referring to his own violence against rival Spaniards as well as acts he considered appropriate if native "idolaters" resisted Catholicism. He considered that the highland city-states "must have some system of justice for punishing the wicked," recounting public beatings and confinements for thefts and other offenses (Cortés [1519] 2001: 210–11, Second Letter). Punitive actions appear to have been the domain of political elites, who also provided reverence and care for supernatural entities that maintained the conditions necessary for human life.

After the devastating European invasion, chroniclers compiled accounts of Mexica religion, identifying deities and their attributes. Some, like the Franciscan Bernardino de Sahagún [1577] (2021), organized them into a pantheon based on their supposed resemblance to Greek gods, while other accounts emphasized the Indigenous (in)compatibility with Christian doctrine. In recent decades, the analysis of precontact Nahua religion has diverged from such comparisons, recognizing that the hundreds of named "gods" personified elements of overlapping cosmological themes, such as creation/cosmic rulership, rain/agricultural fertility, and warfare/sacrifice/death (Nicholson 1971). Nevertheless, ethnohistorical studies have often synthesized postconquest sources without carefully addressing the foreign elements that penetrated discourses on pre-Christian religiosity. As Guilhem Olivier (1997: 40) notes, painstaking documentary analysis is required to reconstruct precontact beliefs since Indigenous Christians often portrayed their ancestral religions as anticipating the fundamental cosmological truths that the Catholic priests were eager to teach.

This raises questions about Tezcatlipoca, depicted by some modern scholars as an all-seeing, paramount god who punished humans for moral transgressions (cf. Baquedano 2015; Olivier 2003). Sahagún [1577] (2021) likened Tezcatlipoca to the Roman god Jupiter, but he also compared him to Lucifer, saying that he was the origin of "war, vice, and filth." Rather than watching over humans to enforce their morality, this Tezcatlipoca was a trickster who lured humans into immorality. This description was written during a time when Spanish writers emphasized the diabolical deception of Native Americans prior to the arrival of Catholicism. By contrast, some Franciscans likened Tezcatlipoca to the Christian God, and by the early 17th century, there were Indigenous writers, like Fernando de Alva Ixtlitlxóchitl, who claimed that an invisible avatar of his was worshiped in Texcoco before the European invasion (Olivier 1997: 44). It should be noted that neither of these Christian representations of Tezcatlipoca is entirely compatible with preconquest depictions of the god, whose fourfold aspects were born at the time of the first universal creation. Although precontact codices depict avatars of Tezcatlipoca among the supernatural figures associated with the punishment of some moral lapses (e.g., adultery), it is not clear whether those beings were believed to watch over humans or whether they represented the personification (*teotl*) of the *human* punishment of socially inappropriate behaviors (see Klein 1990). Given that the Nahua recognized supernatural beings associated with vice (Tlazoteotl) and drunkenness (Tepoztecatl), interpretive caution is warranted. The portrayal of divine punishments for some moral lapses contrasts with what colonial chroniclers recorded about the actual sanctioning of behavior that was considered immoral or criminal (Berdan 2008).

Overall, while scholarly interpretations of Nahua religion sometimes identify a single high god as an all-seeing arbiter of morality, the available evidence is considerably more complicated. There were avatars of supernatural beings who personified the punishment of human transgressions, but the idea of an all-seeing god who meted out MSP appears to have developed following contact with Catholic missionaries. To the extent that social and legal sanctions for immorality were viewed as the domain of families, communities, and rulers, there does not appear to have been a strongly articulated belief in MSP. Such an interpretation is consistent with the EA coding of Aztec religion as having active gods who did not promote human morality.

Tarascan
Jerónimo de Alcalá's *Relación de Michoacán* [c. 1540] (2021) describes the religion of the Tarascan Empire, maintained by a hierarchy of full-time priests who served as the representatives of a panoply of supernatural beings, caring for their temples and images and personifying them during important festivities. Priests conducted blood sacrifices, including with human victims, which were intended to ensure adequate rainfall and abundant water in local springs. The earth goddess Cuerauáperi was the mother of the gods and the focus of many myths and prayers (Alcalá [c. 1540] (2021), Primera Parte). She sent the other gods to their places on the landscape and provided people with seeds and harvests, but she was also responsible for famines, although not necessarily in response to human immorality. The fire/sun god Curicaueri was the Tarascan patron, and the paramount ruler (*cazonci*) claimed to represent him and consult him in times of war, with prayers that the enemy would fall ill. The *cazonci* was the arbiter of moral justice in the capital and outlying areas, ordering severe punishments for adultery, theft, drunkenness, and other acts.

Overall, early descriptions of Mesoamerican religions show common cosmological themes, as well as significant differences in ecclesiastical structure and belief. Across the region, large numbers of supernatural entities were believed to inhabit local landscapes, represent celestial bodies and cosmographic values, and personify aspects of food production, reproduction, warfare, and human life. MSP appears to have been absent, although some supernatural avatars could represent immoral acts and human punishment for such behavior. There was no all-seeing high god whose primary interest was human morality, and individual sickness or environmental perturbations do not appear to have been viewed as punishments for improper interpersonal behaviors. It was the Mesoamerican rulers, local communities, and families who took responsibility for moral surveillance and sanctioning.

Inca

The Pizarro expedition of 1532 produced the first documented accounts of the central Andes, a region where plant cultivation and animal domestication developed independently and urban states rose and collapsed from the first millennium BCE. Eyewitness descriptions of the Inca coastal regions mention the worship of a creator called Pachacamac, whose temple had male and female priests. Pilgrims fasted for 20 days to access the outer shrine, while only those who fasted for a year were permitted to enter an inner patio to consult with a high-ranking priest about weather and crop yields (Pizarro [1533] 1959). Coastal populations sent gifts to the powerful image kept in the inner sanctum, fearing "that it could drown them if they annoy it and do not serve it well, and that the things of the world are in its hand" (Miguel de Estete in Xérez [1534] 1968: 249; my translation). As the world's creator, Pachacamac threatened destruction if not supported generously, but there was no mention of the creator taking any interest in human morality.

Outside the temple, some claimed that Pachacamac appeared as a puma or a serpent and was often angry when people consulted it. To mitigate that anger, the people made sacrifices that included animals and human blood. Elsewhere on the coast, people revered *huacas*, powerful entities that inhabited the world around them, "but not all of them, just those that gave an answer, and not all the time, but rather when they considered it appropriate" (Castro and Ortega Morejón [1558] 1867: 219; my translation). When the Incas conquered the coast, they reportedly brought the *huacas* and their caretakers to Cuzco, where the ruler punished the false ones and granted resources to the others. Having done so, the Incas left the local lords and their people to worship as they thought appropriate.

In the highlands where the Incas originated, local people recognized different creators, including Viracocha, who raised up the Andes and guided the waters to their sources (Betanzos [1550s] 1996; Cieza de León [c. 1553] 1880). After shaping the world, he fashioned the first pairs of men and women and sent them out to their origin places, after which he departed from the human world. Although Inca religion commemorated Viracocha's acts of creation, their principal deity was the Sun, whom they claimed as a royal ancestor. They built sun temples at important highland centers, staffed with priestesses, who prepared food, drink, and cloth as offerings. In Cuzco, these women cared for a golden image of the Sun, which resided within the Qorikancha temple, where only its priestly wives and the Inca ruler interacted with it.

The early chronicle of Betanzos notes that the Inca used offerings to maintain reverent relationships with powerful ancestral mummies, statues, and sacred objects. These beings did not actively monitor the human world but could cause harm if humans did not provide for them. Betanzos clearly identifies Inca moral surveillance and punishment as the unique domain of the Inca ruler, who had special spies watching the city of Cuzco. When the Inca ruler presided over the denunciation and punishment of immoral behavior each year, there is no indication that he was accompanied by sacred objects or guided by their oversight. In the provinces, the Inca ruler sent inspectors called *tukuyrikhuq* (the one who sees all) to watch over people and ritual specialists (*huchakamayuq*) to punish crimes against his interests. The early chronicler Pedro de Cieza de León said that Inca punishment was so feared that people policed their own behavior – "they knew that if they should be bad on their part, then the punishment would have to be carried out ... so that no amount of begging or bribing would suffice" (Cieza de León [c. 1553] 1880: 45–6, chapter 13, my translation).

Early Spanish sources indicate that Andean creators were largely absent or withdrawn from the human world. The *huacas* (including the Sun) expected to be cared for by humans – sometimes offering good weather, abundant crops, and health in return – but they populated the natural world and were not invested in the oversight of human morality. The Incas preferred to gather the physical instantiations of sacred beings in places where they could control access to them and speak for them. They also established themselves as patrons of rural pilgrimages so that they could monitor ritual performances. Andean sovereigns claimed the authority to supervise the moral life of elites and commoners and to punish individual violations. The overall lack of MSP in the Inca world is consistent with the coding of Inca supernatural beings as Otiose in the EA.

Conclusions

Although the SCCS and EA have been used for decades to test hypotheses regarding religious evolution, both databases represent Native American societies in problematic ways. Sample selection is flawed, and the reconstruction of the ethnographic present downplays the impact of colonization and missionization in the Americas. The underrepresentation of complex societies prevents the active consideration of hypotheses regarding beliefs in morality-enforcing "high gods," raising issues about the global models developed using the ethnological databases. Moralizing religions appear to be less prevalent in the Americas than in other regions, and they are absent in the earliest and most complex Native American samples. The regional sample is problematic, and its limited coding for moralizing religions does not support general evolutionary models like the Big Gods Hypothesis.

A brief ethnohistoric review of early Spanish sources suggests that contact period chiefdoms, states, and empires in the Americas recognized *supernatural punishment* in the form of natural disasters and perhaps individual illness. These were responses to lapses in the care that humans were expected to provide the powerful entities that generated rainfall, fertility, and resource abundance. Local elites, rulers, and full-time priests performed necessary acts of ritual care intended to avoid negative consequences. By contrast, *moralizing punishment* was associated with the sovereignty of human rulers, rather than all-seeing gods. Religious differences in contact period chiefdoms, city-states, and empires suggest that religious practices coevolved with sociopolitical complexity, becoming more hierarchical, ecclesiastical, and materially costly in diverse and territorially expansive states. However, there is no reason to associate such coevolution with MSP beliefs, which remained underdeveloped (if not absent) in the largest and most complex societies to develop across the Americas. This does not mean that MSP beliefs were universally absent in the precontact Americas, but it challenges the fundamental sociocultural dynamics that the Big Gods Hypothesis and earlier studies of religious evolution have assumed. Addressing these issues requires a more sustained engagement with the global historical record – the kind of work currently conducted by Seshat collaborators – as well as archaeological meta-analyses to identify material patterning in prehistoric ritual practices. The question of prehistoric religious evolution remains far from resolved, and careful consultation of the direct evidence is the only meaningful way to move beyond entrenched ethnological speculations.

References

Alcalá, Jerónimo de. (c. 1540) 2021. *Relación de Michoacán* [Relation of Michoacán]. Edited by Germán Vázquez Chamorro and Leoncio Cabrero Fernández. Barcelona: Linkgua Ediciones.

Arrom, José J. 1980. "Taíno Mythology: Notes on the Supreme Being." *Latin American Literary Review* 8 (6): 21–37.

Baquedano, Elizabeth, ed. 2015. *Tezcatlipoca: Trickster and Supreme Deity.* Boulder, CO: University Press of Colorado. doi: 10.5876/9781607322887.

Bellah, Robert N. 1964. "Religious Evolution." *American Sociological Review* 29 (3): 358–74. doi: 10.2307/2091480.

Berdan, Frances. 2008. "Living on the Edge in an Ancient Imperial World: Aztec Crime and Deviance." *Global Crime* 9 (1–2): 20–34. doi: 10.1080/17440570701862710.

Betanzos, Juan de. (1550s) 1996. *Narrative of the Incas.* Translated by Roland Hamilton. Austin, TX: University of Texas Press.

Botero, Carlos A., Beth Gardner, Kathryn R. Kirby, Joseph Bulbulia, Michael C. Gavin, and Russell D. Gray. 2014. "The Ecology of Religious Beliefs." *Proceedings of the National Academy of Sciences* 111 (47): 16784–9. doi: 10.1073/pnas.1408701111.

Bunzel, Ruth. 1952. *Chichicastenango, a Guatemalan Village.* Locust Valley, NY: J. J. Augustin.

Castro, Cristóbal de, and Diego de Ortega Morejón. (1558) 1867. "Relacion y declaracion del modo que este valle de Chincha y sus comarcanos se Gobernaban ántes que hobiese ingas y despues que los hobo hasta que los cristianos entraron en esta tierra." [Relation and declaration about the mode by which this valley of Chincha and its environs were governed before and after there were Incas, until the Christians entered into this land]. *Coleccion de documentos inéditos para la historia de España* 50: 206–220.

Cieza de León, Pedro de. (c. 1553) 1880. *Segunda Parte de la Crónica del Perú: Que Trata del Señorío de los Incas Yupanquis y de Sus Grandes Hechos y Gobernación* [Second part of the Chronicle of Peru: Dealing with the lordship of the Yupanqui Incas and their great deeds and government]. Edited by Marcos Jiménez de la Espada. Madrid: Manuel Ginés Hernández.

Columbus, Christopher. 1969. *The Four Voyages of Christopher Columbus.* Edited and translated by J. M. Cohen. New York: Penguin.

Conzemius, Eduard. 1932. *Ethnographical Survey of the Miskito and Sumu Indians of Honduras and Nicaragua.* Washington, DC: U.S. Government Printing Office.

Cortés, Hernán. (1519) 2001. *Letters from Mexico.* Edited and translated by Anthony Pagden. New Haven, CT: Yale University Press.

Divale, William, and Albert Seda. 2000. "Cross-Cultural Codes of Modernization." *World Cultures* 11 (2):152–70.

Dow, James. 2006. "The Evolution of Religion: Three Anthropological Approaches." *Method & Theory in the Study of Religion* 18 (1): 67-91. doi: 10.1163/157006806776142910.

Edmunds, R. David. 1983. *The Shawnee Prophet.* Lincoln, NE: University of Nebraska Press.

Ellwood, Charles A. 1923. "Social Evolution and Christianity." *Journal of Religion* 3 (2): 113-31. doi: 10.1086/480339.

Farriss, Nancy M. 2018. *Tongues of Fire: Language and Evangelization in Colonial Mexico.* New York: Oxford University Press. doi: 10.1093/oso/9780190884109.001.0001.

Flannery, Regina, and John Cooper. 1953. *The Gros Ventres of Montana: Part II, Religion and Ritual.* Washington, DC: Catholic University of America Press.

Foster, George M. 1945. *Sierra Popoluca Folklore and Beliefs.* Berkeley, CA: University of California Press.

Hickerson, Daniel A. 1996. "Hasinai-European Interaction, 1694-1715." *East Texas Historical Journal* 34 (2): 6.

Johnson, D. D. 2005. "God's Punishment and Public Goods." *Human Nature* 16 (4): 410–46. doi: 10.1007/s12110-005-1017-0.

Jones, William. 1939. *Ethnography of the Fox Indians.* Edited by Margaret Welpley Fisher. Washington, DC: U.S. Government Printing Office.

Kirby, Kathryn R., Russell D. Gray, Simon J. Greenhill, Fiona M. Jordan, Stephanie Gomes-Ng, Hans-Jörg Bibiko, Damián E. Blasi, et al. 2016. "D-PLACE: A Global Database of Cultural, Linguistic and Environmental Diversity." *PLOS One* 11 (7). doi: 10.1371/journal.pone.0158391.

Kirchhoff, Paul. 1948. "The Warrau." In *Handbook of South American Indians*, vol. 3: *The Tropical Forest Tribes*, edited by Julian Steward, 869-82. Washington, DC: U.S. Government Printing Office.

Klein, Cecelia F. 1990. "Snares and Entrails: Mesoamerican Symbols of Sin and Punishment." *Res: Anthropology and Aesthetics* 19 (1): 81-103. doi: 10.1086/RESvn1ms20166828.

Kroeber, Alfred L. 1907. "The Arapahoe. IV, Religion." *Bulletin of the American Museum of Natural History* 18 (4): 279-454.

Lang, Martin, Benjamin G. Purzycki, Coren L. Apicella, Quentin D. Atkinson, Alexander Bolyanatz, Emma Cohen, Carla Handley, et al. 2019. "Moralizing Gods, Impartiality and Religious Parochialism across 15 Societies." *Proceedings of the Royal Society B: Biological Sciences* 286 (1898). doi: 10.1098/rspb.2019.0202.

Lenski, Gerhard, and Jean Lenski. 1974. *Human Societies: An Introduction to Macrosociology*. 2nd ed. New York: McGraw-Hill.

Lothrop, Samuel K. 1928. *The Indians of Tierra del Fuego*. New York: Museum of the American Indian/Heye Foundation. doi: 10.5479/sil.472342.39088016090599.

Lowie, Robert H. 1936. *Primitive Religion*. London: George Routledge and Sons.

Lumholtz, Carl. 1912. *New Trails in Mexico*. New York: Charles Scribner's Sons.

Mathews, Shailer. 1911. "The Evolution of Religion." *American Journal of Theology* 15 (1): 57–82. doi: 10.1086/478976.

Murdock, George Peter. 1940. "The Cross-Cultural Survey." *American Sociological Review* 5 (3): 361–70. doi: 10.2307/2084038.

Murdock, George Peter. 1949. *Social Structure*. New York: Macmillan.

Murdock, George Peter. 1957. "World Ethnographic Sample." *American Anthropologist* 59 (4): 664–87. doi: 10.1525/aa.1957.59.4.02a00090.

Murdock, George Peter. 1967. "Ethnographic Atlas: A Summary." *Ethnology* 6 (2): 109–236. doi: 10.2307/3772751.

Murdock, George Peter. 1968. "World Sampling Provinces." *Ethnology* 7 (3): 305–326. doi: 10.2307/3772896.

Murdock, George P., and Douglas R. White. 1969. "Standard Cross-Cultural Sample." *Ethnology* 8 (4): 329–69. doi: 10.2307/3772907.

Naroll, Raoul. 1961. "Two Solutions to Galton's Problem." *Philosophy of Science* 28 (1): 15–39. doi: 10.1086/287778.

Nicholson, Henry B. 1971. "Religion in Pre-Hispanic Central Mexico." In *Handbook of Middle American Indians*, vols. 10 and 11: *Archaeology of Northern Mesoamerica*, edited by Robert Wauchope, Gordon F. Ekholm, and Ignacio Bernal, 395–446. Austin, TX: University of Texas Press. doi: 10.7560/701502-016.

Nordenskiöld, Erland. 1929. "Les rapports entre l'art, la religion et la magie chez les Indiens Cuna et Chocó" [The relationships between art, religion, and magic among the Cuna and Choco Indians]. *Journal de la Société des Américanistes* 21 (1): 141–58. doi: 10.3406/jsa.1929.3663.

Norenzayan, Ara. 2013. *Big Gods: How Religion Transformed Cooperation and Conflict*. Princeton, NJ: Princeton University Press. doi: 10.1515/9781400848324.

Norenzayan, Ara. 2015. "Big Questions about Big Gods: Response and Discussion." *Religion, Brain & Behavior* 5 (4): 327–42. doi: 10.1080/2153599X.2014.928359.

Norenzayan, Ara, and Azim F. Shariff. 2008. "The Origin and Evolution of Religious Prosociality." *Science* 322 (5898): 58–62. doi: 10.1126/science.1158757.

Norenzayan, Ara, Azim F. Shariff, Will M. Gervais, Aiyana K. Willard, Rita A. McNamara, Edward Slingerland, and Joseph Henrich. 2016. "The Cultural Evolution of Prosocial Religions." *Behavioral and Brain Sciences* 39: e1. doi:10.1017/S0140525X14001356.

Olivier, Guilhem. 1997. *Moqueries et métamorphoses d'un dieu aztèque: Tezcatlipoca, le «Seigneur au miroir fumant»* [Mockery and metamorphoses of an Aztec god: Tezcatlipoca, the""Lord of the Smoking Mirro""]. Paris: Institut "Ethnologie, Musée de "Homme.

Olivier, Guilhem. 2003. *Mockeries and Metamorphoses of an Aztec God: Tezcatlipoca, "Lord of the Smoking Mirror."* Boulder, CO: University Press of Colorado.

Pané, Ramón. (c. 1498) 1999. *An Account of the Antiquities of the Indians.* Edited by José Juan Arrom and translated by Susan C. Griswold. Durham, NC: Duke University Press. doi: 10.1215/9780822382546.

Peoples, Hervey C., and Frank W. Marlowe. 2012. "Subsistence and the Evolution of Religion." *Human Nature* 23 (3): 253–69. doi: 10.1007/s12110-012-9148-6.

Peregrine, Peter. 1996. "The Birth of the Gods Revisited: A Partial Replication of Guy Swanson's (1960) Cross-Cultural Study of Religion." *Cross-Cultural Research* 30 (1): 84–112. doi: 10.1177/106939719603000104.

Pizarro, Hernando. (1533) 1959. "A los magníficos señores, los oidores de la Audiencia Real de Su Majestad, que residen en la cibdad de Sancto Domingo" [To the magnificent gentlemen, the judges of the royal audience of His Majesty, who reside in the city of Santo Domingo]. In *Cartas del Perú* [Letters of Peru], edited by Raúl Porras Barrenechea, 77–84. Lima: Sociedad de Bibliófilos Peruanos.

Purzycki, Benjamin Grant, Coren Apicella, Quentin D. Atkinson, Emma Cohen, Rita Anne McNamara, Aiyana K. Willard, Dimitris Xygalatas, et al. 2016. "Moralistic Gods, Supernatural Punishment and the Expansion of Human Sociality." *Nature* 530 (7590): 327–30. doi: 10.1038/nature16980.

Purzycki, Benjamin Grant, Aiyana K. Willard, Eva Kundtová Klocová, Coren Apicella, Quentin Atkinson, Alexander Bolyanatz, Emma Cohen, et al. 2022. "The Moralization Bias of Gods' Minds: A Cross-Cultural Test." *Religion, Brain & Behavior* 12 (1–2): 38–60. doi: 10.1080/2153599X.2021.2006291.

Roes, Frans L. 1995. "The Size of Societies, Stratification and Belief in High Gods Supportive of Human Morality." *Politics and the Life Sciences* 14 (1): 73–77. doi: 10.1017/S0730938400011795.

Roes, Frans L., and Michel Raymond. 2003. "Belief in Moralizing Gods." *Evolution and Human Behavior* 24 (2): 126–35. doi: 10.1016/S1090-5138(02)00134-4.

Rohner, Ronald P., D. Scott Berg, and Evelyn C. Rohner. 1982. "Data Quality Control in the Standard Cross-Cultural Sample: Cross-Cultural Codes." *Ethnology* 21 (4): 359–69. doi: 10.2307/3773766.

Sahagún, Bernardino de. (1577) 2021. *Historia general de las cosas de la Nueva España* [General history of the things of New Spain], vols. 1 and 2. Barcelona: Linkgua Ediciones.

Sanderson, Stephen K., and Wesley W. Roberts. 2008. "The Evolutionary Forms of the Religious Life: A Cross-Cultural, Quantitative Analysis." *American Anthropologist* 110 (4): 454–66. doi: 10.1111/j.1548-1433.2008.00078.x.

Scherer, Andrew K., Charles Golden, and Stephen Houston. 2018. "True People, Foreigners, and the Framing of Maya Morality." In *Bioarchaeology of Pre-Columbian Mesoamerica: An Interdisciplinary Approach*, edited by Cathy Willermet and Andrea Cucina, 159–99. Gainesville, FL: University Press of Florida. doi: 10.5744/florida/9780813056005.003.0007.

Simpson, John H. 1984. "High Gods and the Means of Subsistence." *Sociological Analysis* 45 (3): 213–22. doi: 10.2307/3711478.

Snarey, John. 1996. "The Natural Environment's Impact upon Religious Ethics: A Cross-Cultural Study." *Journal for the Scientific Study of Religion* 35 (2): 85–96. doi: 10.2307/1387077.

Swanson, Guy E. 1960. *The Birth of the Gods: The Origin of Primitive Beliefs*. Ann Arbor, MI: University of Michigan Press. doi: 10.3998/mpub.6484.

Thomassen, Einar. 2014. "Are Gods Really Moral Monitors? Some Comments on Ara Norenzayan's Big Gods by a Historian of Religions." *Religion* 44 (4): 667–73. doi: 10.1080/0048721X.2014.937074.

Tschopik, Harry, Jr. 1951. "The Aymara of Chucuito, Peru. 1. Magic." *Anthropological Papers of the American Museum of Natural History* 44 (2): 133–308.

Underhill, Ralph. 1975. "Economic and Political Antecedents of Monotheism: A Cross-Cultural Study." *American Journal of Sociology* 80 (4): 841–61. doi: 10.1086/225893.

Vail, Gabrielle. 2000. "Pre-Hispanic Maya Religion: Conceptions of Divinity in the Postclassic Maya Codices." *Ancient Mesoamerica* 11 (1): 123–47. doi: 10.1017/S0956536100111022.

Wallace, Anthony F. C. 1966. *Religion: An Anthropological View*. New York: Random House.

Whyte, Martin King. 1978. *The Status of Women in Preindustrial Societies*. Princeton, NJ: Princeton University Press.

Xérez, Francisco de. (1534) 1968. "Verdadera relación de la conquista del Perú" [True account of the conquest of Peru]. In *Biblioteca peruana: El Perú a travé de los siglos, primera serie* [Peruvian Library: Peru through the centuries, first series], vol. 1, 191–272. Lima: Editores Técnicos Asociados.

CHAPTER 2

Great and Little Traditions
Mark Stanford

It is often thought that a newfound concern with morality is a defining characteristic of major world religions born in the Axial Age. This is so not only for theorists but for many religious believers themselves. The word for "morality" in the languages of some Buddhist countries is simply the vernacular equivalent of the Pali *sila*, or the five precepts, while Christianity, Judaism, and Islam all make claims to define the nature of right and wrong through the teachings of their doctrine. Religious practices and beliefs falling outside of doctrine, such as consultation of shamans, astrologers, or practitioners of magic, or propitiation of local saints or spirits, are typically portrayed as morally unconcerned superstitions – perhaps helpful for practitioners seeking practical benefits but unrelated to the definition of morality (Byrne 2012; Goossaert 2005; Josephson 2006).

This holds too for scholars who have noted the advent of moralizing high gods around the time of the Axial Age. Typically, a contrast is drawn between these moralizing doctrinal religions and the kinds of religions that preceded them, in which practitioners made sacrifices to morally unconcerned gods, whose rewards and punishments for those sacrifices depended not on the behavior of humans toward one another but only on their behavior toward the gods (Norenzayan 2013: 6). This line of inquiry has tended to take doctrinal orthodoxy at its word on this point. That is, the source of morality and moral behavior is the official religion, backed up by supernatural punishment either from an omniscient moralizing god or an omnipresent moralizing force of karma.

On this account, then, not only was supernatural punishment that preceded moralizing high gods morally unconcerned, so are the myriad supernatural punishments that have accompanied doctrinal religions throughout history but that originated elsewhere than from their moralizing high gods. For alongside the orthodoxy and orthopraxy of every major doctrinal religion, we find complex, unofficial systems of belief and practice that posit a variety of forms of supernatural punishment and reward of their own (Stanford and Jong 2019). The same practitioners may partake in both official and unofficial forms of religiosity, and the presence of both moralizing high gods and unofficial supernatural forces may be equally important in their lives. Some of these forces appear to recapitulate patterns found before the advent of moralizing high gods; religious practitioners worldwide have continued to venerate local saints, spirits, or demigods who often appear to be morally unconcerned but reward or punish followers depending on the quality of their vows or sacrificial offerings.

Others continue what may be still older patterns, such as the belief that supernatural harm may come from other humans in the community, like witches, sorcerers, or werewolves. According to the standard account, although these survivals might be an important part of the religious tapestry, they are unrelated to morality, and certainly to moralizing supernatural punishment and reward (MSP).

This chapter will present evidence for a different view. If we consider more carefully the emic perspective on both propitiatory obligations to local demigods and beliefs in supernatural harm by community members, we find that the associated supernatural punishments can indeed be thought of as moralizing. The morality concerned, however, is not the high morality of doctrinal religions, which, although textually universalistic, typically gives the highest rewards for helping the extended religious ingroup. Instead, these are punishments and rewards for adherence to a more local, particularistic form of morality.

But first, a word about terminology. There has been a long and tortured debate about how best to conceptualize the relationship between these two sides of doctrinal religion (Davis 1982). Distinctions such as "folk" or "popular" versus "elite" religion have rightly been rejected on the basis that in many cases, elites and religious officials also participate in unofficial practices while the "folk" participate too in official ones (D. H. Green 1994; Moore 1994; Watkins 2004). Nor do strict distinctions between rural and urban, literate and illiterate quite fit the picture (Christian 1981). Robert Redfield's (1956) distinction between "great" and "little" traditions, that is, that actual religious life anywhere is a fluctuating amalgam of local, unofficial practices and beliefs with a local interpretation of centrally prescribed doctrinal ones has been attacked on various fronts. It has been pointed out that great and little traditions are constantly borrowing from each other (Frankfurter 2015; Marriot 1955; Parladir 2014), that in any given context there may be multiple great and little traditions coexisting and interacting rather than just one of each (Nordberg 2018), and that this is an analytical distinction sometimes but not always shared by practitioners themselves (Obeyesekere 1963). Taking into account all these provisos, however, the distinction remains useful: Some practices and beliefs in the overall tapestry of a religious system are propagated and enforced by official translocal institutions, while others are not. Redfield's terminology captures this contrast well enough.

Because of the breadth and heterogeneity of little traditions worldwide, it is not possible to provide a comprehensive survey. But an important point to emphasize at the outset is that many little tradition supernatural agents do engage in direct moralizing punishment. Indeed, even the supposedly morally unconcerned agents of nondoctrinal religions often do so. In a study cited by Ara Norenzayan (2013: 126) as evidence of their lack of moral concern, Christopher Boehm (2008) in fact found that in all of the 18 hunter-gatherer societies he surveyed, at least some interpersonal transgressions were supernaturally sanctioned. It is true, however, that the relevant moral concerns varied much more than they tend to do under universalistic moralizing high gods; and the same holds true for little tradition agents across doctrinal religions. Fairies in mediaeval European Christianity might enforce local rights to a spring or protect peasants who resisted oppression; or they might punish insufficiently vigilant parents by abducting their children and transforming them into changelings (R. F. Green 2016: 22, 39, 111). Muslim saints might reward people for helping the poor, while local spirits might punish them for breaking rules enacted by the community (Mittermaier 2008; Werthmann 2008). But while the specifics of MSP across little traditions are many and varied, what follows will focus on two key recurring features: (1) supernatural agents setting up collective obligations to sustain a local social unit through propitiatory contributions and (2) supernatural harm by human community members, directed at those who arouse envy, break local social norms, or otherwise sow discord.

Collective propitiatory obligations

As noted above, a paradigm example of supposedly amoral supernatural punishment is the vengeance wreaked by a god as a result of improperly or insufficiently performed propitiation. But although the gods themselves may appear morally unconcerned, lack of proper propitiation frequently results in collective punishment. This creates a moral obligation to the community on the part of those designated to make offerings; if they fail to do so, the ensuing supernatural punishment is a direct result of their having failed in their obligations not only to the god but also to the community.

Thus, for example, it was the duty of early Chinese kings, and subsequent emperors, to manage relationships with the god Shangdi and various other deities on behalf of their people. If they failed in their propitiatory duties to the gods, society as a whole would be punished through disasters such as floods. In such cases, the king was seen as failing in his duty to the people; he might be forced to make public penitence or even legitimately be overthrown (Baum 2004). Similarly, ancient Roman elites took up the responsibility of organizing sacrifices to gods in order to ensure the protection of society at large, and they could be held responsible for failing in this duty in the event of calamities befalling the populace. They were thus frequently at pains to sponsor sacrifices and ensuing festivals as a demonstration of their commitment to the public good through proper propitiation of the gods (Knapp 2018: 18). In Egypt, Pharaonic ideology held from early times that it was the king's responsibility, as chief priest, to maintain the necessary cults in order to keep good relations with the gods, lest they take vengeance on the people as a whole by bringing about natural disasters (Richards 2010). Following a pattern of what Azfar Moin and Alan Strathern (2022: 39) have called "cosmic kingship," such rulers were constrained and divinized in equal measure by virtue of their unique role as intercessors between divinities and the populace. In all of these contexts, while the sacrificial relationship between leaders and gods may not itself count as a moral one, the collective consequences of leaders' actions in that relationship mean that they have a moral obligation to their people to manage divine relationships skillfully, and that supernatural punishment is the result of their failure in this obligation.

But while the state cults of ancient polities functioned in part to enable rulers to display their moral commitment to the society over which they ruled, smaller local cults were of far more salience to everyday life for most people. Across the Roman Empire, local elites sponsored festivals and sacrifices to local protector gods to demonstrate their commitment to particular towns and cities (Knapp 2018: 69). The empire was crisscrossed with allegiances to local cults pertaining to families, clans, hills, tribes, neighborhoods, and other social units (Rüpke 2018: 110). Central to such cults were sacrificial offerings to tutelary divinities. Typically, such offerings were the responsibility of the leader of the relevant social unit; the head of a household might be responsible for making offerings to household deities, while the public priests of a city might be obliged to organize sacrifices to relevant local gods (Scheid 2007). This proliferation of heterogeneous cultic obligations to local and household deities was a source of concern for some who saw it as a potential source of "confusion," leading practitioners astray from the official cultus (Rüpke 2018: 217). Nevertheless, it thrived and, mirroring the imperial cult, created a moral obligation on the part of the heads of local social units to maintain good relations with gods on their behalf.

In addition to the duty of designated individuals to make offerings on behalf of the collective, many local cults have historically demanded participation and sacrifices from every member of the community. Jews and early Christians in the Roman Empire came under attack in part because their refusal to take part in offerings to communal gods was seen as endangering the community as a whole, and thus an attack on society (Knapp 2018: 167). When propitiatory obligations of local cults become fully collective, binding every individual member of the relevant social unit to contribute to offerings, they become a public goods provision problem. Those who fail to contribute to the collective welfare bring a collective punishment for their lack of commitment to the community. This might also be seen as a punishment for those who fail to enforce contributions from others – a supernatural answer to the second-order free rider problem.

While doctrinal religions after the Axial Age largely refocused great tradition MSP away from collective propitiatory obligations (Dunbar 2022: 195), little traditions have continued throughout history to reproduce the practice of binding individuals into a moral obligation to a collective through supernatural punishment and reward for sacrificial duties. In the Theravada Buddhist world, we find a proliferation of spirits pertaining to households, villages, and other local social units, which must be propitiated for the well-being of the unit (Brac de la Perrière and

Munier-Gaillard 2019; Spiro 1978). Often such spirits are seen as potentially malevolent, and it is therefore a collective duty to keep their wrath at bay. In many parts of the Muslim world, jinn have played a similar role (Reinhart 2020: 42).

A particularly instructive example is the relationship with local patron saints in mediaeval Europe. Especially in Iberia and around the Mediterranean, many communities entered into contractual relationships with patron saints, offering vows in exchange for collective protection (Wilson 1983: 21). These saints were frequently in competition with centrally recognized saints of the great tradition. All members of the corresponding social unit, whether a village, town, or guild, were obliged to contribute – often by making a monetary or other material contribution to festivals – as part of the collective vow (Sanchis 1983: 274). Anyone failing to do so could be sanctioned by having their rights as a member of the town or guild stripped of them, a punishment occasionally even enshrined in law (Christian 1981: 74). While supernatural punishment for failed vows was generally collective, at times it was said to single out those individuals who were responsible (Christian 1981: 55).

It is noteworthy too that patron saints were often appealed to for collective protection in battle against other groups, including against other Christians (Wilson 1983: 36–7). The Venetian Empire is a case in point, having made the physical acquisition of the remains of Saint Mark, and his subsequent role as a patron saint, a central part of its founding myth. Saint Mark offered protection to the Venetians, and his flag flew from their ships as a universally recognized brand. More importantly, Venetian sailors, as well as the doge, swore loyalty to him and answered to the battle cry "He who loves Saint Mark, follow me!" (Crowley 2011: 204). When doing battle against fellow Christians, for example, in their siege of Constantinople, symbols of the Christian great tradition would hardly have distinguished their loyalty. Here instead, their obligation to the saint was an obligation to one another – in this case, to fight and win battles as part of their compact with him.

Thus, both in the great traditions of ancient religions and in little traditions then and since, much supernatural punishment centered around the idea that a group would be punished as a result of individuals failing to make the necessary sacrificial contributions on its behalf. As with the neglect of maintenance of a dam or a collective commons, the ensuing calamities could be seen as the result of a moral failure on the part of either authority figures or community members. On these grounds, this can arguably be classified as a form of MSP. Moreover, it is a form of MSP with real consequences. In the first place, it provides an individual signal of commitment to the group. And insofar as contributions to collective welfare also spur others to commit themselves further, it may provide an indirect impetus for other forms of cooperation within the group.

It might be objected, however, that punishments meted out by morally unconcerned supernatural agents – who punish with no explicit intention of reprimanding people for their treatment of one another – cannot possibly be seen as moralizing, in the sense of being concerned with interpersonal obligations. That may be the case if our definition of MSP relies on the intentions of the supernatural agent. But we can apply the same argument to many great tradition doctrines. After all, in the Judeo-Christian tradition, we find statements to the effect that the trouble with murder is that it is a sin against God – in other words, as in the case of an improper sacrifice, God is displeased because His commands have been disobeyed (Krausmüller 2004). In the karmic tradition, there is no intention behind supernatural punishment, as karma is not a conscious agent. Intentionally violating moral precepts simply brings about punishment as if by the workings of a natural law (Harvey 2018). What these forms of MSP have in common is simply that supernatural punishment is caused by an act that happens to be a moral violation. The same holds true in the case of collective propitiatory obligations: failure to propitiate correctly is, de facto, a transgression against the community; thus, although the result is a punishment for incorrect propitiation, this punishment is also, de facto, a punishment for an interpersonal transgression.

Mystical harm beliefs
While collective propitiatory obligations posit supernatural harm from failure to meet obligations to a group, another body of little tradition beliefs posits harms arising from arousing the envy, spite, or unwanted attention of other members of the community. So-called mystical harm beliefs are beliefs in the capability of human individuals in the community to inflict harm on one another using supernatural means (Singh 2021). Examples include witches, sorcerers, werewolves, and the evil eye. Such beliefs have been documented in a wide range of human societies and appear close to being a human universal (Antweiler 2016: 215). Notably, mystical harm is often invoked as an explanation for medical problems, and practitioners of magic and related arts are often called upon to remedy such problems. In the context of doctrinal religions, mystical harm is almost always found squarely within little traditions – taught and transmitted alongside the great tradition, and within its cosmological framework, but not forming a part of orthodoxy.

On the face of it, mystical harm may appear to be unrelated to MSP. Some agents of mystical harm, such as werewolves, may appear to strike at random rather than to punish moral violators. Suspicion that others are witches may lead to social discord and conflict (Singh 2021). Rather than enforcing moral behavior, it may spark witch hunts, in which those seen as outcasts, undesirables, or simply convenient scapegoats are subjected to punishments that are anything but supernatural. Thus, while individuals may seek supernatural protection from mystical harm or magical remedies for it, on one view, these are simply practical, morally unconcerned measures.

But for a contrasting view, consider the example of the evil eye. The evil eye belief complex appears likely to have originated in ancient Egypt and Mesopotamia, and from there spread around the Mediterranean and as far as South Asia, and has persisted in some form to the present day (Elliott 2015). The belief suggests that in certain circumstances, the human gaze has the power to inflict harm and misfortune on others. In some forms of the belief, anyone can cast the evil eye, while in others, it belongs only to certain people, usually outcasts suspected of inflicting mystical harm on others (Herzfeld 1981). In general, however, it is involuntary, and incantations are often made or other precautions taken to avoid inadvertently casting it on others.

Typically, the danger of the evil eye is considered to be greatest when envy is involved. In order to avoid the evil eye, it is crucial to avoid showing off one's well-being to others, whether this be wealth, health, or healthy offspring. Arousing envy may result in supernatural harm even from those who have no intention of causing it. It has been argued that this developed as a way of suppressing conflict in unequal societies, encouraging those who gain more to avoid behaviors that might inflame tension (Gershman 2015). More broadly, ethnographic studies of envy, including in societies with evil eye beliefs, have suggested that fear of envy can function to drive prosocial behavior in a number of ways, including by instigating people to share envied objects with, or otherwise help, others around them. This appears particularly strong in the case of kin and neighbors; fear of envy is an ongoing regulator of social interaction within long-term relationships that may be fraught with tensions between cooperation and competition (Hughes 2020).

Why, though, the need for a supernatural punishment, rather than simply ordinary social norm enforcement? One answer is that it may not always be obvious that others are either disposed toward envy or capable of enforcing a mundane punishment for arousing it. Experimental work has suggested that fear of envy increases prosocial behavior but only toward those actually suspected of exhibiting envy (Van de Ven, Zeelenberg, and Pieters 2010). Belief in the evil eye as involuntary and possessed, or potentially possessed, by everyone may serve as a moral motivator even when others are not seen to have particularly envious personalities, or any other means to inflict punishment.

A second possible explanation is that the evil eye often serves to dissuade people from expressing or entertaining envy. In many societies, envy itself is considered a moral violation (Hughes 2020). Given the desire to avoid inflicting inadvertent mystical harm on others – and especially to avoid being branded as a wielder of the evil eye – it becomes particularly important to adhere to norms against the expression of envy. To cast the evil eye can, in other words, be seen as comprising a form of supernatural punishment for the person who casts it too.

But the evil eye can be taken to be much broader than simply a punishment for arousing and displaying envy. Clara Gallini (1973) argues that the evil eye should be understood, at least in some contexts, as falling on anyone who steps out of line with local social norms. That is, whether or not an emotion like jealousy is involved, those who visibly deviate from accepted behavior risk arousing the attention of others. This attention alone is enough to result in mystical harm. Disease, in particular, is then seen as a supernatural punishment for disturbing the social equilibrium by failing to live in the same way as others in one's surroundings (Marcogiuseppe 2018). The evil eye thus becomes a method of punishment for the violation of local social norms. These might be the sorts of violation that are too minor or too locally particular to have much interest for moralizing high gods. Nonetheless, supernatural consequences await those who dare to break these norms.

Similar arguments can be made for witches and other agents of mystical harm, who are often thought to prey on those who arouse their envy or spite, either by having conspicuous health or material well-being, or, again, simply by breaking local norms. Witches in the Christian tradition, for example, have been typically thought of as harming others through uncontrolled emotions of envy, pride, or spite, in a similar pattern to the evil eye (Ostling and Kounine 2016). These wrathful emotions were often thought to be aroused, in both witches and sorcerers, by the violation of interpersonal norms, such as by quarrelling or committing adultery (Kieckhefer 1976: 98–9). Beyond Christianity, the fear of witches and sorcerers as a fear of the consequences of arousing envy or spite is a common phenomenon, not only within the little traditions of doctrinal religions but in smaller-scale societies too. Witches are often perceived to be particularly likely to come from within one's own kin group, suggesting punishment for creating discord within these relationship networks (Koning 2013; Geschiere 2003).

It might be argued, of course, that norms against boasting, envy, and nonconformity with one's peers cannot really be thought of as moral. True, they are norms governing conduct toward other humans, and they have clear consequences for coexistence and cooperation. Nonetheless, "morality" may be taken to imply a higher, more universalistic form of concern with graver sorts of harm. There are, however, reasons to doubt that we can make such a clear-cut distinction between social and moral norms (Dubreuil and Grégoire 2013). Moreover, from an emic perspective, these sorts of concerns are often in fact the most salient in people's lives – the sort of morality necessary to avoid harm to long-standing, locally embedded relationships, in which predictability and dependability are key and envy and pride may be highly destructive.

Great versus little tradition MSP

Other chapters in this volume amply explore MSP in great traditions. But in light of the above observations, it is worth outlining some broad ways in which great tradition MSP and little tradition MSP tend to differ.

A frequent theme of great tradition morality, especially since the Axial Age, is supernatural punishment for the violation of universalistic rules. Unlike particularistic moral injunctions based on the specific character or history of a given interpersonal relationship, universalistic rules enable cooperation between those with no prior relationship history, and even those who lack a shared social network through which norms may be enforced by indirect reciprocity. Such rules have facilitated trade between strangers in far-flung locales, from Buddhist merchants spread across Central Asian trade routes to Muslim merchants plying the seas of the Indian Ocean and Southeast Asia. In practice, although rules may be textually formulated as universalistic, they tend to be interpreted as ingroup directed – either implicitly, when people favor interacting with coreligionists, or explicitly, when doctrine dehumanizes nonbelievers or otherwise exempts them from holding moral status (Bartholomeusz and de Silva 1998; Hanke 1994).

In addition to MSP as a result of actions toward other individuals – but in practice, largely toward coreligionists – great traditions have tended to propagate belief in MSP for another set of actions, namely, those directed at maintaining or propagating the religion itself. A central example of this is the notion of merit – that is, the ability to mitigate supernatural punishment or secure supernatural reward by making donations to religious institutions. Mediaeval Christianity awarded indulgences not only to those willing to perform devotional acts but also to those who donated to church institutions, proselytized, or went on crusades (Swanson 2007). Buddhism from ancient times to the present day has encouraged donations to the monkhood, with the claim that they would bear rich karmic rewards (Stanford, "Buddhism," Part II, Chapter 4, this volume).

Doctrinal religions are, by their nature, complex and expensive to maintain and propagate. They require organized bodies of religious experts, institutions capable of enforcing orthodoxy and orthopraxy, and often elaborate texts and groups of literate clergy capable of reading and interpreting such texts. It is no surprise, then, that doctrinal officialdom has tended to promote forms of MSP that serve to furnish the resources necessary for such religions to flourish. On the one hand, nominally universalistic morality promotes, in practice, ingroup-directed prosociality on a large scale, thus enabling the growth of vast imagined communities in which coreligionists benefit from complex and geographically dispersed forms of cooperation. On the other hand, supernatural rewards are offered for those who directly contribute resources to the institutional hierarchy itself, to attracting more followers, or to combatting competitors. Underpinning these ingroup-directed obligations are a variety of specific forms of MSP, from big gods to karma. What they seem to have in common is that they apply universally to any member of a religious community regardless of status; all such members are enjoined to cooperate with one another and to work for the benefit of the collective. Great tradition MSP revolves mainly around supporting this injunction.

In general, doctrinal religions have had equivocal relationships with their little traditions, and the MSP that has gone along with them. In Europe, the Reformation attempted to subsume local patron saints into a centralized Vatican system to avoid competition between loyalties – a measure that resulted, if anything, in the consolidation of local religion (Christian 1981: 201). Buddhism in both Theravada and Mahayana contexts allowed practitioners to continue with both ancestor worship and propitiation of local spirits – reframing both of these within a Buddhist cosmology. The focus, however, was on individual salvation through participation in the extended ingroup of Buddhists, not through local loyalties. Doctrinal religions tended not to stamp these local loyalties out but to avoid allowing them to trump allegiance to the wider religious community.

As for mystical harm, more often than not, doctrinal religions have not denied its reality but instead have attempted to dissuade followers from engaging in it and from seeking remedies for it outside the great tradition. The example of the evil eye is again instructive here. The eye is not denied, for example, by Islamic texts. Instead, the texts advise against seeking protection from the evil eye from little tradition magical practitioners, or indeed by working to avoid arousing the envy of others, for true protection can only be found by taking refuge in Islam (Qamar 2013). Similarly, mediaeval Christianity did not, on the whole, deny the reality of magic and witchcraft, but it condemned magical and other folk protections against mystical harm as a distraction from piety or as demonic, and enjoined Christians to seek protection from God instead (Kieckhefer 2014: 181). That is, doctrinal religions tend to accept that mystical harm beliefs are part of the fabric of practitioners' lives but attempt to divert their energies and allegiances away from local, particularistic remedies and toward a focus on great tradition alternatives for protection.

It is hardly surprising that great and little traditions have often had an uneasy relationship. Both allegiances to local spirits, saints, and demigods, and practices to avoid the evil eye or remedy witchcraft can be seen as threats to the loyalty of followers to the extended religious community. This is not only because such forms of religiosity may be seen as a distraction from orthodoxy but also because they appear to engender forms of moral concern that are local and particularistic, in contrast to the moral mission of doctrine to spur followers to contribute to the imagined community of coreligionists.

Yet in practice, little traditions tend to be tolerated. It is striking that even those doctrinal religions explicitly intent on denying or even replacing competing religions tend to allow their followers, albeit reluctantly, to continue partaking in little tradition religiosity. There is a range of plausibly complementary social and psychological explanations for the persistence of little traditions (Boyer 2019). But in light of the preceding discussion, it is worth highlighting one in particular: that is, it may be that the moral functions of little and great traditions are complementary (Stanford and Whitehouse 2021). Doctrinal religions grow and thrive by virtue of their ability to spur followers to invest resources in them. But local cooperation between kin and neighbors remains vital for the survival of followers. If local, particularistic moral engagements were replaced entirely by obligations to the extended ingroup, this might undermine the well-being of adherents. Thus, the success of doctrinal religions might be aided by reaching an accommodation with complementary forms of religiosity that sustain cooperation in local relationship networks.

Conclusion

Little traditions, by their very nature, exhibit a baffling variety of forms, including forms of supernatural punishment and reward. Nevertheless, this chapter has pointed to some recurring patterns. Collective propitiatory obligations, often read as amoral relations between devotees and gods, in fact often constitute moral obligations between members of a social group. Belief in mystical harm, whether or not it actually has the effect of promoting prosocial behavior, enforces another kind of local morality, punishing people for stepping out of line with local social norms or acting so as to arouse envy or destabilize relationship networks. Taken together, these two recurring themes suggest that little traditions may have a role in buttressing local, particularistic morality. By contrast, great tradition MSP typically focuses on cultivating loyalty to the extended ingroup of coreligionists, thus motivating followers to provide the resources necessary for that ingroup to thrive and spread. The tension between these two kinds of moral allegiance seems likely to be a key factor behind the overall tension within doctrinal religions between officially enforced beliefs and practices, and the complex forms of local, unofficial religiosity that consistently grow up around them.

References

Antweiler, Christoph. 2016. *Our Common Denominator: Human Universals Revisited.* New York: Berghahn Books. doi: 10.2307/j.ctvpj7h57.

Bartholomeusz, Tessa J., and Chandra R. de Silva. 1998. "Buddhist Fundamentalism and Identity in Sri Lanka." In *Buddhist Fundamentalism and Minority Identities in Sri Lanka*, edited by Tessa J Bartholomeusz and Chandra R. de Silva, 1–35. New York: SUNY Press.

Baum, Richard. 2004. "Ritual and Rationality: Religious Roots of the Bureaucratic State in Ancient China." *Social Evolution & History* 3 (1): 41–68.

Boehm, Christopher. 2008. "A Biocultural Evolutionary Explanation of Supernatural Sanctioning." In *The Evolution of Religion: Studies, Theories, & Critiques*, edited by Joseph Bulbulia, Richard Sosis, Erica Harris, Russell Genet, Cheryl Genet, and Karen Wyman, 143–52. Santa Margarita, CA: Collins Foundation Press.

Boyer, Pascal. 2019. "Informal Religious Activity Outside Hegemonic Religions: Wild Traditions and Their Relevance to Evolutionary Models." *Religion, Brain & Behavior.* doi: 10.1080/2153599X.2019.1678518.

Brac de la Perrière, Bénédicte, and Cristophe Munier-Gaillard. 2019. *Bobogyi: A Burmese Spiritual Figure*. Bangkok: River Books.

Byrne, Denis R. 2012. "Anti-Superstition: Campaigns against Popular Religion and Its Heritage in Asia." In *Routledge Handbook of Heritage in Asia*, edited by Patrick Daly and Tim Winter, 295–310. New York: Routledge.

Christian, William A. 1981. *Local Religion in Sixteenth-Century Spain*. Princeton, NJ: Princeton University Press. doi: 10.1515/9780691241906.

Crowley, Roger. 2011. *City of Fortune: How Venice Won and Lost a Naval Empire*. London: Faber & Faber.

Davis, Natalie Z. 1982. "From Popular Religion to Religious Cultures." In *Reformation Europe: A Guide to Research*, edited by Steven Ozment, 321–43. St. Louis, MO: Center for Reformation Research.

Dubreuil, Benoît, and Jean-François Grégoire. 2013. "Are Moral Norms Distinct from Social Norms? A Critical Assessment of Jon Elster and Cristina Bicchieri." *Theory and Decision* 75 (1): 137–52. doi: 10.1007/s11238-012-9342-3.

Dunbar, Robin. 2022. *How Religion Evolved and Why It Endures*. New York: Penguin Random House.

Elliott, John Hall. 2015. *Beware the Evil Eye: The Evil Eye in the Bible and the Ancient World*, vol. 1. Eugene, OR: Cascade Books.

Frankfurter, David. 2015. "The Great, the Little, and the Authoritative Tradition in Magic of the Ancient World." *Archiv Fur Religionsgeschichte* 16 (1): 11–30. doi: 10.1515/arege-2014-0004.

Gallini, Clara. 1973. *Dono e Malocchio*. Palermo: Flaccovio Editore.

Gershman, Boris. 2015. "The Economic Origins of the Evil Eye Belief." *Journal of Economic Behavior & Organization* 110: 119–44. doi: 10.1016/j.jebo.2014.12.002.

Geschiere, Peter. 2003. "Witchcraft as the Dark Side of Kinship: Dilemmas of Social Security in New Contexts." *Etnofoor* 16 (1): 43–61.

Goossaert, Vincent. 2005. "The Concept of Religion in China and the West." *Diogenes* 52 (1): 13–20. doi: 10.1177/0392192105050596.

Green, Dennis H. 1994. *Medieval Listening and Reading: The Primary Reception of German Literature 800–1300*. Cambridge. doi: 10.1017/CBO9780511518720.

Green, Richard Firth. 2016. *Elf Queens and Holy Friars: Fairy Beliefs and the Medieval Church*. Philadelphia, PA: University of Pennsylvania Press. doi: 10.9783/9780812293166.

Hanke, Lewis. 1994. *All Mankind Is One: A Study of the Disputation Between Bartolomé de Las Casas and Juan Ginés de Sepúlveda in 1550 on the Intellectual and Religious Capacity of the American Indians*. DeKalb, IL: Northern Illinois University Press.

Harvey, Peter. 2018. "Karma." In *Oxford Handbook of Buddhist Ethics*, edited by Daniel Cozort and James Mark Shields, 7–28. Oxford: Oxford University Press. doi: 10.1093/oxfordhb/9780198746140.013.14.

Herzfeld, Michael. 1981. "Meaning and Morality: A Semiotic Approach to Evil Eye Accusations in a Greek Village." *American Ethnologist* 8 (3): 560–74. doi: 10.1525/ae.1981.8.3.02a00090.

Hughes, Geoffrey. 2020. "Envious Ethnography and the Ethnography of Envy in Anthropology's 'Orient': Towards a Theory of Envy." *Ethos* 48 (2): 192–211. doi: 10.1111/etho.12275.

Josephson, Jason Ananda. 2006. "When Buddhism Became a Religion." *Japanese Journal of Religious Studies* 33 (1): 143–68. doi: 10.18874/jjrs.33.1.2006.143-168.

Kieckhefer, Richard. 1976. *European Witch Trials: Their Foundations in Popular and Learned Culture, 1300–1500*. Berkeley, CA: University of California Press. doi: 10.1525/9780520320581.

Kieckhefer, Richard. 2014. *Magic in the Middle Ages*. 2nd ed. Cambridge: Cambridge University Press. doi: 10.1017/CBO9781139923484.

Knapp, Robert. 2018. *The Dawn of Christianity: People and Gods in a Time of Magic and Miracles*. London: Profile Books. doi:10.4159/9780674981591.

Koning, Niek. 2013. "Witchcraft Beliefs and Witch Hunts: An Interdisciplinary Explanation." *Human Nature* 24 (2): 158–81. doi: 10.1007/s12110-013-9164-1.

Krausmüller, Dirk. 2004. "Killing at God's Command: Niketan Byzantios' Polemic against Islam and the Christian Tradition of Divinely Sanctioned Murder." *Journal of the Medieval Mediterranean* 16 (1): 163–76. doi: 10.1080/0950311042000202579.

Marcogiuseppe, Mariano. 2018. "La Parola Come Azione. Il Malocchio in una Comunità del Sud" [Word as action: The evil eye in a community of the South]. *Antrocom Online Journal of Anthropology* 14 (2): 27–38.

Marriot, McKim, ed. 1955. "Little Communities in an Indigenous Civilization." In *Village India: Studies in the Little Community*, 171–222. Chicago, IL: University of Chicago Press.

Mittermaier, Amira. 2008. "(Re)Imagining Space: Dreams and Saint Shrines in Egypt." In *Dimensions of Locality: Muslim Saints, Their Place and Space*, edited by Georg Stauth and Samuli Schielke, 47–66. Bielefeld: Transcript. doi: 10.1515/9783839409688-002.

Moin, A. Azfar, and Alan Strathern. 2022. "Sacred Kingship in World History: Between Immanence and Transcendence." In *Sacred Kingship in World History: Between Immanence and Transcendence*, edited by A. Azfar Moin and Alan Strathern, 18–65. New York: Columbia University Press. doi: 10.7312/moin20416.

Moore, Robert Ian. 1994. "Literacy and the Making of Heresy c. 1000–c. 1150." In *Heresy and Literacy, 1000–1530*, edited by Peter Biller and Anne Hudson. Cambridge: Morey.

Nordberg, Andreas. 2018. "Circular Flow of Tradition in Old Norse Religion." *Fornvännen* 113 (2): 76–88.

Norenzayan, Ara. 2013. *Big Gods: How Religion Transformed Cooperation and Conflict*. Oxford: Princeton University Press. doi: 10.1515/9781400848324.

Obeyesekere, Gananath. 1963. "The Great Tradition and the Little in the Perspective of Sinhalese Buddhism." *Journal of Asian Studies* 22 (2): 139–53. doi: 10.2307/2050008.

Ostling, Michael, and Laura Kounine. 2016. "Introduction: 'Unbridled Passion' and the History of Witchcraft." In *Emotions in the History of Witchcraft*, edited by Laura Kounine and Michael Ostling, 1–16. London: Palgrave Macmillan UK. doi: 10.1057/978-1-137-52903-9.

Parladir, Halil Saim. 2014. "When Folk Religion Meets Orthodoxy: The Case of Imam Birgivi." *Eskişehir Osmangazi Üniversitesi Sosyal Bilimler Dergisi* 15 (1): 65–86. doi: 10.17494/ogusbd.78921.

Qamar, Azher Hameed. 2013. "The Concept of the 'Evil' and the 'Evil Eye' in Islamic Faith-Healing Traditions." *Journal of Islamic Thought and Civilization* 3 (2): 44–53. doi: 10.32350/jitc.32.06.

Redfield, Robert. 1956. *Peasant Society and Culture: An Anthropological Approach to Civilization.* Chicago, IL: University of Chicago Press.

Reinhart, A. Kevin. 2020. *Lived Islam: Colloquial Religion in a Cosmopolitan Tradition.* Cambridge: Cambridge University Press. doi: 10.1017/9781108629263.

Richards, Janet. 2010. "Kingship and Legitimation." In *Egyptian Archaeology*, edited by Willeke Wendrich, 55–84. Chichester: Wiley-Blackwell.

Rüpke, Jörg. 2018. *Pantheon: A New History of Roman Religion.* Princeton, NJ: Princeton University Press. doi: 10.1515/9781400888856.

Sanchis, Pierre, ed. 1983. "The Portugese Romarias." In *Saints and Their Cults: Studies in Religious Sociology, Folklore and History*, edited by Stephen Wilson, 261–90. Cambridge: Cambridge University Press.

Scheid, John. 2007. "Sacrifices for Gods and Ancestors." In *A Companion to Roman Religion*, edited by Jörg Rüpke, 263–71. Chichester: Blackwell. doi: 10.1002/9780470690970.ch19.

Singh, Manvir. 2021. "Magic, Explanations, and Evil: The Origins and Design of Witches and Sorcerers." *Current Anthropology* 62 (1): 2–29. doi: 10.1086/713111.

Spiro, Melford E. 1978. *Burmese Supernaturalism.* Philadelphia, PA: Prentice Hall.

Stanford, Mark, and Jonathan Jong. 2019. "Beyond Buddhism and Animism: A Psychometric Test of the Structure of Burmese Theravada Buddhism." *Plos One* 14 (12): e0226414. doi: 10.1371/journal.pone.0226414.

Stanford, Mark, and Harvey Whitehouse. 2021. "Why Do Great and Little Traditions Coexist in the World's Doctrinal Religions?" *Religion, Brain & Behavior* 11 (3): 312–34. doi: 10.1080/2153599X.2021.1947357.

Swanson, R. N. 2007. *Indulgences in Late Medieval England: Passports to Paradise?* Cambridge: Cambridge University Press.

Van de Ven, Niels, Marcel Zeelenberg, and Rik Pieters. 2010. "Warding Off the Evil Eye: When the Fear of Being Envied Increases Prosocial Behavior." *Psychological Science* 21 (11): 1671–7. doi: 10.1177/0956797610385352.

Watkins, Carl. 2004. "'Folklore' and 'Popular Religion' in Britain During the Middle Ages." *Folklore* 115 (2): 140–50. doi: 10.1080/0015587042000231246.

Werthmann, Katja. 2008. "Islam on Both Sides: Religion and Locality in Western Burkina Faso." In *Dimensions of Locality: Muslim Saints, Their Place and Space*, edited by Georg Stauth and Samuli Schielke, 125–48. Transcript. doi: 10.1515/9783839409688-006.

Wilson, Stephen. 1983. "Introduction." In *Saints and Their Cults: Studies in Religious Sociology, Folklore and History*, edited by Stephen Wilson, 1–54. Cambridge: Cambridge University Press.

CHAPTER 3

Hebrew Bible Traditions
Jutta Jokiranta

The Hebrew Bible *as a book* is a late innovation and owes its origin at least to two processes: (1) the transition from scrolls to codices, which allowed a material sense of a larger fixed or semifixed collection (or within Rabbinic Judaism, also larger scrolls in which all five books of the Torah could fit) and (2) the gradual standardization or canonization of books written in Hebrew (and those translated into Greek). These processes took place in the first centuries of the common era. Before that, we may speak instead of traditions in Hebrew that circulated to varying degrees and in varying forms in Palestine in scroll form and in oral practices. Thus, there was no Hebrew Bible in the modern sense in ancient Israel or in Second Temple Judaism.

This does not mean that there were no authoritative collections or no sense of sacred texts. Scholars widely agree that the Torah, the law of Moses, first became known as an important collection in the Persian and/or Hellenistic period (Collins 2019: 367; Kazen 2019). In written form, *Torah* referred to five books of Moses but potentially also to other texts (such as Jubilees) among some groups. In oral form, *torah* (instruction, teaching) included the traditions of legal interpretation and may have meant different things to different groups. The symbolic significance of the law of Moses contributed to its status as an identity marker that most groups shared; yet they may have disagreed on its interpretation. The process by which the Torah became such an important factor in Judean religion began with the loss of the temple, king, and land in the Babylonian exile (sixth century BCE) and was connected to increased literacy, the rise of scribes, and the opportunity and need to construct a valid but unique identity in the Persian and Hellenistic world.

By speaking of the Hebrew Bible traditions in this chapter, I refer to those books and traditions that were later known from the Hebrew Bible. Most of those traditions as we know them were most probably written down after the exile, and after the disaster, changes were explained by some authors as a deserved divine punishment. Others saw the punishment as still ongoing – and focused on the temple rather than on the monarchy – or developed a periodized view of history where times of testing are set and also ended according to the divine plan.

In the following, we shall first consider to what extent the deity of the Hebrew traditions is moralizing. Then, the will of the moralizing deity is examined, first in explicit moral codes and later in nonlegal material. We shall also see how the nature of punishment and rewards is this-worldly. Finally, we discuss the relation of legal codes and conceptions of deities to moral norms and the distribution of the textual information.

Encounters with nonmoralizing deities

The Hebrew traditions testify to an evolving view of the deity from the Iron Age to the late Second Temple period. The contours of these views in each period are not easy to draw since the texts have been transmitted, collected, and edited through the centuries, while the layers are often difficult to discern and date with certainty. Often, we access the text in a late form from the Persian and Hellenistic periods. In any case, a full-blown idea of a morally interested and all-knowing deity was hardly a reality from the beginning (McClellan 2022).

There is no consensus regarding the earliest history of Yahweh, but it seems clear that the Canaanite attestation of the highest god El with a set of lower-tier gods in the pantheon was also characteristic of the belief system in Palestine (Smith 2001). The frequent occurrences of the name El, theophoric names with -el (Israel, Bethel, Samuel, etc.), and the remnants of the idea of the divine council are testimonies of this (Ps. 82; 1 Kings 22:19–23; Job 1–2). According to the motif of the divine council, an assembly could be gathered, led by the supreme deity, to decide on a current issue or dilemma and to authorize the chosen action (Laine and Jokiranta, 2024; White 2014). When El was the highest god, local gods such as Yahweh could be conceived as His sons. At some point in the early first millennium BCE, Yahweh became the patron deity of Israel. While very similar to the storm god Baal, Yahweh was portrayed as his arch enemy. Eventually, Yahweh was conflated with the high god El or the universalizing designation Elohim (Smith 2002: 32–43). In the process of identity formation, as relations to other nations were rhetorically formulated as polemics against their gods, the worship of foreign deities was strongly condemned as idolatry, and scribal practices occasionally hid the idea of the divine council in fear of recognition of other deities. For example, whereas Deuteronomy 32:8–9 contains the idea of the highest god dividing the earth among the peoples, each having their own god (and Israel being Yahweh's portion), later tradition (already testified by Greek translation in the Septuagint) changed the gods into angels or dissolved the role of other gods altogether (in the Masoretic tradition, the earth was divided according to the number of Israelites, not the sons of God). Angelic "messengers" were still considered legitimate agents in the formation of monolatrism in the seventh century BCE, which attempted to reserve worship by Israel to one God, Yahweh, and one cult place, Jerusalem. Yet the divine council was never fully demolished (as indicated by some evidence in the Dead Sea Scrolls – Ben-Dov 2016), nor were other cult places.

The earliest Hebrew Bible traditions, such as the Song of the Sea (Exod. 15) and Deborah's song (Judg. 5), do not contain an idea of a moralizing deity; rather, this is a deity of war and victory. The texts do reveal much about the limitations of such a deity: this is a tribal god or God of Israel. Not a universal god of all peoples, this god is interested only in one social entity (cf. Larson, Part I, Chapter 2, this volume). Such a nonmoralizing view of the deity occurs occasionally here and there in poetic and narrative texts. The Psalter has several psalms appealing for help or praising God without strong moral implications (e.g., Ps. 8, 20, 29, 30, 47, 61, 93, 104, 121, 147–50).[1] Some of these are dated early (e.g., royal Ps. 20, Zion Ps. 46, enthronement Ps. 47, creation Ps. 104), but not all of them are (e.g., postexilic Ps. 147; Day 2004). However, the majority of psalms construct a strong opposition between the righteous and the wicked, praise God for His help for the weak in society (e.g., Ps. 9, 10, 68, 116), or make a plea for those unjustly accused or persecuted (e.g., Ps. 4, 5, 35, 59, 82). The God of the Psalter is also prayed to for forgiveness of the singer's sins (e.g., Ps. 51). There is no clear chronological division separating morally colored psalms from "nonmoral" ones.

Moses first encountered Yahweh in a burning bush (Exod. 3) without any giving of the law, only a personal mission. Most likely, the Sinai tradition first included an idea of divine theophany, familiar from literary and visual motifs associating deities with high mountains (Ps. 68; Hab. 3; De Hulster 2014; Schmid 2019: 285) and a fiery appearance (cf. Isa. 6), without any association to the revelation of the laws (Edenburg 2019: 157–8). However, the Sinai tradition came to be associated with and remembered particularly for its lawgiving. Similarly, even if the traditions of primeval history (Gen. 1–11) and patriarchs (Gen. 12–50) do not contain a law-giving god, the creation stories represent the desired order of the cosmos, the conception of evil is already present in the flood story, and the patriarchal god gives both commands and promises.[1] In logical continuation, these stories were later reinterpreted from the perspective of laws as if it was a natural order of things or as if God's chosen people always knew the law. For example, the fact that God rested during the seventh day is presented as the motivation for keeping the Sabbath (Exod. 20:11), and according to Jubilees, Abraham already celebrated some of the festivals (Jub. 15:1). Yet there remains tension between the view that the law is revealed and the view that the law is natural and known by everyone.

Explicit moral codes

The earliest law collection in the Hebrew Bible is the Covenant Code (Exod. 21–23), from the beginning of the first millennium BCE. It was reinterpreted and complemented in the Deuteronomic law collection (Deut. 12–26) and further in the Holiness Code (Lev. 17–26). The Priestly Code (esp. Exod. 25–31, 35–40; Leviticus to Numbers) is another distinct collection. Traces of early sets of prohibitions concerning false oaths, murder, theft, and adultery can be found in the prophets (Hos. 4:2; Jer.

---

1   For application of creation and nature as interpretative lenses into biblical ethics, rather than God's salvific acts in history, see Hiebert (2007).

7:9), before the formation of the Decalogue (Exod. 20; Deut. 5), which was then attached to the Sinai traditions. The books of early prophets such as Amos and Hosea are important evidence of moral interests already in the time of the monarchy, not just during and after the exile. Legal texts are thus not primary to prophetic texts but sometimes the other way around (and legal collections themselves are not in unidirectional relationship to each other: Edenburg 2019: 166–9).

All the large law collections include concern for both *interpersonal relations* (e.g., treatment of slaves, widows, and strangers; compensating for injury; property matters; honesty) and *cultic matters* (e.g., worship and festivals), but the latter concern clearly grows stronger in later collections. The Covenant Code is largely made of conditional statements from everyday life, without divine involvement. The Deuteronomic code's innovation is the centralization of the Yahweh cult in Jerusalem (Deut. 12) – never fully successful but contributing to the central position of Jerusalem and Judean rule. This one-temple cult is then protected by other laws, such as condemning idolatry and false prophecy (Deut. 13, 17, 18), ruling about kosher food, tithes, priestly portions, and pilgrimage festivals (Deut. 14, 16, 18, 26), and defining the boundaries of Israel (Deut. 23). Family laws (Deut. 21–5) emphasize solidarity within Israel (Schmid 2019: 225), although it has to be remembered that the laws in general reflect a male perspective and show little interest in women, poor people, and non-Israelites (Anderson 2007). The Priestly laws focus on cultic matters (building of the sanctuary, rules on sacrifices), relevant at the time of the building of the Second Temple in the Persian period, whereas the Holiness Code, even more than the Deuteronomic code, mixes social concerns with cultic ones.

These collections become more understandable when they are viewed from the point of view of ancient Near Eastern covenant making and changing imperial settings. Most influentially, the book of Deuteronomy is seen to be modeled after Neo-Assyrian vassal treaties: absolute loyalty in the language of love is demanded from the vassal toward the ruler, the covenant's stipulations are documented, and curses and blessings seal the covenant (Römer 2007: 74–81; Weinfeld 1972). In applying this model, the Assyrian king is replaced by Yahweh: rather than worrying about empires, Israelites should worry about serving Yahweh. Instead of a king, God becomes the legislator (Schmid 2019: 166, 224). This idea is so influential that it also comes to frame the earlier Covenant Code (Schmid 2019: 225). The emergence of the so-called Deuteronomistic history (Deuteronomy, Joshua, Judges, 1 and 2 Samuel, 1 and 2 Kings) then documents Israel (and especially its leaders) as breaking this covenant and thus drawing upon itself the divine curses, the loss of land and exile – that is, it provides an explanation for the disaster that was experienced in the expansion of the Neo-Babylonian Empire, resulting in the destruction of the kingdom and the Jerusalem Temple in 586 BCE and the dispersion or deportation of part of the population.

There are also other covenant models. The Holiness Code draws upon the consecration of cities and their lands to a god who has a sanctuary in the city (Joosten 2019; Weinfeld 1995: 97–120). The divine territory is to be protected from all violations to sanctity and purity, and the inhabitants are divine property. In another model, during the Persian period, the covenant is a signed document where human parties commit to a set of detailed practices (Neh. 10), or it is a universal peace treaty (Gen. 9; Bautch and Knoppers 2015) or not a covenant at all but a "testimony" (Exod. 25:22; Cook 2019: 283–4). Different covenant traditions draw from different contextual, imperial and court models and send varying messages to their recipients. Some covenant models emphasize laws more than others, but once this association is made, "covenant" is almost taken as a synonym for legal and religious obligations, even if the divine–human relationship is also conceptualized with many other metaphors.

The nature of punishments

Haim Shapira (2011) argues that the Hebrew Bible testifies to two different schemes of judgment: "divine judgment," directly coming from God but performed by special actors, such as priests and prophets (often by special means such as lots or test of ordeal), and "human judgment," where God only authorizes the human judges (e.g., elders or the king) to act.

The divine judgment functions in the context of an immediate threat that has to be resolved. For example, those who challenge the leadership of someone sanctioned by the deity are punished by a sudden disease or death (e.g., the leprous Miryam in Num. 12; death of the rebellious Korah and others in Num. 16; death of the doubting spies of the land in Num. 14:36–8; death of Aaron's sons who carried the unholy fire in Lev. 10:1–2). If someone is considered the cause of a disaster, by violating a rule in a war context or cult, the guilty party is to be revealed by the casting of lots and punished (Josh. 7; 1 Sam. 14; Jonah 1:7). In the legal sphere, divine judgment functions also through oath taking: suspicion of a legal offense is cleared by taking an oath and submitting oneself to divine punishment in case one is lying (e.g., Exod. 22:6–10; 1 Kings 8:31–2). Suspicion of adultery by a woman is cleared through a complex ritual (Num. 5). Shapira (2011) also includes in this scheme important decisions like the appointment of a king (e.g., 1 Sam. 10). However, decision making does not involve a punishment, only divine/prophetic advice on how to proceed or whom to select for a task (e.g., Num. 27:5, 21; Lev. 16:8). All in all, the scheme of divine judgement draws upon magical efficacy: a natural event is explained as caused by supernatural agents, and such agents are believed to communicate through concrete material substances and artifacts such as the Urim and Thummim, which belonged to the priests and were tools for casting lots.

Shapira (2011) presents several cases that are in the process of moving from a divine judgment scheme to a human one: for example, in Leviticus 24:10–23, a man has blasphemed the divine name, and the case is brought to Moses. The decision is considered to be Yahweh's (Lev. 24:12), but it comes as a revelation of a new law to Moses (similarly, celebration of the Passover in case of impurity or travel, Num. 9:1–14; punishment of a Sabbath offense, Num. 15:32–6; inheritance of daughters, Num. 27:1–11).

By contrast, the fully developed human judgment is "rational" and exemplified in Deuteronomy. The judgment of legal offences and advice are outsourced by Moses to judges or elders (Deut. 1, 16:18 to 17:7); only the most difficult cases are solved by Moses (Deut. 1:17; cf. Exod. 18; Num. 11) and later by Levitical priests and the judge in Jerusalem (Deut. 17:8–13). Moses himself appoints the judges (Num. 11, however, portrays them as divinely inspired). Connection to the divine now comes through studying and preserving the law (Deut. 4–11); prophets are to be listened to, but their words need to be tested (Deut. 18:9–22), while prophets who support idolatry are always false prophets (Deut. 13). The king is also under the law and is not given the judge's role (Deut. 17:14–20) – which is understandable in the context where the kingdom is lost (cf. McClellan 2022: 175–93; elsewhere, texts reveal a close link between the king and judgment, e.g., 1 Sam. 8; 2 Sam. 14; 1 Kings 3 and 10).

How the human judges in principle punish individual offenses is hinted in a few cases (e.g., death penalty, Deut. 13:11, 24:7; "eye for an eye," Deut. 19:21; lashes, Deut. 25:2), but the problem of disobedience is not covered by such a judicial system. In the vassal treaty model of Deuteronomy, offenders of the covenant laws are cursed. The first, probably a later set of Levitical curses is in the third person ("Cursed be anyone who ...," Deut. 27:11–26), with an "Amen" response by the people. These curses present a somewhat random collection of offences in comparison to the laws just presented: they include some offences from the Decalogue and the Covenant Code, as well as some from the Holiness Code that are not present in the Deuteronomic collection (e.g., illicit sexual relations, Deut. 27:20–23; cf. Lev. 18); but the final curse seeks to be comprehensive: "Cursed be anyone who does not uphold the words of this law by observing them. All the people shall say, 'Amen!'" (Deut. 27:26; cf. Jer. 11:3).

In the second set of curses, the misfortunes resulting from the offences are listed in the second person ("Cursed are you / your ...," Deut. 28:15–19) and as a long list of Yahweh's punishments (e.g., "Yahweh will send upon you ...," Deut. 28:20–68). The list shows the nature of divine curses as "this-worldly"; they effect all kinds of disaster: physical and mental disease; war and loss of land, property, and family; and rupture in kin relations. Curses are depicted in the most sinister shades: mothers eat their own children due to hunger (Deut. 28:57), God takes pleasure in destroying His people (28:63), and not even the Egyptians will buy the Israelites as slaves (28:68).

Thus, Judah's exile and diaspora become one of the paradigmatic punishment schemes (2 Kings 25; Jer. 52): divine punishment is a *collective* and *historical* thing. But as strongly as these biblical authors blame the leaders and take the blame on themselves, they also envision a future restoration, judgment of foreign nations, and return to the land (Deut. 4:25–31). Restoration is possible when people know the law (Jer. 31).

By contrast, priestly texts conceptualize punishment differently (Schmid 2019: 153, 376). They may even claim that the punishment has already taken place in the past (in primeval history, the flood) and the covenant is unconditional and unbreakable. Yet in the Holiness Code, the promises are conditional, and punishment is cumulative: each disaster is sevenfold harder if the people will not learn their lesson (Lev. 26). The defiled land vomits out its inhabitants (Lev. 18:25; cf. 2 Chron. 36:21), and Yahweh abandons His temple (Ezek. 10). Restoration demands altogether a new creation (Ezek. 36–7) and a new temple (Ezek. 40–48), and salvation is judged on an individual basis (Ezek. 18 and 20:38, 33). It is easy to see why some Judeans thought this sort of restoration lay only in the future and saw their exile as extending far beyond the building of the Second Temple (Staples 2021).

It is clear that the majority of Hebrew Bible traditions do not entertain any idea of punishment in the afterlife. Losing the possibility of having future descendants and continuity of the family name is losing one's "afterlife."

The nature of rewards

Covenantal blessings in Deuteronomy 28:1–14 and Leviticus 26:3–13 are the opposite of curses: Israel will flourish, multiply, and defeat its enemies – and be the first among the nations. There is no otherworldly implication, only the idea of continuity and that by being blessed, Israel is a blessing to other nations (cf. the blessing of Abraham, Gen. 12:3). This idea is later expanded in the visions of a future Jerusalem to which other nations come to bring their riches (Isa. 60), enjoy a feast in the holy mountain (Isa. 25), and gain access to the temple (Isa. 56).

The few passages that speak of the dead coming to life may well be interpreted metaphorically or as a special reward for the few. The prophet Isaiah (Isa. 25) contrasts past dead leaders who do not rise again and whose memory is wiped out with the chosen people whom God has increased and made alive: people are only able to give birth to wind, but God re-creates the dead from the dust. The Book of Ecclesiastes rejects any speculation on the afterlife and turns attention to the joys of everyday life and fair conduct during one's lifetime.[2] The prophet Daniel (Dan. 12) acknowledges true teachers as stars (with semidivine status) and claims that "many" shall awake, some to everlasting life and some to everlasting shame and contempt. Apocalyptic literature, in which wise persons make heavenly travels, participate in

---

2 Compare also Ben Sira, which is partly preserved in Hebrew. Ancestors are praised but only for their legacy and name (Sir. 44); death is inevitable, and one should be concerned for one's name (Sir. 41); the dead should be mourned but then also allowed to rest in peace (Sir. 38:16–23).

heavenly worship, or spectate the divine throne (e.g., Dan. 7; 1 Enoch), contributed to ideas of God's mysterious, otherworldly kingdom. Later scenes of the final judgment (cf. Revelation; see Czachesz, Part II, Chapter 3, this volume) owe much to the genre where heavenly items and beings are portrayed around the divine throne (Isa. 6; Ezek. 1); even nonliving things such as temple structures are animated and praise God, as testified by some Dead Sea Scrolls (e.g., Songs of the Sabbath Sacrifice, 4Q400–407, 11Q17, Mas 1k).[3] This idea drew from a long-standing temple ideology: human participants have access to the divine via worship, and the cult represents the cosmos and everything there is to know about the world. Sacred space and the sphere of death do not belong together (Num. 19 explains the preparation of purificatory water, needed after contact with the dead). Few, if any, in ancient Israel denied Yahweh's power to bring the dead back to life (as Elijah brought back the widow's son, 1 Kings 17:17–24), but this was not expected for everyone. Yet very probably, ancient Israelites had intuitive beliefs about the dead continuing their life in some form, often referred to as the shadowy Sheol, and also testified by beliefs in necromancy (1 Sam. 28), but such beliefs were suppressed rather than encouraged by the biblical authors.

Implicit moral codes

A major part of the Hebrew Bible consists of texts other than explicit legal material. The extensive narrative corpus, prophetic books, wisdom traditions, and prayers also mediate moral principles and ideals, even if only implicitly and ambiguously (Barton 2003). Scholars have shown a growing interest in this as it is acknowledged that human moral intuitions are strongly connected to emotions and situational value judgments (Teehan 2010: 15–21), which are triggered in a different way by nonlegal material. Narrations present readers with moral dilemmas and the possibility of reflection (e.g., Lapsley 2007; Newsom 2021). Teaching of the two ways (e.g., Ps. 1) simplifies life into opposites and functions as a mirror to communities and individuals in their pursuit of the right path.

The ideology of sin and punishment did not go unchallenged. An alternative, more individualistic approach to the future emerged (Ezek. 18). The book of Job challenges the notion that individual misfortunes can simply be explained by that person's sins.

It must also be noted that if the great narrative of the Exodus is implicitly talking about the return from exile and the restoration of the future and the Deuteronomistic history was written after the monarchy was lost (and the Priestly rules about the tent of meeting were written in the interest of rebuilding the Jerusalem Temple),

---

3   For translations of the scrolls, see Vermes (2004). For introductions to various scrolls, their editions, and their genres, see Brooke and Hempel (2019).

then these narrations do not function as a paradigmatic warning of divine punishment or treatises of divine characteristics but rather offer psychological means to cope with the past, construct a new solid identity, and see hope in the future (cf. moralizing supernatural punishment and reward [MSP] as a retrospective idea in Larson, Part I, Chapter 2, this volume). The God of Israel is powerful and faithful, even though he allows His people to suffer. God saves before demanding any obedience. Later, these texts would be read differently; the popular image of the "vengeful God of the Old Testament" comes from ignoring and forgetting the context of these writings and from making a simplified and distorted contrast with the "merciful God of the New Testament" (cf. negativity bias, Johnson 2016: 24).

Different narrators also have a highly varying depiction of the deity. If MSP presupposes a full-access strategic agent (Teehan 2010: 64), that is, a god who knows even the thoughts and intentions of every person, then some narratives fall short of this expectation. Before the cult centralization, Yahweh could be worshiped in several places (e.g., 1 Sam 1:3), and local variations could be expected. Famously, the God of the Edenic paradise (Gen. 3) is depicted in human-like terms, walking in the garden and not knowing what His creation has done. It could be argued that the conversation between God and the human is needed for revealing the state of affairs and its consequences. The "punishment" for eating from the forbidden tree is an etiological explanation of why life is hard and painful, underlying the moral dimension of life as knowing good and evil. But elsewhere, other narrators think that God has to enter a place in order to know what has happened (Sodom in Gen. 18:21), that humans may negotiate with God (Jacob wrestling in Gen. 32), and that truth has to be revealed by human means (e.g., casting lots) rather than by direct divine revelation. Sometimes God scarcely reveals Himself, people do not know God at all (1 Sam. 3), and God may regret His choices (1 Sam. 15:11). Thus, God is not consistently depicted as an all-knowing and powerful deity whom humans always know to fear; God may withhold His punishment or punish collectives, God may contradict Himself and test people with immoral commands (Gen. 22), and God may wipe out all sins and punishment if He so chooses.

Relation to norms
Surely, the divine is the supreme king and judge (even though not a predictable one), according to the biblical authors. What effect then did this idea have in practice? To what extent did the divinely mediated and humanly interpreted laws function as norms in ancient Israel and later Second Temple society? What evidence do we have of beliefs in MSP?

First, we may note the flexible nature of the laws. Even when conceptualized as coming from God, the laws were always being reinterpreted. This is clear from the Hebrew Bible and continues in late Second Temple evidence: the Qumran movement and early Jesus movement largely debate a similar set of themes (the Sabbath, oaths, marriage, property, purity, false prophecy; cf. the Damascus Document; Matt. 5–7). According to the Deuteronomic authors, the law was not mysterious or hard (Deut. 30:11–14). Yet, on the basis of the Deuteronomic division between the hidden and the revealed (Deut. 29:28), there also emerged an idea (known at least from the Qumran movement and rabbinic Judaism) of a hidden law that was given to Moses and that wise persons could study and reveal. This idea enables continuous revelation. Therefore, not everything of the divine will was known, and this enabled scribes and teachers to transmit their views of the law or create new laws.

Second, moral and cultic laws always belonged together (cf. Larson, Part I, Chapter 2, this volume). Mosaic discourse became the trademark of piety and a good life. Even though there may have been disagreement between groups about legal interpretation, and scribal vs. priestly discourse may appear distinct, cultic interests and ethical interests were not separated. Some traditions reminded the people that the God who has set rules for proper sacrifices and cultic acts is the same God who demands social justice (e.g., Ps. 50; Isa. 58). Entering the temple is proclaimed to involve moral aspects, not only following cultic rules to safeguard the sancta, as in Psalm 24 (cf. Ps. 15):

Who shall ascend the hill of LORD?
And who shall stand in his holy place?
Those who have clean hands and pure hearts,
who do not lift up their souls to what is false,
and do not swear deceitfully. (Ps 24:3–4, NRSV)

Yet none of the prophets demanded abolition of the cult. Even the Qumran movement in the second and first centuries BCE, which was critical of the temple establishment and used the metaphorical language of the cult (the community as a temple, offering thanksgiving), looked forward to the proper restoration of the temple.

This brings us to the third point, that is, the limited function of laws within a particular social entity. Even if the God of Israel is seen to become a high god in the Hebrew scriptures and claims an exclusive position in Israel, and even among a wider population (ridiculing other nations' conceptions of gods, Isa. 44), the moral codes are for Israel to keep. Other nations too are punished, but mostly for their wickedness and brutality toward Israel and for defying the divine plan. Only a few visions of a future without war and conflict set these nations also under God's divine rule and instruction (Isa. 2:2–5; Mic. 4:1–5).

John Teehan (2010) shows how the Decalogue, the Ten Commandments, is based on and reveals human moral intuitions. He concludes,

The first four commandments serve the evolutionary goals of uniting the group into a moral community under the watch of a powerful and concerned deity, and of establishing signals of commitment to the moral bonds of society via commitment to that deity. Commandments six through ten shift our focus to the basic moral obligations to members of the community. (Teehan 2010: 92)

The demand for exclusive worship of Yahweh, and all its accompanying cultic rules, had an important function in creating a community and maintaining it through various means: coming together regularly during rituals, signaling commitment by paying careful attention to ritual rules (e.g., Sabbath, purity rules), having symbolic markers of identity (circumcision; the temple, Sabbath; dress; use of the divine name, etc.), acknowledging leaders (priests, scribes, teachers), and simply being a successful idea transmitted through the centuries.[4] Therefore, the MSP was not only about behavior in interpersonal relations outside the cult. The cultic rules as such demanded cooperation and trust, and likely contributed to the cohesiveness of communities throughout the times.

To what extent then were the moral codes known and functioning in Israel? The rule in Deuteronomy 31:9–12 to read the law in public every seventh year hardly suffices to teach the law to the entire people. Elsewhere, continuous teaching and education of children are emphasized (Deut. 6). The Dead Sea Scrolls provide important evidence of the implementation of the law and the distribution of ideas in writing. There was a continuous tradition of legal interpretation (*halakhah*). Most probably, the study and the interpretation of the law were restricted to the learned elite, but the ideal of instructing all the people, including women and children, continued in the regular (annual) covenant ceremonies (1QSa) as well as through prayers and worship. The figure of the wisdom teacher (*maskil*) represents a mediator between God and the people, whom members of the community could identify with or seek to emulate (Uusimäki 2017) – they did not need to (fully) know the law as they relied on their leaders to guide them. The Qumran movement consisted of small groups regularly coming together for meals, prayer, and counsel, resembling in many ways Greco-Roman association meetings and having the potential to function as fictive-kinship groups (cf. Martin 2016: 209). Even though later synagogue assemblies had various functions and recent research suggests the actual buildings only housed a limited number of people from the local community (Bonnie, Hakola, and Tervahauta 2020), Torah reading and study were to some extent associated with synagogues.

---

[4] The successful transmission of Yahweh's name is dependent on the people who worship Him: "For the LORD will not cast away his people, for his great name's sake, because it has pleased the LORD to make you a people for himself" (1 Sam. 12:22, New Revised Standard Version [NRSV]).

The earliest tefillin and mezuzot were discovered at Qumran; these are miniature scrolls following the rule of binding the laws to the hand and forehead (Deut. 6:8-9; Feldman 2022). Such artifacts function as a tangible reminder of the importance of the law. For most ancient Israelites, the monitoring deity was not present in statues, images, or a royal throne (the Ark of the Covenant) but in words and traditions, in ideas of his presence in the temple (cf. Cook 2019: 283), and in the ritual practices materializing the traditions.

Disciplinary measures are occasionally implied. The apostle Paul mentions having received lashes (2 Cor. 11:24).[5] The Qumran movement had a penal code for improper behavior in the assemblies and defiance of authorities, resulting in reductions of food and/or exclusion from decision making for a period of 10 days to two years (e.g., Community Rule, 1QS 6 and 7); for disobedience of Mosaic laws, the punishment was exclusion from the movement (1QS 9:1). Sin and disease were commonly linked, but at the same time, the afflictions of the righteous were conceived of as caused by evil spirits, according to the Two Spirits teaching (1QS 3:23). The movement was the recipient of blessings, and outsiders were the recipients of curses (1QS 2). Divine punishment turned into testing, and members could be sure of their salvation as long as they belonged to the (right) community.

In conclusion, the deity of Hebrew traditions evolves from a war and family deity to a national and cosmic deity but always preserves intimate ways of being in contact with his worshipers and has intermediaries who transmit his plan to his followers. He is capable of judging his people, but he may also choose not to; in several traditions, the deity is portrayed in very human terms. The deity is interested in keeping his name, and thus he must keep and support his followers even if they act against his will. The divine will is both revealed to and learned by the people. The law demands both social justice and careful attention to the cult and worship. Access to the cult depends, ideally, on social justice and contributes to the formation of the people and their distinct identity. Judgments are executed by extraordinary (supernatural) means, which are ministered by select humans, or by human representatives of the deity who study his laws. The idea of a collective punishment in exile is used as a means to define what is valuable in the future. Israel has a special responsibility, but the deity has power over both Israel and the nations.

---

5   The value of the mention is debated. Recently, Oehler (2021) argued that Paul received these lashes in the Judean or Galilean court. Roman officials may also have been involved in the execution of the sentence given by the Judean authorities.

References

Anderson, Cheryl B. 2007. "Biblical Laws: Challenging the Principles of Old Testament Ethics." In *Character Ethics and the Old Testament: Moral Dimensions of Scripture*, edited by M. Daniel Carroll R. and Jacqueline E. Lapsley, 37–49. Louisville, KY: Westminster John Knox Press.

Barton, John. 2003. *Understanding Old Testament Ethics: Approaches and Explorations*. Louisville, KY: Westminster John Knox Press.

Bautch, Richard J., and Gary N. Knoppers, eds. 2015. *Covenant in the Persian Period: From Genesis to Chronicles*. Winona Lake, IN: Eisenbrauns. doi: 10.1515/9781575063577.

Ben-Dov, Jonathan. 2016. "The Resurrection of the Divine Assembly and the Divine Title El in the Dead Sea Scrolls." In *Submerged Literature in Ancient Greek Culture*, vol. 3. *The Comparative Perspective*, edited by Andrea Ercolani and Manuela Giordano, 9–31. Berlin: De Gruyter. doi: 10.1515/9783110428650-003.

Bonnie, Rick, Raimo Hakola, and Ulla Tervahauta, eds. 2020. *The Synagogue in Ancient Palestine: Current Issues and Emerging Trends*. Göttingen: Vandenhoeck & Ruprecht. doi: 10.13109/9783666522147.

Brooke, George J., and Charlotte Hempel, eds. 2019. *T&T Clark Companion to the Dead Sea Scrolls*. London: T&T Clark. doi: 10.5040/9780567669858.

Collins, John J. 2019. "The Law in the Late Second Temple Period." In *The Oxford Handbook of Biblical Law*, edited by Pamela Barmash, 367–82. Oxford: Oxford University Press. doi: 10.1093/oxfordhb/9780199392667.013.20.

Cook, Stephen L. 2019. "The Law and the Prophets." In *The Oxford Handbook of Biblical Law*, edited by Pamela Barmash, 275–88. Oxford: Oxford University Press. doi: 10.1093/oxfordhb/9780199392667.013.2.

Day, John. 2004. "How Many Pre-exilic Psalms Are There?" In *In Search of Pre-exilic Israel*, edited by John Day, 225–50. London: T&T Clark.

De Hulster, Izaak J. 2014. "A God of the Mountains? An Iconographic Perspective on the Aramean Argument in 1 Kings 20:23." In *Image, Text, Exegesis: Iconographic Interpretation and the Hebrew Bible*, edited by Izaak J. de Hulster and Joel M. LeMon, 226–50. London: Bloomsbury.

Edenburg, Cynthia. 2019. "The Book of the Covenant." In *The Oxford Handbook of Biblical Law*, edited by Pamela Barmash, 157–75. Oxford: Oxford University Press. doi: 10.1093/oxfordhb/9780199392667.013.14.

Feldman, Ariel. 2022. *Tefillin and Mezuzot from Qumran: New Readings and Interpretations*. Berlin: De Gruyter. doi: 10.1515/9783110725377.

Hiebert, Theodore. 2007. "Beyond Heilsgesichte." In *Character Ethics and the Old Testament: Moral Dimensions of Scripture*, edited by M. Daniel Carroll R. and Jacqueline E. Lapsley, 3–10. Louisville, KY: Westminster John Knox Press.

Johnson, Dominic. 2016. *God Is Watching You: How the Fear of God Makes Us Human*. New York: Oxford University Press.

Joosten, Jan. 2019. "Covenant." In *The Oxford Handbook of Biblical Law*, edited by Pamela Barmash, 7–18. Oxford: Oxford University Press. doi: 10.1093/oxfordhb/9780199392667.013.19.

Kazen, Thomas. 2019. "The Role of Law in the Formation of the Pentateuch and the Canon." In *The Oxford Handbook of Biblical Law*, edited by Pamela Barmash, 257–74. Oxford: Oxford University Press. doi: 10.1093/oxfordhb/9780199392667.013.29.

Laine, Lauri, and Jutta Jokiranta, 2024. "The Divine Council in Light of Cultural Evolution: Why Should Ancient Near Eastern Scholars Care about Evolution?" In *Changes in Sacred Texts and Traditions: Methodological Encounters and Debates*, edited by Martti Nissinen and Jutta Jokiranta, 365–408. Atlanta, GA: SBL Press.

Lapsley, Jacqueline E. 2007. "A Feeling for God: Emotions and Moral Formation in Ezekiel 24:15–27." In *Character Ethics and the Old Testament: Moral Dimensions of Scripture*, edited by M. Daniel Carroll R. and Jacqueline E. Lapsley, 93–102. Louisville, KY: Westminster John Knox Press.

Martin, Luther H. 2016. "Great Expectations for Ara Norenzayan's Big Gods." In *Conversations and Controversies in the Scientific Study of Religion: Collaborative and Co-authored Essays by Luther H. Martin and Donald Wiebe*, edited by Luther H. Martin and Donald Wiebe, 206–218. Leiden: Brill. doi: 10.1163/9789004310452.

McClellan, Daniel O. 2022. *Yhwh's Divine Images: A Cognitive Approach*. Atlanta, GA: SBL Press.

Newsom, Carol A. 2021. *The Spirit within Me: Self and Agency in Ancient Israel and Second Temple Judaism*. New Haven, CT: Yale University Press. doi: 10.12987/yale/9780300208689.001.0001.

Oehler, Markus. 2021. "The Punishment of Thirty-Nine Lashes (2 Corinthians 11:24) and the Place of Paul in Judaism." *Journal of Biblical Literature* 140 (3): 623–40. doi: 10.15699/jbl.1403.2021.9.

Römer, Thomas. 2007. *The So-Called Deuteronomistic History: A Sociological, Historical and Literary Introduction*. London: T&T Clark.

Schmid, Konrad. 2019. *A Historical Theology of the Hebrew Bible*. Translated by Peter Altmann. Grand Rapids, MI: Eerdmans.

Shapira, Haim. 2011. "'For the Judgement Is God's': Human Judgment and Divine Justice in the Hebrew Bible and in Jewish Tradition." *Journal of Law and Religion* 27 (2): 273–328. doi: 10.1017/S0748081400000400.

Smith, Mark S. 2001. *The Origins of Biblical Monotheism: Israel's Polytheistic Background and the Ugaritic Texts*. New York: Oxford University Press. doi: 10.1093/019513480X.001.0001.

Smith, Mark S. 2002. *The Early History of God: Yahweh and the Other Deities in Ancient Israel*. 2nd ed. Grand Rapids, MI: Eerdmans.

Staples, Jason A. 2021. *The Idea of Israel in Second Temple Judaism: A New Theory of People, Exile, and Israelite Identity*. Cambridge: Cambridge University Press. doi: 10.1017/9781108906524.

Teehan, John. 2010. *In the Name of God: The Evolutionary Origins of Religious Ethics and Violence*. Malden, MA: Wiley-Blackwell. doi: 10.1002/9781444320695

Uusimäki, Elisa. 2017. "Maskil among the Hellenistic Jewish Sages." *Journal of Ancient Judaism* 8 (1): 42–68. doi: 10.30965/21967954-00801004.

Vermes, Géza. 2004. *The Complete Dead Sea Scrolls in English*. Rev. ed. London: Penguin Books.

Weinfeld, Moshe. 1972. *Deuteronomy and Deuteronomic School*. Oxford: Oxford University Press.

Weinfeld, Moshe. 1995. *Social Justice in Ancient Israel and the Ancient Near East.* Jerusalem: Hebrew University Magnes Press.

White, Ellen. 2014. *Yahweh's Council: Its Structure and Membership.* Tübingen: Mohr Siebeck.

Chapter 4

"We Don't Want to Hear Any More About Jesus": Christian Expansion and Immanentist Indifference
Jenny Reddish

In his fascinating book *Don't Sleep, There Are Snakes* (2008), the ex-missionary Daniel Everett described how his efforts to introduce the Pirahã people of the Brazilian rainforest to the Christian gospel failed miserably. He had come to bring the good news: a man named Jesus Christ had died for their sins; he would give them everlasting life if they believed in him and were truly sorry for what they had done wrong.

Everett studied the Pirahã language intensively, created a recording of the Gospel of Mark in Pirahã, and shared it with his hosts using hand-cranked cassette players. But although they understood the translation, the tapes had "little or no spiritual influence" (Everett 2008: 269). Nor did his heartfelt account of his own conversion. The Pirahã did not "want Jesus" because neither they nor anyone they knew (including Everett) had personally met him. "The Pirahã were not in the market for a new worldview. And they could defend their own just fine; … no Pirahãs are known to have 'converted' at any period of their history" (Everett 2008: 269).

As Everett came to realize, for the Pirahã, Christianity was a solution to a nonexistent problem. "There was no sense of sin among the Pirahãs, no need to 'fix' mankind or even themselves" (Everett 2008: 271). They "did not feel lost, so they didn't feel a need to be 'saved' either" (Everett 2008: 270). The book is a reverse conversion narrative: seeing that these people were content without Jesus, Everett eventually lost his faith. He left the missionary life and became a linguistic anthropologist instead. He argued that certain features of the Pirahã language (e.g., lack of numbers and color terms, absence of subordinate clauses) and culture (e.g., lack of creation myths and of "individual or collective memory of more than two generations past") show that many characteristics we think of as human universals are in fact culturally constrained (Everett 2005).

According to Everett, then, this society has much to teach us about the sheer diversity of human experience, which should caution us against making sweeping generalizations about language, religion, or ritual. Partly through his efforts, the Pirahã have become poster children for the benefits of life untainted by religion. In 2009, Everett gave a speech at the Freedom from Religion Foundation's annual conference, titled "The Pirahã: People Who Define Happiness without God" (Everett

2010). It was picked up by Richard Dawkins on Twitter, who called the Pirahã a "happy, trouble-free, worry-free, religion-free Amazonian tribe."[6]

I am not a linguist and so cannot comment on the debate about universal grammar, and I have never spoken to a Pirahã person, whereas Everett has spent years of his life living among them. However, their response to his missionizing – in effect, a shrug – struck me as not particularly atypical, seen in cross-cultural perspective. Indifference to moralizing religion – including expressions of irritation and ridicule – crops up in a wide variety of sources describing encounters between Christian missionaries and those whose religious traditions do not prioritize interpersonal morality enforced by supernatural agents or forces. For short, I will refer to the latter traditions as "nonmoralizing religions" (NMR). However, it is worth emphasizing at the outset that this does not imply that the *culture* is unconcerned with morality, only that an abstract system of moralizing supernatural punishment and reward (MSP) is absent.

In this chapter, I juxtapose sources written by Christian missionaries in regions beyond Amazonia with what Everett tells us about the Pirahã. I focus on the activities of Jesuits in seventeenth-century eastern North America, especially their work among the Innu people (also called Montagnais or Naskapi); and on the encounters of nineteenth- and twentieth-century Protestant missionaries with Australian Aboriginal groups.

Texts written by missionaries suffer from significant biases. The authors' aims were generally to drum up support and funds for their cause, or to justify their activities, rather than to present an accurate picture of the host society. On the other hand, arriving at a realistic and nuanced understanding of local religion was sometimes thought essential to conversion efforts – especially for Jesuits, whose detailed accounts of Indigenous lives and worldviews in the *Jesuit Relations* (Thwaites 1906) have been read as an early form of ethnography (Rubiés 2017; True 2015). Given the diversity of motivations and rhetorical strategies behind these missionary writings, it is striking how often they mention broadly similar types of reluctance, and similar arguments and responses from the NMR practitioners they tried to convert. The commonalities in these reactions to Christianity highlight what is unusual about it – especially its focus on MSP and its "transcendentalist" character, discussed below – and how it differs from NMR. Seen in this light, the Pirahã appear not as lone atheists or materialists but as people practicing a form of religion that has much in common with other traditions in Amazonia and beyond.

---

6   Richard Dawkins (@RichardDawkins), Twitter, July 30, 2015, https://mobile.twitter.com/richarddawkins/status/626675206799663104.

You want us to live like Americans

When Everett had been living in one Pirahã village on and off for over a year, a man named Kóhoi told him,

> The Pirahãs know that you left your family and your own land to come here and live with us. We know that you do this to tell us about Jesus. You want us to live like Americans. But the Pirahãs do not want to live like Americans. We like to drink. We like more than one woman. We don't want Jesus. But we like you. You can stay with us. But we don't want to hear any more about Jesus. OK? (Everett 2008: 246)

Everett's own former missionary organization, the Summer Institute of Linguistics, takes a relatively hands-off approach. Officially, it relies on translations of the Bible to spread the Christian message and avoids active preaching or attempts to change local cultural practices.[1] But evidently, Kóhoi had had previous experience of missionaries who tried to make the Pirahã "live like Americans," insisting on monogamous marriage and sobriety.

This is a common sticking point for attempts to spread Christianity: the objection to "moralizing" in the everyday sense of the term, without reference to supernatural reward and punishment. Often it is not the doctrines of sin and salvation, or the narrative of Jesus' sacrifice that are at issue, but the imposition of new styles of clothing, etiquette, family structures, material culture, and subsistence.

In the seventeenth century, French Jesuits arrived in New France with a package of ideas about what was needed to make good Christians out of the Innu (Montagnais-Naskapi), Haudenosaunee (Iroquois), Wendat (Huron), and other Indigenous groups. It was not enough for converts to accept the tenets of Christianity and receive baptism. Jesuits also "called for ordered settlement, the uprooting of superstition, the reformation of the family, and the close regulation of individual behavior, or *civilité*" (Goddard 1998: 219–20).

While the Wendat lived in palisaded agricultural villages as French peasants did, and so seemed to be good candidates for a speedy conversion, the Innu and other Algonquian-speaking groups were nomadic forager-hunters (Anderson 2010: 128). At that time, they were selling furs from the northern forests to French traders in exchange for iron tools, dried food, and clothes (Leacock 1980). This lifestyle was seen as incompatible with Christianity. The Jesuit Paul Le Jeune wrote in a letter in 1638

---

1 A page on their website (as of October 2022) includes the following statement: "SIL's service with ethnolinguistic minority communities is motivated by the belief that all people are created in the image of God, and that languages and cultures are part of the richness of God's creation" (https://www.sil.org/about/discover). Not everyone has been convinced: Hartch (2006) describes political controversies over their work with Indigenous communities in Mexico.

that he and his fellow missionaries were "trying to fix the wandering Savages," that is, inducing them to settle and cultivate the land. This strategy was a "divine trap" to snare Indigenous souls for Christ (JR 14:127).² Elsewhere, he lamented, "Alas! If someone could stop the wanderings of the Savages, and give authority to one of them to rule the others, we would see them converted and civilized in a short time" (JR 12:126). The Jesuits also attempted to change Innu family structures, insisting on monogamy in place of polygyny and "sexual freedom after marriage" (Leacock 1980: 30–35).

In other words, as a prerequisite for conversion, the Innu had to become sedentary farmers, accept formal political hierarchies, and replace their polygamous and flexible living arrangements (Leacock 1980: 30–35) with something resembling a European family unit. These demands came up against Innu reluctance. There were many obstacles to becoming farmers like the Wendat: threats from Haudenosaunee raiders armed with European guns, for instance, as well as lack of storage facilities. They laughed at Le Jeune for suggesting that they store food instead of eating it all at once in communal feasts, which were "one of their great devotions" (JR 6:139). Innu women as well as men were at first displeased with his diatribes against polygyny:

> Since I have been preaching among them that a man should not have more than one wife, I have not been well received by the women; for, since they are more numerous than the men, if a man can only marry one of them, the others will have to suffer. Therefore this doctrine is not according to their liking (JR 12:165).

In Aboriginal Australia, Protestant missionaries of the late nineteenth and early twentieth centuries had similar concerns. They placed great emphasis on "industriousness" as a Christian virtue (Mitchell 2004). Ernest Gribble (1868–1957), an Australian-born Anglican reverend and devotee of an austere, "muscular" Christianity, took over the mission at Yarrabah, Queensland, from his father in 1893 (Halse 2006). The task of the Yarrabah mission was "the elevation and the evangelization of the Aboriginals by preaching the Gospel, and by teaching them habits of industry," he wrote (cited in Loos 1975: 48). Aboriginal people from various Queensland groups (Gunggandji, Yidindji, Wanjuru, etc.) were settled, sometimes forcibly, at Yarrabah (Halse 2006; Queensland Government n.d.). They slept in dormitories, wore uniforms and were subjected to Gribble's authoritarian discipline (including corporal punishment). They worked for free on the mission or for poor wages on nearby sugar and coffee plantations. All Indigenous forms of ceremony – burial and marriage rites, male initiation – as well as polygamous practices had to be abandoned (Halse 1996:

---

2 JR refers to the Jesuit Relations (Thwaites 1906).

224, 231–2). Of course, this strategy generated discontent. Many residents left, either permanently or to carry out traditional rites of passage and join corroborees (sacred dances), activities incompatible with Gribble's form of Christianity (Halse 1996: 232).

Gribble was a highly authoritarian missionary even by the standards of his time. Not all Australian missions sought to be total institutions in the mold of Yarrabah (which had its own law court, fire brigade, and cricket club). For instance, Presbyterian missions in Central Australia generally refrained from trying to change Indigenous customs (Edwards 2005: 134–5). But as in eastern North America in the early modern period, the pushback that Christian missionaries in Australia encountered may have been more to do with their insistence on sweeping changes in lifestyle than with the content of the Gospels. Indeed, in the early decades of the Yarrabah mission, many of those baptized could speak little English, and Gribble, unlike the French Jesuits, made no attempt to learn the local languages (Halse 1996: 232). Some converts may not have fully understood the belief system to which they were outwardly committing. In an article on missions in British Columbia and Southwest Australia, Brock (2000: 171) summarizes the missionaries' position: "Christianity could not be attained until the Indigenous peoples wore European clothes, lived in nuclear, monogamous families, worked regular hours and received wages."

Why did the agents of Christian expansion sometimes insist on changes in cultural practices that arguably had little to do with the core moral values of their faith? (Marriage is a borderline case: Christian moral norms as they had developed over the centuries certainly frowned on polygamy. In Corinthians 7, Paul says that it is better to remain celibate, but failing that, marriage between one man and one woman is the next best thing).

It is relevant to point out here that moralizing religions of all stripes have often spread hand in hand with imperial expansion, colonization, and state consolidation: Buddhism with the Mauryan Empire, Christianity with Rome, Islam with the conquests beginning after the death of Muhammad. This cozy relationship continued long after the religions had first emerged. For example, although winning souls for Christ was the stated aim of the French Jesuit presence in North America, they were also unashamedly partisan in their support of French rather than British colonization in the region. Bronwen McShea (2019: 256) argues that they were "apostles of French empire, not simply of the kingdom of Christ they strove to populate with Native American souls." Historically, Catholic orders including the Jesuits as well as the Franciscans, Dominicans, and Augustinians received funding and tax breaks from the Spanish crown for their missions in the New World. In return, they were to help produce Europeanized, sedentary, taxable subjects (Merrill 1993: 129). Buddhism has sometimes played a similar role. Keyes (1971: 562–6) describes the Thammacarik program instigated by the Thai state in the 1960s. Increasingly concerned about security in the border areas where animist groups such as the Karen and Hmong lived, the government sent Buddhist monks to spread the dharma among them. According to the architect of the policy, Pradit Disawat (cited in Keyes 1971: 562),

> the propagation of Buddhism among the different tribal groups would be likely to advance administrative and development goals among the tribal people because the integration of our people into a large community depends upon the ties of custom and religion.

From this angle, some missionaries' insistence on changes in customs is not a counterproductive obsession incidental to the work of evangelizing but an integral part of the colonial project of producing more tractable populations. This meant settled farmers rather than mobile foragers. It sometimes meant literacy, a new work ethic, and integration into a monetary economy. Indigenous marriage practices and living arrangements were to be abandoned in favor of nuclear families headed by a *paterfamilias*. This is not the only way in which moralizing religious traditions have historically gained adherents, however. Wherever they have spread largely via informal networks of merchants and scholars, as Islam did in the medieval western Sahel, the imported religion adapted more flexibly to local kinship structures and subsistence practices. The North African Muslim traveler Ibn Battuta was shocked to find women freely associating with unrelated men among Muslims south of the Sahara. But as one scholar in the town of Walata (in the Mali Empire) reassured him, "The association of women with men is agreeable to us and a part of good conduct, to which no suspicion attaches" (Dunn 2012: 299–300).

In cases of strong overlap between colonization and missionization, resistance to moralizing religion may be read as resistance not (only) to systems of MSP but to the "civilizing" processes by which states and empires attempt to absorb new populations. As we have seen, the Pirahã were not alone in their reluctance to undergo such a transformation. But is this the only sticking point when moralizing religions seek to expand? What about their doctrines and ethical systems: how are they received by practitioners of NMR?

A useless and foolish tale?

The Pirahã, Everett reports, were not interested in his tales of a far-off Heaven and a man who lived 2,000 years ago. When he tried to "bear witness," explaining how accepting Jesus as his personal savior had transformed his life, they merely laughed. He puts this response down to the "immediacy of experience principle," which he believes constrains Pirahã language and culture: topics of speech are restricted to the concrete experiences of the interlocutors or of someone who was alive at the time of speaking (Everett 2005: 622). (This claim has been challenged on linguistic grounds by Nevins, Pesetsky, and Rodrigues 2009.)

Responses like this are not confined to a particular corner of the Amazon; they are also reported from Australia, Polynesia, and Indigenous North America, for instance. Time and again in Christian missionary accounts, we find missionaries trying to redirect attention away from the ordinary appetites, desires, and satisfactions of human life and toward a "future state." From sources where a dialogue between a missionary and the missionized population is recounted (albeit filtered through the missionary's perspective), we can gain an impression of how this was received. There is often a two-pronged response: skepticism toward the truth claims of the moralizing religion and a reassertion of the value of this life, with its feasting, ceremonies, warfare, and other arenas for action.

In seventeenth-century New France, French Jesuits struggled to translate the concepts of the fall of man, sin, and salvation through Christ into the Innu language (Goddard 1998: 229). In a passage quoted by Goddard, Le Jeune wrote of an Innu woman he was trying to convert:

> My only trouble was to make her feel sorrow for her sins. The *sauvages* have not this word "sin" in their language, though they certainly have it in their customs. The word for wickedness and malice, among them, means a violation of purity, as they have told me. So I was puzzled to know how to make her understand sorrow at having offended God. (JR 6:137)

The lack of a distinction between interpersonal offenses and transgressions against ritual purity aligns well with what we know about other NMRs. More generally, it seems that this woman, like her fellow Innu and like the Pirahã, did not experience the world of everyday existence as inherently "fallen" or unsatisfactory. Here's Everett, musing during his furlough from the Amazon:

> I thought again of the challenge of the missionary: to convince a happy, satisfied people that they are lost and need Jesus as their personal savior. My evangelism professor at Biola University, Dr. Curtis Mitchell, used to say, "You've gotta get 'em lost before you can get 'em saved." If people don't perceive a serious lack of some sort in their lives, they are less likely to embrace new beliefs, especially about God and salvation. (Everett 2008: 266)

This may explain why the prospect of judgment after death and the potential for eternal life in Heaven did not always have the desired effect in early modern New France. One of the most interesting relationships Le Jeune formed among the Innu was with a man called Carigonan, whom he called "the Sorcerer" – to the Innu, a *manitousiou*, a kind of ritual specialist (JR 7:67). The two clashed repeatedly, and Le Jeune wrote that he was a "very wicked man" (JR 7:201–209). But the *Jesuit Relations* also speak to a mutual curiosity and openness. Carigonan insisted that Le Jeune spend a winter with him, and Le Jeune set down some of the "conversations I had with him when we were enjoying a truce" (JR 7:209).

> The Sorcerer asked me if I really did love the other life, that I had described as so full of all blessings; having replied that I did, indeed, love it, "And I," said he, "I hate it, for to go there one must die, and that is something I have no desire to do; and yet if I thought and believed that this life was miserable, and that the other was full of delights, I would kill myself, to be freed from the one and to enjoy the other." I answered that God forbade us to kill ourselves, or to kill any one else, and if we destroyed ourselves we would go down into a life of misery, for having acted contrary to his commands. "Oh well," said he, "thou needst not kill thyself; but I will kill thee, to please thee, that thou mayest go to Heaven, and enjoy the pleasures that thou tellest about." I smiled, and replied to him that I could not without sin agree to have my life taken. "I see plainly," said he, sneeringly, "that thou hast not yet the desire to die any more than I have." "None," said I, "to bring about my own death." (JR 7:85–6)

In this exchange, which verges on the comic, Carigonan appears to be calling Le Jeune's bluff. Could the black-robed foreign shaman really believe what he was preaching – that the feasts, hunting, and games of this life were nothing compared to the bliss that awaited the true Christian after death? In this case, Carigonan was unconvinced. Elsewhere, Le Jeune complained that though the Innu were quite willing to discuss biblical teachings and asked him many questions (Will people be married after the resurrection? Will animals also be revived? Where did you get the Bible from?), his answers had no visible emotional impact. "They are as cold as marble, and are so imbued with this indifference that you would say they are surprised at nothing" (JR 11:209). In contrast, they took great joy in eating together and in lavish hospitality to guests (including the Jesuits).

> When they are eating something that they are very fond of, you will hear them say from time to time ... *tapoué nimitison*, "I am really eating," as if any one doubted it. This is the great proof that they offer of the pleasure they experience at your feast. (JR 6:147)

What about Aboriginal Australia? Ian Keen writes in "Australian Aboriginal Religions and Morality" (Volume Two),

> Aboriginal religions are refreshingly free from a concept of sin, in terms of an offence against God, for which an individual may be divinely judged and punished,

and of the concept of original sin from which humankind as a whole need to be "saved."

As a rule, for Aboriginal cultures ethical behavior – meeting obligations to kin, being generous, performing certain ceremonies – means following ancestral precedent, set down in the long, long ago (and yet still present) time of the Dreaming. This orientation made the work of Christian missionaries challenging.

In 1891, a German Moravian (i.e., Protestant) missionary named Nicholas Hey landed in northern Queensland and established a mission for the local Tjungundji people (Ludewig 2020). It was named Mapoon. Aside from the task the Mapoon evangelists set themselves of reforming Aboriginal lifeways – patently the work of Satan in Hey's view (Loos 1975: 48) – introducing Christian universalizing morality and ideas about the afterlife was not a simple matter. Hey tried to "impart a sense of guilt or sin, which is quite foreign to the native mind. They could not see that there was anything wrong in themselves" (Bowles 2007: 215). Describing the early missions in northern Queensland as a whole, Loos (1975: 50–51) writes,

> Initially there was a rejection of Christian ideology and morality. It was thought to be irrelevant to the Aborigines. Indeed, the white man's religion often produced scorn and hostility. Thus, at Bloomfield [another German Moravian mission], the Aborigines were astonished that the Ten Commandments were meant for all human beings.

Evangelizing led to some roughly comparable reactions in the arid zone. In 1877, missionaries from the Hermannsburg Mission Society, a German Lutheran organization, arrived on the Finke River in Central Australia (Schmiechen 1971: 69). There they attempted to convert the Arrernte (also known as Aranda) people. The response was initially tepid. Schmiechen (1971: 79) summarizes the Lutherans' difficulties in terms that recall the Jesuits' complaints on a different continent several centuries earlier:

> Every heathen on the station was supposed to take part in [the church] services, however, the only ones who usually attended were those receiving food. Those attending showed a definite indifference to the proceedings and the missionaries remarked bitterly that all the Aborigines' efforts were directed towards their stomachs. Life after death did not interest them and they knew no difference between Heaven and Hell. In any case these were initiates perfect in Aboriginal law and they had no sense of sin or salvation; they were reincarnations of dream time heroes, men whose spiritual desires were all fulfilled, men reconciled with death.

The missionaries became discouraged by the Aborigines' continued indifference to their preachings, and it seemed to them that the adults sat in church as if in a dream.

According to Aram Yengoyan (1993), an anthropologist who did fieldwork with the Pitjantjatjara people of the Western Desert, attempts by Presbyterians (based at the Ernabella mission) to convert them in the mid-twentieth century were largely unsuccessful. The Christian message had no relevance in the context of Indigenous social life and religion. "For the Pitjantjatjara, salvation, damnation, and the future of each person are non-issues" (Yengoyan 1993: 248). It was the deep ancestral past – the source of moral law, ceremonies, and the landforms seen today – that was the focus of communal religious activity, not the prospect of eternal life for the individual. (Yengoyan's interpretation has been challenged, however, as we'll see below.)

But the clearest expression of the two-pronged response (affirmation of the value of this-worldly existence plus skepticism toward talk of Heaven and postmortem judgment) I have seen is quoted by Alan Strathern in *Unearthly Powers* (2019: 36). It comes from nineteenth-century Tahiti.

> The Welsh missionary John Davies in Tahiti found that even when working among people terribly afflicted by the new diseases brought by the English ships, they were irritated by talk of the next world and "would say we want no other salvation but to live in this world." "They cannot be persuaded that as to them, there is anything to be feared, or hoped for beyond the present life. Salvation from sin and its consequences is utterly despised. It is what they look upon as a useless and foolish tale."

Transcendence, immanence, and MSP

It is easy to understand why those who met missionaries hell-bent on civilizing them would be reluctant to move to new, ordered settlements, learn to read and write, or give up ceremonial feasts or initiation rites. The unimpressed response of many NMR practitioners to the moralizing doctrines and eschatology of Christianity, however, needs a bit more thinking through. If missionaries were "selling" an afterlife of eternal bliss, why were the Arrernte and Queensland Aboriginal groups, the Innu in New France, the Tahitians, and others so reluctant to buy it?

Here is where Strathern's theoretical framework comes in handy. As Larson notes in Part I, Chapter 2, this volume, our rough division of religious traditions into moralizing and nonmoralizing overlaps substantially, though not perfectly, with Strathern's distinction between "transcendentalist" and "immanentist" forms of religion. The proselytizing religions that emerged in Eurasia from about 1000 BCE onward are both transcendentalist and moralizing. They posit a realm or dimension that is above and beyond the ordinary plane of human life. For Christians, this is Heaven, or the kingdom of God, while for the karmic traditions that originated in South Asia, nirvana or moksha is the release from the endless cycle of birth, suffering, and death. In general, there is a moral valorization of the transcendent realm, while the mundane sphere is characterized by suffering, sin, and transience. The ultimate goal of human life is salvation from this-worldly suffering, which is accessible at least partly through adherence to a universalized code of interpersonal ethics. That said, acting in ethically sanctioned ways is never a sure route to liberation. The tension between good works and faith or grace as roads to salvation runs throughout the history of Christianity (see Czachesz, Part II, Chapter 3, this volume). In Buddhism the accumulation of karmic merit through generous and compassionate action is not in itself sufficient to achieve liberation.

By contrast, Strathern's immanentist religions align with our definition of NMR in that "metapersons (and their relations with persons) are defined by power rather than ethics" and the purpose of religion is not to achieve salvation but "to access supernatural power for the flourishing of existence in the here and now" (Strathern 2019: 36–7). Gods and spirits are fellow persons in a network of mutual obligations, not infallible supervisors of human behavior.

In immanentist systems, there is no stark divide between earth and Heaven. The divine, or the numinous, suffuses the human social world and the surrounding environment, though it may be particularly potent or concentrated in certain people, animals, objects, or places. Precontact Polynesians, for instance, might have agreed with the pre-Socratic philosopher Thales that "everything is full of gods" (gods in this case being roughly equivalent to *atua* or *akua*). For seventeenth-century (and later) Innu, game animals, weather phenomena, and celestial bodies were all animate. "They believe[d] that the hail has understanding and knowledge," scoffed Le Jeune (JR 6:89).

What the Jesuits in North America and various missionaries in Australia took to be an unseemly obsession with food and hunting was not hard-headed materialism or a focus on the belly above all else. Rather, hunting, eating, and disposing properly of the remains were in themselves "religious" acts, modes of interaction with metapersons. The anthropologist Frank Speck spent several years in the early twentieth-century with the Innu of the Labrador Peninsula, the cultural descendants of those who had received Le Jeune. He observed that "to them hunting is a holy occupation" (Speck 1977: 72) and the game feast was akin to a "ceremonial religious assembly," for the bear, caribou, and beaver have souls just as humans do (Speck 1977: 206). Many Australian Aboriginal societies have traditionally performed rites to ensure the abundance of food species (Keen, "Australian Aboriginal Religions and Morality," Volume Two). Among the Arrernte of Central Australia in the early twentieth century, the missionary-ethnographer Carl Strehlow saw that, when done in the proper way, hunting and gathering, food preparation, and eating were all in some sense sacred activities because they had originated with the ancestors (Kenny

2013: 147–8). Marshall Sahlins (2022) gives many more examples of the sacrality of food production and consumption in what he calls "enspirited societies," which overlap to a large extent with Strathern's immanentist ones, and have generally practiced NMR. For instance, at the great feasts of the Araweté of the Middle Xingu, the living share their food and maize beer with the gods and the dead (Viveiros de Castro 1992: 126, cited in Sahlins 2022: 61). In the Trobriand Islands of the Western Pacific, food is laid out on platforms for the *baloma* spirits. They consume the "shadow" of the offerings and leave their life-giving saliva behind as residue. The food is now charged with divine power, which it transmits to the humans who eat it (Mosko 2017: 180, cited in Sahlins 2022: 63–4). Eating is a religious act, a way to consume the gods. (The parallels with the Eucharist are irresistible, but Christian missionaries have rarely been willing to concede the similarity.)

In terms of morality, it is not that the cultures we have been discussing here are not concerned with what researchers of cultural evolution call prosocial behavior. On the contrary, they all had (or have) complex and nuanced ethical systems. For Aboriginal Australians, as a general rule, "the totemic ancestors bestowed 'law' – the precepts and practices that shaped human social life – on the people who followed them" (Keen, "Australian Aboriginal Religions and Morality," Volume Two). A "good" person is generous, supports kinsmen in disputes, and is not unduly quarrelsome. The *Jesuit Relations* are brimming with observations of Indigenous behavioral norms, and in some respects – for instance in generosity, hospitality, and patience – Le Jeune admitted that the conduct of the "*sauvages*" was preferable to that of Europeans back home (JR 6:103–4). And of course, Everett found that the Pirahã did not need the threat of divine punishment or the promise of salvation to make them cooperative and peaceful. Rather, what is absent from the cosmologies of immanentist religions is a *generalized* sense of sin or unsatisfactoriness that applies to the visible, tangible world as a whole. The world is not experienced as fallen. What need for a transcendent paradise then?

When compared not with doctrinal, universalizing, moralizing religions but with other immanentist societies, the Pirahã's response to Christianity starts to look far less unusual. Their skepticism ("Have you met Jesus?") is consonant with that of the Innu who asked Le Jeune where he had got the Bible from or the Arrernte folk who were unmoved by Lutheran preaching in the late nineteenth century. Although Everett was converted to atheism by his experiences, the Pirahã worldview is very different from that of a European or North American nonbeliever. According to the ethnographer Marco Antonio Gonçalves (2018), they have a multitiered cosmology populated by various metapersons, including a demiurgic figure, Igagai, and the transformed spirits of the dead. Shamanic ritual involves entering into relations with these other kinds of being. In these respects, they resemble other Amazonian groups (Nevins, Pesetsky, and Rodrigues 2009). It is not that they have no religion, only that they are not Christians or Muslims, or adherents of any of the other moralizing religions that emerged in Eurasia during the last millennium BCE and first millennium CE. From a cross-cultural perspective, as many chapters in this volume show, it's quite possible to lack systematic MSP, to be the "ultimate empiricists," as Everett described them (Barkham 2008), and still engage in religious activity.

Overcoming indifference

There is a looming problem here. Although the Pirahã and some other Amazonian cultures to this day have not converted to Christianity, they are in the minority. Over the *longue durée*, moralizing, transcendent religions have proved remarkably successful and durable, spreading from their origin points in Eurasia across the globe, so that (according to the Pew-Templeton Global Religious Futures Project) around 78% of people worldwide professed one of them in 2020.[3]

Small-scale societies are not immune to the appeal of these religions. Among some New Guinean groups, Christianization has been both rapid and profound, transforming both collective religious life and individual subjectivity. Joel Robbins describes how the Urapmin of the remote highlands underwent an enthusiastic Christian revival beginning in 1977, triggered by charismatic movements spreading from the Solomon Islands.

> They quickly began to see themselves as sinners, and to call out in various rituals to ask the Holy Spirit for help addressing the moral problems their sinfulness caused. … In short, they almost immediately came to construe their lives in the terms of a recognizably Christian culture. (Robbins 2004: 2)

The Innu of eastern Canada and the Arrernte of Australia both eventually adopted the new religion as their own, shaping it to fit Indigenous ways of life. Innu people today are mostly Catholic, some very devout, although older beliefs and rituals connected with animal masters and forest spirits persist (Armitage 1992; Tanner 2021). In the 1990s, the Lutheran Arrernte people at Hermannsburg, where Diane Austin-Broos did fieldwork, spoke of "two laws": Arrernte law and God's law (Austin-Broos 1996). Though these were sometimes in tension with each other, they were both necessary, as one woman explained:

---

3   This figure comes from data available at http://globalreligiousfutures.org/explorer (accessible if you create an account at https://www.pewresearch.org/profile/registration/) and includes Christians, Muslims, Jews, Buddhists, and Hindus. The Global Religious Futures Project's "other religions" category includes some other moralizing religions, for example, Jainism and Zoroastrianism. However, the combined proportion of those belonging to this category is under 1% of the world population.

We keep the stories. That's Aranda law. We know they're not true, but they tell us where we are on the land. We need them to tell us where we are on the land. God's law is a proper one but he doesn't say anything about country. (Austin-Broos 1996: 11)

Above, I mentioned Yengoyan's (1993) chapter on the Pitjantjatjara resistance to Christianity. He argued that because the Pitjantjatjara were oriented toward communal religious life rather than individual salvation, and toward ancestral time rather than future prospects, the incoming religion was fundamentally incompatible. It would be ignored as long as the Pitjantjatjara ritual life and social structure remained intact. Yengoyan claimed that those Aboriginal groups that had retained their traditional kinship structures and initiation rites, like the Warlpiri, saw no need for Christian salvation while others that had been more exposed to "social dislocation" converted in greater numbers.

But Bill Edwards, a missionary who lived among the Pitjantjatjara for some years, tells a different story. By 1980, he writes, around 500 Pitjantjatjara adults had been baptized, out of a population of c. 1,600 (Edwards 2005: 139). Many continued to practice traditional rites, such as initiation, but the Presbyterian missionaries had never demanded that converts give them up. The importance of Christianity continued to grow in the 1970s and 1980s, influenced by pan-Aboriginal movements like the Aboriginal Evangelical Fellowship (Edwards 2005: 140–43). Yengoyan's stress on the fundamental incompatibility of Indigenous Australian worldviews with Christianity is also hard to square with the success of early Aboriginal evangelists like Blind Moses Tjalkabota (d. 1954) and Nathaniel Pepper (c. 1841–1877) (Edwards 2005: 130).

Yengoyan (1993) appears to have overstated his case and understated the dynamism of Pitjantjatjara culture. However, his point about social dislocation may still stand. A strong link between moralizing, transcendentalist religious movements and the disruption of preexisting sociopolitical structures is supported both by anecdotal evidence from the ethnographic and historic record and by our quantitative comparative analysis. For instance, the Innu and Wendat who hosted the Jesuits in the seventeenth century became more receptive to Christianity as their societies suffered increasingly from smallpox and measles epidemics, armed conflict with the Haudenosaunee, and encroachment from settlers (Goddard 1998: 229–330). The moralizing and ascetic *śramaṇic* movements of Iron Age India, including Buddhism and Jainism, emerged from a context of endemic conflict between many small-scale city-states, republics, and kingdoms (Armstrong 2006: 232–44). And the results of a regression analysis using data collected in the Seshat Databank (Turchin et al. 2022) point to intense interpolity competition – entailing high levels of violence and insecurity – as a driving factor behind the emergence or adoption of moralizing religion.

Such outcomes illustrate the darker side of Everett's old professor's maxim: "You've gotta get 'em lost before you can get 'em saved."

In the carrot and stick of conversion to moralizing religions, this is the stick. As we have seen, despite missionaries' expectations, the promise of liberation or eternal life does not make a particularly good carrot – at least at first. Again, Strathern's (2019) work provides a helpful way of thinking about the inducements to convert to moralizing (or transcendentalist) religions. He points out that wherever these traditions expand into regions where immanentism is the only form of religion, they must first make themselves understood in immanentist terms (Strathern 2019: 219). Unless missionaries prove themselves "more effective at providing prosperity, healing, or victory" (Strathern 2019: 219) than local ritual specialists, the response will be lukewarm or unpredictable. If the "stick" condition – sociopolitical crisis – is present without the carrot, new forms of ritual and devotion to alternative metapersons may emerge. However, there is no guarantee that this will take a form pleasing to the missionaries.

The Jesuits in North America were well aware of this problem. They saw that their deathbed baptisms were interpreted by some Innu and other Indigenous Americans as a potent yet ambivalent rite, with the power to heal or to kill (Morrison 1990: 420). Their writings reveal that they were conflicted about how to respond: promise that baptism would deliver the desired results or insist that the state of the eternal soul was more important than earthly experience? In one case described by Le Jeune in the *Jesuit Relations* (JR 5:231), Father Jean de Brébeuf hedged his bets, offering purification of soul and body. He visited an Innu cabin where a child was ill with fever. The boy's grandmother said that she would agree to have him baptized if de Brébeuf could promise to cure him. This prompted a miniature sermon, delivered via an interpreter:

> You care only for the body ... we care for the soul, which is purified by this Sacrament. ... Baptism always cures the soul, and does no harm to the body, but on the contrary often restores it to health.

On hearing this, the parents agreed to the rite. Le Jeune and another priest returned to the cabin the next day, only to find that the family had engaged a respected manitousiou to perform a healing ceremony. The missionaries had to wait while the "charlatan" used dance, percussive music, and breath to bring down the fever. This was repeated a few days later, and in the meantime, the child recovered – attributed by Le Jeune, of course, to the mildness of the illness rather than the manitousiou's ministrations. He complained,

If I continue this business, the mothers will soon regard me as the little children's physician, for they already come to me with their ailments, but we have a much higher calling; they think only of the body, and we of the soul. (JR 5:237)

The Jesuit Relations contain many similar accounts, showing that the Jesuits understood the economy of ritual efficacy very well. In this case, both carrot and stick were present and reinforced each other: the novel pathogens brought by colonial contact had unleashed devastating epidemics on the Innu and others, throwing the existing ritual system into jeopardy (Morrison 1990: 417). Similar push–pull dynamics are evident in Strathern's (2019: 275–80) discussion of conversion in nineteenth-century Oceania.

In summary, at least two ingredients appear to be necessary for the conversion of NMR practitioners to Christianity: significant sociopolitical disruption and the ability of missionaries to demonstrate that their own God is more powerful than any metapersons venerated within the existing ritual system. Without both these conditions in place, indifference and irritation – "We don't want to hear any more about Jesus" – is a frequent response, and moralizing doctrines struggle to take root.

Conclusions

This chapter has focused on the reception of Christianity: a religion that is both strongly moralizing and transcendentalist, and whose expansion has tended to accompany empire building by European powers, especially since 1500.

There are certainly cases in which adherents to various forms of NMR, or immanentist traditions, resisted Christianity vehemently. In historical cases where proselytization of "heathens" took the form of violent conquest, such as the Polish crusades into pagan Pomerania in the twelfth century (Kling 2020: 169–70), the main mode of resistance was military. But barring cases of conversion at the point of the sword, I suggest that the response was usually more mixed. Missionaries' attempts to bring about far-reaching changes in lifestyle naturally met with resistance. These efforts were, whether consciously or not, part of a civilizing mission, a process of extending state power over new populations. It is interesting to note that where the Christian message was shorn of its extradoctrinal "baggage" – the new, restrictive clothes, the nuclear family, the increased workload – vigorous indigenized forms of it have emerged.

Matters of doctrine and worldview, including abstract systems of MSP, judgment after death, and a cleft between the mundane and the transcendent realm, are often initially received with polite indifference or curiosity tinged with mockery. The early nineteenth-century Tahitians wanted "no other salvation but to live in this world." As the subsequent history of Tahiti shows, this indifference is not a lasting disposition, or evidence of the inherent incompatibility of Indigenous societies with moralizing religions like Christianity. It is only one type of response, or one phase in a longer process of religious accommodation and conversion. That said, it appears to be a rather common one where Christianity expands into immanentist territory.

It would also be interesting to explore whether moralizing religions other than Christianity – Zoroastrianism, Manichaeism, Islam, Buddhism, and so on – have elicited similar responses. The karmic traditions approach preexisting gods, spirits, and rituals in a different way from the Abrahamic monotheisms. To generalize, instead of denouncing the veneration of immanentist metapersons, Buddhism incorporates them into its cosmology (e.g., fierce, wrathful deities become guardians of the dharma: Bailey 2022; Lewis 2000: 109–18). Does this strategy also butt up against immanentist indifference? Maybe so, but it may also be the case that this indifference poses less of an obstacle to the spread of religions that do not require people to give up practices and beliefs seen as idolatrous.

We began this chapter with a discussion of Everett's failure to convert the Pirahã. Due to certain features of their language and culture, the Pirahã have come to be seen as a cautionary tale against claims for the universality of any cultural or linguistic trait. But seen from a cross-cultural vantage point, their lack of interest in Everett's evangelizing is not unique. They are not "religion-free" (Dawkins's term) if we define religion broadly as forms of interaction with metapersons. Christianity has faced similar obstacles wherever it has expanded into societies practicing immanentist religions without systematized MSP.

Cross-cultural comparisons suggest that two factors increase the likelihood of conversion to Christianity by followers of NMR. The "stick" of sociopolitical disintegration (e.g., catastrophic defeat in warfare, deadly epidemics) throws preexisting modes of relating to metapersons into question. The "carrot" is the demonstration of Christianity's superior ritual efficacy, that is, its ability to provide this-worldly benefits. It appears that neither was present during Everett's stay with the Pirahã. Without them, neither Everett's communication of Christian doctrine via translations of the Gospel nor previous missionaries' attempts to introduce social mores thought more appropriate to Christians (e.g., monogamy and abstemiousness) succeeded. This does not make Pirahã culture an anomaly. On the contrary, their response helps reveal common patterns in how encounters between moralizing religions and NMR unfold.

References

Anderson, Emma. 2010. "Blood, Fire, and 'Baptism': Three Perspectives on the Death of Jean De Brébeuf, Seventeenth-Century Jesuit 'Martyr.'" In *Native Americans, Christianity, and the Reshaping of the American Religious Landscape*, edited by Joel W. Martin and Mark A. Nicholas, 125–58. Chapel Hill, NC: University of North Carolina Press. doi: 10.5149/9780807899663_martin.10.

Armitage, Peter. 1992. "Religious Ideology among the Innu of Eastern Quebec and Labrador." *Religiologiques* 6: 63–110.

Armstrong, Karen. 2006. *The Great Transformation: The Beginning of Our Religious Traditions.* New York: Knopf.

Austin-Broos, Diane J. 1996. "'Two Laws,' Ontologies, Histories: Ways of Being Aranda Today." *Australian Journal of Anthropology* 7 (3): 1–20. doi: 10.1111/j.1835-9310.1996.tb00334.x.

Bailey, Cameron. 2022. "Guardian and Protector Deities in Tibetan Buddhism." In *Oxford Research Encyclopedia of Religion.* doi: 10.1093/acrefore/9780199340378.013.1045.

Barkham, Patrick. 2008. "The Power of Speech." *The Guardian.* November 10, 2008. Accessed April 20, 2024. https://www.theguardian.com/world/2008/nov/10/daniel-everett-amazon. doi: 10.1016/S0262-1762(08)70232-3.

Bowles, Devin. 2007. "Sinful Enough for Jesus: Guilt and Christianisation at Mapoon, Queensland." In *Transgressions: Critical Australian Indigenous Histories*, edited by Ingereth Macfarlane and Mark Hannah, 211–29. Canberra: ANU E Press. doi: 10.22459/T.12.2007.10.

Brock, Peggy. 2000. "Mission Encounters in the Colonial World: British Columbia and South-West Australia." *Journal of Religious History* 24 (2): 159–79. doi: 10.1111/1467-9809.00107.

Dunn, Ross E. 2012. *The Adventures of Ibn Battuta: A Muslim Traveler of the Fourteenth Century.* Berkeley, CA: University of California Press. doi: 10.1525/9780520951617.

Edwards, Bill. 2005. "Tjurkurpa Palya – The Good Word: Pitjantjatjara Responses to Christianity." In *Indigenous Peoples and Religious Change*, edited by Peggy Brock, 129–53. Leiden: Brill. doi: 10.1163/9789047405559_008.

Everett, Daniel L. 2005. "Cultural Constraints on Grammar and Cognition in Pirahã." *Current Anthropology* 46 (4): 621–46. doi: 10.1086/431525.

Everett, Daniel L. 2008. *Don't Sleep, There Are Snakes: Life and Language in the Amazonian Jungle.* New York: Vintage Departures.

Everett, Daniel L. 2010. "The Pirahã: People Who Define Happiness without God." *Freethought Today* 27 (3). Accessed April 20, 2024. https://ffrf.org/about/getting-acquainted/item/13492-the-pirahae-people-who-define-happiness-without-god.

Goddard, Peter A. 1998. "Converting the 'Sauvage': Jesuit and Montagnais in Seventeenth-Century New France." *The Catholic Historical Review* 84 (2): 219–39. doi: 10.1353/cat.1998.0069.

Gonçalves, Marco Antonio. 2018. "Pirahã." *Povos Indígenas No Brasil.* Accessed April 20, 2024. https://pib.socioambiental.org/pt/Povo:Pirah%C3%A3.

Halse, Christine. 1996. "The Reverend Ernest Gribble: A Successful Missionary?" In *Lectures on North Queensland History*, no. 5, edited by B. J. Dalton, 218–47. Townsville: James Cook University.

Halse, Christine. 2006. "Gribble, Ernest Richard Bulmer (Ernie) (1868–1957)." In *Australian Dictionary of Biography.* Canberra: National Centre of Biography, Australian National University. Accessed April 20, 2024. https://adb.anu.edu.au/biography/gribble-ernest-richard-bulmer-ernie-10367.

Hartch, Todd. 2006. *Missionaries of the State: The Summer Institute of Linguistics, State Formation, and Indigenous Mexico, 1935–1985.* Tuscaloosa, AL: University of Alabama Press.

Kenny, Anna. 2013. *The Aranda's Pepa: An Introduction to Carl Strehlow's Masterpiece Die Aranda – Und Loritja-Stämme in Zentral-Australien (1907–1920)*. Canberra: ANU E Press. Accessed April 20, 2024. https://www.jstor.org/stable/j.ctt5hgz6k. doi: 10.22459/AP.12.2013.

Keyes, Charles F. 1971. "Buddhism and National Integration in Thailand." *Journal of Asian Studies* 30 (3): 551–67. doi: 10.22459/AP.12.2013.

Kling, David William. 2020. *A History of Christian Conversion*. Oxford: Oxford University Press. doi: 10.1093/oso/9780195320923.001.0001.

Leacock, Eleanor. 1980. "Montagnais Women and the Jesuit Program for Colonization." In *Women and Colonization: Anthropological Perspectives*, edited by Mona Etienne and Eleanor Leacock, 25–42. New York: Praeger.

Lewis, Todd T. 2000. *Popular Buddhist Texts from Nepal: Narratives and Rituals of Newar Buddhism*. Albany, NY: SUNY Press.

Loos, Noel A. 1975. "A Conflict of Faiths: Aboriginal Reaction to the First Missionaries in North Queensland." In *Lectures on North Queensland History*, no. 2, edited by B. J. Dalton, 47–55. Townsville: James Cook University.

Ludewig, Jasper. 2020. "Mapoon Mission Station and the Privatization of Public Violence: Transnational Missionary Architecture on Queensland's Late-Nineteenth-Century Colonial Frontier." *ABE Journal: Architecture beyond Europe* 17. doi: 10.4000/abe.8032.

McShea, Bronwen. 2019. *Apostles of Empire: The Jesuits and New France*. Lincoln, NE: University of Nebraska Press. doi: 10.2307/j.ctvgc62ns.

Merrill, William L. 1993. "Conversion and Colonialism in Northern Mexico: The Tarahumara Response to the Jesuit Mission Program, 1601–1767." In *Conversion to Christianity: Historical and Anthropological Perspectives on a Great Transformation*, edited by Robert W. Hefner, 129–64. Berkeley, CA: University of California Press. doi: 10.1525/9780520912564-007.

Mitchell, Jessie. 2004. "'Country Belonging to Me': Land and Labour on Aboriginal Missions and Protectorate Stations, 1830–1850." *Eras Journal* 6. Accessed April 20, 2024. https://www.monash.edu/arts/philosophical-historical-international-studies/eras/past-editions/edition-six-2004-november/country-belonging-to-me-land-and-labour-on-aboriginal-missions-and-protectorate-stations-1830-1850#notes.

Morrison, Kenneth M. 1990. "Baptism and Alliance: The Symbolic Mediations of Religious Syncretism." *Ethnohistory* 37 (4): 416–37. doi: 10.2307/482862.

Nevins, Andrew, David Pesetsky, and Cilene Rodrigues. 2009. "Pirahã Exceptionality: A Reassessment." *Language* 85 (2): 355–404. doi: 10.1353/lan.0.0107.

Queensland Government. n.d. "Yarrabah." Queensland Government. Accessed April 20, 2024. https://www.qld.gov.au/firstnations/cultural-awareness-heritage-arts/community-histories/community-histories-u-y/community-histories-yarrabah.

Robbins, Joel. 2004. *Becoming Sinners: Christianity and Moral Torment in a Papua New Guinea Society*. Berkeley, CA: University of California Press.

Rubiés, Joan-Pau. 2017. "Ethnography and Cultural Translation in the Early Modern Missions." *Studies in Church History* 53: 272–310. doi: 10.1017/stc.2016.17.

Sahlins, Marshall. 2022. *The New Science of the Enchanted Universe: An Anthropology of Most of Humanity*. Princeton, NJ: Princeton University Press. doi: 10.1515/9780691238166.

Schmiechen, H. J. 1971. "The Hermannsburg Mission Society in Australia 1866–1895: Changing Missionary Attitudes and the Effects on the Aboriginal Inhabitants." Master's thesis, University of Adelaide. Accessed April 20, 2024. https://openresearch-repository.anu.edu.au/handle/1885/267409.

Speck, Frank G. 1977. *Naskapi: The Savage Hunters of the Labrador Peninsula*. Norman, OK: University of Oklahoma Press.

Strathern, Alan. 2019. *Unearthly Powers: Religious and Political Change in World History*. Cambridge University Press. doi: 10.1017/9781108753371.

Tanner, Adrian. 2021. "Innu (Montagnais-Naskapi)." In *The Canadian Encyclopedia*. Accessed April 20, 2024. https://www.thecanadianencyclopedia.ca/en/article/innu-montagnais-naskapi.

Thwaites, Reuben Gold, ed. 1906. *The Jesuit Relations and Allied Documents*. 71 vols. Cleveland: Burrows Brothers.

True, Micah. 2015. *Masters and Students: Jesuit Mission Ethnography in Seventeenth-Century New France*. Montreal: McGill-Queen's Press. doi: 10.1515/9780773581999.

Turchin, Peter, Harvey Whitehouse, Jennifer Larson, Enrico Cioni, Jenny Reddish, Daniel Hoyer, Patrick E. Savage, et al. 2022. "Explaining the Rise of Moralizing Religions: A Test of Competing Hypotheses Using the Seshat Databank." *Religion, Brain & Behavior* 13 (2): 167–94. doi: 10.1080/2153599X.2022.2065345.

Yengoyan, Aram A. 1993. "Religion, Morality, and Prophetic Traditions: Conversion among the Pitjantjatjara of Central Australia." In *Conversion to Christianity: Historical and Anthropological Perspectives on a Great Transformation*, edited by Robert W. Hefner, 233–57. Berkeley, CA: University of California Press. doi: 10.1525/9780520912564-010.

CHAPTER 5

The Evolution of Moralizing Supernatural Punishment: Empirical Patterns
Peter Turchin

One of the fundamental questions in the evolutionary study of religion concerns the relationship between moralizing religion and sociopolitical complexity (Alexander 1987; Johnson 2005; Norenzayan 2013; Norenzayan and Shariff 2008; Swanson 1960). An early analysis of Guy Swanson (1960) seemingly confirmed that there is a positive correlation between these two variables, but his study was conducted at a time when cross-cultural research was in its infancy. A later replication by Peter Peregrine (1996), while confirming a positive association between sociopolitical complexity (proxied by levels of political organization) and beliefs in a high god, did not find a relationship between complexity and supernatural sanctions on morality. More recently, Aaron Lightner, Theiss Bendixen, and Benjamin Grant Purzycki (2023) argued that moralizing supernatural punishment is *not* positively associated with social complexity and, thus, there is no pattern that needs explaining by invoking theories of evolutionary causation. Overall, the relationship between big gods and big societies continues to be subject to much controversy (Whitehouse et al. 2023).

One empirical problem bedeviling this debate is the tendency of the previous investigations to reduce the complexity of moralizing religion to binary (absent/present) measures. Thus, the analyses of the Standard Cross-Cultural Sample and the Ethnographic Atlas focus on the construct of "moralizing high gods" (MHGs) because this is how the data are coded in these ethnographic databases. Lightner, Bendixen, and Purzycki (2023), instead, argue that the *high* god variable's coding criteria, defined by whether or not a god is the creator or director of the universe, is irrelevant to the question about whether gods are moralizing or punitive. Reanalyzing Swanson's (1960) data, they show that whereas there is a strong positive correlation between the presence of MHGs and social complexity (again, proxied by the number of jurisdictional levels), this statistical association is greatly diminished, or even disappears, when MHG is replaced with the construct of punitive "moralizing gods" (MGs) who are not necessarily "high" (Lightner, Bendixen, and Purzycki 2023: figure 5). Their conclusion, thus, echoes an earlier analysis by Peregrine (1996).

The construct of MHG (and that of MG), furthermore, excludes nonagentic forces, such as karma or *ma'at* (see the chapters on MSP in South Asia and ancient Egypt in Volume Two). To remedy this problem, several investigators proposed an alternative measure of "broad supernatural punishment" (BSP) that may have contributed to the transition to large-scale, complex sociopolitical organization in different parts of the world (Raffield, Price, and Collard 2019; Watts et al. 2015).

The problem with all these constructs (MHG, MG, BSP, etc.) is, once again, that they reduce the potentially multidimensional and (certainly) nonbinary nature of MSP to stark, binary distinctions. Yet the proponents of the big gods theory (BGT) state its main prediction in quantitative terms: gods in small-scale societies tend to be "weak, whimsical, and not particularly moral," while "big powerful moralizers" are associated with complex, large-scale societies because they motivate an expansion of cooperation that kin selection and reciprocity cannot sustain (Henrich 2020: 130–31).

One of the goals of the Seshat project has been to shift away from such Procrustean approaches and attempt to capture the quantitative and potentially multidimensional nature of sociocultural evolution. This philosophy is exemplified in our approach to coding the sociopolitical complexity of past societies (Turchin et al. 2018). The Seshat measure of sociopolitical complexity (SPC) aggregates 51 Seshat variables coding different dimensions of sociopolitical complexity. This set includes seven quantitative variables: polity population size, population size of the largest settlement, polity territory size, and the number of levels in administrative, military, religious, and settlement hierarchies. The rest of the variables are binary, which at the analysis stage are aggregated into quantitative measures of polity-produced infrastructure, sophistication of government institutions, information systems, and economic exchange. Our investigation of the dimensions of sociopolitical complexity characterizing the polities in the Seshat sample showed that they are well captured with the first principal component (PC1), which explains more than three-quarters of the variance in the data (Turchin et al. 2018). Although we focus (here and elsewhere) on this particular measure, our analysis indicated that other dimensions of complexity may also be of interest. For example, the second principal component captures the difference between social scale and hierarchy, on the one hand, and informational and institutional variables, on the other (Turchin et al. 2018). An independent team of investigators subsequently performed a deep dive into this rich data set, analyzing how increases in scale interact with improvements in information processing and economic systems (Shin et al. 2020). The broader implication of this development is that, by publishing all the raw Seshat data – which has been the guiding philosophy of the Seshat project – we enable subsequent investigators to question our analysis decisions and propose alternative approaches to conceptualizing the variables of interest. Our approach to coding a quantitative measure of MSP was informed by the same philosophy (and is summarized in the section "A Coding Scheme for MSP"; see also Covey on MSP beliefs in the Americas in Part III, Chapter 1, this volume).

Another empirical problem (in addition to the crude binary measures used by previous investigators) has to do with data biases that may influence our ability to make inferences about the possible coevolution of moralizing religion and sociopolitical complexity in the deep past. First, much of our knowledge about religion practiced by small-scale societies – which provide the bulk of data for the ethnographic databases – comes from missionaries, agents of European empires, and early anthropologists who were laboring under a variety of cultural ethnocentric biases. Second, and conversely, while we have much better knowledge of contemporary small-scale societies, they all have lived for centuries (and sometimes millennia) in geographic proximity with large-scale societies, characterized by religious systems with well-developed MSP. It is a serious fallacy, thus, to assume that the contemporary small-scale societies studied by academic anthropologists give us an unbiased insight into the small-scale societies during the early Holocene.

Third, as we move deep into the past, the extent of our knowledge about historic and, especially, prehistoric societies diminishes drastically. Some critics go so far as to argue that it is impossible to infer the absence or presence of beliefs in big gods in societies that lacked writing (Beheim et al. 2019; Purzycki, Bendixen, and Lightner 2022). However, as the region-specific analytic narratives in Volume Two (and Covey, Part III, Chapter 1, this volume) demonstrate, this view, when stated in absolute terms, is wrong. It is surprising how much scholars whose life work was focused on a particular society can reconstruct about religious practices, even in societies that lacked records and texts. At the same time, an investigation into how the decline in the quantity and quality of records, when we move deeper into the past, affects our ability to make inferences about MSP is both warranted and possible (this will be taken up in the section "MSP and Information Systems"; see also François, "Bridging the Quantitative/Qualitative Divide," Volume Two).

These problems are real but not insurmountable. As Harvey Whitehouse explained in the introduction to this volume (Part I, Chapter 1), a combination of coded data together with analytic narratives on a large sample of past societies provides us with a uniquely powerful way of resolving questions of sociocultural evolution (see François, "Bridging the Quantitative/Qualitative Divide," Volume Two). A formal statistical analysis of data allows us to discover general principles that may underlie the cultural evolution of features such as moralizing religion, and to distinguish the general from specifics. The information on specific societies summarized in the analytic narratives, on the other hand, provides a check of validity of statistical results, as well as giving them additional depth.

The main goal of this chapter is to explore the empirical patterns that are revealed by the Seshat data on moralizing religion and various features of sociopolitical complexity. I start with an explanation of how we quantified the degree of MSP in past societies and then review "static" correlations between MSP and several important variables. Next, I summarize the results of a dynamic regression analysis that utilizes the time-resolved nature of Seshat data to empirically test various *causal* theories that have been proposed to explain the evolution of MSP. Finally, I provide an overview of the historical-geographical patterns revealed by our data. Some material in this chapter follows (and summarizes) articles that were previously published in scientific journals (Mullins et al. 2018; Turchin et al. 2023; Whitehouse et al. 2023).

A coding scheme for MSP

To test hypotheses concerning the role of MSP in the rise of social complexity, we seek to capture features that could plausibly facilitate cooperation as increasingly anonymous social interactions become harder to monitor and as cross-cutting structural tensions in society grow more intense. We also attempt to capture the degree of penetration of a particular religion into the society under consideration.

The geographical regions covered in this volume were primarily determined by the availability of data previously compiled in the Seshat Databank. This approach was essential in order to explore the possible causal influence of key factors – sociopolitical complexity, intensity of interpolity competition, and production/resources – on the rise and spread of MSP. The unit of analysis here, as in all other analytic Seshat articles, is not a particular region (such as a Natural Geographic Area [NGA]) but a *Seshat polity*, an independent political unit ranging in scale from autonomous self-governing local communities (e.g., Neolithic villages) through simple and complex chiefdoms, to states and empires (Turchin et al. 2018). In the static correlation analysis (see below) we look for associations between different characteristics of Seshat polities, for example, the degree of MSP and the level of social complexity (these variables will be explained below; see also François, "Bridging the Quantitative/Qualitative Divide," Volume Two).

For the dynamic regression analysis, which tests causal hypotheses attempting to explain the evolution of various characteristics (e.g., MSP, social scale, or the sophistication of governance), we need time-resolved data. We create time sequences for the analysis by determining the historical polities that occupied each of our sample regions (NGAs) over time, starting with the early modern period and working back in time to the Neolithic, or as far as available evidence allows (Turchin et al. 2015).

For each of the polities in our sample, we gathered data for 10 variables of supernatural moral enforcement (see Table 1). All the variables are "binary" in the sense that they attempt to capture the presence or absence of a particular feature of religion practiced in the polity. The extent to which it is possible to code variables in this way varies between different world regions and chronological periods (as is readily seen in the analytic narratives in Part III). We employ the now established Seshat approach for capturing uncertainty and disagreement. Thus, codes of "absence" and "presence" can be modified with "inferred." "Unknown" is also a possible code. Finally, codes of "absent-to-present" and "present-to-absent" (which are different from "unknown") are used to code a particular aspect of MSP during transitional periods that cannot be precisely dated (see Table 1).

Table 1. Summary of the Supernatural Moral Punishment/Reward Variables Used in Constructing the Measures of MSP Used in the Analysis

Components of the Quantitative Measure of MSP

Primary	The principal concerns of supernatural agents or forces pertain to cooperation in human affairs (rather than the behavior of humans toward the supernatural realm, for example, the discharging of ritual obligations)
Certain	MSP is certain and predictable (rather than arbitrary or capricious)
Broad	MSP enforces norms across a broad range of moral domains (instead of just a few domains)
Targeted	MSP is targeted specifically at culpable individuals (instead of the whole group)
Rulers	Moralizing supernatural forces or agents punish and/or reward rulers
Elites	The elites of the polity subscribe to MSP
Commoners	The commoners of the polity subscribe to MSP

Additional Characteristics of MSP

AfterLife	Moralizing enforcement in the afterlife: punishment is delayed until after the death of the transgressor
ThisLife	Moralizing enforcement in this life: punishment occurs during the transgressor's lifetime
Agency	Moralizing enforcement is administered by a supernatural agent, such as a deity or spirit (as opposed to an impersonal supernatural force, such as karma)

Note. For a more detailed explanation, see François, "Bridging the Quantitative/Qualitative Divide," Volume Two.

We obtain a quantitative measure of MSP by combining the first seven MSP "traits" (Table 1: Primary through Commoners) into an integrated measure of moralizing supernatural enforcement, MSP. In the publication that reported statistical analyses of these data (Turchin et al. 2023), we explored both an additive and a multiplicative way of combining the seven MSP traits and determined that we obtain qualitatively identical results with either measure. Here, for specificity, I will use an additive measure: simply summing up values (equating present with 1, absent with 0, and transitional periods with 0.5) and scaling the resulting measure to be between 0 and 1. The resulting MSP measure is a categorical variable with 15 levels (due to "half-tones" introduced by transitional periods). MSP = 0 indicates that no MSP traits are present, and MSP = 1 indicates that the religion of the polity in question is characterized by fully developed MSP.

The additional three variables (AfterLife through Agency) were used to explore whether the immediacy of punishment (in this life or the afterlife) and the mechanism of punishment (by a supernatural agent or a supernatural force) affect our results. These results are reported in Peter Turchin et al. (2023), and I don't make a further reference to them in this chapter.

MSP and information systems

Making inferences about the features of religion in past societies is a challenging task, and a variety of potential biases can affect the availability and quality of the data (François, "Bridging the Quantitative/Qualitative Divide," Volume Two). As a result, quite a number of our analytic narratives acknowledge that no inferences about MSP can be made for this or that society, and where this holds, the data table contains missing values ("unknown"). Overall, as the sophistication of the information systems used by a society declines, the proportion of missing MSP values increases (Figure 1). But this correlation is not absolute. While MSP is coded as "unknown" in about half of the societies that lack writing, quite a lot is known, or can be inferred, for the other half. Note also that even for societies with well-developed writing and several kinds of texts, there are some missing data.

There are several reasons why experts can make inferences about religion in societies without writing. In some cases, we have copious texts resulting from contacts between nonliterate and literate societies (see the analytic narratives on the Americas). In other cases, scholars have reconstructed the probable content of religious beliefs using phylogenetic methods (see the analytic narratives on the regions to which Indo-Europeans spread and on Polynesia).

As a result, despite the missing values, the Seshat sample explores enough variation in the cultural characteristics of past societies to allow strongly supported statistical conclusions. This can be seen by plotting the measures of MSP (omitting missing values) and information systems (Info) against each other (Figure 2). The analysis of these data shows that although MSP and Info are correlated (R^2 = 0.47), there is enough variation for the analysis to be able to disambiguate the effects of the two variables. For example, there are two point concentrations at low Info values: one for MSP near zero, suggesting absence of moralizing features, and the second one around MSP = 0.6, corresponding to relatively strong presence of MSP (and a few cases of full MSP).

The case of the Uyghur Khaganate in Mongolia (c. 800 CE) illustrates why the correlation between Info and MSP is imperfect. From the abundant records originating in nearby agrarian societies, we know that the state religion in the Uyghur Khaganate was Sogdian Manichaeism, a moralizing tradition including belief in divine punishment or reward after death (see the analytic narrative on Mongolia).

Similar logic underlies the code of "inferred absent" for many societies without writing in the Americas, for which we have abundant contact-era documents (these societies populate the lower left corner of the plot in Figure 2). Of course, the authors of these documents wrote under the influence of various kinds of biases, which need to be taken into account when interpreting the information they transmit. For an example of such an approach, see the narrative on Central Andes (Volume Two) and Alan Covey's survey on MSP in the Americas (Part III, Chapter 1, this volume).

MSP and social complexity

As we have seen, previous analyses of ethnographic data discovered that there is a positive and statistically significant correlation between beliefs in a high god ("a spiritual being who is believed to have created all reality and/or to be its ultimate governor") and the number of jurisdictional levels in a society (Roes and Raymond 2003; Swanson 1960). However, Peregrine (1996) and Lightner, Bendixen, and Purzycki (2023) did not find evidence for a positive correlation between *moralizing* religion and social complexity. I now revisit this debate with more comprehensive Seshat data, which have two advantages over the ethnographic databases. First, Seshat uses a quantitative measure of MSP instead of binary variables such as MHG, MG, or BSP. Similarly, SPC1[1] integrates 51 Seshat variables capturing various dimensions of social complexity and scale (instead of reliance on the hierarchical levels). Second, Seshat systematically samples past societies at all levels of complexity, unlike the ethnographic databases, which are biased toward the lower end of the complexity scale.

Analysis of the Seshat data finds that there is a substantial degree of correlation between the Seshat measures of MSP and SPC1. The correlation coefficient is $r = 0.71$ ($r^2 = 0.51$). Different ways of "slicing up" multidimensional social complexity yield similar correlation coefficients. Thus, the correlation between MSP and Scale (the first principal component of polity population, polity territory, population of the largest settlement, and number of hierarchical levels) is $r = 0.64$. NonScale (integrating governance, public goods, information, and money) is correlated at $r = 0.74$. Figure 3 provides an overview of the statistical associations between these and other Seshat variables.

The next question with which we can interrogate the Seshat data is how lack of writing may affect the estimated correlation between MSP and SPC1. As Figure 4 shows, the negative relationship between Info and missing MSP values is primarily due to the high frequency of unknowns for low values of Info (Info ≤ 0.1; these polities are depicted as hollow circles in Figure 4). Omitting these points from the regression, we still estimate a very similar, and strongly positive, relationship between

---

[1] "SPC" refers to sociopolitical complexity in general, whereas "SPC1" is a particular measure of SPC in Seshat: the first principal component of the eight Seshat complexity components (log polity population, log polity territory, log population of the largest settlement, number of hierarchical levels, sophistication of governance institutions, provision of public goods, informational complexity, and sophistication of economic exchange).

MSP and SPC (dashed line in Figure 4). Omitting points with Info ≤ 0.2 yields a regression line lying nearly on top of the solid line (not shown in order to avoid cluttering up Figure 4). The relationship between MSP and SPC1 is robust with respect to different levels of Info.

This analysis using an independent data set thus disagrees with the analyses of ethnographic data by Peregrine (1996) and by Lightner, Bendixen, and Purzycki (2023). There are several reasons why. First, as I noted above, the Seshat analysis uses a quantitative measure of MSP. The (re)analysis of Lightner, Bendixen, and Purzycki uses two binary measures: MHG (for which they find a positive association with social complexity) and MG (for which they find no correlation). The researchers argued that the relevant measure is the second one. However, the definition of MG used by them is very broad: essentially, any element of moralizing punishment results in MG coded as "present." But the proponents of the big god theory don't postulate a complete absence of any MSP features in small-scale societies, instead proposing that there was a *quantitative* change. Our analysis with the Seshat MSP measurement supports such a quantitative pattern, as we also observe a number of small-scale societies with a substantial degree of MSP (Figure 4). Lightner, Bendixen, and Purzycki's "binarization" of moralizing religion, thus, introduces an upward bias in their estimate. We can see it clearly in Figure 5, which depicts two alternative binarizations of the quantitative MSP, one in which any MSP element is enough to code moralizing religion as present (MG) and the opposite, where all elements need to be present in order to yield presence (MSP_max). As expected, the MG curve is shifted substantially higher than the MSP_max curve.

But even taking this bias into account, we still find a statistically significant relationship between the minimal MSP and SPC (logistic regression: $P < 2e^{-16}$). There is more going on than just the binary/quantitative distinction. The second major difference between the Seshat and ethnographic data sets is that Seshat samples societies with higher complexity more thoroughly. Indeed, when we restrict the analysis of the Seshat data to polities with SPC1 < 5 (which is the midpoint of the SPC1 distribution), we find that the positive association between MSP and SPC1 disappears (Figure 4c; logistic regression, $P = 0.12$).

The difference between samples is even more stark between Seshat and the data used by Peregrine (1996). The Peregrine sample consisted of 72 native North American societies. The polity within North America (excluding Mesoamerica) that has the highest SPC1 score is Cahokia (SPC1 = 4.25). Furthermore, only 2 (out of 72) societies in this sample were coded as possessing "present, active, moralistic" high gods. Such paucity of MHG in the Peregrine sample is consistent with the general rarity of MSP in the Americas (see Covey, Part III, Chapter 1, this volume). I will return to the difference in the prevalence of MSP between the Old World and the New World in the section "Historical Geography of MSP."

A third reason for the discrepancy between this analysis and that of Lightner, Bendixen, and Purzycki (2023) may be that whereas their data come from *recent* small-scale societies, the Seshat Databank samples societies deep into the past. Thus, the difference in our results may arise from cultural diffusion of MSP elements from large-scale complex societies located in geographic proximity to the small-scale societies in the Swanson sample (and, more generally, in the ethnographic data sets). This inference is supported by the observation that minimal MSP in the Seshat sample of less complex (SPC1 < 5) polities occurs at a level of 0.5 or less (Figure 5c). In contrast, the prevalence of MG in the analysis by Lightner, Bendixen, and Purzycki (2023) is located at a level of 0.75 or more (their figure 5B). This bias, mistakenly treating contemporary small-scale societies as a faithful reflection of early Holocene societies, is even more glaring in the social-psychological studies, such as that of Martin Lang et al. (2019), in which the experimental results from analyses conducted with subjects in societies influenced for centuries by world religions such as Hinduism, Christianity, and Buddhism are used to make inferences about the cultural evolution of religion during the Holocene (see also Covey, Part III, Chapter 1, this volume).

The evolution of MSP: a causal analysis

Our analysis, thus, finds a statistically significant correlation between MSP and SPC1 (with the caveat that the relationship is revealed only for the full spectrum of SPC1, and that there are important continental effects, on which more in the following section). The next question is what the causal mechanisms are that gave rise to this pattern. The best-known and most discussed hypothesis is the Big Gods Hypothesis (Norenzayan 2013; Norenzayan et al. 2016). This argument starts with the premise that religious beliefs and behaviors originated as an evolutionary by-product of ordinary cognitive tendencies, such as mind–body dualism (Bering 2006) or teleological reasoning (Kelemen 2004). These intuitive biases were later exploited by culturally evolved beliefs in supernatural surveillance and punishment because such beliefs increased the ability of groups to sustain complex social organizations and successfully scale up. Competition among cultural groups gradually aggregated these elements into cultural packages, in the form of organized religions. Thus, big gods (supplemented possibly by other evolutionary factors) enabled the rise of big societies (Norenzayan 2013).

Whereas in the initial formulation of the Big Gods Hypothesis by Ara Norenzayan (2013) the causal arrow goes from moralizing religion to sociopolitical complexity (SPC), in a subsequent article, Norenzayan et al. (2016) described a more complex scenario of mutual causation, in which not only prosocial religion enabled the rise of complex societies but higher SPC also had a positive feedback effect on religion. As a result, highly moralizing religion and sociopolitical complexity coevolved in a mutually supportive fashion.

Both versions of the Big Gods Hypothesis, thus, assert that MSP played a causal role in the evolution of SPC. An alternative set of theories points to other driving forces underlying the rise of highly moralizing religions, such as warfare (Bellah 2011; Geertz 2014; Turchin 2006, 2016; Whitehouse et al. 2017), animal husbandry (Peoples and Marlowe 2012), resource scarcity (Botero et al. 2014; Snarey 1996), and rising affluence and material security (Baumard et al. 2015). Furthermore, multiple factors may work together to drive the evolution of moralizing religion. For example, writing more than 35 years ago, Richard D. Alexander proposed that between-group competition, taking the form of warfare, favored larger groups. Because larger groups are more vulnerable to fission, the same evolutionary driver favored the rise of moralizing religion, which would counteract such centrifugal tendencies in larger groups (Alexander 1987).

What this quick theoretical review suggests, therefore, is that a positive correlation between MSP and SPC can arise as a result of multiple causal processes. More formally, we can distinguish four causal scenarios resulting in a pairwise correlation between variables X and Y (Table 2).

Table 2. Four Causal Scenarios That Can Give Rise to Pairwise Correlations

No.	Causation	Equation
1	Simple causation	$X_t \rightarrow Y_{t+1}$ (with no feedback from Y to X)
2	Simple causation	$Y_t \rightarrow X_{t+1}$ (with no feedback from X to Y)
3	Mutual causation	$X_t \rightarrow Y_{t+1}$ and $Y_t \rightarrow X_{t+1}$ (feedbacks in both directions)
4	Indirect causation	$X_{t+1} \leftarrow Z_t \rightarrow Y_{t+1}$ (no direct causal effect between X and Y but correlation between them because they share a common driving factor or factors, Z)

Note. Arrows indicate the direction of causation. Note also that this formulation makes explicit the informal notion that "causes precede effects" by the use of the subscripts indicating time dependence.

Because many forces may interact in driving cultural evolutionary change, Turchin (2018) proposed that this coevolutionary process can be formalized mathematically as a discrete-time nonlinear dynamic system:

$X_{t+1} = f(X_t, Y_t, ...Z_t, U_t, ...V_t)$
$Y_{t+1} = g(X_t, Y_t, ...Z_t, U_t, ...V_t)$
...
$Z_{t+1} = h(X_t, Y_t, ...Z_t, U_t, ...V_t)$

(Eq. 1)

Here, X_t, Y_t, ...Z_t are state variables reflecting the cultural characteristics of a polity at time t, which are treated as endogenous variables representing dynamic feedbacks; U_t, ...V_t are exogenous factors that are not involved in feedback loops; and f, g, ...h are nonlinear functions specifying how the variables interact with each other. The time step is one century, here chosen to operationalize the temporal resolution of the Seshat Databank. This general dynamic model allows us to capture the "descent with modification" nature of the evolutionary process because current values of state variables are conditioned not only on potential causal factors ("modification") but also on their own past values ("descent"). Exogenous variables can represent a variety of processes: white noise, random walks, or a single discontinuous change of the environment (for further details, see Turchin et al. 2022).

This conceptual framework can be used both for modeling cultural macroevolution and as a basis for empirically testing rival theories proposing alternative causal scenarios. Details can be found in specialized publications (Turchin 2018; Turchin et al. 2022), but the general logic underlying this approach is straightforward. Let's say, for the sake of concreteness, that we are interested in the factors influencing the evolution of SPC. This is our *response* variable (these are the variables on the left-hand side, with subscript $t + 1$). Different theories propose different *predictors* (right-hand side, with subscript t). The goal of statistical analysis is to determine which combination of predictors at time t generates the best level of prediction for future values of the response variable (at time $t + 1$). If including MSP in the model increases its ability to predict SPC1, and this increase is statistically significant, then the Big Gods Hypothesis is supported. If not, then we reject it. A more nuanced way of stating this is that the results of this analysis either elevate or depress our degree of belief in the theory (all statistical results are tentative because, in the future, better-quality and more abundant data as well as new and improved statistical methods may further change the theory's level of empirical support).

Time-resolved data are key for this kind of analysis because it uses the time arrow to move from purely correlational analysis toward inference about causality. Thus, an observation that increases in MSP tend to follow, rather than precede, increases in SPC1 is evidence against the hypothesis of simple causation (Scenario 1 in Table 2: $MSP^t \rightarrow SPC1^{t+1}$). But distinguishing between other scenarios requires a more elaborate analysis (e.g., using the dynamic regression framework). For example, depending on the details of the interaction between MSP and SPC1, Scenario 3 (mutual causation) can lead to a similar time delay between MSP and SPC1 dynamics as Scenario 2 (simple causation from SPC to MSP). The most difficult problem is distinguishing Scenario 4 (indirect causation) from other causal scenarios, because we can never know whether we have tested for the effects of all possible common drivers (Z). The only way forward is to continue adding to the analysis alternative hypotheses, proposed by various researchers, gather data on empirical proxies, and test them in an overall statistical analysis. This general research strategy has informed data collection in the Seshat project from its inception (Turchin et al. 2015) and resulted in the publication of two articles helping us to answer the question raised in this section: which causal scenario is best supported by the data (Turchin et al. 2022, Turchin et al. 2023)?

The first article (Turchin et al. 2022) focused on the evolutionary drivers of sociopolitical complexity. We used three measures of sociopolitical complexity: (1) social scale (the first principal component of log-transformed polity population, polity territory, and population of the largest settlement), (2) vertical or hierarchical complexity (the average number of levels in administrative, military, and settlement hierarchies), and (3) specialization of governance (combining 11 measures of government sophistication). These three measures served as the response variables in the statistical analysis. Using the general model (Equation 1), the analysis then tested 17 potential predictor variables proxying mechanisms suggested by five major classes of theories of sociopolitical complexity (agriculture, functionalist theories, internal conflict, external conflict, and religion). The results indicated that there was a high degree of agreement between the best combinations of predictors in their effect on the three response variables. The best-supported model indicated a strong causal role played by a combination of increasing agricultural productivity and invention/adoption of military technologies (most notably, iron weapons and cavalry in the first millennium BCE). While this global historical analysis identified warfare and agriculture as the main drivers of sociopolitical complexity in human societies, it found that including MSP as a possible predictor did not increase the ability of the model to predict future values. This result, thus, is strong evidence against two of the causal scenarios, 2 and 3 (Table 2, interpreting X as SPC1 and Y as MSP).

The second article (Turchin et al. 2023) performed a similar analysis but focused on MSP as the response variable. The predictor variables were sociopolitical complexity (SPC1), warfare intensity (proxied by the invention/adoption of military technologies), productivity of agriculture, pastoralism, and two environmental variables (the first capturing the overall suitability of the region for agriculture and the second reflecting the cline from cold to hot and dry environments). Our analyses indicated that intergroup warfare, supported by resource availability, played a major role in the evolution of MSP (Table 3). We also found that including pastoralism as a predictor significantly improved the model. Both environmental factors, suitability for agriculture and hot and dry environments, were also supported. On the other hand, adding SPC1 as a predictor failed to improve the model's performance. This result, therefore, provides strong evidence against Scenarios 1 and 3 in Table 2, which postulate a direct causal effect of SPC1 on MSP (whether acting by itself or in a mutual causation loop).

Table 3. Regression Results with MSPt+1 as the Response Variable

	Estimate	SE	t	Probability
(Intercept)	0.000	0.011	0.000	0.501
MSP	0.613	0.057	10.835	0.000
MSP.sq	−0.200	0.048	−4.212	0.000
MilTech	0.052	0.022	2.366	0.016
Cavalry	0.095	0.020	4.814	0.000
Agri	0.095	0.034	2.804	0.019
Agri.sq	−0.061	0.029	−2.115	0.044
Pastor	0.031	0.013	2.318	0.008
EnvPC1	0.030	0.014	2.196	0.052
EnvPC2	0.037	0.014	2.582	0.033

Notes. Estimate: standardized regression estimate; *SE*: standard error of the estimate; *t*: the *t* statistic associated with the estimate; Probability: the proportion of bootstrap values greater than 0 (lesser than 0 for the negative terms MSP.sq and Agri.sq). The predictor variables are all lagged. Thus, MSP is an autocorrelation term (MSPt), reflecting the influence of the past value (one century before) of MSP on its future value.

Source. Turchin et al. (2023: table 2).

These analyses together, thus, support Scenario 4, that correlation between SPC1 and MSP arises not because of direct causal influences but indirectly, as a result of sharing the same evolutionary drivers. Specifically, these drivers include intensity of warfare and productivity of agriculture. In addition, increases in MSP are also more likely in societies practicing pastoralism and living in hot and dry environments.

How do these results agree with/extend the insights from the analyses of the ethnographic databases? Keep in mind that the Seshat Databank includes the temporal dimension, which enables us to approach evolutionary causality more effectively than correlations on simultaneous data. Furthermore, the Seshat sample, by design, explores the full range of social complexity, whereas the ethnographic data are heavily biased toward small-scale, low-complexity societies. Finally, the ethnographic data only provide information about moralizing high gods (the binary MHG variable), while the analysis of the Seshat data is based on a more quantitative MSP variable (as well as more quantitative predictor variables, such as SPC1).

The Seshat analysis also tested the effects of multiple variables, possibly acting together, allowing us to untangle the multifarious effects of the potential causal variables on the evolution of MSP. Considering first the effects of resources and the environment, we see that EnvPC1, capturing the general suitability of the environment for agriculture, appears to have a positive effect on the evolution of MSP (however, note that its effect is associated with a weak degree of statistical significance, $P = 0.05$). The productivity of agriculture also has an overall positive effect but with a nonlinear twist. The negative quadratic term Agri.sq suggests that high values of Agri do not promote evolution of MSP. Next, we observe that pastoralism and EnvPC2, possibly acting in synergy (as EnvPC2, possibly acting in synergy (as EnvPC2 reflects hot and dry environments), also have a positive effect on MSP.

These results are in general agreement with previous analyses of the ethnographic databases, which found both a positive effect of resource base (Roes and Raymond 2003) and a positive effect of ecological stress, such as dry environments (Botero et al. 2014; Snarey 1996), and animal husbandry (Peoples and Marlowe 2012). Thus, both the historical data in Seshat and the ethnographic data suggest that the environment and resources have a complex, multifarious effect on the evolution of moralizing religion.

This discussion should be tempered by the observation that the magnitude of the environmental influences is dwarfed by the effects of warfare proxies, especially the spread of cavalry (as indicated by both the high standardized regression coefficient and the low P value; see Table 2). This result validates the cultural group selection theory advanced by Alexander (1987) and further developed in Turchin (2016). This theory was empirically supported by the analysis of the ethnographic data (SCCS) by Frans Roes and Michel Raymond (2003) and by the analyses of the Seshat data described here. Note that SCCS and Seshat use different approaches to quantify external conflict. The main variable in the SCCS analysis by Roes and Raymond was frequency of external warfare, which was supplemented by variables such as hostility toward other societies and acceptability of violence toward people in other societies (Roes and Raymond 2003: 129). In Seshat, the main proxy for the intensity of interpolity warfare is a measure of the realized sophistication and variety of military technologies used by polities, MilTech (for details, see Turchin et al. 2021). A large variety of sophisticated means of attack and defense serves as a quantitative proxy for the intensity of warfare in the environment of the polity because people tend to invest in expensive armor and in settlement defense when their societies are threatened by their neighbors. The Seshat Databank also contains direct measures of warfare intensity: warfare severity variables coding the consequences of warfare for polities and their populations, ranging from relatively mild, such as annexation and looting, to acute, such as massacre and ethnocide. Our analysis showed that the relationship between MilTech and war severity variables is approximately linear and characterized by a high correlation coefficient (more than 0.9), suggesting that MilTech adequately captures the increasing intensity of interstate conflict and threat (Turchin et al. 2022: supplementary materials). War severity variables, however, are much harder to code, and as a result, these variables are characterized by high proportions of missing values, making MilTech a better predictor variable in a comprehensive analysis. Abstracting from these details, the general point here is that different ways of quantifying warfare intensity in two different databases (SCCS and Seshat) yield similar results, thus strengthening the overall conclusion.

Dynamic regression results throw additional light on the correlation analysis reported in the section "MSP and Social Complexity." We now see that a positive correlation between these two variables arises as a result of shared evolutionary drivers (Scenario 4 in Table 2). Furthermore, the main driver of MSP revealed by this analysis is intensity of warfare, proxied by the development of military technologies. This result helps to explain continental differences, most notably between Afro-Eurasia and the Americas. As it happened, the evolution of military technologies was more rapid in Afro-Eurasia, triggered by military revolutions – most famously the one resulting from the development of gunpowder weapons and ocean-sailing ships (Parker 1996; Roberts 1956), as well as earlier ones, such as advances in bronze and iron metallurgy or the domestication of the horse (Turchin 2006). This observation suggests a possible explanation for the relative paucity of MSP in the precontact Americas. The next section delves into this and other questions by considering the historical and geographic patterns of the rise and spread of "world religions" with full MSP.

Historical geography of MSP

MSP is a topic adjacent to many investigations of comparative religion and to the debate over the so-called Axial Age.[2] This pivotal era has been variously described as the "moral revolution," the "prophetic age," "*die Achsenzeit*," the "ecumenic age," the "age of transcendence," "an age of criticism," and more recently as "the great transformation," a "revolution in worldviews," and "the moral Axial Age" (for references, see Mullins et al. 2018). Although the specific temporal boundaries and geographic extent of the Axial Age phenomenon are debated, there is a nearly universal agreement among scholars that some kind of transformation in the moral and religious realm did occur. There is also substantial debate about whether terms such as "monotheism" and "transcendence" can be applied across cultures (Larson, Part I, Chapter 2, this volume). Nevertheless, several classification proposals have attempted to define the nature of religious change during the Holocene.

In her chapter, Larson discusses two such conceptual schemes: the distinction between "primary" and "secondary" religions made by Jan Assmann and between "immanentist" and "transcendentalist" religions by Alan Strathern. In addition,

---

2   See the chapter by Jennifer Larson in this volume (Part I, Chapter 2); the Axial Age is a historical period in the mid-first millennium BCE, during which a cluster of changes in cultural traditions are said to have occurred in some of the complex social formations in a wide band of Eurasia, stretching from China to Greece (Hoyer and Reddish 2019).

Harvey Whitehouse (Part I, Chapter 1, this volume) proposes a three-stage transition from "wild" to "doctrinal" religions. A common thread through all these schemes is that the moral dimension of human religion during the Holocene was transformed. In primary/immanentist religions, the ritual dimension of morality typically takes precedence over interpersonal ethics. In transcendental religions, on the other hand, interpersonal morality is central; evolution from immanentisms to transcendentalisms involves a radical shift toward a universalizing ethics enforced by infallible supernatural powers (Larson, Part I, Chapter 2, this volume).

Narrowing our focus to moralizing supernatural punishment, what the different classification schemes (Assmann, Strathern, and Whitehouse, as well as the "big gods" theorists) imply is the shift from rare or minimal (but not necessarily completely absent) MSP at the beginning of the Holocene to common and well-developed (but not necessarily universal) MSP by the end of the pre-industrial era (leaving religious evolution during the past two centuries outside these brackets; but see Whitehouse, Part I, Chapter 1, this volume, for a possible "fourth phase"). This evolution occurred in parallel with the great transformation in the scale and complexity of human societies during the Holocene.

The MSP data in the Seshat Databank are consistent with such a quantitative pattern. Minimal MSP is estimated to be present at the level of 10% to 20% in societies with low levels of SPC1 and saturates at 100% for high SPC1 (Figure 5a). Full MSP, on the other hand, is absent at low social political complexity, but reaches a level of about 90% for high levels of SPC1 (Figure 5b).

While Figures 4 and 5 map the association between MSP and SPC1, another useful approach is to map MSP in time and space. Figure 6 is an attempt to do so. The focus is on Eurasia (including North Africa) because the spread of transcendentalisms with full MSP outside this region by European empires and missionaries occurred recently and is well understood (see also Covey, Part III, Chapter 1, this volume).

The pattern of the spatiotemporal evolution of MSP, as mapped in Figure 6, departs significantly from the "averaged" ideas of the Axial Age reviewed in Daniel Austin Mullins et al. (2018: figures 1 and 2). Most importantly, the region that evolved full MSP the earliest, according to the Seshat data, is Egypt, which is not even included in the standard list of Axial regions (Mullins et al. 2018: figure 2). A well-developed form of MSP appeared in Egypt no later than c. 2400 BCE, and MSP elements were likely present earlier, although in forms that have left little unequivocal evidence. From the New Kingdom on (after 1600 BCE), Egypt possessed a full set of MSP characteristics – a millennium before the Axial Age as it is usually dated (800–200 BCE).

On the other hand, China was comparatively slow to develop full MSP. The first appearance of any MSP elements occurred during the Western Zhou period

(1045–771 BCE), but the primary concern of Chinese religion remained with ritual, while moralizing aspects were limited. The Mandate of Heaven (Tian) never evolved into a fully moralizing supernatural force/agent. Fully developed MSP arrived in China only with Buddhism, which first became the official ideology c. 300 CE and later became a mass religion during the Tang period (eighth century) – that is, a millennium after the Axial Age.

The regions that shifted to full MSP during the Axial Age were West Asia (Mesopotamia and Iran, Figure 6) and South Asia (Pakistan and India, Figure 6). All contemporary forms of transcendentalisms with full MSP are evolutionary offshoots of these two "progenitors" – the West Asian moralizing big god and the South Asian moralizing supernatural force (karma). Furthermore, it is quite possible that these two religious innovations did not evolve independently. Mesopotamia and North India had been in close cultural contact at least since the Third Millennium BCE Interaction Sphere (Robbins Schug et al. 2012). In the middle of the first millennium BCE, they became part of a single political-military network, "Central PMN" (Chase-Dunn and Hall 1997), with a central role played by the Achaemenid empire, which stretched from Egypt and Anatolia to Sogdiana and northwest India. It stands to reason that cultural elements originating in different religions within this Central PMN mixed and recombined promiscuously, giving rise to new forms that competed against each other. Striking similarities between the West Asian and South Asian transcendentalisms – beliefs in punishment/reward in the afterlife, internalization of moral norms, and an emphasis on salvation, liberation, or enlightenment (Strathern 2019) – coupled with their nearly simultaneous rise in closely culturally connected regions argue against independent evolution.

Conclusion

The social life of human beings was utterly transformed during the Holocene. Agriculture, large-scale organized warfare, elites, rulers, bureaucracies, writing, and monumental architecture evolved independently in many world regions at markedly different times. But as the data buttressed by the analytic narratives in Volume Two attest, the evolutionary history of moralizing religion in different world regions varied substantially. Although limited forms of MSP are found in many different parts of the world and have substantial antiquity, fully developed MSP evolved in one particular world region, stretching from eastern Mediterranean to northern India, during a period that can reasonably be called the Axial Age. However, moving away from the multiple competing notions of the Axial Age advanced by previous researchers (Mullins et al. 2018), the Seshat MSP project, by focusing on one particular aspect, defining its dimensions, and gathering systematic data across the world regions and historic eras, provides us with a quantitative, empirically based approach to delineating the spatial and temporal boundaries of this "MSP Age."

Full MSP first developed in Egypt (see the chapter on Egypt, Volume Two). The central MSP concept of *maʿat* presages later developments in West Asian monotheisms and South Asian karmic religions, because although *maʿat* was primarily imagined as a supernatural force or universal principle, it was also personified and depicted as a supernatural (or superhuman) agent. In the next millennium, full MSP became firmly associated with the rise of what Strathern calls transcendentalisms, such as Zoroastrianism, Judaism, Buddhism, and Jainism. This evolution took place within the Central PMN, which provided an "incubator" for religious ideas originating from Egypt, the Steppe, North India, and other geographically adjacent regions to mix and recombine in new ways. Interestingly, the East Asian PMN was not part of this religious interaction sphere, although by that point the Central and East Asian Prestige Goods Networks had already merged (Chase-Dunn and Hall 1997) and religious ideas could travel together with the merchants (which, indeed, happened but a millennium later, when Buddhism arrived in China and Manichaeism in Mongolia).

What was so special about the Central PMN in the Axial Age? Analysis of the Seshat data points to the role of military revolutions and the overall intensification of warfare as the primary causal drivers of MSP. The invention and spread of cavalry, in particular, was the strongest predictor of the increases in MSP (Table 3). This statistical result helps us understand why world religions with full MSP evolved in the Central PMN at that particular point in time. Cavalry – horse-riding military units – was invented on the Great Steppe around 1000 BCE. It spread to Iran by 900 BCE and to North India by 600 BCE. Cavalry revolutionized warfare within the Central PMN, leading to a cascade of other military innovations (Turchin et al. 2021). Intensification of warfare in the early first millennium BCE, associated with the spread of cavalry, resulted, after a time lag of 300–400 years, in the rise of the first mega empires, which were an order of magnitude greater in scale than preceding states (Turchin and Gavrilets 2021: table 2). And it was these mega empires, most notably Achaemenid Persia and Mauryan India, that adopted and spread religions with full MSP.

All transcendentalisms with full MSP that exist today are evolutionary offshoots of the religions that developed within the Central PMN in the first millennium BCE. The main mode of evolution of MSP was by military conquest, long-distance traders, and missionaries (see also Larson, Part I, Chapter 2, this volume; Reddish, Part III, Chapter 4, this volume). Apart from the initial evolution in the Central PMN, we know of no examples of independent evolution of full MSP, as is imagined by the big gods theorists (although world religions often incorporated cultural elements from local religious traditions once they were introduced to new regions). Instead, world religions spread through Afro-Eurasia following the arrival of military technologies such as horse-riding and iron weapons and armor. Later, another military revolution took place in Europe in the fifteenth and sixteenth centuries. Following it, world religions with full MSP spread to the rest of the world carried by the European empires.

The connection between military revolutions and the spread of MSP suggests an interesting hypothesis. One (limited) form of MSP that we find in many regions of western and southern Eurasia is the combination of supernatural enforcement of oaths and hospitality. As discussed in several analytic narratives in Volume Two, it is a fairly secure inference that this form of MSP was already present in Indo-European religion. Evidence is now accumulating that the spread of Yamnaya people, who most likely spoke an early version of Indo-European language, was anything but peaceful (Kristiansen 2020). Whether the spread of Yamnaya groups was propelled by an advantage in military technology is controversial, but one possible candidate is their use of horses (not as cavalry, which was a much later development, but for logistics). This reconstruction – military use of horses and intense warfare leading to the spread of MSP elements – is highly speculative but should warrant additional investigation.

To reiterate, the evolution of MSP is distinct in its mode from other aspects of the Holocene transformation, which, unlike full MSP, arose repeatedly and independently in different parts of the world. Instead, full MSP evolved in a particular world region at a particular time and then spread from there. Furthermore, full MSP is not a necessary condition for effective functioning of large-scale societies. Large bureaucratic empires in China, for example, functioned well enough without otherworldly supernatural punishments. Instead, they relied on a combination of this-world cultural devices: cultivation of personal virtue and societal harmony due to Confucianism and state-administered punishments and rewards. Big brother may be as effective as (if not more so than) the big god. A sequence of large states in the Central Andes, culminating in the Inca empire, also attests that MSP is not a necessary institution for the growth of complex societies. Well-functioning secular modern states, such as Denmark or Austria, in which religion plays a minor (at best) role is more evidence for this idea. Finally, other aspects of world religions may be of greater importance than MSP for sustaining large-scale societies: their ability to symbolically unify large ethnically heterogeneous populations, their emphasis on doctrinal rituals, and their literate clergies, who often served in government bureaucracies.

The evolution of moralizing religion is an interesting puzzle that is clearly amenable to investigation using the tools of cultural evolution. Much progress has been made, and the data reviewed in this volume yield many new insights. However, and perhaps disappointing to some, the conclusion they point to is that moralizing religion was not a particularly important force in the evolution of large-scale complex societies.

Figures

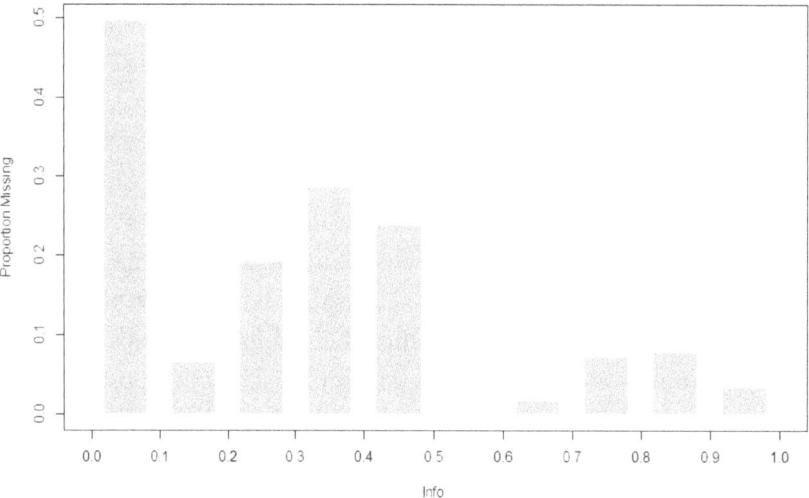

Figure 1. Proportion of Seshat polities for which MSP data are coded as "unknown," as a function of the sophistication of information systems (Info). Info, a measure of information complexity, combines data from 13 binary Seshat variables: four provide the basis for measuring the sophistication of the writing system (Mnemonic devices, Nonwritten records, Script, Written records), and nine variables code for presence or absence of various kinds of texts (lists, calendar, sacred texts, religious literature, history, philosophy, scientific literature, fiction; see Turchin 2018).

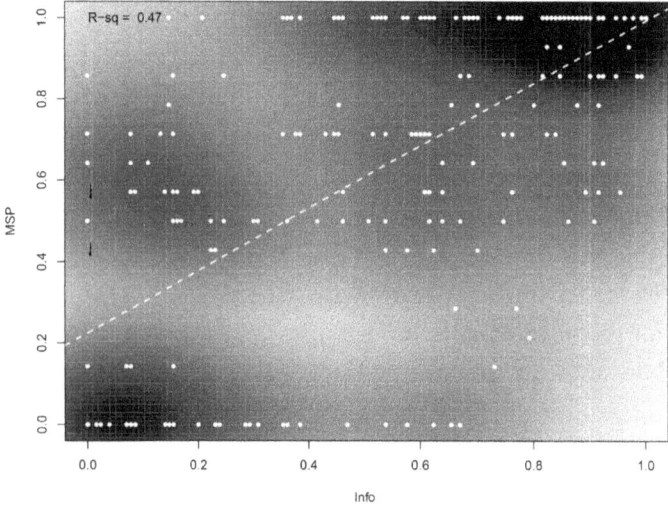

Figure 2. Statistical association between MSP and Info. The color indicates point density from low (blue) to high (red). The dashed line represents linear regression, and $R2$ is the proportion of variance explained by the linear regression.

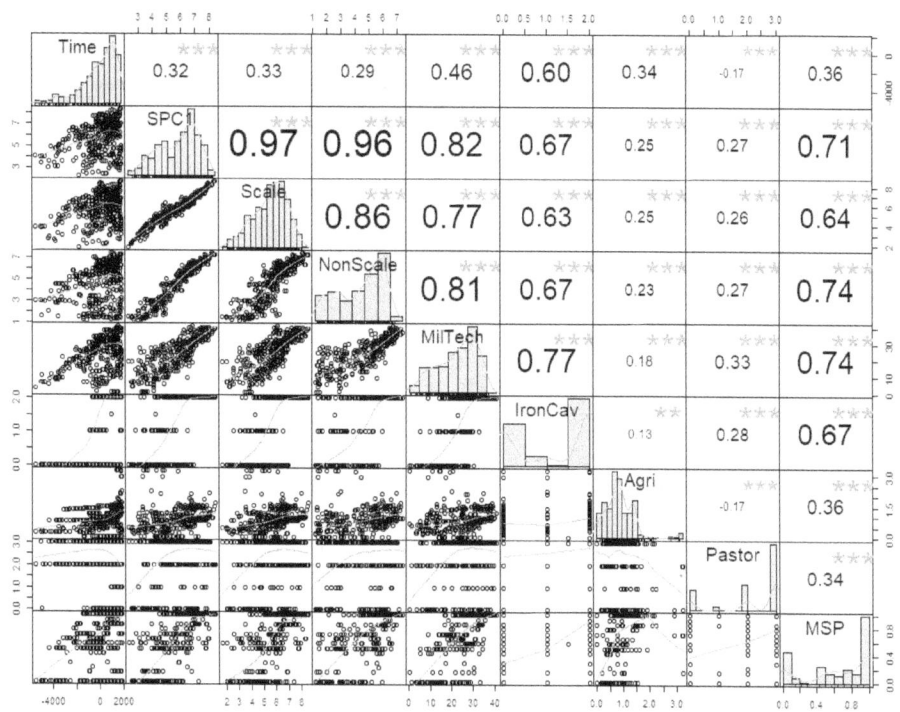

Figure 3. Correlation matrix between MSP and other variables reflecting various aspects of the sociocultural evolution of polities.

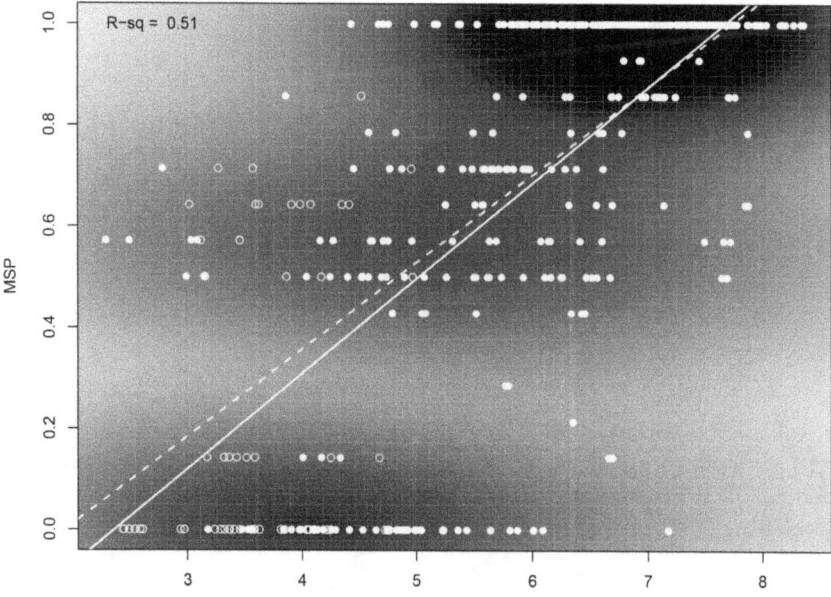

Figure 4. Statistical association between MSP and sociopolitical complexity (SPC1). The color indicates point density from low (green) to high (red). Hollow points are for polities with Info ≤ 0.1, solid points for polities with Info > 0.1. The solid line is linear regression on the whole data set ($R2$ is the proportion

of variance explained); the dashed line is regression on polities with Info > 0.1. SPC1 is the first principal component of the eight Seshat complexity components (log polity population, log polity territory, log population of the largest settlement, number of hierarchical levels, sophistication of governance institutions, provision of public goods, informational complexity, and sophistication of economic exchange; see Turchin 2018).

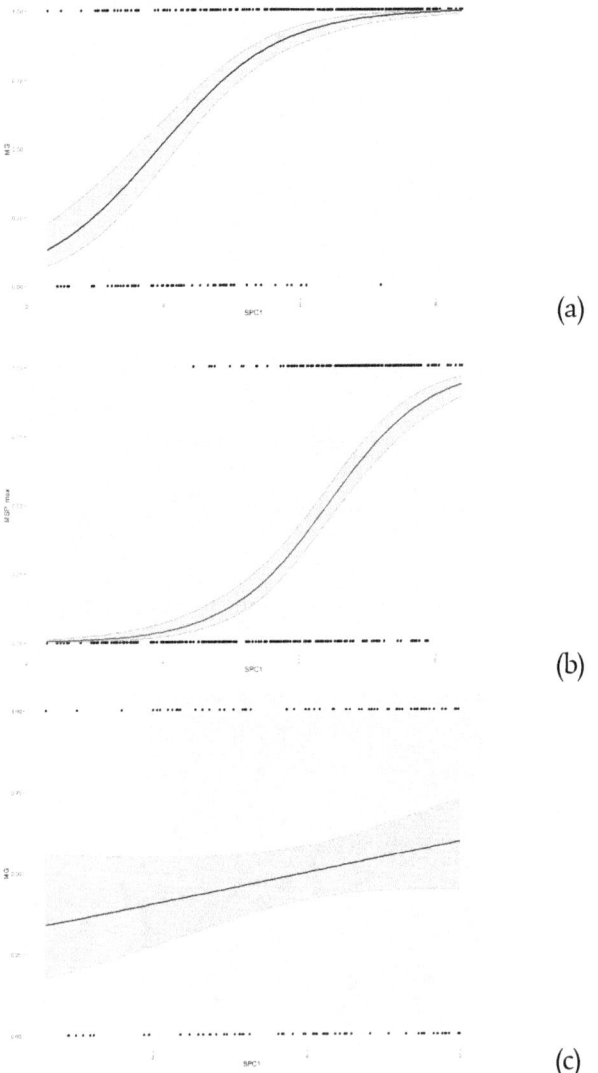

Figure 5. Logistic regression models showing the probability of moralizing supernatural punishment as a function of social complexity: (a) minimal MSP (any MSP element present), (b) full MSP (all MSP elements present), and (c) minimal MSP for the lower range of complexity (SPC1 < 5). The shaded area represents 95% confidence intervals.

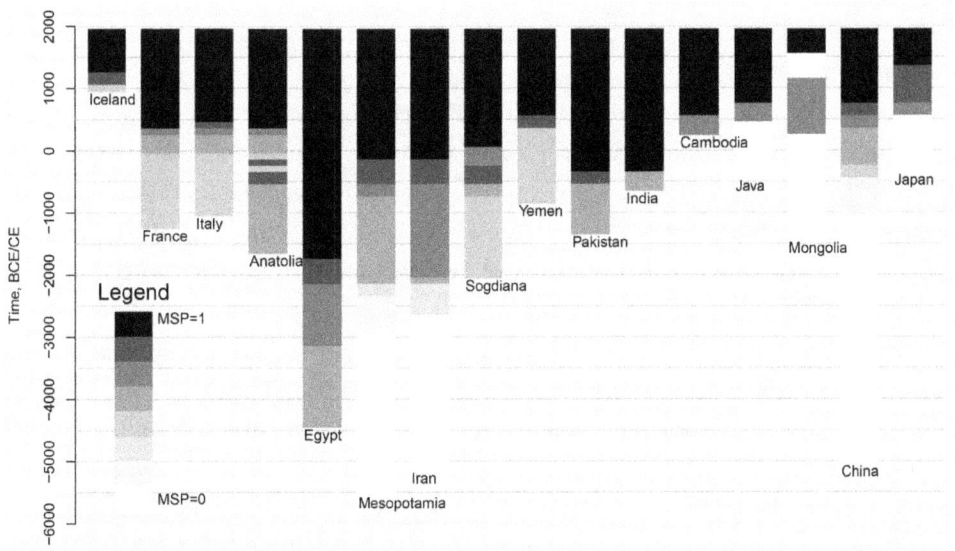

Figure 6. Mapping the evolution of MSP in space and time. Colors from blue to dark red indicate the level of MSP (see "Legend" in the lower left corner). Regions are arranged in a rough west–east order.

References

Alexander, Richard D. 1987. *The Biology of Moral Systems*. New York: Aldine De Gruyter.

Baumard, Nicolas, Alexandre Hyafil, Ian Morris, and Pascal Boyer. 2015. "Increased Affluence Explains the Emergence of Ascetic Wisdoms and Moralizing Religions." *Current Biology* 25 (1): 1–6. doi: 10.1016/j.cub.2014.10.063.

Beheim, Bret, Quentin Atkinson, Joseph Bulbulia, Will M. Gervais, Russell Gray, Joseph Henrich, Martin Lang, et al. 2019. "Corrected Analyses Show That Moralizing Gods Precede Complex Societies but Serious Data Concerns Remain." *PsyArXiv Preprints*. doi: 10.31234/osf.io/jwa2n.

Bellah, Robert N. 2011. *Religion in Human Evolution: From the Paleolithic to the Axial Age*. Cambridge, MA: Harvard University Press. doi: 10.4159/harvard.9780674063099.

Bering, Jesse M. 2006. "The Folk Psychology of Souls." *Behavioral and Brain Sciences* 29 (5): 453–62. doi:10.1017/S0140525X06009101.

Botero, Carlos A., Beth Gardner, Kathryn R. Kirby, Joseph Bulbulia, Michael C. Gavin, and Russell D. Gray. 2014. "The Ecology of Religious Beliefs." *Proceedings of the National Academy of Sciences of the United States of America* 111 (47): 16784–9. doi: 10.1073/pnas.1408701111.

Chase-Dunn, Christopher K., and Thomas D. Hall. 1997. *Rise and Demise: Comparing World-Systems*. Boulder, CO: Westview Press.

Geertz, Armin W. 2014. "Do Big Gods Cause Anything?" *Religion* 44 (4): 609–613. doi: 10.1080/0048721X.2014.937052.

Henrich, Joseph. 2020. *The WEIRDest People in the World: How the West Became Psychologically Peculiar and Particularly Prosperous*. New York: Farrar, Straus and Giroux.

Hoyer, Daniel, and Jenny Reddish, eds. 2019. *Seshat History of the Axial Age*. Chaplin CT: Beresta Books.

Johnson, Dominic D. P. 2005. "God's Punishment and Public Goods." *Human Nature* 16: 410–46. doi: 10.1007/s12110-005-1017-0.

Kelemen, Deborah. 2004. "Are Children 'Intuitive Theists'?: Reasoning About Purpose and Design in Nature." *Psychological Science* 15 (5): 295–301. doi: 10.1111/j.0956-7976.2004.00672.x.

Kristiansen, Kristian. 2020. "The Archaeology of Proto-Indo-European and Proto-Anatolian: Locating the Split." In *Dispersals and Diversification: Linguistic and Archaeological Perspectives on the Early Stages of Indo-European*, edited by M. Serangeli and T. Olander, 157–65. Leiden: Brill. doi: 10.1163/9789004416192_009.

Lang, Martin, Benjamin G. Purzycki, Coren L. Apicella, Quentin D. Atkinson, Alexander Bolyanatz, Emma Cohen, Carla Handley, et al. 2019. "Moralizing Gods, Impartiality and Religious Parochialism across 15 Societies." *Proceedings of the Royal Society B: Biological Sciences* 286. doi: 10.1098/rspb.2019.0202.

Lightner, Aaron D., Theiss Bendixen, and Benjamin Grant Purzycki. 2023. "Moralistic Supernatural Punishment Is Probably Not Associated with Social Complexity." *Evolution and Human Behavior* 44 (6): 555–65. doi: 10.1016/j.evolhumbehav.2022.10.006.

Mullins, Daniel Austin, Daniel Hoyer, Christina Collins, Thomas Currie, Kevin Feeney, Pieter François, Patrick E. Savage, Harvey Whitehouse, and Peter Turchin. 2018. "A Systematic Assessment of 'Axial Age' Proposals Using Global Comparative Historical Evidence." *American Sociology Review* 83 (3): 596–626.

Norenzayan, Ara. 2013. *Big Gods: How Religion Transformed Cooperation and Conflict*. Princeton, NJ: Princeton University Press.

Norenzayan, Ara, and Azim F. Shariff. 2008. "The Origin and Evolution of Religious Prosociality." *Science* 322: 58–62.

Norenzayan, Ara, Azim F. Shariff, Aiyana K. Willard, Edward Slingerland, Will M. Gervais, Rita A. Mcnamara, and Joseph Henrich. 2016. "The Cultural Evolution of Prosocial Religions." *Behavioral and Brain Sciences* 39: 1–65. doi: 10.1126/science.1158757.

Parker, Geoffrey. 1996. *The Military Revolution, 1500–1800: Military Innovation and the Rise of the West*. 2nd ed. Cambridge: Cambridge University Press.

Peoples, Hervey C., and Frank W. Marlowe. 2012. "Subsistence and the Evolution of Religion." *Human Nature* 23: 253–69.

Peregrine, Peter. 1996. "The Birth of the Gods Revisited: A Partial Replication of Guy Swanson's (1960) Cross-Cultural Study of Religion." *Cross-Cultural Research* 30 (1): 84–112. doi: 10.1177/106939719603000104.

Purzycki, Benjamin Grant, Theiss Bendixen, and Aaron Lightner. 2022. "Coding, Causality, and Statistical Craft: The Emergence and Evolutionary Drivers of Moralistic Supernatural Punishment Remain Unresolved." *SocArXiv Preprint*. doi: 10.31235/osf.io/qvjfp.

Raffield, Ben, Neil Price, and Mark Collard. 2019. "Religious Belief and Cooperation: A View from Viking-Age Scandinavia." *Religion, Brain & Behavior* 9 (1): 2–22. doi: 10.1080/2153599X.2017.1395764.

Robbins Schug, Gwen, Kelsey Gray, V. Mushrif-Tripathy, and A. R. Sankhyan. 2012. "A Peaceful Realm? Trauma and Social Differentiation at Harappa." *International Journal of Paleopathology* 2 (2–3): 136–47. doi: 10.1016/j.ijpp.2012.09.012.

Roberts, Michael. 1956. *The Military Revolution, 1560–1660*. Belfast: M. Boyd.

Roes, Frans L., and Michel Raymond. 2003. "Belief in Moralizing Gods." *Evolution and Human Behavior* 24 (2): 126–35. doi: 10.1016/S1090-5138(02)00134-4.

Shin, Jaeweon, Michael Holton Price, David H. Wolpert, Hajime Shimao, Brendan Tracey, and Timothy A. Kohler. 2020. "Scale and Information-Processing Thresholds in Holocene Social Evolution." *Nature Communications* 11, art. 2394. doi: 10.1038/s41467-020-16035-9.

Snarey, John. 1996. "The Natural Environment's Impact upon Religious Ethics: A Cross-Cultural Study." *Journal for the Scientific Study of Religion* 35 (2): 85–96. doi: 10.2307/1387077.

Strathern, Alan. 2019. *Unearthly Powers: Religious and Political Change in World History*. Cambridge: Cambridge University Press. doi: 10.1017/9781108753371.

Swanson, Guy E. 1960. *The Birth of the Gods: The Origin of Primitive Beliefs*. Ann Arbor, MI: University of Michigan Press. doi: 10.3998/mpub.6484.

Turchin, Peter. 2006. *War and Peace and War: The Life Cycles of Imperial Nations*. New York: Pi Press.

Turchin, Peter. 2016. *Ultrasociety: How 10,000 Years of War Made Humans the Greatest Cooperators on Earth*. Chaplin, CT: Beresta Books.

Turchin, Peter. 2018. "Fitting Dynamic Regression Models to Seshat Data." *Cliodynamics* 9 (1): 25–58. doi: 10.21237/C7CLIO9137696.

Turchin, Peter, Rob Brennan, Thomas Currie, Kevin Feeney, Pieter François, Daniel Hoyer, Joseph Manning, et al. 2015. Seshat: The Global History Databank. *Cliodynamics* 6: 77–107. doi: 10.21237/C7CLIO6127917.

Turchin, Peter, Thomas E. Currie, Harvey Whitehouse, Pieter François, Kevin Feeney, Daniel Mullins, Daniel Hoyer, et al. 2018. "Quantitative Historical Analysis Uncovers a Single Dimension of Complexity That Structures Global Variation in Human Social Organization." *Proceedings of the National Academy of Sciences of the United States of America* 115 (2): e144–e151. doi: 10.1073/pnas.1708800115.

Turchin, Peter, and Sergey Gavrilets. 2021. "Tempo and Mode in Cultural Macroevolution." *Evolutionary Psychology* 19 (4). doi: 10.1177/14747049211066600.

Turchin, Peter, Daniel Hoyer, Andrey Korotayev, Nikolay Kradin, Sergey Nefedov, Gary Feinman, Jill Levine, et al. 2021. "Rise of the War Machines: Charting the Evolution of Military Technologies from the Neolithic to the Industrial Revolution." *Plos One* 16 (10): e0258161. doi: 10.1177/14747049211066600.

Turchin, Peter, Harvey Whitehouse, Sergey Gavrilets, Daniel Hoyer, Pieter François, James S. Bennett, Kevin C. Feeney, et al. 2022. "Disentangling the Evolutionary Drivers of Social Complexity: A Comprehensive Test of Hypotheses." *Science Advances* 8 (5): eabn3517. doi: 10.1126/sciadv.abn3517.

Turchin, Peter, Harvey Whitehouse, Jennifer Larson, Enrico Cioni, Jenny Reddish, Daniel Hoyer, Patrick E. Savage, et al. 2023. "Explaining the Rise of Moralizing Religions: A Test of Competing Hypotheses Using the Seshat Databank." *Religion, Brain & Behavior* 13 (2):167–94. doi: 10.1080/2153599X.2022.2065345.

Watts, Joseph, Simon J. Greenhill, Quentin D. Atkinson, Thomas E. Currie, Joseph Bulbulia, and Russell D. Gray. 2015. "Broad Supernatural Punishment but Not Moralizing High Gods Precede the Evolution of Political Complexity in Austronesia." *Proceedings of the Royal Society B* 282. doi: 10.1098/rspb.2014.2556.

Whitehouse, Harvey, Pieter François, Patrick E. Savage, Daniel Hoyer, Kevin C. Feeney, Enrico Cioni, Rosalind Purcell, et al. 2023. "Testing the Big Gods Hypothesis with Global Historical Data: A Review and 'Retake.'" *Religion, Brain & Behavior* 13 (2): 124–66. doi: 10.1080/2153599X.2022.2074085.

Whitehouse, Harvey, Jonathan Jong, Michael D. Buhrmester, Ángel Gómez, Brock Bastian, Christopher M. Kavanagh, Martha Newson, et al. 2017. "The Evolution of Extreme Cooperation via Shared Dysphoric Experiences." *Scientific Reports* 7, art. 44292. doi: 10.1038/srep44292.

Index

A

Aboriginal Australia, 210, 214
Aboriginal Australian people, 215–220
   conversion, 210–211
   ethical behavior, 214–215
   on food and hunting, 217–218
   missionary work among, 210–211, 214–216
   prosocial behavior and, 218
Aboriginal Evangelical Fellowship, 220
Aboriginal law, 215
Aboriginal religions, 214–215
Abraham, 80, 97, 134, 136, 193, 197
Abrahamic religions, 14, 155, 159. *See also* Specific types
Achaemenid Empire, 15–16, 243
A'chik, 15, 29, 34, 37
Adam's sin, 83
adultery, 37, 58, 92, 167–168, 193, 195
afterlife, 11, 16, 32, 34–36, 92, 94, 97, 99, 116, 128, 136, 140, 163, 197, 215–216, 231, 243
   beliefs, 25, 91, 101
   in Christianity, 94
   concepts, 34–35
   constructs, universality of, 6
   and MSP, 34
   punishment, 34
   rewards, 32–35, 33
agency, 6, 11, 39, 231
agents, 31, 50, 54, 106–107, 109, 117, 195, 211, 229, 244
   amoral, 112
   counterintuitive, 6
   in little traditions, 179
   personified, 117
aggadah, 72
agriculture, 4, 13, 144, 145, 159, 164, 238–240, 243

Ahom monarchy, 59
Akiva, Rabbi, 71
akua (gods of state-sponsored religion), 30
Algonquian-speaking groups, 209
allegiances, 180, 186
Allāh, 134–141
altruism, 28, 33–34, 163
Amazon, 213
Amazonian cultures, 218–219
American religions, 29
Americas, 29, 54, 155, 157–165, 167, 169–171, 232–234, 241
Amitabha, 114, 116
Anatolia, 16, 30, 34–36, 39, 243
ancestors, 3, 7, 9, 11, 13, 26, 28, 30–31, 35, 73–74, 116, 197, 217
   worship of, 13, 16, 115, 186
      in China, 16
      development of forms of, 13
ancient China, 40
ancient Egyptian religion, 26
ancient Greek culture, 32
ancient Greek gods, 32
ancient Greek teachings, 35
ancient Israel, 95, 191, 198–199
ancient Jewish legal tradition, reinterpretation of, 92
ancient Judaism, 91, 94
ancient Mediterranean world, 92, 94
angelic "messengers," 192
Aniruddhadeva, 55, 57
an-Nadim, Ibn 125
anthropology, 158, 163
antisocial behaviors, 31, 33
Antitheses, 92

aparādha, 58
Apocalypse of Peter, 95–97
apostles, 93–94, 99, 127–128, 202, 211
Arab polytheism, 134
Arab prophets, 136
Arabs, 133–134
Aranda people, missionary work among, 215
    law, 219–220
        missionary work among, 215
Araweté people of Middle Xingu, 218
ascetic religious groups, 51
Aṣoka, Emperor, 51
Assam, 47, 58
Assamese Vaiṣṇava (Mahāpūrūṣiyā), 51, 57
Assmann, Jan, 14, 25, 27, 39, 242
Augustine of Hippo, 100, 123
āśrama and dharma, 48
authoritarian religiosity, 14–15
avarṇas, 52, 60
avatars, 167–168
Axial Age, 5, 14, 25, 177, 180, 184, 241–244
axiality, 11, 27, 38
axial religions, 14
Aymara, 160–161
Azande people of South Sudan, 6–7
Aztecs, 14, 25, 29, 34, 162, 168

B

Babylonian exile, 70, 73–74, 191
Babylonian Talmud, 71–72, 75–76, 82
Babylonization, 72
bad karma, 106, 109–110, 112–113, 115
baptism, 209, 221, 223
Barnabas, 93–94
basic Islamic teachings, 135
behavior, 6–9, 28, 30–31, 33–34, 54, 79, 97, 106–107, 114–115, 123, 135, 137, 143, 166–168, 170, 177, 183, 201, 231, 235
    antisocial, 28, 31, 33, 36, 62
    sinful, 92, 99
    social, 143
    toward kin, 33
behavioral expectations, 123, 125
beliefs, 3–4, 6–8, 10–11, 14, 16, 26, 33, 40, 50, 91, 93, 98, 105, 109, 115, 117, 140–141, 143, 155–156, 158–159, 161–162, 166, 168, 177–178, 182–183, 185, 198–199, 209, 219, 223, 227, 229, 232–233, 235, 237, 243
    in big gods, 229
    in the evil eye, 182–183
    evolution of, 235
    in hell, 91
    in high gods, 162–163
    in Islam, 140
    in little traditions, 182
    in moralizing gods, 4–5, 14
    in MSP, 185, 199, 243
    Native American, 155
    and norms, 143
    religious, 3, 6, 16, 156, 159, 162, 232, 235
    in supernatural agents, 3–4, 7
believers, 98, 100–102, 134, 138, 140, 177
beybhicāra, 58
Bhagavad Gita, 47–48, 52–53
bhakti, 48, 54–58, 63
    beybhicāra, 58
    inner state of, 56–57
    movement, 55
    and mukti, 56
Bible, 73, 75, 209, 214, 218
Biblical verses, 72, 75
big gods, 4, 10–11, 14, 163, 185, 227, 229, 235
    of states and empires, 163, 227
Big Gods Hypothesis, 4–5, 163, 170, 228, 235–237
blasphemy, 28
bodhisattvas, 113–117
Book of Life, 81, 95
Book of Revelation, 95, 97
Brahma, Puruṣa, Nikā, and Kāla saṃhati, 57
brahminic supremacy, 51–52

broad supernatural punishment (BSP), 227–228
Buddha, 108–114, 117
Buddhism, 5, 10, 16, 25, 27, 34, 36, 39–40, 51, 105–109, 111, 113, 115, 117, 124, 126, 137, 146, 159, 185–186, 211–212, 217, 220, 223, 235, 243–244
    commingled with preexisting religions, 105
    doctrinal, 112
    and Jainism, 108–109, 220
    origin of, 105
    pre-modern, 105–106, 107
    subdivisions of, 105
Buddhism, MSP in, 106
    based on karma, 106–107
    in early Indian Buddhism, 107–110
    in Mahayana Buddhism, 113–115
    and Tang dynasty, 115–117
    in Theravada Buddhism, 110–112
Buddhist, 32–33, 51, 105–106, 110, 117, 145, 186, 219
    cosmology, 105, 186
    doctrines, 105, 112
    ethics, 106
    historiography, 105
    history, 117
    kingdoms, 146
    scriptures, 115
    texts, 128
    traditions, 146
burial practices, 13
Burmese laity, "little traditions" practiced by, 10
Byzantine Empire, 133

C

caciques, 164–165
Caribbean, MSP in complex societies in, 164–165
Carigonan, 213–214
caste, 55–58, 60–61, 108
caste society, 107–108
catechumens, 123–127, 124, 129–130
causally opaque behavior, 7–8
causal thinking, 35–36, 40

cavalry, 238–240, 244–245
cemis, 164–165
Central and East Asian Prestige Goods Networks (Central PMN), 243–244
Central Andes, 27, 29, 33, 36, 164, 169, 233, 245
Central Asia, 39, 105, 125, 134
Central Australia, 211, 215, 217
Central Italy, 28, 30, 33–36
ceremonial killing, 14
charity, 3, 80–81, 92, 96, 116–117, 138
chiefdoms, 163–164
China, 16, 34, 105, 114–115, 145, 241–245
Chinese Buddhism, 115
Chinese concepts of karma, 115
Chinese religions, 243
Christianity, 5, 15–16, 25, 27–28, 40, 54, 69, 71, 77, 91, 93–104, 127, 133, 135, 137, 139–140, 142, 159, 161, 177, 184, 207, 209, 211, 216–220, 222–226, 235
    charismatic, 16
    encounter with local immanentisms, 40
    and Islam, 40, 69, 139
    obstacles to spread, 209
Christianity, MSP in
    catastrophic events as divine punishment, 94
    commandment against adultery, 92
    commandment against murder, 92
    in gospels, 91–94
    gospel sayings, 91–92
    Heaven and Hell, 94–97
    illness as consequence of sin, 93–94
    justification and penance, 99–102
    kingdom of Heaven, 91
    postmortem fate of rich and poor, 91–92, 94
    postmortem punishments, 93–94, 97–99
    postmortem rewards, 93, 94
    ways leading to salvation and damnation, 93
Christianization, 15, 93, 219
    of Cuzco Valley, 15
    of Cyprus, 93–94
    of New Guinean groups, 219

Christian missionaries. *See* Missionaries
Christians, 33, 71, 93, 98, 100, 128, 133, 144–145,
   160–161, 178, 181, 186, 209–211, 216, 219, 222–223
   ascetic practice, 129
   communities, 97, 133
   concept of Hell, 35
   cultures, 91, 219
   doctrine, 165, 167, 223
   god, 160–161, 167
   gospel, 207
   and Muslim missionaries, 159
   traditions, 94, 97, 136, 184
   trinitarianism, 135
   universalizing morality, 215
Christ. *See* Jesus of Nazareth.
Church, 40, 99–101, 126, 215–216
circumambulation, 40, 108, 110, 117
class, 48, 52, 55–56, 58, 60–61, 71, 107–108
coding, 125, 156, 159, 163, 170, 192, 228, 230, 232, 240
   scheme for MSP, 230
coevolution, 163, 228
cognition, 36, 38, 40, 85
cognitive predispositions, 6
coinage, 38–39
collective propitiatory obligations, 179–182
collective rituals, 11, 12, 13, 99, 108
colonization, 14, 164, 170, 211–212
   European, 15
   and missionization, overlap between, 211–212
commoners, 111, 116, 164, 170, 231
Common Judaism, 73, 77
communal identity, 58, 63
communities, 11, 28–29, 32, 47–53, 55, 57–59,
   58–59, 61, 63, 70, 77, 81, 83–86, 100, 106, 109,
   123–125, 127, 136, 138, 155, 168, 178–182, 181, 198,
   200–202
   contemporary Hindutva, 47, 49
   early agricultural, 163
   imagined, 10, 32, 185–186

moral, 201
   persecuted, 47, 49
competition, 11, 128, 181, 183, 186, 235
complex, adaptive, and dynamic systems (CADS),
   49–50, 53
   religions as, 49–50
   understanding Hindu MSP through, 53–63
complexity, 163, 227–228, 233–234, 242, 248
   informational, 233, 248
   low sociopolitical, 242
   and supernatural sanctions, 227
complex social organizations, 235
complex societies, 4, 8, 14, 37–38, 155, 157, 162–164,
   170, 235, 245
   larger-scale,
   and MSP, 37–39, 163
confession, 36, 101, 113, 124
conflict, 13, 83, 141, 144, 182, 238, 240
conquered and colonized peoples, agency of, 39
conquest, 14, 27, 39, 134, 139, 163
contact-era Americas, MSP in complex societies
   in
   Caribbean, 164–165
   Inca, 169–170
   Lowland Maya, 165–166
   Mesoamerica, 165
   Nahua, 166–168
   Tarascan, 168
conversion, religious, 15, 63, 207, 209–210, 221–223
conversion to moralizing religions, 223
   to Christianity, likelihood of, 223
   demonstration of superior ritual efficacy, 223
   push-pull dynamics of, 221
   and sociopolitical disintegration, 223
conviction, religious, 77
cooperation, 9–13, 38, 53, 92, 108, 181, 183–185, 228,
   230–231
cooperative rules, 9
correlation coefficients, 233
cosmic kingship, 179–180

cosmology of heavens, 106–107, 109
counterreligions, 25
courts, 33, 115–116, 128, 145
covenants, 194–195, 197, 202
covenantal blessings, 197
Covenant Code, 73, 193–194, 196
credit-based MSP systems, 80
crime, 31, 34, 35
criminal punishment, 138, 145
cross-cultural comparisons, 223
cross-cultural patterns, 26, 36
cross-cultural research, 157, 227
cross-cultural studies of moralizing religion, 155–56, 158–159, 163
   Big Gods Hypothesis, 163
   Ethnographic Atlas (EA), 156
   Native Americans, 157–162
      agriculture and pastoralism, 159
      belief in "high god," 158–159
      coded in SCCS and EA, 159, 161
      external influences, 159–161
      neo-evolutionary interpretations, 158
      religious beliefs in EA, 162
   Standard Cross-Cultural Sample (SCCS), 156–157
   World Ethnographic Sample (WES), 156
cross-cultural studies of religious evolution, 159
cultic laws, 200
cults, 70–71, 95, 105, 112–114, 180, 195, 198, 200–202
cultural evolution, 34, 229, 235, 245
cultural evolutionary change, 236
cultural evolution of MSP, 40
cultural learning, 9
cultural macroevolution, 237
cultural practices, 13, 39, 143, 209, 211
cultural traditions, 12, 94, 143, 241
cultural Zionism, 86
cultures, 9, 27–29, 33, 36–37, 39–40, 62, 71, 78, 94, 127, 156–162, 207–209, 212, 218, 223, 241
   circum-Mediterranean, 157
   immanentist, 33
   Native American, 162
   prehistoric, 13
   traditional, 27
curses, 194, 196–197, 202
Cuzco, 169–170

D

databases, ethnological, 155, 161, 163, 170
data biases, 228–229
deadly sins, 100
death, conditions after, 34
Decalogue, 194, 200–201
deities, 4, 26, 28, 47–48, 50, 52, 56–57, 63, 76, 107, 114, 179, 191–193, 195, 199, 201–202, 231
   of Hebrew traditions, 202
   household, 180
   and merit transfer, 107
   and moral norms, 192
   pre-Islamic, 146
   of war and victory, 192–193
demerit, 50, 106
demigods, 10, 177, 186
demons, 11, 106–107, 109–110, 126, 130, 135
Densu (Akan deity), 31
denunciation and punishment, 170
Deuteronomic code, 69, 73, 76–77, 80, 83, 193–194, 196–197, 200–202
Deuteronomic theology, MSP in
   exile, 74
   Israel's behavior toward God, 75
Deuteronomistic history, 73, 194, 198
Deuteronomy, 71, 73, 76–77, 86, 192, 194, 196–197, 201
deva-beybhicāra, 58
devas, 50, 54, 57–58, 106, 112–114
devotion, 3, 12, 48, 58, 114–116, 221
devotional practices, 114
dharma, 27, 34, 36, 47–57, 50, 59–63, 137, 212, 223
   conceptions of, 48–49, 53–54

Index | 257

in epics, 52
epistemology of, 48-49, 51-52
evolution of conceptualizations of, 51-52
karmic and theistic implications of, 48-49, 52-53, 54
literature, 51-52
redefining, 53
secondary rules of, 52
subtle nature of, 52
Vedic, 53
dharma-rakṣā, 55, 60-62, 61-62
Dharmaśāstra (DhS), 48-49, 51-52, 56
hegemonic and normative discourse, 60
tradition, 49-52, 51, 52, 60
Didache, 93, 98
Dieu (Cuna deity), 161
diffusion, 159-160
cultural, 156, 163, 235
religious, 159
disaster, 31, 179, 191, 194-197
natural, 111, 135, 165, 170, 179
disciples, 54, 56-57, 59, 110, 123, 128
discourse, 50, 53, 59-62, 72, 94, 139, 167, 200
on divine rewards and punishments, 94
exegetical, 73
hegemonic, 50, 53
religious, 54
disloyalty, 58, 75
diversity, 4, 11, 141-143, 208
divinatory processes, 37
divine, 37, 50, 57, 59, 71, 86, 195-196, 198-200, 202, 217
action, 50
council, 192
curses, 194, 196
intervention, 110, 112
judgment, 99, 123, 195-196
knowledge, 141
law, 99, 137, 160
MSP system, 79

name, 196, 201
plan, 191, 200
punishment, 92, 93-94, 167, 191, 195-196, 199, 202, 218, 232
retribution, 31, 50
revelation, 134, 136-137
reward, 50, 92, 94
throne, 198
divinities, 69, 73, 180
doctrinal religions, 7, 10, 14, 177-180, 178, 182, 184-186, 242
doctrine, 36, 54, 93, 101, 106-107, 109, 116, 123, 133, 140, 177, 186, 209-210, 212, 222
religious, 134
theological, 53, 136, 142-143
domestication of wild religion, 10, 12, 14
donations, 106-110, 112, 115-117, 125, 185
Don't Sleep, There Are Snakes, 207
duty, 48, 52, 179-180

E

early Buddhism, 105, 107, 109-110, 113, 116
early Christianity, 36, 98
early Indian Buddhism, 107, 110
early Jesus movement, 200
early Jewish Christianity, 93
early Judaism, 73, 75-76
early Vedic references to karma, 108
Earth, 69, 73, 85, 95, 127, 136, 140-141, 161, 166, 192, 217
Earthquakes, 35, 94, 141
East Asia, 105, 111, 113
East Asian PMN, 244
Eastern India, 29, 31, 34, 37
Eastern religions, 14
Egypt, 14, 29, 39, 70, 133, 144, 179, 242-244
and Anatolia, 243
authoritarian religiosity associated with, 14-15
religions, 26-27
eka-śaraṇa-nāma-dharma tradition, 55

elect, 124
elites, 14, 34, 164, 166, 170, 178, 180, 231, 243
emotions, 139, 183, 198
end of world, 127
enlightenment, 101, 105, 113–114, 243
environment, 31, 77, 158, 161, 237, 239–240
eternity, 50, 123, 140
ethical systems, 69–70, 212, 218
ethics
   interpersonal, 28, 217, 242
   universalizing, 26, 242
Ethnographic Atlas (EA), 156–157, 159, 161–162, 168, 170
ethnographic data, 4, 233–234, 239–240
ethnographic databases, 227, 229, 234–235, 239–240
ethnographic record, 3, 13, 157
Eurasia, 27, 145, 216, 219, 241–242, 245
Eurasian immanentist traditions, MSP in, 34
Europe, 101, 185, 245
Everett, Daniel L., 207–209, 212–213, 218–219, 221, 223
evil, 140–141
evil eye, 16, 182–184, 186
evil spirits, 96, 202
evolution, 13, 16–17, 27, 49, 51, 53–54, 157, 230, 241–242, 244–245
   of dharma conceptualizations, 51, 53
   of large-scale complex societies, 245
   of moralizing beliefs, 157
   of MSP, 49, 51, 229, 235, 238–240, 244–245
   of religion and morality, 155
   social, 155
   of social complexity, 16
   sociocultural, 228–229, 247
   of sociopolitical complexity, 4, 6, 236–237
   spatiotemporal, 242
Evolution of Religion and Morality project, 155
evolutionary approaches to MSP, 155
evolutionary drivers, 236, 238–239

evolution of moralizing religion, 5, 12, 155, 236, 240, 245
   ancestor worship, 13
   authoritarian religiosity, 14–15
   collective rituals, 13
   human sacrifice, 14
   imagistic rituals, 12–13
   Neolithic transition, 13–14
   secondary religions, 14
   supernatural powers, 13
   transcendentalisms, 14, 15
exile, 74, 83, 191, 194, 197–198, 202

F

faith, 78, 99, 114, 116, 125, 129, 207, 211, 217
family laws, 194
fasting, 124–125, 129, 138
fate, 11, 78, 92, 97–98, 117, 127
fear
   of envy, 183
   of God, 129, 140
fertility, 3, 135, 165, 170
food, 33, 124, 138, 140, 202, 210, 215, 217–218
food production and consumption, sacrality of, 217–218
forces
   impersonal, 50, 117
   of moral evil, 140–141
   nonagentic, 31, 47, 227
   omnipresent moralizing, 177
foreign deities, 192
French Jesuits, 162, 208, 209, 211, 213
   activities in seventeenth-century eastern North America, 208
   missionary work among Innu people, 208–209
      difficulties, 213
      prerequisites for, 210
   missionary work among Wendat people, 209–210
      prerequisites for, 210

G

Geenna, 94
ghosts, 7, 11, 106–107, 110
god, 3, 9, 28, 30–32, 34, 37, 48, 50, 58, 69, 71, 73–77, 80–84, 86, 93, 95–96, 98–101, 106–107, 109–110, 112, 127–130, 135–136, 138–142, 160–161, 163, 165, 167–168, 177, 179–180, 182, 192–201, 207, 209, 213–214, 217–220, 222, 227–228
    Baal, 192
    concepts, 4
    El, 192
    local, 39, 155, 180, 192
    and morality, 135
    on Mount Sinai, 78
    and salvation, 213
    and spirits, 217
    of vengeance, 69
God's law, 219–220
good deeds, 84, 100, 109, 112, 128–130, 140
good karma, 105, 109
Gospels, 91–94, 99, 127, 210–211, 223
grave, 78, 80, 82, 140
great traditions, 9–10, 181–182, 184–186
    doctrines, 182
    MSP across, 180, 184–185
        collective propitiatory obligations, 180–182
        little traditions *vs.*, 178, 184–187
Greek gods, 32, 167
Gregory I, Pope, 40
Gribble, Ernest, 210–211
Gros Ventre, 160
group cohesion, 37, 47–48, 58
group formation, 77
group goals, 47, 53, 61–64
group identity, 12, 38, 55, 58
group loyalty, 10, 12
group members, 63, 98–99
guru, 54–55, 57–59
guru-beybhicāra, 58
guru mahimā, 57–58

H

ḥadīths, 136–137, 140, 142
Halakhah, 72
ḥanīf, 134
Haudenosaunee, 33–34, 209, 220
Heaven, 30, 48, 73, 78–79, 83, 86, 91–98, 101–102, 106–107, 109, 112, 114–115, 123, 127–129, 136, 140, 142, 213–217, 243
Hebrew Bible, 69, 71–72, 92, 99, 136, 139, 191, 193, 195, 198–199
    and Jewish tradition, 37
Hebrew Bible traditions, 191, 193, 195, 197, 199, 201, 202
    divine judgment, 195–196
    explicit moral codes, 193–195
    human judgment, 196–197
    implicit moral codes, 198–199
    nature of punishments, 195–197
    nature of rewards, 197–198
    nonmoralizing deities, 192–193
    relation to norms, 199–202
Hell, 33, 35, 78, 91, 94–97, 100–103, 106–107, 109–110, 115–117, 123, 125, 127–129, 140, 142, 215
Hellenism, 39, 72, 94, 98
Hellenistic Judaism, 27
Hellenistic world, 70, 94, 191–192
Hermannsburg Mission Society, 215
hermaphroditism, 28–29
hermeneutical evolution, 49–50
hermeneutics, 50, 53
high gods, 4, 156, 158–161, 163, 170, 177, 179, 184, 227, 234, 239
high MSP, 29–30, 38
Hindu, 32, 53–54, 60–62, 134, 145–146, 219
    canon, 48, 53
    dharma, 55, 60–61
        continuation of, 61–62
        protecting, 60–61
Hinduism, 5, 25, 27, 34, 40, 105, 137, 142, 146, 159, 235

CADS characteristics of, 49–50
elements of, 146
emergent properties of, 54–55
and Islam, 105
Hinduization programs, 62
Hindu law, 137–138
Hindu MSP systems
  divine action, 50
  Hindutva theology, 54–55, 59–63, 60–61
    dharma-rakṣā, 61–62
    and Hindu society, 60–61
    position of Brahman and Kṣatriyaḥ, 60–61
    Rāma-Janambhumi, 60
    Rāma-Rājya, 60, 61
    sevā, 62–63
    social harmony, 60–61
  karma-phala, 50
  Māyāmārā Vaiṣṇavite theology, 54
    Ahom monarchy and, 59
    aparādha, 58
    beybhicāra, 58
    Brahma, Puruṣa, Nikā, and Kāla saṃhati, 57
    guru mahimā, 57–58
    guru-ṛṇa, 58–59
    Nij-Śāstra, 57–58
    nāma dharma, 55–56
    supernatural rewards, 56
Hindu-ness, 53
Hindutva, 47, 49, 51, 53–54, 61–65
  contemporary, 59
  cultural milieu of, 49
  discourse, 60
  ideals of, 62
  ideology, 62
  proselytizing, 63
history, 3–4, 10–12, 27, 38, 57, 91, 106, 109, 123, 130, 141, 144–145, 156, 163, 177, 180, 184, 193, 207, 217, 222, 246
  evolutionary, 4, 243

postmortem rewards and punishments, 91
primeval, 193, 197
Holiness Code, 193–195, 193–197
Holocene, 163, 235, 241–243
hospitality, 30, 33, 218, 245
huacas, 169–170
human sacrifice, 14, 29, 39, 56, 94, 165
hunter-gatherer societies, 178–179
hunting, 214, 217

I

identity fusion, 12, 38
identity markers, 3, 11, 191
idols, 75, 125, 134, 166
imagistic practices, 12–13, 16
imagistic rituals, performance of, 12
immanence, 25, 216
immanentism, 16, 26, 36, 38, 40, 221, 242
  and Buddhism, 16
  historical priority of, 26–28
immanentist cultures, kin-related transgressions among, 33
immanentist religions, 10, 25–26, 27, 28–30, 29, 31–33, 32, 36, 39–40, 216, 218, 223, 241
  afterlife concepts, 34–35
  endogenous development of, 27
  morality in, 28–29
  MSP in, 29–31, 32–34
immoral behavior, 30, 35, 108, 170
immorality, 167–168
imperial expansion and missionization, overlap between, 211–212
Inca Empire, 15, 25, 29, 162, 169–171, 245
  MSP in, 169–170
incest, 28, 33
Indian Buddhism, 105, 109. *See also* Buddhism
Indian lotus, 54
Indian Mahayana, 114
Indian Ocean trade routes, 145
Indian politics, 47, 49, 60

Indigenous belief systems, 155
Indigenous conversion and syncretism, 165
Indigenous cultures, 3, 13
Indigenous marriage practices, 212
Indigenous religions, 25, 155, 159
individualistic nature of karma, 116
inequality, 13-14
Information systems, 228, 232, 246
Initiation rituals, 11
Innu people, missionary work among, 208-209, 219
    difficulties, 213
    prerequisites for, 210
interiorization, 80, 86
interpersonal behavior, 31, 47-48, 51-52, 75, 111, 116, 123
interpersonal morality, 25-26, 28-29, 32-33, 40, 208, 242
interpersonal offenses and transgressions, 33, 35, 213
interpolity competition, 220
Iron Age India, 220
Islam, 5, 25, 40, 69, 77, 105, 133-141, 143-151, 159, 177, 186, 211-212, 223
    adoption of, 212
    emergence of, 143
    encounter with local immanentisms, 40
    historical forms of, 141-143
    history of, 133-135
    Middle East in classical period and, 143-145
    MSP framework in, 136, 139, 141
        afterlife, 140
        divine law, 137-139
        end times, 140-141
        prophets and scriptural texts, 137
        war, 139
    orthodox, 143
    in pre-modern Southeast Asia, 145-147
    promotion of, 144
    teachings of, 135-141

Islamic doctrines, 140
Islamic history, 133, 142-143, 145
Islamicization, 146
Islamic traditions, 145-146
Israel, 72-73, 79, 82-83, 192-194, 197, 199-202
Israelites, 70, 77, 192, 194, 196, 198, 202

J

Jainism, 25, 108-109, 219-220, 244
Jerusalem, 70, 75, 77-78, 94-95, 192, 194, 196-197
Jerusalem temples, 76-78, 194, 198
Jesuit Relations, 208, 210, 213, 218, 221-222
Jesuits, 208-211, 214-215, 217, 220, 221, 222
Jesus of Nazareth, 91-94, 93, 95, 97, 99-101, 123-124, 127, 129-130, 136, 141, 160, 207, 209, 210-211, 211-213, 215, 217-219, 221-225
Jewish communities, 84
Jewish law, 85-86, 93, 98, 137
Jewish legal system, 71
Jewish liturgy, 76
Jewish tradition, 37, 75, 93
Jews, 34, 70, 86, 97, 99, 133, 219
Judah ha-Nasi, Rabbi, 72
Judaism, 5, 25, 28, 69-72, 76-78, 84, 93-94, 98, 133, 135, 137, 139-140, 177, 244
    and Christianity, 28, 133, 140
    Hellenistic, 27
    Late Antique, 77
    prerabbinic, 73
    Ten Commandments, 28
Judaization, 70, 72, 78
Judean religion, 191
judgment, 29, 37, 93-95, 123-124, 127, 129, 140-141, 195-197, 202, 213, 222
    final, 94-95, 100, 123, 127, 198
    postmortem, 123, 125, 127, 129, 216
justice, 32, 40, 51, 74, 127, 139-141, 167
justification by grace, concept of, 100-101

K

Kaaba, 40, 134
Kabbalah, 71
Kali yuga, 53, 55
kamala, 53-54
karma, 27, 34, 36, 48, 50, 52, 55-56, 106-110, 112-120, 177, 182, 185, 227, 231, 243
    beliefs, 113-115
    doctrine, 107, 110, 112
    and supernatural intervention, 106
karma-phala, 50, 55
karmic demerit, 52, 56, 58, 63
karmic implications, 47-49, 51-52, 54, 63, 106, 107-108, 110, 114
karmic merit, 62, 217
karmic punishment, 107, 115
karmic rewards, 111, 185
kindness toward strangers, 34
Kingdom of God, 95, 99, 217
Kingdom of Heaven, 91, 94
Kingdom of Light, 123, 125-127, 130
kin-related transgressions, 33
Konya Plain, 15-16

L

laity, 110-111
Late Antique and medieval Judaism, 81
Late Antique Christian texts, 94
Late Antique Jewish mysticism, 82
Late Antique religions, 135-137, 140, 142
Late Antique world, 133, 135, 139
Late Antiquity, 27, 71-72, 77, 135, 143
Late Postclassic Mesoamerican religions, 165
Law of Moses, 191
Letter of James, 93
liberal Christianity, 101
liberation, 48, 50, 53, 100, 217, 221, 243
life
    eternal, 33, 93, 99, 213, 216, 221
    everlasting, 34, 197, 207
    everyday, 180, 194, 197
    family, 138, 145-146
    human, 52, 137, 161, 164, 167-168, 213, 216-217
    moral, 170
    social, 16, 216, 243
lifestyle, 209, 211, 222
light particles, 123-124, 126, 130
light souls, 126, 130
literacy, 38, 111, 212
literature, 52, 70, 97, 100, 145
    apocalyptic, 95, 197
    early ethnohistoric, 157
little traditions, 9-10, 32, 110, 177-187
    breadth and heterogeneity of, 178
    forms of, 187
    MSP across
        collective propitiatory obligations, 179-182
        features of, 179
        great tradition MSP vs., 184-187
        mystical harm beliefs, 182-184
        supernatural agents, 178-179
liturgy, 76-78, 83
local cults, propitiatory obligations in, 179-180
local religions, 186, 208
local spirits, 114, 179, 186
love, 73-75, 80, 86, 138, 140, 194, 214
    for God, 86, 139
    of God, 140
Lowland Maya, MSP in complex societies in, 165-166
Lurianic Kabbalah, 82-83

M

Mādhavadeva, 55
magic, 8, 16, 125, 177, 182, 186
magical automatism, 33
magical ritual, 8
Mahāpūrūṣiyā dharma, 52-53
Mahayana Buddhism, 105, 107, 110, 113
Mahayana religiosity, 113

Mahayana societies, 113-114
Mahayana world, 111, 113, 115
mahimā, 55, 57-59
Makka
  city of, 134, 138, 146
  shrine of, 40
Mani, 123-131, 136
Manichaean catechumens, 123, 125-126
Manichaean community, 123, 125-129
Manichaean polemical texts, 124
Manichaean teachings, 125
Manichaeism, 5, 25, 123, 125, 127, 129, 131, 133, 135, 140, 223, 244
  adherents of, 124-125
  foundation of, 123
  postmortem rewards and punishments in, 125
    end of world, 127
    Heaven and Hell, 127-129
    psalms and memorial services for dead, 129-130
    reincarnation, 126
    salvation of elect, 126
  teachings, 123
Manu, 51
Mapoon, 215
Mark, Saint, 181
martyrs, 80, 95, 124, 223
Masoretic tradition, 192
mass human sacrifice, moral basis of, 29
material culture, 8, 123, 126, 209
Mauryan Empire, 16, 51, 211
Mauryan India, 244
Mayan deities, 165-166
Māyāmārā rebellion, 59
Māyāmārā Vaiṣṇavites, 49, 55, 57-58
Mecca. *See* Makka.
medieval Christianity, 179, 185-186
medieval European Christianity, 179
medieval art, 97, 100
medieval Judaism, 81

meditative practices, 10, 105, 107
memorial services, 129-130
mercy, 74, 93, 96
merit, 50, 80, 84, 86, 100, 105-109, 111, 113, 115-118, 185
  books, 111, 114
  making activities, 110, 117
  transfer, 107, 115, 117
Mesoamerica, MSP in complex societies in, 164-165, 234
Mesopotamia, 30, 32, 34, 70, 72, 133, 182, 243
messiah, 83, 85-86, 140-141
metaggismos, 126
metapersons, 26-31, 30, 31-32, 35-37, 39, 217-218, 222-223
Middle East, 133, 143-146
  in classical period, 143-145
  monotheism, 27, 145
Middle Yellow River Valley, 15
military aristocracy, 144, 146
military revolutions, 241, 244-245
military technologies, 16, 238, 240-241, 244-245
mind-body dualism, 6, 235
misfortune, 3, 6-8, 11-12, 26, 35-37, 110, 112, 183, 196
  forms of, 6-7
  MSP concepts in relation to, 35-36
  supernatural explanations for, 7
Mishnah, 72, 76, 78-82, 85
missionaries, 27, 40, 61, 134, 139, 159-160, 162, 208-209, 211-213, 215-217, 218, 220-224, 229, 242, 244
  challenges of, 213
  insistence on changes in customs, 211-212
  texts written by, 208
  work among Aboriginal people, 210-211, 214-216
  work among Aranda people, 215
  work among Innu people, 209
  work among Pitjantjatjara people, 216
  work among Tjungundji people, 215

work among Wendat people, 209–210
missionization, 15, 157–158, 170, 212
mitzvot, 75, 80, 83, 86
monarchy, 52, 58–59, 191, 194, 198
monasteries, 9, 105, 111, 116
Mongolia, 31, 232, 244
monotheism, 25, 135, 241
monotheistic worship, 134
moral behavior, 91, 116, 135, 140, 177
    enforcing, 182
    and merit, 116
    source of, 177
moral character, 105, 140
moral codes, 115, 200–201
moral dimension, 199, 242
    of life, 199
    of religion, 242
moral domains, 9, 31–32, 231
moral foundations theory, 9
morality, 8–9, 12–14, 26, 28, 30, 32, 92, 101, 105, 108, 112–113, 116, 135, 139, 167–168, 177–178, 184, 208, 214–215, 217–218, 242
    Confucian, 115
    definition of, 177
    and future of humanity, 16–17
    in great traditions, 184
    of human relations, 9
    important components of, 28
    Mahayana, 111
    in primary/immanentist religions, 28–29
    and religions, 177
    source of, 177
    and wild religions, relationship between, 8–10, 12
morality as cooperation (MAC), theory of, 9
moralizing beliefs, 157, 159–163
moralizing doctrines, 216
moralizing gods (MGs), 4, 8, 14, 69, 159–160, 191–192, 227
moralizing high gods (MHGs), 227

and social complexity, correlation between, 227
moralizing punishment, 165, 178, 227, 234
moralizing religions, 3, 25–26, 234
    addressing puzzle of, 4–6
    associated with complex societies, 4
    category of, 25–26
    in ethnographic record, 3
    evolution in world history, 12–16
    history, 3
    postulates of, 4
    prosocial commitment and, 4–5
    and sociopolitical complexity, 227, 235, 236
    sources of, 27
    spreading with imperial expansion, 211
moralizing supernatural punishment and reward (MSP), 5, 11, 14, 27–38, 40, 47–51, 53, 55, 57, 62, 69, 91–92, 94, 97–98, 100, 106–107, 109, 111, 113–114, 117, 123, 125, 129, 133, 136, 155, 157, 159, 161, 163–166, 165, 167, 168, 169, 170, 178–179, 181–182, 185, 199, 201, 208, 212, 216, 222, 227–248, 229, 231, 233, 235, 237, 239, 241–243, 244, 245, 247–248. *See also* Buddhism, MSP in; Christianity, MSP in; Contact-era Americas, MSP in complex societies in; Deuteronomic theology, MSP in; Hindu MSP systems
    approach to coding quantitatively, 228
    beliefs, 115, 155, 164, 228
    and causal thinking, 35–36
    characteristic features of, 31
    coding scheme for, 230–232
    and complex societies, 37–39
    definition of, 28, 182
    degree of, 30, 229–230, 234
    in early Indian Buddhism, 110
    elements of, 234–235, 242, 245, 248
    evolution of, 235–231, 245
    general rarity of, 234
    in great traditions, 184
    in Hinduism, 47, 49, 63
    historical geography of, 241–243

and human moral enforcement, 36–37
incremental development of, 40
and information systems, 229, 232–233, 246–247
in Islam, 137
in Judaism, 86
logistic regression models of, 248
at low levels, 33
in Manichaeism, 125
measures of, 228, 231, 232, 233–234
and misfortune, 36
nonbinary nature of, 228
prevalence of, 234
in primary/immanentist traditions, 29–31
punishment, reward, and afterlife, 32–35
in Rabbinical Judaism, 86
resistance to, 212
in small-scale societies, 234
and social complexity, 33, 233–237, 241–242, 247–248
systems, 47, 49, 54, 56, 63, 75, 77–79, 81, 86, 212
in Torahized Early Judaism, 72
way of resolving questions of, 229
moral justice, 76, 168
moral laws, 47–48, 53, 60, 62, 200–201, 216
morally unconcerned superstitions, 177
moral intuitions, 31–32
moral norms, 36, 136–138, 184, 192, 211, 243
moral obligations, 12, 111, 138, 179–180
moral principles, 13, 32, 198
moral surveillance, 168–169
moral values, 70, 211
Moses, 69–71, 76–78, 84, 136, 191, 193, 196, 200
mosques, 144, 146
Mount Sinai, 71, 76–78
Muḥammad, 134, 136–137, 140–141
Mueller, John, 49
mukti, 50–51, 55–56, 58, 63
murder, 28, 30, 36, 58–59, 92, 114, 182, 193
Murdock, George Peter, 155–156

Muslim communities, 138–139, 141
Muslim countries, 134–135
Muslim populations, 134–135
Muslim societies, 143, 145
Myanmar, 10
mystical harm, 182, 184
  agents of, 182, 184
  beliefs, 182–184, 186
mysticism, 83–84, 141–142

N

Nahua religion, 167–168
nāma dharma, 53, 55–56
nāmaghara, 56
Native Americans and religious evolution, 155, 157–158, 158–162, 161, 167, 170, 211, 223
  agriculture and pastoralism, 159
  belief in "high god," 158–159
  coded in SCCS and EA, 159, 161
  external influences, 159–161
  neo-evolutionary interpretations, 158
  religious beliefs in EA, 162
natural disasters, 111, 135, 165, 170, 179
Natural Geographic Areas (NGAs), 14–15
neo-evolutionism, 158
Neolithic transition, 11, 13
Neoplatonism, 27
New France, 209, 216
New Testament, 34, 38, 69, 91, 93, 98, 136, 199
Nij-Śāstra, 57–58
Nirvana, 33, 105, 108, 111, 217
non-Manichaeans, 123, 126–127
nonmoralizing religions (NMR), 207, 208, 212–213, 217, 222–223
Norenzayan, Ara, 163, 178, 235
norms, 3, 26–28, 38, 50, 137–138, 142–143, 146, 183–185, 199, 231
  cultural, 11
  local social, 179, 183–184
  religious, 144

of worship, 138
North Africa, 134, 143, 242
North America, 156–157, 211, 217, 221, 234
North American societies, 157–158
North China, 15, 30, 34, 40
North India, 30, 34, 61, 134, 243–244
nuclear families, 212

O

oaths, 31, 33, 37, 195, 200, 245
obligations, 33, 61, 76, 84, 111, 117, 138, 179–182
   propitiatory, 178, 180
   religious, 195
offerings, 31, 36, 116, 166, 169, 179–180, 218
   sacrificial, 3, 112, 177, 180
Old Testament. *See* Hebrew Bible
omniscient gods, 30
ontology and epistemology of dharma, 48, 51
Onyakopon (Akan god), 30
Oral Law, 71
Oral Torah, 71, 78, 80
order, 74, 83, 86, 193, 244
   cosmic, 48, 60, 62
   natural, 29, 193
   social, 3
Orthodox Church, 101
otiose gods, 156, 158, 162, 170
outcasts, 182–183
overimitation, 7

P

Pachacamac, 169
Palestinian Talmud, 72
pāpa (demerit), 50, 58
Parama Brahman, 48
Paris Basin, 16
pastoralism, 38, 133, 159, 238–240
paterfamilias, 212
patron saints, 181, 186
Paul (apostle), 93, 99, 202

Pentateuch, 70–71, 73, 76, 78–79, 83, 86
persecution, 59, 96, 117, 127
Petersen, Anders Klostergaard, 72
phala beybhicāra, 58
pharisees, 71
pilgrimage, 77, 80, 138
Pirahā language and culture, 207, 212
Pirahā people, efforts to convert, 207–209, 212–213, 223
   Pirahā's response to, 218
   prosocial behavior and, 218
   resistance to Christianity, 209
Pirahā worldview, 218
Pitjantjatjara culture, 216, 220
Pitjantjatjara people
   missionary work among, 216
   resistance to Christianity, 220
Pizarro, Hernando, 169
Platonism, 27
policing, 31
political Hinduism, 47, 49, 51, 53
polities, 16, 38, 228, 230–231, 233–235, 237, 240, 247–248
   historical, 230
   small-scale, 15–16
polygyny, 210
Polynesia, 28–31, 36, 213, 232
polytheisms, 39
polytheistic religiosity, 134
Popoluca, 160
postmortem judgment, 123, 125, 127, 129, 216
postmortem rewards and punishments, 91, 93–95, 98, 101, 125, 128
power, 3, 14, 26–27, 34, 52, 100, 109, 113, 116–117, 135–136, 183, 202, 217, 221
prayers, 81, 101, 125, 129–130, 138, 144, 168, 198, 201
prehistoric religious evolution, challenges to study of, 155
prehistoric societies, knowledge about, 229
prerabbinic Judaism, 73

Presbyterian missionaries, 220
pride, 11, 101, 184
Priestly Code, 193–194
primary religions, 25–30, 32, 39. *See also* Immanentist religions
progroup action, 12
property, 9, 13, 54, 138, 196, 200
prophets, 14, 73–74, 76, 127, 134, 136–137, 141–142, 193, 195–196, 200
   false, 127, 196
   and scriptural texts, 137
propitiation, 10, 35–36, 177, 179–182, 186
proselytizing religions, 216
prosocial behavior, 28, 32–33, 76, 78–79, 81, 97, 109, 117, 183, 218
   cultural evolution, 218
   incentivizing, 33
prosocial commitment and moralizing religions, 3–5
prosocial effects of religious beliefs, 3
prosociality, 60, 62–63, 163
prosocial religions, 163, 235
Psalms, 124, 129–130, 193, 200
Purāṇas 49, 52
Pure Land Buddhism, 114, 116
puṇya (merit), 50, 56, 62–64

Q

Qumran movement, 199–200, 199–202
Qur'ān, 136–137, 140, 142, 144

R

Rabbinical Judaism, 69–73, 75, 77–83, 85–86, 191, 200
   attitude of, 86
   Babylonization, 72
   legal and exegetical discourse in, 73
   rabbinization, 70–72
   as reflected in Mishnah, 78–82
   Torahization, 70

rabbinization, 70–71, 70–72, 77–79, 86
rabbis, 71–72, 78–80, 82, 85–86
Rāma-Janambhumi, 60
Rāma-Rājya, 55, 59–62
Rashtra Sevika Samiti, 62
Rashtriya Swayamsevak Sangh (RSS), 62
rebirth, 35, 50, 105–106, 110–111, 113–115, 117, 123
reciprocity, 12, 14, 26, 28, 30–33, 31, 36, 228
recitation, 113–114
Reformation, 101, 185
reincarnation, 33–34, 105–106, 110, 114–115, 126, 129, 215
religions, 3, 5 6, 11, 13–28, 32–33, 37, 40, 49, 53–54, 60–62, 70, 75, 98, 100, 108–109, 111, 123, 125, 135, 137, 139, 145–146, 157, 168, 177, 185, 207–208, 211–212, 215–219, 221–224, 229–233, 235–236, 238, 243–245
   adaptive, 54
   ancestral, 167
   in archaic states, 13–14
   classifying, 25–26
   comparative, 25, 241
   as complex, adaptive, and dynamic systems (CADS), 49–50, 53
   definition of, 54
   degree of antiquity, 26
   dominant themes in, 3
   dynamic nature of, 54
   and future of humanity, 16–17
   karmic, 34, 36
   and morality, 9, 13–14
   official, 100, 133, 177
   organized, 7, 14, 16, 235
   proliferation, 13
   secondary, 31–32, 40
   transcendentalist, 32–41, 242–243
religiosity, 177
   authoritarian, 14
   in little traditions, 186
   neo-Hittite, 15

polytheistic, 134
pre-Christian, 167
religious change, 39, 159, 241
religious evolution, 155-156, 158-159, 170, 242
religious life, 164, 178, 219-220
religious practices, 3, 143, 164, 166, 177, 229
religious systems, 11, 16, 39, 53-54, 178, 229
religious traditions, 10-11, 13, 49, 123-124, 127, 133, 142, 145-146, 208, 212, 216, 244
repentance, 36, 52, 58, 81, 99, 109, 113
resistance
    to intrusion of secondary/transcendentalist religions, 40
    to moralizing religion, 212
respect for authority, 31
resurrection of dead, 78-79, 83, 99, 140, 214
retribution and reward, mechanisms, 50
Ṛgveda, 51, 52
righteousness, 74, 96, 99, 127, 141
rituals, 3, 7-8, 10-13, 28, 37-38, 40, 52, 59, 77-78, 107-108, 113, 130, 160, 201, 207, 219, 221, 223, 243
    for amelioration of misfortune, 7
    collective, 11-13
    complex, 195
    doctrinal, 38, 77, 245
    efficacy, 11, 16, 222
    imagistic, 12, 38, 81
    logics, 48, 52, 63
    norms, 28
    obligations, 13, 231
    practices, 7, 11, 73, 202
    purity, 138, 213
    spaces, exclusion from, 60
Roman Empire, 15, 40, 77, 91, 100, 180
Roman religions, 16, 100

S

sacredness, 26
sacred texts, 32, 191, 246
sacrifices, 71, 77, 109, 116-117, 169, 177, 179-180, 194
    human, 14, 29, 39, 56, 94, 165
    to tutelary divinities, 180
sacrificial relationship between leaders and gods, 179-180
sādhāraṇa dharma, 52
Śaiva and Śākta, 52
Sakha people, 33
salvation, 26, 35, 39-40, 53, 93, 99-100, 107, 114, 117, 126-127, 130, 186, 197, 202, 209, 213, 215-218, 217, 220, 222, 243
Samaritanism, 70-72
Samaritans, 70
sāmājik samarasatā, 55, 59-60
sampling flaws, 155, 161-162
sangha, 105-112, 117
Śaṅkardeva, Śrīmanta, 53, 55, 57
Sarapis, 39
Sasanian Empire, 79, 123, 128, 133, 135
Sasanian Mesopotamia, 123
Satan, 98, 215
śatras, 56, 58-59
scripture, 55, 70, 105, 109-110, 113-114, 136-137, 139
Secondary religions. *See* Transcendentalist religions
Second Temple, 75, 194, 197, 199
Second Temple Judaism, 191
sectarianism, 141
Sefirot, 83-84
selfishness, reputational costs of, 5
self-sacrifice, 11, 12
Seshat complexity components, 233, 248
Seshat data, 33, 39, 228-229, 233-234, 239-240, 242, 244
Seshat Global History Databank, 16, 163, 220, 228, 230, 235, 237, 239-240, 242
Seshat sampling, 228, 232, 235, 239
Seshat variables, 228, 233, 246
sevā, 55, 59-60, 62-64
Shamanic ritual, 218-219
Sharīʿa, 137-139, 142, 144-145

courts, 144–145
norms, 137, 142
Shema, 76–77, 86
Sheol, 78, 94
Shulhan Arukh, 72
simulation constraint hypothesis, 6
Sinai tradition, 193
sinners, 95–96, 126–127, 129, 219
sins, 48, 55–56, 74, 81, 83, 93–94, 96–101, 109, 111, 114, 124, 129, 182, 198–199, 202, 207, 209, 213–217
Śiva, 50
slavery, 34, 73, 86, 96, 130, 194, 196
small-scale societies, 219, 229
social cohesion, 11, 35, 37, 53, 55–57, 63
social complexity, 4, 16, 27, 33, 38, 163, 227, 230, 233–234, 239, 248
social harmony, 55, 59–61, 60, 111
social hierarchies, 52, 163
social justice, 200, 202
sociocultural evolution, multidimensional nature of, 228
sociopolitical complexity (SPC), 4–6, 14–15, 155, 161, 227–230, 228, 233–237, 235–236, 238, 247
  and moralizing religion, relationship between, 227
  and MSP, 233–235, 247–248
  Seshat measure of, 228
  SPC1, 233–235, 237–239, 242, 247–248
Socrates, 97
Sogdiana, 15, 30, 34, 39, 243
Solomon Islands, 219
sorcerers, 95, 178, 182, 184, 213–214
souls, 35, 53, 73–74, 84, 125–127, 129–130, 200, 217, 221–222
South Asia, 123, 134, 143, 183, 217, 227, 243
Southeast Asia, 105, 107, 115, 134, 143, 145–146, 185
spirits, 3–4, 7, 10–11, 26, 28, 33, 84, 107, 109–110, 112, 114, 156, 177, 180–181, 217–218, 223
Sri Lanka, 105, 111–112, 114

Standard Cross-Cultural Sample (SCCS), 156–157, 156–159, 161–162, 170, 227, 240–241
state religions, 39
subsistence practices, 159, 212
śudras, 48, 52, 57, 60
Sufis, 142–144
Sufism, 142, 146
Summer Institute of Linguistics, 209
Sunni Islam, 141–142, 144
supernatural agents, 3–4, 7, 9–12, 31, 54, 106–107, 109–110, 113, 117, 165–166, 168, 178, 181–182, 195, 208, 231–232
  and forces, 3
  ubiquity of beliefs in, 7
supernatural attention, 40
supernatural force, 3, 231–232, 243–244
supernatural harm, 107, 178–179, 182–183
supernatural punishment and reward, 27–29, 31, 40, 48, 56, 76, 78, 81–82, 106, 170, 177, 179–185, 227, 245
superstition, 25–26, 209
Synagogal Judaism, 77–78
syncretism, 39–40, 141–143
systems theories, emergent properties in, 54

T

Tang Buddhism, 117
Tang dynasty China, 114–115
Taíno, 165
Tarascan Empire, 168
targums, 71
Teaching of the Twelve Apostles. See Didache
temples, 40, 60, 70, 77–78, 111, 116, 165, 168–169, 191, 197, 200–202
Ten Commandments, 28, 69, 71, 75–77, 80–84, 86, 92, 96, 124, 126, 130, 200–201, 215
Tezcatlipoca, 167
Thailand, 105, 112
Thammacarik program, 211–212
Theology, 9, 55, 75, 78–79, 141

of punishment, 75
and Sharī'a norms, 141
Theravada Buddhism, 10, 105, 107, 110–111, 113, 180
Theravada MSP, 110–111
Theravada societies, 110–112
Theravada world, 110–111, 114
Tikkun olam (repairing the world), 82–85, 84–85
Tjungundji people, missionary work among, 215
Torah, 70-73, 71, 73, 75–77, 79, 82–86, 137, 191, 201
Torahization, 70, 72, 75, 78
Torahized early Judaism, MSP in, 72–78, 73
Torahized Judaism, 72
Torah law, 76–77
Tosefta, 72
traditional culture, transcendentalist critiques of, 27
traditional religions, 3, 15
transcendence, 25–26, 39, 216–217, 222, 241
transcendentalism, 14–15, 27, 38–39, 242–244
transcendentalist movements, 27, 36, 38–39, 216, 220–222
transcendentalist reaction and denunciation, 27
transcendentalist religions, 10, 14, 25–27, 26, 32, 33–36, 39, 216, 219–220, 241
    afterlife concepts, 35
    MSP in, 33
    policing in, 31
transcendent realm, moral valorization of, 217
transgressions, 3, 31, 33–35, 52, 57, 74–75, 82, 86, 182, 213
    interpersonal, 28–30, 33, 35, 58, 178, 182
    moral, 98, 167
    against nonkin, 33
transmigration, 34
Trobriand Islands of Western Pacific, 218

U

universalistic morality, 107, 185
untouchability, 60
Urapmin people of New Guinea, 219

utilitarian, wild religion as, 12

V

Vaiṣṇava sects, 52
Vaisya, 48
Vajrayana Buddhism, 105
Varṇāśrama dharma, 52
varṇa, 48, 51–52, 56, 60
    and dharma, 48
    meaning of, 52
varṇāśrama dharma, 57
Vedas, 51, 52
Vedic ideology, 51–53
Venetian Empire, 181

W

warfare, 11, 38, 54, 138–139, 145, 166–168, 192, 196, 200, 202, 213, 223, 236, 238–241, 244–245
wealth, 14, 39, 74, 92, 183
Wendat people, missionary work among, 209–210
    prerequisites for, 210
    receptivity to Christianity, 220
Western Europe, 16, 30, 33–34
wild religions, 6–14, 16, 26
    constructs associated with, 6
    cross-cultural patterns of, 26
    domestication of, 10–12, 16
    and morality, 8–10, 12
    and moral reasoning, 9
    solutions for misfortune, 7
    as toolkits, 7–8
    universal foundations of, 6–7
witchcraft, 7, 186
witches, 11, 178, 182, 184
World Ethnographic Sample (WES), 156
world religions, 3–4, 5, 9–11, 14, 161–162, 177, 230, 235, 241, 243, 244–245
worship, 27, 55–56, 73, 105, 110, 134, 138, 142, 144–145, 169, 192, 194, 198, 201–202

Y

Yahgan, 160
Yahweh, 192–193, 194, 196–197, 199, 201
Yahwistic cults, 70, 75
Yarrabah mission, 210–211
Yiddish-speaking secular socialist movement, 84

Z

zekhut, 80, 84
Zoroastrian, 128, 133, 138
Zoroastrianism, 5, 14–16, 15, 25, 124, 133, 135, 139–140, 219, 223, 244

www.ingramcontent.com/pod-product-compliance
Lightning Source LLC
Chambersburg PA
CBHW080730300426
44114CB00019B/2542